R. Douglas Clark

5,15

MUSIC IN THE ROMANTIC ERA

Books by Alfred Einstein

A SHORT HISTORY OF MUSIC
MOZART—HIS CHARACTER, HIS WORK
GREATNESS IN MUSIC
MUSIC IN THE ROMANTIC ERA

ALFRED EINSTEIN

MUSIC
In The
ROMANTIC ERA

New York

W · W · NORTON & COMPANY · INC ·

PRINTED IN THE UNITED STATES OF AMERICA
FOR THE PUBLISHERS BY THE VAIL-BALLOU PRESS
0123456789

CONTENTS

PART II. The History

Contents   vii

PART III. The Philosophy

ILLUSTRATIONS

FOREWORD

THE present volume of the Norton History of Music differs not only in outward degree but in its essential attitude from the customary approach to a period of history. It is an attempt to characterize the Romantic movement through its center: music. My aim has been to show how the Romantic movement was manifested in music and how music affected the Romantic movement. This book is not a "History of Music in the 19th Century from the Death of Beethoven to That of Wagner" but rather a history of musical thought in the period that is closest to us and hence best known in its outward course. Accordingly one will find in it no information about such musicians as Ferdinand Ries, Pierre Louis Philippe Dietsch, or William Sterndale Bennett; and even about the life and work of the great masters of the Romantic movement only as much as is essential for the comprehensive treatment of the main theme. This choice of treatment is not made on arbitrary grounds but is dictated by the nature of the period itself.

The same reason that dictated this approach and treatment compelled me to present my work without musical examples. Such examples are feasible for the earlier epochs of musical history because of their relative shortness, and they are necessary because they are for the most part unknown to the reader and often available only in remote and unique sources. But examples are almost impossible to furnish for the 19th century owing to their length and abundance, and are furthermore almost unnecessary because the major—and many of the minor—works of the Romantic era, from Schubert to Brahms, from Weber to Wagner, from Rossini to Verdi, and from Berlioz to César Franck, are alive, known, and accessible to everyone. The radio alone provides illustrations almost every day.

Since the emphasis laid on the national element is one of the essential marks of Romanticism, I may perhaps be permitted to offer for the critical reader a little experience of my own. Some years ago the unwelcome task befell me of re-editing a Dictionary of Modern Music, which owed its existence to the contributions of trustees of all nations and nationalities. The original and its revised edition were, in general, well received, but the critic of the Republic of San Marino (here one may substitute any state or political unit to suit his fancy) objected to the brevity with which the music and musicians of San Marino were treated. If in this book the presentation of the Romantic movement in Germany occupies a wide space, it might be remembered that it is, at least in the eyes of a later generation, perhaps not a matter of pride for any nation to have been the one most strongly affected by the Romantic virus.

ALFRED EINSTEIN

Northampton, Massachusetts.

PART I

Antecedents, Concepts, and Ideals

CHAPTER I

Contrasts

MUSIC AND THE ROMANTIC SPIRIT

FROM the pen of one of the earliest and most significant standard-bearers of the Romantic movement in literature, August Wilhelm Schlegel, there is a dramatic skit in the manner of Hans Sachs, the title of which might be translated *A Highly Amusing Carnival Play of the Old and the New Century, Performed on the First of January in the Year of our Lord 1801.* This play depicts in broad fashion how, on New Year's Eve, the Old Century—dried-up, ugly, fulsome old hag, rattling on with would-be wisdom and rationalism—proclaims that she is the mother of the New Century, who lies in the cradle, a blissful babe. For this impudent lie, the Devil wrings her neck and marches off with her to hell. Then out of the clouds appear the true parents of the rosy child, a godlike pair, Genius and Freedom. The Herald, who opens and closes this one-act play, invites the audience at the conclusion to come again a hundred years later and see the second act,

> Which well may please us even more, . . .
> Either in this our stay on earth,
> Or when in heaven we find rebirth.

But in the end, unfortunately, the poet was not right: the pleasure afforded by the second act was limited; the Zukunftsträume, "Dreams of the Future," for the 20th century have found no joyous fulfillment. Also in denying the relationship between the 19th and the 18th centuries he was wrong, for the 19th *is* the daughter of the 18th, even if the family resemblance is not very striking; it will be one of the aims of this book to establish just what was like and what unlike about them. But in one respect he was right: around 1800 there did begin a new chapter in the history of the human mind—that chapter which is commonly referred to as the

Romantic period. The spirit of that age is one which pervades all realms of life—art, philosophy, politics. It is a spirit whose effects no nation of Europe could avoid or remain entirely immune to, though various countries succumbed in differing degrees, the northern ones being more susceptible than the southern. It is a spirit which did not manifest itself as a single, one-time occurrence either among all the nations or among all the arts, but as a series of occurrences: among the nations it appeared first in England, Germany, and France; among the arts, first in poetry, then in painting, and finally in music. But in music this Romantic spirit found not only its latest expression in point of time, but also its strongest. No history of European Romanticism can be complete without a history of Romantic music, and whoever undertakes to write a history of 19th-century music may well hope to get at the essence of the movement.

ANTITHESES IN ROMANTIC MUSIC

We seek in vain an unequivocal idea of the nature of "musical Romanticism." One need only glance at the names of the great Romantics, in chronological order—Weber and Schubert, Mendelssohn and Berlioz, Chopin and Schumann, Liszt, Wagner, and Brahms—in order to see that here within one frame are brought together the greatest contrasts. They are within one frame, for there must indeed be some common ground among the members of a given period. The contrasts are very great, yet not mutually exclusive. True, these contrasts may *seem* irreconcilable. Romanticism in music is, by its very nature, a revolutionary movement directed against the fathers and grandfathers of the revolutionary generation; accordingly, Romanticism hates Classicism—or what it considers to be Classical. Berlioz recognized fundamentally only two great masters of the past whom he approved of, Gluck and Beethoven; he hated Bach and entertained the greatest contempt for Handel. Still less did the past have significance for Wagner, though he edited Palestrina's *Stabat Mater,* concerned himself with Gluck's operas, applied certain practical features of the style of the early Classics to *Die Meistersinger,* and proclaimed his veneration of Mozart and Beethoven: he vanquished them for himself and his retinue by an act of violence which was in keeping with his natural disposition, even though he loved these earlier composers. In contrast, we might consider Schumann, who likewise was a revolutionary, but who looked upon the past with awe; and again we might consider, in contrast, Brahms, whose art is not completely intelligible apart from its continuous though changing relation to the art of Beethoven, Mozart, Haydn, Bach, Handel—indeed, to that of the masters of the earlier centuries.

Another pair of contrasts is that between theatricality and intimacy. It might seem as if Romanticism, as a movement of greater subjectivity, of withdrawal into the more secret and personal areas of the soul, must have been an important period of intimate musical impulses; and, as a matter of fact, the pianistic art of Chopin or Schumann speaks for this conception of the movement. But this intimacy, strangely enough, consorts very well with the utmost brilliance and the most undisguised exhibition of virtuosity; consider Carl Maria Weber, whose piano music was entirely of a brilliant character and whose entire production as a composer reached its culmination in the opera. He would probably be forgotten today if he had written only sonatas and variations for piano, concertos, and songs. There is, moreover, Wagner, who—even though he was recognized by Nietzsche as one of the greatest masters of the miniature—was able to speak out fully only in the realm of opera: he required a public which, never too large for him, played the part of a *mass* to be coerced, as a people, or a nation, or the world.

This contrast leads to a further pair of antitheses: subjectivity and objectivity of the musical idiom. From composition to composition, Wagner made his idiom ever more personal, ever more refined; and it is one of his greatest triumphs that he nevertheless captivated the world. Other Romantics—Weber, Schubert, Schumann, Brahms, each in his own way— did not wish to break the ties that linked them with the popular mind. They loved homely things; they were afraid of departing too far from them, so they reworked these elements without changing the content. They thought primarily of the people—or, rather, what they considered to be the people. Different, again, was Berlioz, who thought only of a metropolitan public, of Paris, London, Berlin, Vienna, or other cities that offered a place for his boundless creations. Even in the special fields of chamber music, of piano composition, of the symphony, of song, and of the opera, the contrasts reappear. To speak only of opera, consider Wagner and Verdi—Wagner the revolutionary, who began in a highly conventional manner but who struck out on a road that was ever more individual (one might almost say bachelor-like) and egocentric, and, in the end, forced all the world to follow him; Verdi, with his roots in a two-hundred-year-old tradition whose soil he never left, more and more lifted up, borne on high, and idolized by his public, by his nation, which understood him from his first to his last step.

As another contrast we might mention clarity and a "profound" or "mystical" quality. There is Mendelssohn: perhaps a Romantic Classicist, but nevertheless a Romantic by virtue of his new relationship to the past and his new feeling for sound. He was a master of clarity and symmetrical form; nothing was more odious to him than a disturbance of the harmony in the part or the whole, an unnecessary violation of the rules, an affront to musical respectability. On the other hand, nothing was more odious to Berlioz than the punctilious observance of musical respectability, the servile following of rules. Both derived from Beethoven; but the one saw in Beethoven only the master who perfected form, subdued all violence, brought order out of chaos; the other saw in him only the master who revolutionized the symphony and unchained dark and chaotic forces. They were antipodal, but even the antipodes belong to the same world.

Another contrast in Romantic music is that between absolute and program music. For this contrast also Berlioz and Mendelssohn offer a classic example. For the former, music was inconceivable without an admixture of elements from the other arts. His symphonies flowed from a white-hot crucible, fired by his feelings and fancy; without fancy or the fantastic, they would be meaningless—that is, meaningless in the very narrow sense of the word. They needed the stimulus of poetry, even when they followed purely musical laws. On the other hand, let us turn to Mendelssohn, whose instrumental works, even when they were called "songs without words," or when they may be referred to specific suggestions—the *Italian,* the *Scottish* Symphonies, the overtures—were never based on a program in the same sense of the term as Liszt's or Berlioz's works were. We are indebted to Mendelssohn for the finest statement ever made in justification of absolute music: in a letter of October 15, 1842, he said that the thoughts which good compositions express are not too vague to be contained in words, but too definite. Good music, he says, does not become more significant or intelligible through "poetic" interpretations; instead, it becomes less significant, less clear.

From contrasts such as these we may infer the contradictory views that were taken towards the instrumental works of Beethoven, the idol of the Romantics: for some, his sonatas and symphonies were the highest model of fully realized *form;* for others, they were no more than program music, the poetical key to which Beethoven had, unfortunately, committed to the deep.

These contrasts or apparent contradictions are found not only between the representatives of various aspects of Romantic music, but also within the character of the individual personalities themselves. Schumann—composer of the most intimate piano works, entirely comprehensible only to one who knows Jean Paul's and E. T. A. Hoffmann's novels, secretive to the point of mystification—also wrote his characteristic pieces for the young and his popular or patriotic choruses. Liszt, the greatest of all virtuosi except Paganini, wrote—alongside glittering and hair-raising paraphrases of favorite opera themes—Masses and oratorios and intimate songs. Wagner translated an amorous experience into a heroic opera and displayed it in such form for two thousand to see and hear.

UNIFYING PRINCIPLES IN ROMANTIC MUSIC

These contrasts, however, are not all mutually exclusive, like day and night, or white and black. They are contrasts like the positive and negative poles in an electro-chemical state. A relationship of tension always exists between these poles, a lively stream which flows from the one to the other. In Romantic music the enemies are not conceivable one without the other. We say Weber *and* Schubert, Liszt *and* Brahms, Wagner *and* Verdi. This is an entirely different relationship from that existing between Handel and Bach, whom we arbitrarily consider together but who, as a matter of fact, differ greatly and belong to separate worlds; they have not much more in common with each other than the fact that they were born in the same year. Today we smile at the strife which once drove the public of about 1860 into two camps, the "neo-Germans" on one side and Mendelssohn, Schumann, and Brahms on the other; today we recognize the deep affinities, the close connection between the erstwhile enemies.

The question is: wherein does this close connection lie. The answer is two-fold. The first of these affinities is a purely musical one; the connection lies in the relationship of all these musicians to sheer sound. In the development of music, sheer sound has always played a role; never, to be sure, a completely negligible one—for music which does not sound is hardly music at all—but an ever-changing role, and never the significant one that it did in the Romantic period of the 19th century. We need only think of the transition from the symphonies, sonatas, or operas of Haydn, Mozart, and Beethoven to those of Schubert and Weber, in order to grasp the mighty change. In this connection it should be emphasized that new sonority is inseparable from new harmony. Haydn, Mozart, and Beethoven were themselves the great conquerors in this realm. How could they have avoided being so? Haydn, one of the most original experimenters in the orchestral field; Mozart, the possessor of the most discriminating ear that any musician had yet been gifted with; Beethoven, whose very deafness led him into the most sublime regions of sound! Yet, with the first Romantics, sound took on a new meaning. It was a stronger factor in the body of the music than it had ever been before; it won a higher value purely in and for itself.

Today we argue about the best medium for the performance of Bach's keyboard works; but it is not really important whether we play them on a harpsichord, clavichord, modern piano, or organ—though, to be sure, there is always the danger that the piano may lend them a too sensuous tone-quality. Bach's keyboard works are by no means abstract, yet their sonority does not belong at all to their essential nature. The only thing, however, that a Romantic is *un*able to make is abstract music. Real abstract music first appears when Romanticism is dead, or apparently dead; it comes as the utter revulsion, the most violent reaction to the Romantic spirit. The unifying principle that links all the composers from Weber and Schubert to the end of the neo-Romantic movement and brings together such seemingly antipodal composers as Wagner and Brahms is this: their relationship to the most direct and perceptible element of music, its sound.

The immediate expression of this new relationship was the development of the orchestra in the 19th century. Great as had been the experimenters in this field, such as Haydn, Mozart, and Beethoven, orchestration was as yet no problem for them and their predecessors—there was no "textbook of orchestration" in the 18th century. Instruments had in both the orchestra and the score their fixed, conventional role, in spite of exceptions to the rule. Even Beethoven's instrumentations were worked out schematically: the oboes under the flutes, the clarinets under the oboes, the bassoons under the clarinets—not to mention the traditional role of the horns and trumpets. But what new possibilities and combinations were discovered, even in Beethoven's lifetime, by Weber and Schubert! What would Berlioz be without his orchestra! And in 1844 appeared his *Traité d'Instrumentation,* the bible of the new orchestral sonority.

The new relationship to sound was the new refinement in the art, and yet at the same time it was a *retrogression* to the primitive relationship that man had had to music—to the mysterious, the exciting, the magical. It was a union of the refined and the elemental, as is characteristic of all late periods in artistic development. And this union, this fusion of unlike things, shows perhaps more clearly than anything else the polarity of the contrasts in Romantic music.

The other feature that all the Romantics had in common is indicated by the one word "late." (While the 19th century may have been a youthful century in many fields, for example, in that of technology, a great many of its problems—problems which never cease to hold a magical fascination for the historian—lie in the contradiction between its youthfulness and its aged or "late" quality. For in the field of art in general it was an old century, and especially so in that of music. It already had a vast inheritance and, on coming into possession of it, was thrown into great confusion.

All of us feel that the time around 1800 was a boundary-line or watershed, that something new had entered into the history of our civilization. It was the new relationship of the individual, and especially of the artist, to the whole, as symbolized by the French Revolution—symbolized by it and not, as it were, caused by it. For the Revolution of 1789 was indeed, as a historical event, only the visible expression of a change that had been slowly prepared in the course of the 18th century: the emancipation of the personality to the extent of complete freedom. And this emancipation was recognized by all. Jean-Jacques Rousseau was persecuted, but he never stood before the Inquisition as did Galileo; Giordano Bruno was burned at the stake, but Voltaire died the most honored man not only of his nation but also of the whole of European society. This alteration in the attitude of the individual towards society made itself most conspicuously felt in music; and there it was symbolized by the name and work of Ludwig van Beethoven, the Son of the Revolution.

CHAPTER II

The Individual and Society

SOCIAL FUNCTION OF THE COMPOSER

THE relationship of the creative musician to society underwent a distinct change about 1800. Ever since the Middle Ages—since the days of the jongleurs and minstrels—the musician had taken his definite place in the organization of the body politic. And it is especially significant that even the wandering minstrel, who during many periods and in many lands was despised and outlawed, improved his lot, in the 13th century, by becoming a member of a corporation or a guild, which would protect him, guarantee his opportunity of making a living, and bring him into relationship with the well-organized world of the townsman.

Up to the end of the 18th century, even the greatest among the creative musicians knew whom they served and where they belonged. The most powerful employer was the Church; other agencies upon which music was dependent were the princes, the aristocrats, the cities, the patrician circles. "Free" music was not written, any more than an architect erects a building for his personal gratification or as a kind of protest against the prevailing style. As in the graphic arts, so also in music the creator was free within the outlines of his commission. Michelangelo painted the ceiling and wall of a chapel, and no one prescribed to him what limits his fancy had to observe. He painted, however, sibyls and prophets, Biblical scenes, and the Day of Judgment. Monteverdi, who is justly considered one of the greatest revolutionaries in the history of music, was very careful to point out in his defense of himself against his critics that his innovations had in no wise aroused the displeasure of his employer, the Duke of Mantua; and, later on, after he had left the service of the Duke, he had to be careful not to offend the seigniory of Venice. If—as happened in rare instances—society made demands of an aesthetic nature, as, for example, the Church did in its "reform" of Church music at the Council of Trent, the musician did not feel that this was an encroachment upon his rights. He was not revolutionary-minded; he felt that he was the servant of powerful social institutions and of the times into which he had been born.

One may say that until late in the 18th century there was scarcely any music conceivable that was not utilitarian, *Gebrauchsmusik,* or that would not have served an immediate purpose: occasional music, music made-to-order, in the real sense of the phrase. There was no "art for art's sake." Even apparently subjective art, which had the appearance of having arisen solely from the creative impulse of the musician, reveals itself on closer examination to have been bound to society, to have been commissioned music. In the 17th century, music was still thought of exclusively either as church music, which could not be separated from its connections with worship, or as "house"-music, which was almost always ensemble music. Solitary music-making was rare.

To be sure, at the beginning of the 17th century new phenomena appeared: the development of virtuosi, both vocal and instrumental, and the rise of opera, at first serving only as a sumptuous ornament for princely feasts, but a little later, in Venice, being opened to a larger public. Then there came into existence, for the first time, the idea of a new public audience which appreciated art as art—entirely different from the religious congregation, for whom music was only a means of achieving more intense devotion and exaltation. But this new audience of the opera was still aristocratic; and, in the new branch of art, taste was determined by the aristocracy, even if occasionally there appeared clumsy and bourgeois-looking imitations, such as the operas in a few German cities and French provincial centers.

THE EIGHTEENTH-CENTURY COMPOSER

The most striking example of a composer whose art was bound closely to the society in which he lived is that supreme genius, Johann Sebastian Bach. He was the mightiest of all creative musicians, but by no means the most independent. There are scarcely any works of his that might be considered "free works of art." His cantatas, his Passions, his Magnificat were all written for immediate use; and his High Mass, too unwieldy to be performed as a whole in Dresden, and which for us is a most highly personal revelation, was for him primarily a document attesting to his superior skill, a proof of his right to bear the title of Court Composer. We scarcely need cite the chorale-preludes, the organ preludes and fugues, which today, in brilliant transcriptions, are show-pieces of the concert hall, but which then had their fixed place in the liturgy. We scarcely need cite the *concerti grossi* or the orchestral suites written for the use of *collegia musica*. We would even be mistaken if we considered Bach's most intimate works, such as the *Well-Tempered Clavier* or the Two- and Three-Part Inventions, "free" works of art in the sense that Chopin's *Préludes* are. Bach excused them, as it were, on the grounds that they had a pedagogical intent, or a value as entertainment: nothing is more revealing than the title page of the manuscript of the *Well-Tempered Clavier:* ". . . for the use and practice of young musicians who are eager to learn, and as a special means of passing the time for those who already have some facility in this study."

All of Bach's suites and sonatas, moreover, were created with this end in view of serving to provide a means of "passing the time"—even, in the case of one of his greatest works, the *Goldberg Variations,* of passing the time at night—for the entertainment of a nobleman who suffered from insomnia. The 18th century was quite right in looking upon *The Art of the Fugue* as a document attesting to its author's supreme contrapuntal skill, i.e., as a model for pedagogical purposes; and it remained for the 20th to misinterpret it as a "free" work of art and to transplant it into the same concert hall in which Tchaikovsky's *Pathétique* and Richard Strauss's *Ein Heldenleben* resound. The fact that all Bach's compositions are incidentally works of the highest art, are as "eternal," as valid for all ages as works of art can be, is quite beside the point, and was, at all events, beside the point for Bach himself. He created them for his own day, for the nobles whom he served, for the congregation by which he was employed, for Arnstadt, Mühlhausen, and Leipzig, and not, so to speak, for Halle or Magdeburg or Hamburg.

What was true of Bach was true also for most of the composers of the 18th century—for Haydn, and even for Mozart. Haydn was the conductor of the court orchestra for Prince Esterházy, to whom he was under obligation for the entire output of his creative powers; and it is more than a mere symbol that he had to appear at the concerts in Esterház and Eisenstadt dressed in lackey's costume. He, of course, felt this dependent status deeply; but he did not free himself from it, and was satisfied with making it as bearable as possible. Mozart did free himself from it, but failed, in a materialistic sense, for his independence cost him his security. After 1782 he was a "free artist," even though in the last years of his life he again bore the title of Imperial Court Composer. Yet, in spite of all this, Mozart was closely linked to the society in which he lived, deeply bound to the Vienna of 1782–1791. He wrote piano concertos so long as society esteemed him as a virtuoso, and ceased to write them when it neglected him; he wrote no operas "for eternity," but only when he had an order for one. In 1785 Anton Klein, a very influential public official in Mannheim, asked him to compose music for one of his libretti; but Mozart refused, as long as a performance was not assured. All of Mozart's works were pieces written to order or for a definite occasion. Only, it should be noted, the order usually roused his own inner impulse.

The only great 18th-century musician who knew how to create his own public was George Frideric Handel. For more than thirty years Handel was a composer of operas, and the opera had quite obviously prepared the way for him to capture his public. Opera seems, as a matter of fact, to have been the first institution to serve the need for a free art. Yet actually, in its beginnings it served exclusively the love of splendor of several courts—the Medici, the Gonzagas, the Roman cardinals, the Emperor's court, the king of France, and a few German princes. And it would be entirely wrong to call the Venetian opera, which in 1637 opened its doors to a paying public, a popular opera. It was maintained by merchant princes, and counted on aristocratic attendance; the populace that was let in for the last act was nothing more than an intruder. It was a long time before the opera became even a middle-class institution. Previous to the 1740's, Handel himself had done nothing more than provide operatic entertainment for the English aristocracy; and in this undertaking he had failed. Then he became the creator of the oratorio—a new type of music that no longer had any essential connection with the devotional oratorios of Carissimi, nor with the opera-substitutes that were used by the Italians during Lent; the oratorio, completely released from worship in the church; the appeal of a single individual to the religiosity, to the moral consciousness of a nation, to the imagination of an international free congregation. It is noteworthy that the idea of the modern concert took shape in connection with the Handel oratorio. The *Messiah* was the first work that was given mass-performances, with masses on the stage, masses in the auditorium—first in Ireland and England, then in northern Germany. It was the Handel oratorio which, for the first time, found the aristocratic concert hall and the *aula* of the academic or civic *collegium musicum* too small: new, festive auditoriums had to come into existence, the secular, clear, free counterparts to the dark and solemn halls of the church. In the church was assembled the congregation; in the new concert auditorium was assembled the public, the anonymous mass of people. This revolution—and it was precisely that—corresponds closely to the proceedings that began with the taking of the Bastille: the leveling of classes, the abolition of aristocratic prerogatives, the advance of the lowest classes of society, the creation of the *citoyen*. The musical *amateur* gave way to the *citoyen* of the concert hall.

Mozart lived to see this development without really taking part in it. His piano concertos are still highly elegant art for aristocratic society, and even his last three or four great symphonies stand just between the chamber and the concert hall—significantly enough, one of them, that in G minor, renounces trumpets and timpani; it is still chamber-art. Haydn, too, became a "free" musician only in the last decade of his life, through his acquaintance with the metropolis—with London and with the spirit of that Londoner, Handel. The real representative and heir of this revolution, however, was Beethoven.

BEETHOVEN'S CONCEPT OF HIS ART

Where Mozart failed, Beethoven—in the same Viennese locale and only a few years later—was successful, thanks to his intractable and independent personality. He placed himself no longer in the service of the aristocracy; instead, he placed the aristocracy in his own service. A dozen anecdotes testify to the recklessness with which he treated his patrons—counts, princes, archdukes. It was an unprecedented thing for a circle of aristocrats to come together in order to assure a musician—without obligation for any service in return—the freedom to create, and for this musician to dare to complain if the sum of money put up should shrink during an inflation, through no fault of the patrons. Here for the first time appeared a musician without any ties to bind him. He took up a position as an individual facing the world, and often even opposing the world. This new relationship showed itself in the smallest as well as in the largest aspects of his work. It appeared, for example, in the degree of technical difficulty of performance. Haydn and Mozart scarcely wrote anything that exceeded the technical ability of their day—as a matter of fact, Clementi's solo sonatas are more "brilliant" than Mozart's piano concertos, and when Haydn and Mozart exceeded the ability of their day to *understand* their music, they tried to conceal the fact. On the other hand, it was not deaf-

ness, but independence in Beethoven that created the new technical problems in his piano works, quartets, and symphonies.

Beethoven was the first composer who, in many of his works, seems
to have followed the "art for art's sake" principle. Here a parallel with
Romantic poetry is easily found. (Samuel Taylor Coleridge in his *Essay
on Taste* (1810) had already formulated a point of view opposed to that
of the 18th century which considered as beautiful only the morally useful,
when he said that beauty is subservient to nothing but itself.) Beethoven's
sonatas are compositions no longer written for entertainment, for "society"; instead, they are pure documents of art. Of course, Beethoven often
came to terms with his times. But he no longer catered to a definite or
limited public; instead, he addressed an imaginary one, limited by neither
social stratification nor national boundary. To us today it seems hardly
appropriate that the *Eroica* should have had its first performances in the
palace of Prince Lobkowitz before a small circle of nobles: no concert hall
in the world can be too large for a work such as this Opus 55, or for the
Fifth, the Seventh, the Ninth Symphonies. Beethoven appealed to the
masses; he conquered, uplifted, transformed them; he united them.

On the other hand, he sometimes forgot his public entirely. His music
may be divided into two groups, one of which contains those works he
would have wished to be *heard:* among the sonatas, for example, the
brilliant ones in C major—Op. 2, No. 3, and the *Waldstein* Sonata; among
the quartets, Op. 59, No. 3, and the *Quartetto Serioso,* Op. 95. But the
last sonatas and the last quartets become soliloquies, which we are permitted only to overhear, and which Beethoven wrote for himself and his
God—confessions of a solitary. With Bach, there are likewise such confessions; but they are, with him, hidden in pedagogical guise. Beethoven
no longer needed that excuse.

THE ROMANTIC MUSICIAN

With this new attitude towards society and the world, Beethoven became a model for the Romantic movement. It was a dangerous model.
And it was principally the figure of Beethoven that provided the Romantic era with a model for its conception of the "artist." Of course, the
"musician," who rendered direct service to society, did not entirely disappear: the cantor, the church organist, the choir singer, the music director in the theater, and all the others connected with opera, mostly state-

appointed, continued to perform an official function. But the union of this officialdom with the *creative* was no longer present, or at least was considerably diminished. The cantors of the Thomas-Kirche in the 19th century no longer composed a cantata every week, as J. S. Bach had done of old; and the directors of opera and of concerts no longer wrote their own operas and symphonies, as Handel, Hasse, Gluck, or Haydn had done. Or if they did, their work was spoken of disparagingly as "band-master music." Hector Berlioz was simply a composer and nothing else, unless possibly he could also be called an occasional conductor of his own works and a writer; and in civil life he came to be only librarian of the Conservatoire. By way of a trade, Richard Wagner in his youth held the post of conductor of a theater orchestra; but the more powerfully the creative spirit stirred in him, the more he limited himself to the presentation of his own works. Robert Schumann, at the end of his short life, had become Municipal Director of Music—but he was a very poor director of music. More and more the creative musician freed himself from society; he placed himself more and more in opposition to it, and he became increasingly isolated when he did not succeed in conquering it.

The Romantic era created the opposition between the "artist" and the "Philistine," which Robert Schumann in his *Carnaval* expressed also in musical form. Was not Bach himself a "Philistine," like his fellow citizens of Leipzig? Does anyone think that Mozart felt himself to be an "artist"? He wrote, according to his own statement, for all kinds of ears, except the long ones! The Romantic musician, on the contrary, was proud of his isolation. In earlier centuries the idea of misunderstood genius was not only unknown; it was inconceivable. The creative artist produced for his own time for the purpose of immediate consumption: hence the vast amount of music written during the three centuries from 1500 to 1800.

With Beethoven there began a period in which symphonies, oratorios, lyric and choral chamber music of every kind, and even operas were written without being ordered, for an imaginary public, for the future, and if possible for "eternity." Pre-19th-century music, even when it is mediocre or empty, has always the charm of its relation to its own present, to the social life of its time—much as, for instance, do the "weekly" symphonies which appeared in Paris and London after the middle of the 18th century, and among which the symphonies of Haydn are to be distinguished only by their quality, not by their immediate purpose. The

Romantic musician, on the other hand, considered those of his works the most noble that were the most purposeless, those with which he pushed forward farthest into the future. Frequently he wrote with greater zest against than for his times.

It is significant that a sharp-sighted observer, Ludwig Börne, on October 30, 1830, wrote from Paris thus about the French Romantics, and particularly about Victor Hugo: ". . . the more senseless, the better; for Romantic poetry is wholesome for the French, not because of its creative but because of its destructive principle. It is a joy to see how the industrious Romantics apply the match to everything and tear it down, and push great wheelbarrowfuls of rules and Classical rubbish away from the scene of conflagration."

What was true of poetry was true to a still greater degree of music. And thus Romanticism brought forth a succession of revolutionary, and nothing but revolutionary, musicians; thus the Romantic 19th century has left us a profusion of ambitious and ill-starred works, which slumber in libraries as an eternal and unfulfilled appeal to the contemporary and the future world. Even the purpose behind the printing of music changed between the 18th and 19th centuries. In the 18th, a composition was published because a demand for it existed; in the 19th, compositions were often printed only for the purpose of arousing a desire for them.

The isolation of the Romantic musician—his working, as it were, in a vacuum—did not exist without a retroactive effect upon his personality and the character of his works. Before 1800, a composition—a Mass, an opera, a symphony, a quartet—had to be susceptible of immediate appreciation; too great a deviation from old custom, from tradition, was not without its dangers, as many an innovator had to learn by experience: Monteverdi or Gluck or Haydn. At all events, the striving for originality was the exception and not the rule. The generations followed each other as sons and grandsons follow their forefathers in a well-ordered family; and where there were revolutions, they were subdued without too loud an outcry. The Romantics, on the other hand, struggled against tradition. Not only did they cease to avoid originality, they actually sought it, and esteemed their work all the more highly the freer of presuppositions it appeared to be. Romantic music, that of the 19th century, seems filled with a more colorful procession of personalities, a more sharply defined group of profiles, than does that of all the earlier centuries; and it is a difficult task to draw the line of development neatly.

THE NATIONALISTIC IDEA

It is one of those strange tensions between the positive and negative poles, so significant for the Romantic era, that along with the emancipation of the creative artist and his isolation from society, from the everyday life of the community there should go hand in hand a closer connection with the *nationalistic* idea. It goes without saying, of course, that even before 1800 the historical development of music had taken place in national currents; but they flowed, to some extent, in a common stream bed. There are centuries in which one may speak of a universal art even in music, e.g., the 15th century with its art of polyphony, usually referred to as Burgundian.

There have also been international and supra-national composers whose classification is so difficult that it can be determined reliably only according to their musical style. So considered, Rore and Lassus become Italians, albeit Italians of Netherlandish origin. Girolamo Frescobaldi becomes a semi-northern composer. To what nation is one to ascribe Handel—to Germany, which gave him birth, to Italy, which formed his style, or to England, without which his art would never have achieved its magnitude? How is one to begin to classify Gluck, who presumably came from the Upper Palatinate, but who was a composer of operas half-Italian, half-French, or—more precisely stated—an opera composer of strongly individual cast, belonging to neither Italy nor France, and least of all to Germany, a cosmopolite in the domain of the opera? How is one to place Haydn, who has been acclaimed by one group a Croatian composer, and by another a "pure German"? How identify Mozart, who was too universal and too Mozartian to be entirely German or entirely Italian, entirely Salzburgian or entirely Viennese? Nor is Beethoven to be forced behind a boundary-line. He was not only a world-citizen of the symphony, but also a cosmopolite of music in general; and it is supremely unimportant whether his Flemish origin on his father's side is emphasized by one writer, or his native origin in Bonn on his mother's side, by another.

Before 1800 a strongly national coloring was shown only by those composers whose stature did not reach the lofty heights of greatness. In France, distinctively "French" traits were shown by the small craftsmen who wrote for the harpsichord and whose work culminated in the compositions of François Couperin *"Le Grand."* In Italy, characteristically "Italian" traits are found in Pergolesi and Domenico Scarlatti.

During the Romantic period the national profile became sharper.

Granted that Weber was not the "most German" of all composers (an epithet which Wagner applied to him in commendation), yet his *Freischütz* and his patriotic men's choruses were closely linked with nationalistic matters. Rossini was, in a peculiar way, more "Italian" than Paisiello or Cimarosa; Berlioz showed, more strongly than any of his predecessors, a liking for the descriptive, which is a traditional trait of French music; and Wagner, the most international of all composers in his influence, reached the point of chauvinism in the emphasis that he gave to the Teutonic. It is no wonder that Romanticism, in the course of the 19th century, appealed to all the musical nations successively, from the greatest to the smallest—Russia, Bohemia (the Czechs), Hungary, Poland, Denmark, Norway, Sweden, Finland—until the movement, going to extremes, either wore itself out or suddenly was transmuted into provincialism or abstraction.

CHAPTER III

Music as the Center of the Arts

TENDENCY TOWARDS MERGER OF THE ARTS

THE beginning of the Romantic era occurred within the period of the Napoleonic Empire, and this strange coincidence of opposites is one of the further examples of the Romantic tension between opposing poles. The 18th-century stylistic period that preceded the Empire, the Rococo, had been a last tremulous echo of the grandeur of the Baroque—entirely dependent upon the finest taste, upon the utmost elegance, upon a choice frame within which a reminiscence of antiquity blended very well with impulses from the Far East, particularly China. The Empire, however, weeded out everything Oriental, everything artificial, and concentrated on a stiff and monumental antiquity, which it magnified to gigantic proportions—Classicism of a kind that has given us some of its most ludicrous examples in certain of Canova's statues. It involved, from the artistic point of view, a suffocation, exhaustion, a rationalization of the Rococo. It had to rid itself of its extreme opposite, and found this extreme opposite in music.

The 18th century had tried to *separate* the arts. True, Lessing, one of the most clearheaded men of his time, was not favorably disposed towards Rationalism. He was an opponent of the neatly-measured-off "Classical" French tragedy with its three unities and exhibited a particular dislike for Voltaire, while admiring the "rule-less" Shakespeare. His love of the unconventional permitted fresh air to stream into the dusty chambers of German literature. Yet he advocated in his most significant essay on art, the *Laocoön,* a strict separation of the pictorial and the poetic, and drew for both areas as sharply as possible the boundary-lines of what was there representable. Had he lived longer (he died in 1781), he would have resisted passionately the intrusion of the "musical" into poetry and painting, on the grounds that it was a mysterious, disruptive, uncontrollable in-

20

gredient. Here also he would have insisted upon clear separation and would have sharply put music in its place.

To the Romantics, however, the arts merged into one. This tendency was so strong that it could not be resisted even by certain very great spirits born and reared in the clear air of the 18th century. Schiller, in his *Braut von Messina* (1803), reintroduced the Greek chorus with the express intention of achieving in the tragedy "a certain liberation from the confines of the actual," just as he had found it achieved in opera. Both Schiller and Goethe looked with some envy on the nature and development of opera; Mozart's *Don Giovanni* made a deep impression on Schiller, *The Magic Flute*, a deep impression on Goethe—so deep that he tried his hand at a continuation, a second part. It is significant that this period straightway supplied musical background for Shakespeare's later works, particularly *The Tempest*, which has much in common with *The Magic Flute*. More than once *The Tempest* was reworked into an opera—for example, in 1798 by the South German Johann Rudolf Zumsteeg, and again in the same year by the North German Johann Friedrich Reichardt. What is the second part of Goethe's *Faust* but the literary counterpart to a "magic opera"—to, one might almost say, a "grand opera"? At all events, it is impossible to think of *Faust II,* or to present it, without music.

MUSIC AND WORD

If the great "Classics" of German literature were unable to avoid the Romantic trend towards music, the genuine Romantics actually regarded music as the primal cause, the very womb from which all the arts sprang and to which they were again to return. There was no poet of the Romantic era who did not think of his artistic medium—language—as inadequate. "O lovers," cried Ludwig Tieck, one of the founding fathers of Romanticism, "never forget, when you would entrust a sentiment to words, to ask yourselves: what, after all, is there that can be said in words!" Music, the mysterious force, stirring every depth, bursting every form, seemed alone capable of making the ultimate, the most direct statement. Bettina Brentano, the highly eccentric little friend of Goethe and Beethoven, likewise declared how inadequate language seemed to her; unable to give something a poetical *form,* she asserted, "I know very well that form is the beautiful, inviolable body of poetry, in which it is engendered by the spirit of man; but then ought there not also to be an intuitive revelation of poetry, which perhaps more deeply, more thrillingly penetrates right to the quick, without fixed limits of form?" What a conception of the nature of poetry! It is surprising that Bettina did not straightway add, "This intuitive revelation, without fixed limits of form, is music!" But it was not Bettina alone who demanded that the art of poetry have a physiological effect. There was virtually a general flight of the Romantics into the ostensibly indefinite, engulfing depths of music.

Not only in Germany but also in England and France, the Romantic poets strove to create a new verbal music—at best, to strengthen the musical pulsation with which every genuine lyric is animated; at worst, to be satisfied with the sheer sound of the words, the play of vowels and consonants. The more "musical" a poem, the surer seemed to be its advance into new, unexplored regions of feeling. Limits melted away, not only between poetry and music, but also between music and painting: Philipp Otto Runge, whose symbolical pictures delighted the Romantics, wrote a dialogue about the similarity between colors and tones; and as for William Blake, how is he ultimately to be disposed of—was he a Biblical prophet, a painter, a poet, a musician? At all events, he was a Romantic. We must not be surprised, then, if E. T. A. Hoffmann—whom we shall shortly have to consider in greater detail—gives definitive expression to the point of view in his famous critique of Beethoven's C-minor Symphony: "Music is the most Romantic of all the arts—in fact, it might almost be said to be the sole *purely* Romantic one."

The contrast with the 18th century in this respect could not have been more sharply drawn, the metamorphosis that took place in the very meaning of music more distinctly marked. Music became a medium through which the ineffable could be made palpable to sense, through which the mysterious, magical, and exciting could be created. To the great philosopher of the 18th century, Immanuel Kant, "nature" had been something hostile, the overcoming of which was one of the tasks of ethics. Along with his English predecessors and most of his contemporaries, he harbored a rationalistic mistrust of the unconscious, the subconscious, the impulsive. Even music had to be clear, formal, orderly, restrained. But the Romantics began to respect the unconscious; they began to relax the form; they let the reins hang loose. And they honored Beethoven because he seemed to them to have shattered clear form—one of their great misconceptions and misinterpretations—and because he seemed to have opened up for them not only unknown but also uncontrollable regions of feeling and agitation.

They honored Beethoven for still another reason: that he was so great and substantial an *instrumental* composer—and, as a matter of fact, the instrumental portion of Beethoven's creative activity does by far exceed the vocal. Just as the Romantics considered music the center, the kernel, the fountainhead of all the arts, so also did they think of purely instrumental composition as the center of all music. They did so, moreover, precisely because of the seemingly indefinite, ambiguous nature of music for instruments. What exactly occurred is too characteristic to be denied special and more detailed treatment in the following chapter. But—again the two opposing poles—Romanticism felt at the same time the necessity of investing music with a new comprehensibility, through a new convergence and amalgamation with poetry: through program music.

Yet, be it noted, this fusion was to take place along a new way. In all periods of history, of course, there has been program music, from Sakadas's *Nomos* for the aulos, of 586 B.C., representing Apollo's fight with a dragon, to Kuhnau's Biblical sonatas and Beethoven's *Battle* Symphony. But Romantic program music has little in common with the program music of earlier times. The older program music was quite childlike in its attempt at pictorial representation; frequently it consisted only of a mere fanciful title, as in François Couperin or Jean-Philippe Rameau, in many of whose compositions scarcely any relationship exists between the title and the "content." It was happy to take its cues from the most immediate associations of the audible: tumult of battle, bird-song, peal of bells, or thunderstorm and pastoral sounds. Even when Kuhnau narrated Old Testament episodes or when Vivaldi tried to represent the four seasons symphonically, or Dittersdorf wrote actual symphonies on Ovid's *Metamorphoses,* these composers still continued to preserve the limits of form, keeping within the framework of the sonata, the concerto grosso, or the symphony; and —what is more important—they addressed themselves to the clear, serene intellect of the listener. To use an 18th-century expression, there was more "play of wit and understanding."

Here again Beethoven put a new face on things. With his *Pastoral* Symphony and his sonata *Les Adieux,* he addressed himself more to the listener's feelings—entirely so in the Sonata, and almost entirely so in the Symphony, despite a few remnants of childlike tone-painting and a few traits of a new impressionism that were there present. This combination of elements became the pattern for Romantic program music, except for the addition of a new ingredient, stimulus from literature.

The Romantic composer was no longer, so to speak, his own poet, but sought incitement to composition in the sister art of poetry: for example,

Berlioz in Victor Hugo's Romantic thrillers, in Lord Byron's *Weltschmerz*-tinted scenes, in Sir Walter Scott's novels, and in Shakespeare's dramas. Liszt, moreover, summoned to his aid not only literature—Victor Hugo, Lamartine, Schiller, Goethe, Dante, Tasso, Shakespeare—but also painting, in the person of one of its worst representatives, Wilhelm Kaulbach. But in this instance it was possible to use Kaulbach as a source of suggestions, for he himself also painted "ideas." Liszt was even of the opinion that in the symphonic poem a more intimate union of poetry and music might be possible than in song, oratorio, or opera.

From time immemorial the sung word has occasioned or developed a *connection* between music and literary or quasi-literary works. The present attempt, however, is intended as a *fusion* of the two, which promises to become more intimate than any heretofore achieved. More and more the masterpieces of music will absorb the masterpieces of literature. After all that has been said and after music has developed so far in the modern era, we ask ourselves, "Is it possible that this fusion—which unmistakably has blossomed out from a modern way of feeling and from the connection of music with poetry—could become harmful? On what grounds should music, which was so inseparably associated with Sophocles's tragedies and Pindar's odes, hesitate at the thought of becoming fused—differently, but yet more fittingly—with literary works of post-Classical inspiration, of becoming identified with names such as Dante and Shakespeare?" [1]

Whatever the validity of these pontifical assertions and rhetorical questions, they are characteristic of a tendency on the part of the Romantics to wipe out the boundary-lines between music and poetry. Music assumed a position, however, in these programmatic symphonies and "symphonic poems" (what a characteristic title!) not, as it were, in the service of poetry. Quite the contrary: music, it was felt, was doing a favor to poetry in trying to represent by more direct, sensuous, striking means what was ostensibly the essence of the poem or painting. What happened was a complicated matter, at once egoistic and altruistic. But if it was an egoistic act, designed to further music's best interests, yet it was one committed in good faith. It involved, at all events, a mixture of literary and musical elements, unthinkable for the 18th century and typically Romantic. In the new program music the Romantics again showed clearly that, for them, the limits of the arts were dissolved, but that within the combinations resulting from this strange alchemy, music was always the stronger element—the expressive center.

A similar mixing and shifting of the musical components in a quasi-

---

[1] *Gesammelte Schriften* (Leipzig, 1882), IV, p. 58 f.

chemical change took place in Romantic opera. True, the rule of music over drama had been established for almost two hundred years in Italian opera, and while occasionally it was made the subject of apparent controversy, for example by Gluck, in actuality, this hegemony had not for an instant faltered. Drama, the libretto of Italian opera, made no attempt whatsoever to shatter the bonds of its serfdom; it knew that the success of the opera depended entirely on the quality and achievement of the composer and the singers. In this relationship Romantic opera also made no change, although it felt that it was in fundamental opposition to its Italian rival. This was so because Romantic opera also discerned and acknowledged the overwhelming might, the superior power of music in the complicated whole of opera. Nothing was really changed in this situation by Wagner's demand that in opera the drama must have supremacy over the music, and that music should be the feminine, drama the masculine principle. The effect of his own work gives the lie to his theory, for this effect rests almost entirely on the music. The only difference is that, in the Wagnerian music drama, it was no longer the singer who bore the brunt of the expression, but the symphonically enlivened orchestra.

NEW VERSATILITY OF THE ARTIST

The obliteration of the boundary-lines between the various arts, especially between music and verse, corresponds to the sudden appearance of double talent among the Romantic artists. This was a new phenomenon. To be sure, Guillaume de Machaut had been both poet and musician, the greatest literary and musical figure of 14th-century France; and among the musicians of the 16th century there were many like Girolamo Parabosco and Thomas Campion, who were able to make up their own texts. Johann Kuhnau wrote a satirical novel, and Grétry wrote his memoirs. Bach had an aptitude for sketching—a gift which held exclusive sway in one of his grandsons. Jean-Jacques Rousseau was a great writer, but also an amateur in the field of music. Dozens of musicians were able to become theoreticians or aestheticians of their art: Zarlino, Morley, Marcello, Rameau, Gluck.

But about 1800 there came a time when musicians began to vacillate between their talents. Weber was the first example of a new versatility, even though—being still a child of the 18th century—he never went entirely astray from his status as a musician. He tried his hand at a novel, with the characteristic title "The Life of a Musical Artist" (*Tonkünstlers Leben*)—for the simple musician of the 18th century became, in the Romantic period, a "musical artist." Weber was already a man of letters and a publicist, in the 19th-century sense; he was the first musician to have at his disposal the entire cultural equipment of his time, in quite another way than did Beethoven, who—even though on occasion he also called himself a "tone poet"—still felt that he was entirely a musician, and also in quite another way than did Schubert, whose nature was incompatible with journalism.

How dangerous the double talent could be to one thus gifted is seen in Schumann, who—being the son of a bookseller—was, as it were, born under a literary star, and had to undergo long struggles, both inner and outer, before he became inwardly sure of his musical calling. He did not have the apprentice-like training which, up to 1800, had been a matter of course for a musician; and it was the violence, the convulsive effort, with which he conquered his technique that lamed his later work and prematurely broke the buoyancy of his spirit. Berlioz, too, came to music much too late; yet, if he had lived a hundred years earlier, he would probably not have been spared the physician's career which he began. For him, to be sure, his double talent as musician and writer was—from the business point of view—a piece of good fortune. One might say that he was a *professed* musician, but by *profession* he was a critic, belles-lettrist, writer of fiction—for what are his memoirs but an autobiographical novel!

The perfect type of the "cultured musician" in the 19th century is represented by Franz Liszt, who was an essayist and salon philosopher, airing his views on every conceivable subject in his essays on music and musicians, but least of all dealing with his own real forte. In his *Frédéric Chopin,* for example, the reader learns very little about Chopin's work or Chopin's music, but very much about Poland.

One of the most noteworthy examples of double talent among the Romantics, and at the same time the special herald of the Romantic era, is Ernst Theodor Amadeus Hoffmann. His life was roughly contemporary with that of Beethoven—he was six years younger than Beethoven, and died five years before him. Thus Hoffmann did not live to hear the last and "most Romantic" works of his great contemporary; yet he had already become the originator of the misunderstanding, the Romantic light in which the 19th century viewed Beethoven. What was Hoffmann? Was he a man of letters? Was he a musician? Was he a government official? For he *was* a government official; he was active as adviser to the Prussian highest court of appeal, without giving his superiors too much cause for complaint. Was he a painter? At least he was remarkable at drawing caricatures. Out of the disunion between his activity as an official and that as an artist, he achieved the highly unusual effect of his stories: the clash of the everyday with the fantastic, the gruesomeness of the common-place, the ghostliness of the humdrum. This tension is also hinted at in his music: Hoffmann, in general a "Mozartian," to whom music was a loosening of all tensions, recognized the senselessness of counterpoint—of the late, *post*-Bach counterpoint, which was no longer alive. The center of his many talents was perhaps literary, but he had trouble bringing them into harmony. A dissonance remained unresolved in his nature.

A more fortunate successor of Hoffmann's was Richard Wagner, for the many-sidedness of his native ability found its center of gravity at last —late, but yet early enough—in music, or more precisely in opera. Noth-ing, however, was more characteristic of him than his *decision* one fine day, "to become a musician." Try to imagine such an utterance on the part of Bach, Haydn, Mozart, Beethoven, or Schubert! They had no other choice than to become musicians.

In "A Communication to My Friends" (*Eine Mitteilung an meine Freunde,* 1851) Wagner has himself indicated his restless course of de-velopment and his unstable surrender to every possible artistic impression:

Most definitely of all, my zeal for imitation threw itself into the writing of poetry and the making of music—perhaps because my stepfather, a portrait painter, died early, and thus the pictorial element disappeared from among my immediate models; otherwise I would probably have begun to paint too, although I must confess my recollection that the learning of sketching tech-nique very quickly disgusted me. I wrote plays, and my becoming acquainted with Beethoven's symphonies—which, with me, did not take place until I was fifteen—resolved me at last, passionately, on music also. . . . In my study of music the poetic "imitative urge" never quite left me; it subordinated itself, however, to the musical, for whose contentment I brought it in only inci-dentally. . . .

That he did not become a dilettante, or rather that he did not remain the many-sided dilettante that he was at first is a wonder—to be explained only through Wagner's tremendous intellectual gifts and energy. In his youth he wrote a Piano Sonata and a Symphony that are so amateurish, so unoriginal, that one can scarcely consider them without embarrass-ment. He wrote highly attractive stories in the style of E. T. A. Hoffmann. He first composed a "Romantic" opera in the style of Weber or Marsch-ner, and then a comic opera in the French style—like those of Hérold or

Auber—with some Italian admixture. At last, in *Rienzi,* he became an imitator, with better taste, of the Parisian "grand opera." He was a long time in finding himself. And there were various steps in the maturing of his talents. The poet—or, rather, the dramatist conscious of his aim—was ready first; and again there was a rather long period before, in *Lohengrin,* the musician caught up with the dramatist. But Wagner, all his life, thought of himself not merely as a poet-musician, but also as much more: a critic of culture, a philosopher, a statesman, or even more a "Redeemer through art." Only after the passing of the era in which men were carried away by Wagner's achievements has it again been permissible to express the opinion that in these particular fields he remained, throughout his life, a dilettante. What a contrast, here, to Goethe's universality, which was assured by the strictest research and the most cautious restraint! But it is characteristic of the Romantic period that in it even dilettantism was permitted.

SOCIAL BACKGROUND OF THE ROMANTIC COMPOSER

It is only an outward sign of this change in the training of the Romantic musicians that they almost all came from a different civic or social stratum than did the majority of their predecessors in the 17th and 18th centuries. Handel as the son of a surgeon, Schütz as the son of an innkeeper, Gluck as the son of a forester, Haydn as that of a wheelwright, were exceptions; as a rule, the great musicians came from musicians, or were the last members of whole generations of musicians. Bach was not merely a last member of such a family, but was also the father of three important members of the musical profession: Wilhelm Friedemann, Carl Philipp Emanuel, and Johann Christian. Beethoven was the grandson and son of musicians, Wolfgang Amadeus the son of vice-Capellmeister Leopold Mozart. In this respect also, Schubert and Weber occupy a middle and transitional position. Weber was the son of an adventurer, whom a passion for the theater led into the career of impresario; the whole Weber family, which played such an important part in Mozart's life, shared this theatrical and musical bent. Schubert was the son of a Viennese schoolmaster, and it can almost be said of him that he was the son of a musician, for in the life of an Austrian schoolmaster music played a most important and decisive role.

This situation changed with the advent of the Romantic era. Berlioz's father, like Louis Spohr's, was a physician, a man of high literary and philosophical culture, who precisely as a result of this culture hindered his son as much as possible from following his natural inclination to the musical profession. Prejudices such as these were not encountered in the Mendelssohn family, which belonged to the enlightened and cultured Jewish circle in Berlin: there, sufficient freedom and wealth permitted the superior musical gifts of Felix Mendelssohn to take their course. And in this instance it might have been well if there had been obstacles to overcome, just as it would have been in that of Meyerbeer, who could allow himself to experiment in all possible styles and wait for the success of his works. Of Schumann, it has already been stated that he was, so to speak, the offspring of a library, just as it might be facetiously said of Rembrandt, that miller's son whose pictures are so full of semi-darkness, that he was the son of a mill. Schumann was to have been a lawyer, and he might also have become a writer. In a famous letter to his mother (July 30, 1830), written in his twenty-first year, he remarked: ". . . now I stand at the crossroad"; and he pressed her for a decision on the question of whether he should follow his own genius. Chopin came from a home in which culture was pursued professionally, even though his own upbringing was somewhat desultory and imperfect. Adam Liszt, the father of Franz Liszt, was an official in the house of Prince Esterházy.

The case of Richard Wagner is quite curious. Even if he may not have been the natural son of his stepfather, the actor and painter Ludwig Geyer (presumably he *was* Geyer's son), in the Wagner family the proclivity for theater was as endemic as it was in the Weber family, even though the mother came from the respectable middle class. The sisters Rosalie, Luise, Clara, and the brother Albert showed the younger brother Richard the way to the stage. But the actual direction of his intellectual powers he received through his uncle Adolph Wagner, who was a learned and literary man, a member of the middle class—though a very freethinking one. Without the Geyer heredity, Richard Wagner would perhaps have become a literary person anyway; without the influence of Adolph Wagner, he might have become a composer for the theater and a conductor of theater orchestras, with no other works to his credit than some in the style of *Die Feen* or *Das Liebesverbot*. He became, however, something other and greater than a mere musician.

One need only recall, furthermore, the names of the French Romantics —Félicien David, Gounod, Saint-Saëns—to see how very closely they were bound up with the *salon,* i.e., the literary and aesthetic culture of the middle class. Though César Franck was the son of a banker, he still was a member of a long line of painters—the artistic talent seems simply to have been transferred to another field.

We need not multiply the examples. If it was the rule before 1800 that musicians came from musicians, it was the rule in the Romantic period that they came from the educated middle class. Even the aristocracy no longer played a part. In the 16th, 17th, and 18th centuries, Europe teemed with aristocratic musicians, among whom were dukes, princes, and emperors. In the 19th, particularly, the high German aristocracy of kings, archdukes, and princes still retained the patronage of music—or, more precisely, of opera—but only as a highly external matter of inheritance and duty. The cultivation of music had become an affair of the middle class.

LITERARY CONSCIOUSNESS OF THE ROMANTICS

The transition from the "handicraft" stage to the "cultured" stage of musicianship appears in the fact that the representatives of the latter all knew how to write. Even if they were not all professional litterateurs like Weber, Berlioz, Schumann, Wagner, and Liszt, at least they were great letter-writers. The only exception was Anton Bruckner, who in many ways was an anachronism, and might just as well have come into the world as a contemporary of Haydn. Even Mozart and Beethoven wrote a considerable body of wonderful letters—Mozart, the most beautiful ones ever written by a musician. But these letters are, heaven knows, not "literary." The letters of the Romantics are, however—even when they are as charming and unaffected as those of Chopin to his friends and his family. Wagner, especially, never wrote a line in which he was not conscious of how it would show up biographically—that is, in terms of eternity. That is the reason why his letters are so seldom straightforward and yet so often contradict statements in his autobiography (*Mein Leben*). Brahms, who knew that his letters, too, would have to serve some day as biographical source material, was exactly for that reason so unwilling a correspondent—somewhat like Verdi, the straightforward, honest, simple composer, who once protested passionately against the publication of such intimate documents as letters.

The formulation of an articulate program for the new relation between musician and society was attempted by Franz Liszt in six articles "On the Position of Artists" (*Zur Stellung der Künstler*), written in 1835.[2]

[2] *Ibid.*, II, pp. 3–54.

They are, as he emphasizes, the result of a "great religious and philosophical synthesis," the model for which he had found in the writings of Count Claude-Henri Saint-Simon: the system of a new social movement, Saint-Simonism, in which the artist assumed the highest rank, for to him was entrusted the moral upbringing of mankind. Liszt asked:

How has it been possible that music and musicians have lost all authority and consciousness of their mission, while thanks to their effort and unbelievable self-sacrifice the tonal art has developed further and further?

artist vs. society

"How could it come to pass that the social status of artists has been buried in complete insignificance, while they have created this multitude of wonders and masterpieces, to which they have given their lives with pain?

"How, finally, has it been possible that so many great men have not cast off by force the yoke of a deplorable degradation? And through what misfortune has it come to pass that those who were the first are now become the last?"

It is clearly seen that Liszt here set forth a thoroughly Romantic conception of the musician. A Romanticized Mozart or Beethoven was present in his mind, for of Bach it can hardly be asserted that "he gave his life to his masterpieces with pain." The end to which Liszt, thoroughly disgusted above all by the condition of French music, exhorted all musicians, "all who possess a wide and deep feeling for art," was "to form a holy band of fellowship, of brotherhood, to found a general world-association whose task it should be:

1) to call into existence, to encourage, and to exemplify aspiring activity and unlimited development of music;

2) to raise and ennoble the position of artists through abolition of the abuses and injustices with which they are faced, and to take the necessary steps to preserve their dignity."

This was a new order of things, in which the artist, and particularly the composer, exercised a more or less high-priestly power. Gone were the mere musicians; there were only artists, in the service of a Romantic ideal. "We believe," Liszt continued, "as steadfastly in art as we do in God and Man, both of whom find therein a means and type of elevated expression. We believe in one unending progress, in one untrammeled social future for the social artist; we believe in these with all the strength of hope and of love! . . ." If it is recalled that Bach, for example, created his masterpieces within the narrowest "social trammels," it will be seen that the reversal of the relationship could not have been more complete.

CHAPTER IV

The Supremacy of Instrumental Music

MUSIC AS SOUND

IT IS a matter of great historical significance that Beethoven, who stood at the threshold of the Romantic era and was claimed by the Romantics as one of their group, was essentially an instrumental composer. To be sure, we would have been immeasurably poorer if he had not composed *Fidelio,* the *Missa Solemnis,* and the song-cycle *An die ferne Geliebte;* but with the piano sonatas, the string quartets, the concertos, and the symphonies, the complete well-roundedness and the full greatness of his stature would have been preserved and would have shone forth in undiminished glory. For the Romantics, however, Beethoven was above all the creator and perfecter of the symphony, the sonata, and the quartet; they tried to understand him only as such, and used that alone as their point of departure. Bach, too, had been essentially an instrumental composer: the flowering of his entire work sprang from "organistic" soil; and not only do his choruses and arias have a *concertante* origin but even his recitatives have a strict form that has been conceived instrumentally, however conscientiously and imaginatively they may follow the words. But Bach's fundamentally instrumental conception had no historical continuation; the entire 18th century still remained a century of vocalism.*

The reason that Beethoven, with his instrumental inclinations, became so influential a model lies in the fact that the Romantics saw something different in the symphonic, in chamber music, in *wordless* music, than did the preceding generation. With them, instrumental music lost its class-art character. It became the choicest means of saying what could not be said, of expressing something deeper than the *word* had been able to express.

As early as 1810, E. T. A. Hoffmann, in the critique of Beethoven's Fifth Symphony previously referred to, stated the point clearly: "When

* Bach & his sons were primarily instrumental composers; Haydn was primarily a symphonist; Mozart's instrumental works — symphonies, string quartets, concertos — were at least as important as his operas. Handel + Gluck are not enough evidence for Einstein's assertion.

one speaks of music as an autonomous art, one should always think only of instrumental music, which, disdaining any help, any admixture from another art, gives pure expression to the peculiar and otherwise unrecognizable nature of the art." Schumann too, at the beginning of his career, could think of no other means for expressing his poetically engendered art than the instrumental, and wrote twenty-three works entirely for piano before he found in song a new method of expression.

The wordless—a negative thing—acquired a new, positive value. The word—music with text—was too definite, too rational. It was not by chance that in the rediscovery or revival of J. S. Bach, his instrumental works, beginning with the *Well-Tempered Clavier,* aroused much quicker response than did his Passions, cantatas, and motets) And it was due to a characteristic misunderstanding of Beethoven by the Romantics that they admired his symphonies not because of the definiteness and clearness of the form, the taming of all the chaotic impulses, but because of the manifold possibility of interpreting them. Somewhat the same thing happened in the attitude of the Romantics towards Christianity: they turned away from all the forms of Christianity to which some element of rationalism clung—away from Lutheranism, from Calvinism. It has often been pointed out how many Romantics cherished an inclination to Catholicism, an inclination which in many instances led to formal conversion. The Romantics felt themselves drawn to Catholicism because it was the least rational manifestation of the Christian impulse, because it was the nearest to the mystical. *Credo quia absurdum!* Thus, to the Romantics, instrumental music appeared also as a manifestation of the mystical. They turned aside from the music of the past, which did not permit this plunge into the "depths," and especially from the clear, witty music of Haydn, which was deep merely in terms of the sensibilities but not "deep" in the Romantic sense of the word. They even lost a proper relationship to Mozart, in spite of all their marveling at his work. They felt, finally, that Beethoven was especially "deep"—because they did not quite understand him.

Music became a matter of *withdrawal.* Beethoven prepared the way for this change. He began to place various of his movements, as it were, on a pedestal. He began to "withdraw," not so much with the two rhythmic strokes that precede the entrance of the theme in the first movement of the *Eroica,* as with the mysterious measure, composed later, which lifts the beginning of the Adagio of the *Hammerklavier* Sonata, Op. 106, as if it were on two temple steps. In general, moreover, the Classical sonata

and symphony began with the theme, it set it forth. The Romantics, on
the other hand, led the hearer first away from the world; they introduced
the theme only after preparation, to emphasize that it belonged to another, new region of feeling. This was a common trait of all the Romantic
instrumental composers, beginning, perhaps, with Mozart's G-minor symphony or his last piano concerto, but certainly with Schubert. The most
convenient example in his work is the A-minor Quartet, which creates a
sonorous background of two murmuring measures for the entrance of the
theme. As the most diametrical opposite, the Romantic era also first developed the instrumental "surprise," as in Schumann's G-minor Sonata,
though he may already have had before him the example of Beethoven's
impetuous compositions.

In the Romantic era music became something orphic. There was an
escape from clear into the semi-darkness in which visions appear, in which
wonder is again possible. In the end, there was a flight not only into the
dusk but into the night itself. The night became one of the mightiest
symbols of the Romantic movement, and the symbol of night in music
is the original element of magical sound. It has already been pointed out
in these pages that all the Romantics of music, however little they may
have had in common with each other, met in their relation to sound:
they all obeyed this magic. Night, symbolized in sound, had for the Romantic era a quite different significance than it had had for the 18th century. Since Edward Young's *Complaint, or Night Thoughts on Life,
Death, and Immortality* (1742–45), night had become even during the
period of Rationalism a favorite theme or symbol of poetical feeling—or
rather more of "sensibility," sentimentality, melancholy, and of *Weltschmerz*. This theme was not neglected by the Romantics: it is no mere
accident that William Blake was stirred by this very work of Young's
to create for it a set of illustrations. But the total immersion in the unconscious, the orphic quality of night is a special feature of Romanticism.
Novalis—one of the first and most sensitive poets among the German
Romantics—had already struck upon this aspect of the movement; and
the astonishing parallels, almost word-for-word, between his *Hymn to
Night* and the second act of *Tristan* have often been noted. But what
Novalis could barely indicate with dark, Ossianic words found its ultimate fulfillment in Wagner's magical music. There is no more significant
evidence of this than the prelude to *Lohengrin,* the opera in which Wagner the *musician* takes a place of equal rank with Wagner the dramatist,
and a work which is expressly called by its composer a "Romantic opera."

This prelude depends entirely on sound and on a sonorous, dynamic crescendo right up to the glorious entrance of the trumpets. One might refer to it as nothing more than a sonorous, thematic unfolding of the A major chord, which both in the beginning and at the end, as a pure chord, shimmers and dies away in a magical pianissimo.

The Romantics were conscious of this magical effect of music. The position assigned to music among the arts by the philosopher of the Romantic movement, Arthur Schopenhauer, was in essential agreement with this idea of the orphic power of music. If the other arts are but copies of the Platonic idea, the true content and the eternal element in the "appearance" of things, then music is the direct manifestation of the *original* nature of the world, of the "will." It is no wonder that Richard Wagner enthusiastically adopted this interpretation for his music drama, in which the copies of the Platonic idea in the form of the visible proceedings on the stage and the copy of the "will" in the form of his many-tongued symphonic orchestra were merged into one.

THE VOCAL ELEMENT IN ROMANTIC MUSIC

This brings us to those two types of music which the Romantics cultivated with especial fondness: song and opera. It might appear that this fondness offers a contradiction to our assertion of the supremacy of instrumental music among the Romanticists; but, rather, it is a confirmation. For, both in song and in opera, the Romantics had altered the significance of the role which the "accompaniment" played in relation to the vocal parts. This revolution was not without some preparation: it was clearly foreshadowed in Gluck's and Mozart's orchestra, but, in general, the relation of the orchestra and of the piano to the vocal parts remained that of servant, that of accompaniment. Shortly after 1750 the song-writing Berlin purists had even set up the demand that a song—and they were thinking then only of the strophic song—ought to be complete and well-rounded in itself, *without* the accompaniment, purely as melody. In the Romantic era, the accompaniment became a kind of commentary. It conveyed the descriptive and the psychological, and it became more and more important as the strophic song and the "closed" aria in opera declined. In Schubert's songs the two weights in the balance—melody and accompaniment—were still in equilibrium; and the Italian opera had never renounced the supremacy of the human voice, the closed, i.e., musically well-rounded, form. But in later Romantic song, in Romantic opera, the accompaniment laid claim to an ever greater portion, right up to the instrumentally conceived song with a commenting, declamatory voice-part, and right up to the symphonically created operatic scenes with the vocal parts superimposed.

The Romantic period was no longer a century of great vocal composition. There was still a succession of delicate and refined *a cappella* composers, such as Mendelssohn and Brahms, who achieved effects of harmony and color inconceivable to the 16th century, the time when the classical *a cappella* style was in flower. The means of achieving this refinement became, especially in Germany, the composition for men's chorus, which owed its impetus, however, not to purely artistic reasons, as it became more and more an expression of nationalistic or party activity. The major forms that had a vocal basis fell into neglect. The great champions of the Romantic era no longer thought of creating for the church works that would help the Biblical word to get a hearing; and they would not have considered doing so even if the church had still been able to offer them the fixed, complete liturgical orders of worship. The Protestant church turned back to Bach, a master of two centuries before; the Catholic went back still further, to Palestrina and his time, in whose style it fostered a new musical Nazarenism, comparable to the Pre-Raphaelitism of the English school of painters. The big oratorio still lived, because Handel had once lived and had created an influential model; but its life was only a traditional, useless existence, even in a country that joyed in tradition like England, which received the oratorios of Mendelssohn and Spohr with enthusiasm, though not without the opposition of certain orthodox religious leaders. But even Brahms's *German Requiem* lived off the past—even Brahms was driven by his times into specialization and glorious achievement in the instrumental field. Nothing is more significant of the new relationship between vocal and instrumental elements than a minor work of Wagner's, the Biblical scene written in 1843 and entitled "The Love Feast of the Apostles" (*Das Liebesmahl der Apostel*). The whole first half of the scene is filled with *a cappella* music for three-part chorus of men's voices, but the descent of the Holy Ghost to the meek and suppliant is represented by the inflowing tide of the orchestra: it had become an instrument of the suprasensual, of the magical. In his opera the two elements maintained this relationship; moreover, they continued to do so.

CHAPTER V

The Contradictions

GROWING CLEAVAGE BETWEEN ARTIST AND PUBLIC

THE Romantic artist, or more particularly the Romantic musician, did not remain unaware of the danger in his growing isolation. He looked back yearningly towards the Renaissance, in which, as it seemed to him, the musician had been nothing more than the mouthpiece of the people, the transmitter through which the whole immediately revealed itself; and, above all, the Middle Ages appeared to him a true artistic paradise, a time in which art had been nothing more—so he believed—than exalted handicraft.

This, too, was a bit of Romantic self-deception. Art—and especially music—always was at the service of the ruling powers: the Church and the aristocracy. Even in the much-praised Middle Ages polyphony was reserved for "art," for what one might almost call science, and—when tolerated at all by the Church—was merely handed to the people; moreover, the art of the troubadours and trouvères, at once simple and refined, was a privilege of the nobility. Before 1750, or before 1800, there were types of music restricted to certain classes: opera, for example, was at first something exclusively reserved for the highest nobility to present at their very brilliant and sumptuous festivities, and a little later—in Venice—for the aristocracy and their guests; in the 18th century it became for the first time open also to the middle class. Certain types of instrumental music—the symphony in its earliest period, the string quartet—remained long a prerogative or privilege of the nobility; the instrumental overture or suite remained long that of middle-class students.

But this much is true: the musician remained always in the service of a social class; he did not set himself against it. Besides, in the church he had to speak clearly to the whole of the congregation; he had to be intelligible to all. Though in the Catholic Church the composer might still preserve a measure of aloofness, in the Protestant he had to set forth the word of God in such a way that it was fully grasped by the artistic comprehension of the laity: the cantatas of J. S. Bach have been called, not without some justification, a musical *Biblia pauperum*. So far there existed no cleavage between the creative artist and the public; even high art did not cut itself off from general intelligibility. Although Haydn wrote symphonies for his princely masters, these compositions were also usable in the concert halls of Paris and London; and his quartets, from the first to the last, unite the aristocratic with the popular—and with the Most High.

Again, this state of things began to change with Beethoven—not that his work ascended to rarefied strata, but that his symphonies no longer served either the aristocracy, or the masses newly brought into prominence by the French Revolution. True, his works wished to speak to all men, to humanity, but to a humanity that the creative artist had raised to his own level. And what about Beethoven's piano sonatas? We repeat: many of them he consciously made so "brilliant" (e.g., the *Waldstein* Sonata) and so difficult (such as the great Sonatas Op. 106 and Op. 111) that they are no longer accessible to the ordinary player and exceeded the capacity of the dilettante who felt that he had easily mastered Haydn and Mozart. As a matter of fact, one can classify Beethoven's piano sonatas, in general, into intimate and "concert" sonatas, into those that are essentially monologues and those that seem to require listeners—a distinction, incidentally, that is not absolutely identical with that between "simple" and "brilliant." The C-sharp minor Sonata, Op. 27, No. 2, for example, remains intimate despite its stormy Finale, and the C-major Sonata, Op. 2, No. 3, is a concert sonata despite its fervent Adagio. And what about Beethoven's last quartets? Does there still remain alive in them a last trace of that "sociability" that Haydn's and Mozart's quartets, and even Beethoven's own Op. 18 had exemplified? Beethoven's last quartets are esoteric creations, sung by their creator himself, just as God might meditate in his heart, finding no partner of equal rank. Beethoven communicated here only so much as a very deep, inner compulsion forced to become articulate, indifferent to its finding a listener. And everyone knows how long it took, in the 19th century, for listeners to be found.

The Romantic musicians apprehended this separation and imitated it, even if it was not always so much a matter of compulsion and so well grounded with them as with Beethoven. They felt painfully the gulf that began to yawn between them and the world. A cleavage started to make its appearance even as early as Franz Schubert, who distinguished between works that he had written for himself, his circle of friends, and serious music-lovers, and those that he had written for "success": in the one group, the String Quintet or the D-minor String Quartet, in the other the popular *Trout* Quintet or the brilliant Duet for Piano and Violin, Op. 159. Profound and painfully felt was the gulf that isolated one part of the work of the arch-Romanticist Robert Schumann. It was as if he wished to make good the subjectivity of his first works—a subjectivity that goes so far as to become a kind of hide-and-seek, a guessing-game: so he placed his *Bagatelles,* his *Kreisleriana,* his C-major Fantasy over against his *Scenes from Childhood,* his *Album for the Young,* his *Bunte Blätter.* He felt that he had made a sacrifice for his subjectivity, even for his subjectivity linked with virtuosity—though never for his mere virtuosity. But he felt also that in so doing he had relinquished the firm basis of general musical practice, and he wrote his *Home and Life Rules for Musicians,* which originally were incorporated in his *Album for the Young.* "The laws of morals," he there wrote, "are also those of art." And the moral laws apply to all.

All the Romantic musicians felt the contradiction, felt their isolation; but it was felt most passionately of all by Berlioz and Wagner. Berlioz wrote no—or almost no—intimate works: he could have written string quartets or piano pieces only if he had wished to make fun of himself. The more colossal the means that he set in motion, the better he felt. He could not wait, accordingly, till the appropriate mass of people found their way to him; he had to conquer them. Only half of his life was taken up with the creation of his works; the rest of it with presenting them before a great audience—in Paris, in London, in Germany, wherever there was half a chance of subjugating a public. And the greatest tragedy of his life lay perhaps in the fact that the conquest of that mass was so hard, so seldom successful.

With Wagner, finally, the violence required for connecting and bridging over the gap can scarcely be surpassed. From *Rienzi* to *Lohengrin* his obvious demands on the theater public increased more and more. Then, however, he was driven, by his personal misfortune (his exile from Germany) and by his refusal to compromise in artistic matters, to lonelier and lonelier heights, to an ever more personal creed—and that in the field of opera, which is unthinkable without the participation of the public, of a public at once most refined and most vulgar! *Tristan and Isolde,* most personal, passionate—though not most lonely—avowal of faith, was offered to this opera public! Wagner, the most subjective of all artists, must try to form from the mass a congregation—his congregation—and that precisely in a field that placed in his way the very greatest obstacles. And he succeeded halfway, though in the end he resigned himself to his fate and wished that *Parsifal* might be reserved for a more limited congregation.

FOLK SONG AS A CURE FOR ISOLATION

A great number of other musicians attempted to bridge the gap in another manner, that of meeting the audience halfway, of coming to an agreement with the nation by cultivating the most homely kind of song, by cultivating folk song. The veneration of the folk song is typically Romantic; it has even a mystical tinge. For the Romantic movement believed in the anonymous origin of folk song, in its birth from the very womb of the "nation." In actuality, folk song is created by an individual, and taken up by a higher or lower stratum of the people, whereby it is usually changed, simplified, sung over and over again—not always to its advantage.

Earlier centuries were not familiar with this veneration of folk song. On the contrary, in Italy, as the 15th century was giving way to the 16th, it was rather an object of jest and laughter, even of scorn. Although the masters of sacred polyphony drew upon it for motivic suggestions, they did so in anything but a spirit of reverence. For every day new folk songs could well arise.

This attitude first changed at the end of the 18th century; and again, as in literature, England first established the basis for the new relationship with the apparent bit of "nature" or "antiquity" that seemed to be embodied in the folk song. In June of 1793, George Thomson published his first "set" of Scottish songs. He followed up this first half of a volume with six further ones in the years up to 1841, and also brought out collections of Irish and Welsh songs—collections made famous for the part taken in their preparation by Haydn and Beethoven. Thomson's intention was not "Romantic," nor was it purely scholarly; he was trying simply to save these old melodies from oblivion and to make them productive for his day.

The Romantic phase of folklore did not begin to appear until later, especially in Germany, where two arch-Romantic poets, Arnim and Brentano, in 1805 (and later), under the strange title "The Boy's Magic Horn"

(*Des Knaben Wunderhorn*) "brought out a German song collection, in which the cosmopolitan character of Herder's 'Folk Songs' became merely national." [3] The musicians followed the example of the poets. For Schubert, significantly enough, folk song was not as yet an object of veneration and imitation: he lived in Vienna, where the "folk" at that time still sang, and he was himself a child either of the people or of heaven. When he chanced upon a text that had found its way into verse from the heart of the folk, like Goethe's "Heidenröslein" or Wilhelm Müller's "Lindenbaum," he set it to music without wishing himself to create an idealized folk song or, as in the second example, the basis for a folk song. But in the Romantic North men began to collect and reverently to imitate. Mendelssohn published three "folk songs" for mixed chorus in his Opus 41, and sought to use folk motives especially in his songs and choral compositions for men's voices. Schumann's endeavor, above all, was to succeed, in his Romances and Ballades, in striking the genuine tone of folk material. Brahms, finally, cannot be understood without an appreciation of the Romantic—that is, the half mystical—relation of the composer to folk song. It is well known that towards the end of his life he brought out about fifty folk songs with German text, taking special precautions to protect this work in various countries, and that it was secretly a source of particular satisfaction to him that one of his own songs, the very beautiful *In stiller Nacht,* was thus brought out under the folklike, anonymous label. Highest triumph—to have created a folk song! A song of such spontaneous generation that it seemed to be a product of the soul of the people!

NEW FUNCTION OF MUSIC IN THE ROMANTIC ERA

The relation of the Romantic epoch to folk song was a sentimental relationship: impulses were aroused by it that had been foreign to earlier centuries. Thus, in the Romantic period, music was given a new general function. It became a remedy for languor; it became in itself a stimulant. It demanded more of the listener than it had done in earlier times, and the listener demanded more—and something different—of it. Even in the 18th century a few "profane" types of art, notably the opera—quite apart from the edifying, uplifting effect of church music—had endeavored to lead the listener out beyond the limits of his own mind. Gluck sought to renew the dignity and the purifying effect (of catharsis) achieved by

[3] W. Scherer *Geschichte der deutschen Literatur* 9th ed. (Berlin, 1902), p. 636.

Greek tragedy. His operas, from *Orfeo ed Euridice* to *Echo et Narcisse,* left the participants with a different, more sublime memory than that of having enjoyed mere entertainment. It is noteworthy that the real historical effect of Gluck's operas, which are ostensibly so Classical, is an *after*-effect, and first achieved its culminating point in the beginnings of musical Romanticism: in the Berlin of E. T. A. Hoffmann, the Paris of Hector Berlioz, and the Dresden of Richard Wagner. In the field of instrumental music, the symphony took over this "uplifting," arousing function. Nothing of the sort was as yet evident in Haydn and Mozart, whose symphonies always remained within the social frame, even in exceptional works such as Mozart's G-minor Symphony. True, they were born of deepest excitement, but they renounced all pathos, they remained within the limits of the fatalistic; they did not openly appeal to the listener. In general, Haydn and Mozart limited themselves in their symphonies and chamber music to the attainment of noble mirth, to a purification of the feelings, to a catharsis through pure art. In this connection one might ask oneself whether this "limitation," this remaining in a more sublime region, is not a paradise that has been lost by the Romantic movement.

In Beethoven the change began with the *Eroica,* increasing in the Fifth, the Sixth, the Ninth Symphonies. Here began the appeal—to the heroic, to the religious, to the moral. The *deed* itself could always ensue immediately upon the last note in the Finale of each of these works, just as the Belgian movement for independence was linked with the performance of Auber's *Muette de Portici.* Beethoven had not intended it so: he wished to create by the *Eroica* an inner agitation and no external effect; aware of its unusual length he wished it to be placed towards the beginning rather than at the end of a program (*più vicino al principio ch'al fine di un'Accademia*).

Of course, the appeal of music in opera and symphony has only very seldom actually led to the *deed.* All the more deeply this appeal impressed itself upon the consciousness of the hearers. In the Romantic era they demanded of music a new effect, either pacifying or exciting—above all, exciting. It has already been noted, in passing, that the middle-class era which succeeded the Napoleonic wars sought in art a substitute for the heroic experience. We do not wish to do an injustice to the age: it gave birth to the July Revolution and the uprisings of 1848; it was full of bloodshed and horror, of political and social strife scarcely less than other, rougher ages. Despite all that, however, it was also the age of Metternich, of the Citizen-King, of the Prussian, Hanoverian, and Hessian reactionary movement. It was the Victorian era; it was the time of a new, commercial, cultured middle class. This age loved to have its feelings whipped up by art; what life denied it, it sought to behold in a more passionate, a heightened reflection, to experience in *art*.

It is highly noteworthy that Schubert early felt this reversed relationship and lamented it in his "Complaint to the People," a poem that he included in a letter of 1824 to his friend Schober:

> O youth of this our time, you fade and die!
> And squandered is the strength of men unnumbered,
> Not one stands out, so by the crowd encumbered,
> And, signifying nothing, all pass by.
>
> Too great the pain by which I am consumed,
> And in me but one dying ember flashes;
> This age has turned me, deedless, into ashes,
> While every man to bootless deeds is doomed.
>
> In sick old age the people creep along,
> They judge but dreams their youthful deeds impassioned,
> Yea, laugh to scorn the golden rhymes once fashioned,
> Attending not these verses' message strong.
>
> To thee 'tis given, holy Art and great,
> To figure forth an age when deeds could flourish,
> To still the pain, the dying hope to nourish,
> Which never reconciles that age with fate.

Art, and especially music, dissociated itself more and more from life. Meanwhile, in the house of God the musical service declined and, at its best, turned back to Palestrina in the Catholic churches and to Bach in the Protestant. And also, the rooms of the aristocratic and patrician families where once chamber music had been heard became ever more silent. The music-lover sought new excitement or relaxation after the cares of the day, in the opera house or concert hall. The opera, the symphony, even chamber music met this demand. The stirring up or calming down of the feelings became more and more intense, more subjective; out of emotion there arose more and more of exhibition—by the end of the century an exhibitionism of such intensity as is found in Tchaikovsky or Gustav Mahler.

The man of the 16th, 17th, and 18th centuries to whom music was at all available sought in it exaltation, self-composure, and enrichment. The creative artist, if he was a genius, opened up to the listener regions of feeling that otherwise would have remained to him mysterious, confused, deformed, or entirely strange. Even in the 19th century there were still many who felt that way, who demanded no more than that of music: they were the "Mozartians," the opponents particularly of Wagner and Liszt. They were the "classically" disposed souls. But those who had been infected with the Romantic virus demanded something else of music; they demanded that they be "transported." They lived fully only so long as they were hearing something: music became for them a substitute for life. Above all, the operas of Wagner exerted this exciting, intoxicating effect, seeming to heighten the whole individual's potentialities and, in extreme cases, rendering those entranced by this effect unfit for life. What a change from the end of the 18th century, when music was essentially still "applied art," an ornament of life in the service of society, all the way to this exclusion and separation of music from life!

ROMANTIC VIEW OF EARLIER MUSIC

This conception of music affected also the interpretation of the art of earlier periods. The music of the past appeared in a Romantic light. As we have said, the Romantics claimed Beethoven, from the very beginning as one of their number. "Beethoven's music," declared E. T. A. Hoffmann in his discussion of the Fifth Symphony, "touches the springs of horror, of fear, of terror, of pain, and awakens that infinite yearning that is the nature of Romanticism; Beethoven is a purely Romantic (and for that very reason a truly musical) composer. . . ." Later, Hoffmann repeated this description and emphasized it more passionately in his review of the two Piano Trios, Opus 70. He was too good a musician not to reject unequivocally any crudely programmatic interpretation of Beethoven's instrumental music, and not to recognize the formal mastery —he called it "thoughtfulness"—of these works. Nevertheless, he saw in Beethoven the opposite to a "Classical" master.

Although Robert Schumann still saw in Beethoven the great master of absolute music, of inherent musical logic, he took the liberty, about 1835, of reading a concealed "program" into Beethoven's works, just as he did into his own. When he wrote, "I was afraid of being stoned by the Beethovenites if I were to say what kind of a text I would read into the final movement of the A-major Symphony . . . ," he must have had in mind a noisy scene from a novel by his favorite author, Jean Paul. Whom was he thinking of when he used the word "Beethovenites"?

Beethoven's followers who still looked upon the master as a child of the 18th century, the successor to Haydn and Mozart, the last in the triad of "Viennese Classics"? But Beethoven did not become a "Classic" again until well on in the 19th century, and he is as little a Classic as he was ever a Romantic. Nevertheless, shortly after his death he became a Romantic.

Where Schumann was seeking the secret poetical impulses behind Beethoven's compositions, the *Eroica* became for Berlioz entirely a "Homeric Symphony." "In his magnificent musical epic," Berlioz wrote, "which justly or unjustly has been considered as inspired by a modern hero, reminiscences of the ancient *Iliad* play a wonderfully beautiful, but no less evident, role." In the Ninth Symphony Berlioz despaired of finding out "what personal ideas Beethoven may have wished to express in this vast musical poem," but he never for an instant doubted that it was a "musical *poem*." The slow movements were for him "superhuman meditations, into which the pantheistic genius of Beethoven so loves to plunge itself." The "pantheistic genius"!

Berlioz established contact here with Wagner, who went to great trouble, in his paper for the centenary of Beethoven's birth, to characterize Beethoven as the purest and greatest representative of music, quite along the lines of Schopenhauer's philosophical ideas. This description has very much to do with Wagner, but very little with the true Beethoven, the child of the Revolution and of the victory over all that is revolutionary, the child of humanity itself; it certainly has nothing at all to do with the "intuitive idea of the will to life."

We shall not multiply examples and names. As no musician of the Romantic era could remain aloof from the necessity of coming to terms with the mighty phenomenon of Beethoven, this relationship need not be discussed for each individual. Yet to each one Beethoven appeared in a different light.

It was not only Beethoven who appeared to the Romantics in a new, shifting light; it was the musical past in general. To be sure, it was not the entire musical past. Like every living intellectual movement, Romanticism in music had its objects of preference, of antipathy, and of indifference. E. T. A. Hoffmann, himself a child of the 18th century, still thought of Beethoven in connection with Haydn and Mozart; accordingly, he considered not only Beethoven but also the two earlier masters as Romantics, even though he was at some pains to justify his inclusion of Haydn. But the generation of musicians born in the first two decades of the new century was more strongly influenced by the rule of revolt and of contradiction, which usually marks off the sons from the fathers. The "Classicists" in one camp, in the other the "Romantics"! This was true in spite of the growing popularity of Haydn and Mozart in the first half of the century. Mendelssohn, Schumann, Berlioz, Liszt, and Wagner consummated completely their separation from pre-Beethoven music, in spite of all honor for Mozart—and with Berlioz, not even sincere honor. No one has misunderstood Mozart's deepest symphony, that in G minor, more thoroughly than Schumann—unless it be Wagner, with his epithet about "musical genius of light and love." And Haydn particularly, was obliged to suffer from this separation, despite—and perhaps precisely because of—his popularity. People surrendered him to the Philistines; they spoke patronizingly of him as "Papa Haydn"; they even went so far as to keep alive the memory of his pigtail. To the Romantics he appeared much too clear, too full of life and wit, too transparent, for them to know quite what to do with him.

ROMANTICIZED REVIVAL OF THE PAST

An entirely new characteristic, however, of musical Romanticism as well as of the Romantic era in general, was the fact that it cultivated an entirely new relationship with the past. Earlier creative periods had not known a relationship of this sort, in any field. The Baroque had placed its chapels and altars, with their ecstatic saints and chubby angels, nonchalantly in Romanesque and Gothic churches; and only with the 19th century was any effort made towards "correct stylistic restoration." The period of Josquin had completely forgotten not only the musicians of the *Trecento* but also Dufay, the greatest master of the 15th century; and Monteverdi in his maturity was no longer acutely conscious of Palestrina. It is true that after the stylistic change that occurred about 1600— the "discovery" of monody and the *concertante* style—the art of the Palestrina period continued to maintain a semblance of life; but it had become an archaic art. It is significant that the Romantic era rediscovered the art of Tallis, Byrd, and Palestrina, and of their period. It is the same movement that in England brought to maturity the Pre-Raphaelite school of painters and in Germany the "Nazarenes," with their pilgrimages to Rome and their paintings of the Madonna, that led once more to the building of Gothic cathedrals and palaces in Tudor style. Behind this revival of a remote past, there stood the sentimental preference for everything medieval, far away, mellow, and—especially in the field of German church music—the protest against the allegedly secular art displayed by the three "Viennese" masters in their liturgic compositions, and, from the Protestant side, against the flat and rationalistic adornment of the church service. A Protestant monarch, the Prussian King Friedrich Wilhelm IV, sent Protestant musicians to Rome, to study the genuine Catholic style of sacred music, the Palestrina style. This inclination was quite in keeping with the revival of the ancient Greek tragedy, the *Antigone* with music by Mendelssohn.

In the masses, psalms, and motets of the 16th century, people saw the purest embodiment of an ideal church music—unearthly, freed from all passion, seraphic. They constructed an ideal of *a cappella* song that had never existed; they overlooked the many traits of strength, of naïveté, of worldliness, that had also been present in the church music of that time. And thus the archaic imitations of this style throughout the 19th century —those of Ett, Aiblinger, and others—are just as flat and empty as the Gothic or Romanesque churches of correct and scholarly architects.

In consequence of this Romanticizing revival of the past, there arose a new discipline, musicology. This was the time when the Viennese R. G. Kiesewetter wrote his "History of European-Occidental or our Present Day Music" (*Geschichte der europäisch-abendländischen oder unsrer heutigen Musik,* 1834) and his "The Changing Aspects and Nature of Secular Song" (*Schicksale und Beschaffenheit des weltlichen Gesanges,* 1841); the Prussian Carl von Winterfeld his "Giovanni Gabrieli and his Period" (*Johannes Gabrieli und sein Zeitalter,* 1834) and his history of Evangelical sacred song (*Der evangelische Kirchengesang und sein Verhältnis zur Kunst des Tonsatzes,* 1843 ff.). Others, like the Belgian Fétis embarked on vast researches, and associations, such as the Musical Antiquarian Society in London (1840–7), were founded "for the publication of scarce and valuable works by the early English composers," tried to propagandize Byrd and Wilbye, Weelkes and Dowland, Gibbons and Purcell. This interest was something new, something different from the rather antiquarian or archaeological interest of Padre Martini or Forkel in the more distant past of music, or the more amateurish concern of Hawkins and Burney, who never deviated from the point of view of their country. It was objective research and at the same time subjective yearning: it was Romanticism.

NEW VENERATION OF J. S. BACH

Yet before the enthusiasm for Palestrina and his style, there had arisen a still more strange and enthusiastic movement—that towards a new appreciation of Johann Sebastian Bach. This, too, had a certain Romantic coloring. Bach had never been entirely forgotten. He lived in the active memory of his elder sons, Wilhelm Friedemann and Carl Philipp Emanuel, and also in that of the "Bückeburg" Bach, Johann Christoph Friedrich. He lived in the reverence of his pupils, and never entirely died out in the repertory of the Thomas-Kirche, not even under the cantorship of Johann Adam Hiller, a decided adherent of Handel. But in this Rationalistic age, the reverence and admiration was bestowed more on the great organist. It is a question, moreover, whether to the ears of his son in Hamburg, Carl Philipp Emanuel, the works of his father were expressive, singing, sentimental enough. Only the three great masters—Haydn, and especially Mozart and Beethoven—sought to come to terms in a creative way with the work of the "first parent of music." Bach was, to the second half of the 18th century, a scholastic of polyphony. His works had didactic value; he was a masterful model. Quantz, an elder contemporary of Emanuel's, had Bach primarily in mind when he wrote thus about the German masters around 1700: "Their style was . . . harmonious and full-voiced, but not melodious and charming. They sought more to compose in an artistic than in a comprehensible and pleasing manner, more for the eye than for the ear." [4]

About 1800 the figure of Bach emerged from these confines—the confines of a circle of admiration and contemplation. A new enthusiasm was astir in England and Germany. In 1799, the London organist August Friedrich Christoph Kollmann prepared a new edition of the E-flat Trio (No. 1 of the Organ Sonatas), and pleaded for the publication of the *Well-Tempered Clavier*. Bach found a still more fiery English admirer in Samuel Wesley, to whom—as he wrote in his letters to Benjamin Jacob in 1808—Bach's works were "a musical Bible, unrivaled and inimitable." Bach's greatness as an artist attained mystical proportions. Is it not strange that Wesley—like the German Romantic poets Zacharias Werner, Friedrich Schlegel, and Ludwig Tieck—went over to Catholicism? It was no longer the scholastic, didactic Bach whom Wesley praised and exalted to the skies (very characteristically, at the expense of Handel), but it was the pure artist, the consummation of an era, whose greatness and

[4] *Versuch* . . . (Berlin, 1752), XVIII, par. 79.

innocence and purity shone in the past as unattainably as the architecture of the Gothic age.

In Germany, at the same time, it was the Music Director at the University of Göttingen, Johann Nicolaus Forkel, whose book "On Johann Sebastian Bach's Life, Art, and Works (*Über Johann Sebastian Bachs Leben, Kunst und Kunstwerke,* 1802) laid the foundations for a new conception of Bach. Forkel, a violent opponent of Gluck, had been impelled by several emotional factors—by the newly awakened feeling for the historical, by the yearning for an apparently better artistic age in the past, and by nationalistic pride. Bach was to belong no longer simply to a narrow circle of connoisseurs, but to all the people. "Preserving the memory of this great man," he declared, "is not simply a matter of artistic concern—it is a matter of national concern." This was a new point of departure, unknown to the rationalistic, universal, humanistic 18th century, and inapplicable to Handel. Handel had been born in Germany, educated in Italy, and made by England into what he was; but Bach was a *German* composer. This antithesis is true only in the sense that Bach was the "founder" of German music: but it was typical of the Romantic era, which began to separate the nationalities in music.

Carl Maria Weber, too, expressed the same idea when he wrote in 1821, the year of the first presentation of *Der Freischütz:* "Sebastian Bach's characteristic feature was, even in its strictness, really Romantic, of fundamentally German nature, perhaps in contrast to Handel's more Classical greatness." At the same time, Bach's sacred music was being fostered in Carl Friedrich Zelter's Berlin Song Academy, even though Zelter was also of the opinion that there was still much that was learned and pedantic about the old master. Nevertheless, he had a sure feeling for Bach's greatness, although it was not he himself but his friend Goethe who was able to formulate this feeling: "As listeners to Bach's music, we may feel as if we were present when God created the world." In such a way occurred the transition from chaos to cosmos! That is a thoroughly Romantic idea.

Zelter's exertions on behalf of Bach were brought to a conclusion by his pupil Mendelssohn, who staged in 1829 the first public performance of the Passion according to St. Matthew. This was an entirely "Romantic" affair. In the course of a century, how everything had changed! Bach's Passion, a work composed for the Divine service and the liturgical ceremony, transplanted to the concert hall; shortened, mutilated. completely modernized in sound, and—as Zelter expressed it—"rendered practical for the abilities of the performers"! Not merely for the abilities of the performers, but also for the mental capacity of the public. It was no longer the Bach of the Bible, of the Lutheran faith, of the magnificent simplicity, but a Romanticized Bach, reduced to Mendelssohnian formulae. But precisely these Romanticized details were what made the greatest impression on the public. Only in the course of the 19th century was Bach gradually divested of this Romantic costume, and presented in purer outline.

But, however this conception of Bach may have been constituted, it remained—just as with Beethoven—almost impossible for any creative musician of the Romantic period to remain aloof from coming to terms with Bach. Only Schubert—lucky fellow—did not find it necessary. And for Berlioz, who was too passionate to cultivate a historical sense, Bach did not exist at all, except as an object of irony and hate. Bach was indeed a dangerous inheritance for the Romantics. He was antipodal to them in every respect; yet they reverently had to make the best of him. By none of them was he successfully imitated; and by only a few—Chopin, Wagner, Brahms, Bizet, César Franck—was his style successfully fused, in various ways, with the Romantic idiom.

VIRTUOSITY VS. INTIMACY

Among the contradictions of the Romantic movement is the fact that, at the same time that it was reviving the past and manifesting its own tendencies towards extreme intimacy and absorption, it raised virtuosity to unprecedented heights. Virtuosity had not been unknown in the earlier centuries. In the 16th century the lute and *gamba* had brought forth players of especial technical skill unattainable by the mere amateur. The lute and gamba were succeeded by the harpsichord and the violin. And in the 18th century, with the vocal art of the *castrati* and of a few prima donnas, the human voice seemed to have attained a power and flexibility surpassing even that of the singers of Rossini's and Bellini's time. There was still a group of vocal virtuosi of the earlier 19th century, feminine and masculine—Catalani, Pasta, Nourrit, Tamberlick, Lablache—to whom the present day looks back, half with a smile, but also half in envy. The real, new virtuosity, however, occupied itself particularly with two instruments, the violin and the piano. It was connected, of course, with the rise of the new public, the mass, which was no longer to be conquered with Mozart's or even Clementi's sonatas.

The distinction between the intimate and the brilliant became sharper and sharper. It was—as has already been remarked—already perceptible in Beethoven, although the difficulties in Beethoven's sonatas are always subservient to the expression, and are never there simply for their own sake. Still, he made the Rondo of the *Waldstein* Sonata so difficult, he constructed it so much according to his own personal technique that, as he himself said, not everyone could imitate his playing of it. With Carl Maria Weber, intimacy completely disappeared in favor of brilliance. Not only were his variations, polonaises, and rondos intended for performance, for the concert hall, but also his sonatas: all four are "Grand Sonatas," and all four contain movements *di bravura.* And after Weber there followed a host of virtuoso composers, who as musicians were subservient to their instrument—Kalkbrenner and Czerny, Dreyschock and Thalberg, Herz and Hünten, and whatever the names of the rest may be. Even Schubert had to bring a few offerings to the altar of *bravura;* even Mendelssohn had to strew a few flowers.

About 1820, then, there came from Italy to conquer the European concert halls a violinist about whose virtuosity there still breathes today an air of fabulous enchantment, Nicolo Paganini. The clash, the compromise of virtuosity with great art could not be more clearly demonstrated than by the program of a concert of Paganini's in Breslau on July 28, 1829. Between the movements of Beethoven's First Symphony, so mercilessly torn asunder, he played the following: a "Grand Concerto," an "Adagio and Rondo with Bell," "Variations for the G-string on the Prayer from Rossini's *Mosè*," and "Variations on *Nel cor più non mi sento.*" But Paganini was no mere trickster, and his extant works can give us no conception of the demoniac power of his playing. According to the testimony of his contemporaries such as Heinrich Heine, it must have been a way of playing in which the consummation of the mechanical extended into the weird, to the weirdness of E. T. A. Hoffmann's characters. Even Louis Spohr, the leading representative of the German style of violin playing in this period, had to acknowledge, half against his will, Paganini's peculiar power.

Paganini's example then kindled into flame the sparks of resolve in Franz Liszt to bring his art to the same perfection on his own instrument, the piano—and, if possible, to surpass it. And he achieved his end, precisely because he was much more than a mere virtuoso. He began with matters of technique, with the *Études d'exécution transcendante d'après Paganini;* but alongside the Allegro, Rondo, *Grande Valse di Bravura,* beside the Fantasies on Favorite Themes after Bellini, Donizetti, Meyerbeer, there also came into being the *Album d'un Voyageur* and the *Années de Pèleri-nage*. The virtuosity in Liszt became sated with itself. And masters like Schumann and Chopin—along with Liszt, the greatest piano composers of the Romantic era, both Romantics of the first water, both antagonists of the merely virtuoso—struck at virtuosity with their own weapons, virtuosity in the service of poetical expression.

CHAPTER VI

Universal and National Music

UNIVERSALITY IN THE EIGHTEENTH CENTURY

IN THE music of the Romantic era, the peoples began to drift apart. In the 18th century there had been only three nations to which a national character in music and a national development could be definitely attributed: the Italian, the French, and the German. At the beginning of that century, moreover, the German nation was still not quite sure whether it might claim for itself a distinctive character, or whether its music was not simply an Italian-French mixture.

There had been no lack of nationalistic manifestations, even in the 18th century; but they had assumed extensive proportions only in France, where the inhabitants were proud of their traditional leadership in all matters of taste, and where—as early as about 1700—they amused themselves by debating the relative merits of Italian and French music. In so doing, however, they forgot that the style of French opera had been established by a Florentine musician, Giovanni Battista Lulli, on the model of the Roman cantata of 1650. About 1760 and 1780 this controversy over national operatic form grew sharper and sharper, until Gluck closed it with his own form of opera. Gluck was a man who hated all nationalistic limitations; a contemporary of his, Johann Adam Hiller, justly said of him that "the confines of all national music are too narrow for him: out of Italian and French music, out of every people, he has made a music that is his own. . . ."

Outside the field of opera, the public—even in France—was not merely tolerant; it was completely unprejudiced. Nowhere were the symphonies of Stamitz and Haydn more enthusiastically received than in Paris. One has only to recall the names of the Parisian composers fashionable during the period of Mozart's youth—Schobert, Eckardt, Honnauer—to observe that they do not sound very French. Since the arrival of Handel, England had become an importing country, particularly of Italian music; and the parodic protest of *The Beggar's Opera* only bore out how firmly established this import was. The serious rivals of Handel were not, as it happened, English composers, but Italian. In Germany an attempt was made about 1770 to start a "Teutsche Oper," but the "teutsch" in this phrase referred solely to the choice of subject matter—as in Holzbauer's *Günther von Schwarzburg* or Schweitzer's *Rosamunde*.

In Italy itself, moreover, there was no chauvinism in music, no hatred of the French such as that expressed by Alfieri in his poetry. This was so for the simple reason that Italy's leadership, her rule of the world in this respect, stood under no shadow of doubt. Of course, the French too— even the Germans—made music; but one did not need to concern oneself with it: Italian music was world-music.

The music of the greatest 18th-century composers, Haydn and Mozart —and, still more, of the master who stood at the turn of the century, Beethoven—is universal. Haydn would not have understood how a controversy could one day arise over the question of whether he had been a "Croatian" or a "German" musician—a controversy in which a certain advantage lay from the start with the British champion of the "Croatian" Haydn, for his evidence was based on musical characteristics, while the advocate of the "German" Haydn based his case on highly questionable genealogical data. Actually, Haydn wrote his own kind of music, neither German nor Croatian. He wrote, in two of his piano trios, both a *Rondo all'ongarese* and a *Rondo alla tedesca;* and he borrowed many other details from popular music, even where he did not acknowledge the indebtedness in the title. But he was not for that reason either a "Hungarian" or a "German" composer, or any other kind. His *Rondo alla tedesca* is precisely a sign that he cultivated certain relationships with the "German"— that is, with the folklike German—but did not feel himself to be completely German. He spoke to human beings, with sentiment, spirit, and wit; and thus was understood in Paris and London even earlier than he was, for example, in Berlin. He was even understood in Italy. He stands high above everything national, let alone nationalistic.

With Mozart things were no different. We do not need to be told that he was a Freemason, and that one of his last works, *The Magic Flute,* is a document in the struggle against gloom and narrowness of every kind, an apotheosis of humaneness: we feel this universal spirit in all of his music. One will never be able to decide, moreover, whether his music is German or Italian—it is both, or neither: it is Mozartian, and for that reason it is universal. The fact has often been noted and expressed that Mozart's music never receives its suggestions from nature, from the "open air," as did that of Haydn and Schubert, but from either the works of others or previous works of his own; it involves a sort of pure artistic inbreeding. Sometimes—though very seldom—Mozart seems to be "Salz-burgian" or "Viennese"; but, when so, it is more a relationship of condescension, of irony. Mozart is not "folksy": he is always himself. It is significant that throughout his *Don Giovanni,* which is set "in a Spanish city" (*in una città di Spagna*), and throughout his *Nozze,* with its scene in the neighborhood of Seville, Mozart makes use of Spanish coloring only once, in a short ballet intermezzo. His characters may be dressed in Spanish costume; yet costume is not the chief thing. By way of contrast, one need only think of *Carmen,* of the charm that Bizet obtained from the Spanish local color, without, however, forgetting the human beings involved; for he likewise was a great musician.

Even Beethoven would have been very much astonished if he had known that he would one day be called the "Giant of the Lower Rhine" and would be claimed as a national composer from both the Flemish and the German sides, quite apart from his position as the last in the triad of "Viennese Classics." As for him, moreover, there is scarcely need to cite *Fidelio,* and to recall the words there of Don Fernando:

> The brother seeks his brothers . . .

or the Ninth Symphony with its apotheosis of the fraternal union of mankind under the star of divine love. Beethoven never addressed himself to a nation. In his Third Symphony he wished to chant a hymn of praise for the man who had consummated the French Revolution—an event which had driven his electoral patron from his estate—and thus it became a work "to celebrate the *memory* of a great man" (*per festiggiare il Sovvenire di un grand Uomo*); but when Napoleon made himself Emperor of the French, Beethoven tore up the dedication.

NEW ENTHUSIASM FOR REGIONAL COLOR

One would have to search very diligently in Beethoven's musical language to find a trace of national dialect. The reason is that the quality of the melody, as such, had little significance for Beethoven, and that he restamped and recast the melody until it represented his intention, until it was able to render perceptible that music which lay *behind* the music.

Nothing is more indicative of his attitude towards the stock of melodies of each nation than his use of two Russian tunes in his Quartets Op. 59, which he dedicated to Count Rasumowsky. One of these melodies—that in the third movement of the second Quartet (in E minor), or, more specifically, in the *Maggiore* of the Allegretto which stands in place of the Scherzo—is the same as that used by Musorgsky in one of the most colorful folk scenes of his *Boris,* and one can imagine nothing more genuine, more "Russian" than this scene. For Beethoven, however, these melodies were nothing but thematic material, motivic building stones, like any other. Just as he wrote a Polonaise in which there was nothing Polish but the rhythm, so he wrote in the B-flat Quartet Op. 130 a movement "in the manner of a German dance" (*alla danza tedesca*)—not, as it were, an actual "German dance." His relationship to the national idea resembles his relationship to the fugue, "now free, now artful" (*tantôt libre, tantôt recherché*). He reserved for himself the right to take all kinds of liberties. He used national reminiscences, just as he did the stricter forms, for his own purposes.

This state of things was immediately changed with the appearance of the Romantics. We shall be obliged to concern ourselves more closely with the problem of Weber's Germanism later on; and even if the Germanic aspects of *Der Freischütz,* on closer view, may tend to disappear, the nationalistic intention and effect of this "Romantic opera," in contrast to *The Magic Flute* and *Fidelio,* is quite certain. Weber was the first composer with an eye for the intrinsic melodic value of folk melodies. He was to the "universal" musicians of the 18th century what the two compilers of *Des Knaben Wunderhorn,* Arnim and Brentano, were to Johann Gottfried Herder, the editor of that collection of folk songs (1778 and 1779) which was later christened "Voices of the Peoples in Songs" (*Stimmen der Völker in Liedern*). For Herder, poetry was the mother tongue of the human race. He felt a purely humanistic devotion to foreign peoples and remote periods of the past, and did not care much whether a song came from Germany, from Spain, from Lapland, or from Peru. The two Romantics, however, limited themselves to the German, and thus they acquired a new sense for foreign national color, as did also those who held the same opinion among the other nations. In *Richard Cœur de Lion* (1784), old Grétry had used a Provençal melody (later employed by Beethoven for a set of piano variations) as a kind of leitmotif; but one will not discover much that is Provençal or ancient about it. Weber, however, in the first Finale of *Oberon,* used in connection with a little aria sung by his Rezia a genuine Arabian melody for the chorus of harem guards, a tune which he had found in a travel book (by Carsten Niebuhr, 1774) and which was intended to sound Arabian, grotesque, and weird—and it does achieve precisely that effect. He also found the horn motive, which ushers in the happy resolution of the plot, as a *"Danse turque"* in Laborde's *Essai sur la Musique* (1780).

Even Schubert was already affected by the new enthusiasm for the national *as* national. When, alongside his lieder, he composes a series of Italian *canzonette,* they are—one might say—more Italian than those of Rossini himself, without being imitations of Rossini. To be sure, Beethoven had also composed several vocal works with Italian texts and in Italian style, such as his scena *"Ah! perfido,"* his terzetto *"Tremate, empj,"* and several arias and canzonets; but he used Italian merely as one of the universal languages of music. With Schubert, Italian was already a fascinating, colorful costume. And this was true not merely of Italian. Schubert was more Viennese than his predecessors, than—for example—Mozart, who wrote *"Deutsche Tänze"* or *"Ländler"* that might have come from Salzburg or any other place south of the Danube. Schubert's *"Ländler"* turned into waltzes—a development that was something more than a mere change of name. Something more sensuous, flexible, luxurious pulses through them—a feature characteristic of the "City of the Phæacians," as Beethoven called Vienna. And the fact that Schubert lived for a time on a Hungarian estate was not without its effect. How often did he give movements of his works a Hungarian tinge, even when his acknowledgment of it is not so clear as it is in his *Divertissement à l'hongroise,* Op. 54, for four hands: for example, in the Finale of his A-minor Quartet, in the Allegretto of his C-major Fantasy for Violin and Piano, Op. 159, and in the slow movement of his C-major Symphony. He utilized the minor mode, the particular harmonic resources, and the sharp rhythm of the Hungarian music dialect for his own, Schubertian melancholy; he was quite himself, even in Magyar costume. And he also knew how to wear French costume; among his works for piano four-hands are to be found no less than five "on French themes" (Op. 10; 63; 82, 1; and Op. 84, 1 and 2). Among his lieder, how different is his setting of an Ossianic poem from that of one of Hölty's neo-Classical odes, or one of Schiller's neo-Classical ballads! One of his earliest vocal works was a three-part romance, *Don Gayseros,* which displays pronounced Spanish coloring, although the youth of sixteen or seventeen who wrote it had never seen Spain.

This taste for imagining oneself in strange lands or remote periods, this joy in costume, is genuinely Romantic. And as the movement developed, the regions became more and more numerous, and farther and farther away. It is quite in keeping with the art of Carl Loewe, Schubert's rival as a ballad-composer, that the complete edition of his songs is divided into sections according to the national coloring of the individual pieces—into Polish, French, Spanish, Oriental ballads. The feeling for the national, for the provincial, became sharper and sharper.

Berlioz might serve as an example of the way Italian developed from a universal language of music to a national one—even, it might be said, to one peculiar to a region. The first movement of his *Harold en Italie* (1834) presents Byron's Romantic hero in "scenes of melancholy, of happiness, and of joy." But the second and third, the "March of the Pilgrims Chanting their Evening Prayer" and the "Serenade of a Mountaineer of Abruzzi to his Mistress," are ethnographical studies of a tourist—of a tourist who, like Berlioz, has known Italy and the clear sky, the heroic contour of the mountains, and has deeply loved the simple Roman people. The "Scene in the Fields" of the *Symphonic fantastique* (1830-31) is more sharply localized than the "Storm" in Beethoven's *Pastoral* Symphony, and is—if not "more sentiment than painting" (Beethoven's motto)—yet richer in impressionistic traits, with its "pastoral duet," its "light rustling of the trees, gently moved by the wind," and its "distant peal of thunder." To be sure, we always experience this landscape through the passionate soul of the hero; yet it stands more in the foreground than it does in Beethoven. In his *Damnation of Faust,* Berlioz tries to make his Marguérite, in both her songs, speak *German* musical dialect; and he takes his hero to Hungary simply "because he wished to hear a piece of instrumental music on a Hungarian theme." Among his vocal works are to be found pieces like "The Young Breton Shepherd" and an Oriental song entitled "The Captive," both of which seem to be enveloped in the appropriate provincial atmosphere through the use of special harmonic and coloristic means.

Thus the Oriental in music completely changed its character. During the 18th century, it frequently took on a touch of the comic, especially in the many Turkish operas, the fun of which consisted in the noisy instrumentation. This was still true when Mozart wrote his *Entführung,* though in his *Rondo alla Turca* he also had come to understand how to mingle the comic element with a certain spiritual quality. Even Beethoven still demanded for the Chorus of Dervishes in his *Ruins of Athens* (1811-12), "all sorts of incidental noise-making instruments, such as castanets, little bells, and the like"; but this chorus, with the ensuing *Marcia alla Turca,* already had somewhat the character of an ethnographic study. Thus music followed very quickly in the footsteps of the Romantic poets, who for their subject-matter pushed farther and farther afield to the South—to Italy, Spain, Greece, Arabia—and to the East.

The conception of the Orient changed. On one occasion Gustave Flaubert spoke thus of Byron's Orient—the Turkish—as something quite different from that of the 18th century: ". . . the Orient of the scimitar, of the Albanian costume, of the latticed window looking out on azure waves." This was no longer the Orient of the "Turkish operas," but a new, more ethnographic one.

Even as early as 1809, so conservative a Romantic as Louis Spohr, who was two years older than Weber, wrote a Rondo on "genuine Spanish melodies" in his Violin Concerto in G minor, Op. 28. The colors became increasingly rich and bright, until in Félicien David's "symphonic Ode" *Le Désert* (1844) the genre of exotic music was established. It was the musical counterpart to the colorful travel impressions of Chateaubriand in French literature.

In considering all this, one must bear in mind that the ballet had long before discovered costumes, the decorative or picturesque quality of highly remote exoticism. The tradition goes back to the early years of the Renaissance, with its processions, masquerades, and *carri*. Particularly the French *ballet héroïque,* during and after the 17th century, searched the whole wide world for suggestions. The most beautiful of them, Jean-Philippe Rameau's *Indes Galantes* (1735), brought together in its scenes no more nor less than the Ancient World (the Garden of Hebe), Turkey, the Incas of Peru, the Persians, and even—in a celebration of the smoking of the peace pipe—the North American Indians in conjunction with French and Spanish officers: thus, Europe, Asia, and the whole Western hemisphere. But in the dances of the various scenes, Rameau did not as yet make the slightest attempt to give a musico-ethnographic characterization: people from the ends of the earth danced and sang French. The discovery of the world remained something reserved for the 19th century.

NATIONAL DIALECTS IN MUSIC

The discovery of the world led to a new discovery of Europe itself. Out of the universal language there developed national languages. It was not, as it were, a Babylonian confusion of tongues, as in the Bible; the national idioms in Romantic music were to the universal, humanistic language of music more as the popular dialects were to the literary language—as, for example, Venetian, Lombard, or Sicilian is to pure Tuscan, or as the Swabian, Low German, or Saxon is to Luther's unified German. In music as well as literature, dialects are more flexible, colorful, and childlike than the smoother "literary language."

With these dialects, moreover, a great deal depends upon who is speaking them and for what purpose they are being used. If they are spoken by a genuine personality, they soar above the national, the regional, the provincial, and are accepted by the world. This was especially true of Frédéric Chopin. Polish music owes to him something more and something greater than he does to Polish music. From fairly early times the Polish idiom had attracted the attention of musicians. Polonaises are to be found in Bach and Telemann, *Rondeaux en Polonaise* in Mozart, none for the first time. But Polish music would have remained a very provincial affair so long as it was only a matter of the compositions of Joseph X. Elsner, Chopin's teacher, or the operas of K. K. Kurpinski. Chopin employed the Polish national dances, such as the polonaise, mazurka, and *cracovienne;* but he was the first to breathe a soul into them. Are his scherzi, *études,* or nocturnes Polish? The nocturnes are as little Polish as their models, the nocturnes of John Field (1782–1837), are English or Russian. Poland has justly laid claim to Chopin's entire work as a valuable national asset—all the more precious as it is a possession of the spirit.

What happened in Poland was repeated in all the countries of Europe, large and small, and even in very small ones. It was like an echo, except that it became louder instead of softer. National self-consciousness tried to assert itself even in music. Is it not strange that it first became active in the countries that were nearest to the "universal" musical nations?

A very convenient example is Bohemia, restrained for centuries by the Habsburgs from developing a national life, even in the 19th century still referred to by a German poet as one of the "caryatid peoples" and thus relegated to a position of inferiority. In their music, the Czechs since the time of Johann Stamitz and the two Bendas, had already expressed themselves occasionally in folklike tones in Rondo themes and "second" subjects; but, in general, the musicians from Bohemia and Moravia—Koželuch and Mysliweczek, Dussek and Gyrowetz—belonged to the "Viennese" group. Even a master like Johann Wenzel Tomaschek (1774–1850), who spent his life in the midst of the musical activity of Prague, was still a "Viennese" musician of this type; no strong national aspirations are to be found in either his works—among which are some Goethe songs—or his autobiography. Czech music was first established with the work of Bedřich Smetana (1824–1884), and particularly with the first performance of his *Bartered Bride* (1866). Everything is Czech in this opera—the language, the costuming, the setting of the action, and above all the music, with its dances and rhythms of folk origin. But it is also more than national. Anyone who would deliberately limit his analysis to the purely musical would find that it derives from early-Romantic Viennese music, from Schubert, and that nothing is to be found in it that could not have originated from Schubert himself.

The national emphasis of Romantic music was, of course, connected closely with the revived interest in the national or regional folk song. That is not to say that the movement always began with this interest. There had been a kind of music with Spanish emphasis, a Spanish music with folk coloring (the so-called *Casticismo*), long before Felipe Pedrell's manifesto of 1890. In Russia the interest in folk song developed in a mighty crescendo that has continued on into our own times. The demarcations were especially sharp in Russia throughout the area that had anything at all to do with Western music. In the 18th century, since the time of Peter the Great, Russia had been, musically, an Italian province, obtaining from Italy not only compositions but also librettists, singers, orchestras, and composers—Paisiello, Sarti, and others. But one of these Italians, Catterino Cavos (1776–1840) of Venice, began to deal with Russian subject matter and to utilize Russian melodies in his works, for example in his *Ivan Sussanin* (1815): until, with Michael Glinka (1804–1857) and his *A Life for the Tsar* (1836), which deals with the same material, there came into existence a patriotic and national work with which the national music history of Russia seems for the first time to make a genuine beginning. But the fact that it was not "Russian" enough is shown by the appearance of the "mighty Five," Balakirev, Musorgsky, Cui, Rimsky-Korsakov, and Borodin, with their opposition to and struggle against the "Westerners" Serov, Rubinstein, and Tchaikovsky. In this matter it always remains a question how much of this Russianism is genuinely national and how much is "Romantic." One cannot say much more than that this emphasis on the national is one of the distinguishing features of the Romantic era in music.

NATIONALISM AND THE INDIVIDUAL

This emphasis on national matters has nothing to do with the greatness of a composer. Chopin would have belonged among the great men of music even if his work had not had the least to do with Poland. And Grieg certainly does not belong among the great of music, although the charming national color of his work has had international success.

The relationship of a musician whose work displays national coloring to the nationality of his own country remains always an open question. One is reminded of the fact that the first "Danish" composers (and, thereby, the first of the "Scandinavian" musicians, for only later did Sweden and Norway follow suit with their national tendencies) were, without exception, Germans—Friedrich Ludwig Aemilius Kunzen (1761–1817), Christoph Ernst Friedrich Weyse (1774-1842), and Friedrich Kuhlau (1786–1832), together with the founder of the Danish *Singspiel,* Johann Abraham Peter Schulz. Similarly, some of the Danish poets of this time, like Jens Baggesen (1764–1826), first published some of their poems in German; and some of their dramatists, like Adam Öhlenschläger (1779–1850), translated their own dramas into German. It would be a mistake to consider Franz Liszt a Magyar national composer, despite his symphonic poem *Hungaria,* his Gran *Festival Mass,* and his Hungarian Rhapsodies. The history of Romantic-national music in Hungary is not without its humorous touches, for the popular storehouse of melodies upon which it drew—the so-called gypsy music—was a stylistic mixture of very questionable, very slightly national ingredients.

In the course of the 19th century, all the peoples—one after another, from the greatest to the smallest national entities—expressed themselves in music. At the beginning of the century there was only Italian, German, and French music, in which the distinctively national traits were not emphasized, and did not need to be, for there was no particular contest for authority. The purpose of this threefold music as a whole, especially among the German masters, was humanistic or universal. Yet, by the end of the century, Europe had fallen apart into a dozen or so musical provinces; and a map of these boundaries would be as motley as that of the old Holy Roman Empire. After Poland, Hungary, and Bohemia, there came Russia and Spain; after the three Scandinavian countries, there came Holland and Finland; and, finally, there come the Baltic states, the three Yugoslavian entities, Rumania and Bulgaria, and the individual regions of the wide Russian domain. Only England waited until the end of the century to take account of its folk song and of its national claims in music; and, although America in the 18th and 19th centuries had many American—and in the 19th also Romantic—musicians, she had no real American music.

The nationalistic note in Romantic music seemed to be emphasized even among the nations which had previously not exhibited this emphasis at all. Of course, ever since the 16th century there had been certain distinguishing national features among the three great musical nations, and in the course of time regional differences appeared in Germany and Italy—though less so in France, where musical life was centered in Paris. By the end of the 17th century, the art of South Germany and that of North Germany, (even when the popular element played no part), were already noticeably different: Johann Pachelbel and Georg Muffat were masters of the organ with Southern traits, Buxtehude, Lübeck, and Reinken with Northern traits. In Italian music there had existed a Neapolitan manner since Pergolesi, a Milanese since Sammartini, and since Galuppi a Venetian.

But the strengthening of the national character after 1800 was unmistakable, even among the great and well-established musical nations. Rossini, we repeat, seems "more Italian" than Paisiello or Cimarosa; Berlioz, "more French" than Grétry, Méhul, or Le Sueur; Schubert, "more Austrian" than Haydn or Mozart; Schumann, "more German" than Schubert, or even than Haydn, Mozart, or Beethoven. The word "seems" is used here advisedly, for it will be hard to distinguish how much of this new emphasis upon the national belongs to the composer's personality and how much to his origin. When Louis Spohr in 1816 first came to know the works of Rossini—the *Italiana in Algeri*, the *Tancredi*—he tried, not without a certain jealous hostility, to make clear to himself what was new in them: the suspensions in the bass, the dazzling modulations, the instrumental features in the design of the vocal line, the senseless coloratura passages, and the senseless crescendos in the *strette*. All this was quite Rossini's own, and quite characteristic of him; but since Rossini immediately created a school, it became "Italian."

The national element in Berlioz was, as in so many other instances, a matter of renewing or emphasizing an ancient national predilection—that for the descriptive, which was already to be found in the 16th century, in Janequin's representations of battles, bird concerts, city sounds, and hunting scenes, and was still more distinctly marked in the works of Couperin and Rameau. To be sure, this feature of Berlioz's was also an expression of his own genius: his sharp ear for orchestral sonority, his aversion to mechanically produced noise in the orchestra—an aversion which Berlioz often expressed in his letters and other writings. This feeling for sound became, after Berlioz, a tradition of French music—so much so that one can distinguish a French from a German or even an Italian score by merely glancing at it.

In other instances, the national element is a pure legend, fabricated by the composer himself, or a crude bit of materialism, as in Wagner. In Wagner's operas, after *Tannhäuser,* nothing is German or Teutonic or Nordic but the plot and the language; otherwise, they are Wagnerian, and their international effect is to be explained only on the basis of their overpoweringly individual merits. Only in *Die Meistersinger von Nürnberg* has Wagner made a creative compromise with the music of the German past—the polyphonic style of the period of Bach and Handel. This is the usual procedure, and the usual basis for the formation of a national movement in the Romantic music of the 19th century—the linking of traditional folk material with past eras of art music. This is also the formula for the Germanism of Brahms, who not only loved folk song from the beginning and introduced it into his work but also took an interest in the findings of musicology and tried to imitate and revive the old forms.

CHAPTER VII

The Forms and the Content

BEETHOVEN AND FORM

LIKE every new period in the history of art, the Romantic era in music altered its inherited forms and created new ones. In the field of instrumental music, its greatest heritage was the sonata form, which had received its most powerful expression of universal appeal in Beethoven's symphonies. The fate of the Romantic movement was sealed by the greatness of this heritage.

With Haydn, Mozart, and Beethoven, the symphony had been a fully realized form. Haydn had created it, by slow toil and after many experiments, until at last the four-movement structure in its several parts, contrasting and yet brought together into a unity of the highest order, was well established. The so-called "sonata form," which Haydn used for the first movements of his symphonies, was also a favorite of his for last movements. He was almost solely responsible for developing this form: he was the first one to give it meaning. With him, no one development section is like another, for each one has been developed according to the special character of the themes.

This feature was understood by Haydn's greatest contemporary and best pupil, Mozart, who in his last four symphonies increased even more the inner drama of the development (in the G-minor and D-major Symphonies), the monumental quality of the finale (in the C-major Symphony), and the felicitous relationship of the parts. He did this without being false to his own character, for the earliest of these—the so-called Prague Symphony—has only three movements, and those that have four do not have a scherzo, for Mozart not only retains the minuet but even emphasizes the minuet character of the whole.

The Romantics, however, paid more attention to Beethoven than they did to Haydn and Mozart, whom they were rather inclined to look back upon with a certain reverent tolerance. With Beethoven, the symphony achieved for the first time its full, monumental stature, as the call to the individual and the mass, to the individual *in* the mass, an appeal of magnificent pathos, magnificent humor. Its forms were mightily extended without being exaggerated in the way that makes us dislike some of the architectural works of the Baroque, or laugh at many of the creations of the so-called Empire, which flourished in Beethoven's own day. Beethoven—not in all of his works, but in all of his important works—"tamed the forces of chaos," found complete formal expression for his thoughts, and filled outlines of the broadest dimensions with the most energetic expression. The first movement of the *Eroica* is, today just as on the day it was written, one of the wonders of music, supremely alive in every detail yet completely unified, supremely clear yet most powerfully impulsive. And what applies to this movement applies to the whole symphony.

There are no "lengths"—heavenly or otherwise—in Beethoven, because he took over no forms; instead, he created them anew. Beethoven had his characteristic formulae, but they were never empty husks, and he never repeated himself. The Romantics were of the opinion that in his last works —in the piano sonatas from Op. 101 to Op. 111, and especially in the last quartets—he had "burst form asunder"; and from this illustrious model they developed the idea that it was permissible or justifiable that they themselves should deal as freely as possible with form. As a matter of fact, there is not—even in these last works of Beethoven's—a single movement, a single measure, that does not rest on the strictest, immanent musical logic, and that even in the most minute detail would call for extra-musical justification.

FORM IN THE ROMANTIC SYMPHONY

From the very first, there was a relaxed attitude on the part of the Romantics towards symphonic form. It is quite characteristic of Weber that he wrote only two symphonies in his life, both in C major, both in 1807, when he was as yet not quite twenty-two. The *Eroica* had already been written, presented, and published—a model of the highest seriousness, sounding out like a hymn, most pure in structure, a composition in which no instrument obtrudes itself in the ensemble, and each serves the purposes of the symphonic whole. Yet Weber wrote these two highly independent works—compositions which one might almost call formally irresponsible. No one has characterized the first of them better than Weber himself in his later letters to Gottfried Weber (1813) and Friedrich Rochlitz (1815): ". . . Heaven knows, I would write many things in my symphony different now; I am entirely satisfied, really, with nothing but the Minuet and possibly the Adagio. The first Allegro is a senseless fantasia-movement, at the most in the style of an overture, made up of ragged sections; and the last movement could be worked out more fully." Weber was a master of the *concertante* style, but not of the symphonic; and whenever one speaks of Weber as an orchestral composer, one thinks actually of the three overtures to his operas, which connect their brilliant and impressive ideas rather loosely and bring them to an overpowering conclusion. Compared to Beethoven's great overtures, the *Leonore,* the *Egmont,* and the *Coriolanus,* these compositions are merely strung together and arbitrary in structure.

Schumann's famous saying about the "heavenly lengths" leads us to Franz Schubert, for whose C-major Symphony it was intended. Inappropriate as the remark is, it is especially misapplied in this instance, for nowhere else has Schubert shown more clearly that he is a Romantic *Classic,* worthy of carrying on the heritage of Beethoven. Every cut mutilates the unified, monumental structure of this work. Both movements of the *Unfinished* Symphony are masterpieces of the highest concentration: the exposition of the first is a perfect example of demoniac explosion, while, in the first movement of the C-major Symphony the exposition is a piece of inexorable consummation.

But in a few traits the Romantic side of the otherwise classically disposed Schubert makes its appearance. The first is the thematic connection of the introductory *Andante* with the *Allegro ma non troppo,* a motivic "safeguard" that one will not as yet find so clearly stressed in the Classics; and another is the emphasis on the pure, enchanting, "magic" sonority, which becomes most enchanting and most audible in the *Andante con moto,* in that unison call of the two horns, leading back to the theme. (The horn, incidentally, is the Romantic instrument *par excellence;* and solely through its use in instrumentation one could trace the development of the Romantic in music.) It is true, moreover, that Schubert achieved this concentration of the opening movements in but few of his works, such as his two Symphonies and his D-minor Quartet. In his Piano Sonatas, especially, the form is relaxed; the development sections are often mere transitions, indeed sometimes even the place for episodes and for happy idling. Schubert's power of melodic invention was so well rounded, so complete, that unlike Beethoven's motives, his melodies were no longer adapted for the dissection, for the discursive examination of their content, that is, for symphonic and dramatic elaboration.

Mendelssohn was too cultivated, too clever a musician not to master the symphonic form; but both of his principal works in this field, the *Italian* Symphony (1833) and the *Scottish* Symphony (1842), show by their very titles that he did not follow in them the Beethoven of the *Eroica,* the Fifth, the Seventh symphonies, but the Beethoven of the *Pastoral,* with its germinal impulse which comes from without. There is, however, this difference: what had been in Beethoven a hymnlike and religiously inspired feeling for nature became with Mendelssohn a more melancholy and more serene reflection of the landscape in a responsive soul. The relationship of the four movements to one another became looser, and the symphonic or cyclic form appeared less necessary. Even the development sections seemed to be less a matter of necessity and more a merely clever game; and the recapitulation seemed to be a delightful return—no longer, as with Haydn, Mozart, or Beethoven, a return to a new, higher level, a revelation. Where Mendelssohn was filled with extra-musical ideas, as in the Overture to Shakespeare's *Midsummer Night's Dream,* or in the *Hebrides* Overture, even the development section gained at once a special life, free of all that was schematic, of all that was traditional. Schumann found in each of his four symphonies, along with a more limited mastery of the external form, much more original and compelling solutions.

BERLIOZ AND LISZT

The relaxation of symphonic thought appeared most clearly in the work of Hector Berlioz, only a few years after Beethoven's death. The mere proximity in point of time, the passionate reverence for Beethoven, and above all the strange mixture of revolutionary and traditional that is inherent in the general character of French art, these are all that still confine Berlioz to the symphonic frame in his *Symphonie Fantastique—Episode de la vie d'un artiste* (1830-31); five movements instead of four, all animated and accompanied by extra-musical ideas. And it is one of the greatest surprises in the history of music that Berlioz succeeded in bringing the first movement of the symphony into line with traditional form, despite a program of "surge of passion, unending revery, delirious emotion, with all its outbursts of tenderness, jealousy, fury, fear, etc., etc." In the individual movements the typical contrasts of the Classical symphony are still persistently recognizable; yet Berlioz felt the necessity of joining them by unity of theme, i.e., by his famous *idée fixe,* which he derived from a Romance among his earlier juvenilia.

In *Harold en Italie* (1834), Berlioz again returned to the four-movement plan, but omitted the Adagio and made the two middle movements nothing but picturesque scenes—most finely impressionistic, most genuinely akin to French *plein air* painting. Thus there evolved from the symphonic unity more and more a *succession* of movements, although even in this work there was no lack of that uniting bond of an *idée fixe.*

Later (not to mention *Lelio ou Le Rétour à la Vie,* the continuation of the *Symphonie Fantastique*) in *Roméo et Juliette* (1839) and *La Damnation de Faust* (completed in 1846) the mixture of types is even more extensive. Berlioz called the earlier work a *symphonie dramatique,* the later a *légende dramatique.* We are, accordingly, on the way from the symphony to the cantata or even the opera. And one need but think of Mendelssohn's *Lobgesang,* a symphony-cantata, to see how even works that are artistically antipodal, may yet have something in common.

It was no more than logical that a clever musician like Franz Liszt should take the final step and renounce the symphonic outlines almost entirely. Some time between 1849 and 1858 he composed or gave the finishing touches to his "symphonic poems"—*poèmes symphoniques*—each of which, even when not following a program, was yet suggested by a poetical (i.e., an extra-musical) "idea." Each of these works required a poetical or intellectual explanation. How very heavily burdened with feeling and thought these explanations for the most part are may be seen from one of the shortest of them, that for the *Berg-Sinfonie,* after Victor Hugo. This explanation, according to Liszt's request, was to be added to the program every time the work was performed:

The poet hears two voices, one infinite, magnificent, ineffable, singing the beauty and harmony of creation, the other swollen with sighs, with groans, with sobs, with rebellious cries, and with blasphemous oaths. The one is saying, "Nature"; the other, "Humanity." . . . These two strange voices, never heard before, are now reborn, now fade away, in ceaseless alternation; they follow one another, first from afar; then they draw nearer; they cross, mingling their accents now strident, now harmonious, until the meditation to which the poet has been moved reaches silently the borderland of prayer.

In no sense of the phrase did Liszt "burst form asunder." On the contrary, his idea of a symphonic poem was born of the honest recognition of the fact that it would be better to create a new—even if uncertain—form, to venture on an experiment, than to retain something that had become an empty shell, a traditional form. Whether Liszt succeeded in this creation of a new form is another question. He felt, as did Berlioz, the danger of his freedom; and he sought to obviate it by the principle of motivic or thematic uniformity, by extensive and free use of the principle of variety (not that of variation)—the same principle as that by which Wagner held together the symphonic structure of his music dramas. He also applied this principle even where he seemed to be approaching again the old form of the symphony or sonata, as in his *Faust* Symphony (1854) with its subsequently appended vocal conclusion, in his *Dante* Symphony (1855-56), in his two Piano Concertos, and in his B-minor Piano Sonata.

With Liszt, the main stream of instrumental composition parted: on the one side, the enemies of the "New Germans," such as Brahms, and the naïve New Germans themselves, like Bruckner, tried to fill Classical form with new content and life; on the other, genuine Lisztians or innovators like Smetana or Musorgsky wrote no more symphonies. The majority, among whom were Dvořák and Tchaikovsky, bustled about unconcernedly in both fields—which already were approached by the overture. In the overture the strict sonata form had been relaxed from the very beginning, and the overture had always had the character of an introduction, if not actually that of a piece of program music. In this connection it might be recalled that Beethoven had been criticized for having held too fast to the sonata form in his third *Leonore* Overture, or —more precisely—that he had not foregone the recapitulation.

SMALLER FORMS

Another peculiarity of the Romantic era in music is the preference for the miniature. This is, in a way, a complement to the relaxation and enlargement of the great forms. There had been, of course, not only short pieces of music but also genuine miniatures long before the Romantic era, such as the characteristic pieces of the 17th-century French lutenists, perhaps many of the preludes or dance-pieces in the Elizabethan virginal books, certainly the Inventions of Bach, the "programmatic" pieces of Couperin and Rameau, and even some of the compositions of Philipp Emanuel Bach. But in this respect also Beethoven marked a new beginning, with his 25 Bagatelles, Opp. 33, 119, and 126. They are nothing more than ideas—motifs, combinations of sounds, lyrical moments—susceptible of further development, but not requiring it, so great is the concentration of thought.

Beethoven's example was eagerly followed by the Romantics. The only difference was that they were no longer striving solely for concentration, but also for expression of the lyrical feeling inherent in a happy moment of music. Thus Schubert's *Moments Musicaux* came to be written, the purest and most enchanting examples of instrumental lyricism; thus also, Mendelssohn's *Songs without Words,* which suited so admirably the feelings of his age; and thus, Chopin's *Préludes,* some of which say everything that is to be said in a relatively brief period of time—that in A major, Op. 28, No. 7, in eight measures, that in C-sharp minor, Op. 28, No. 10, in but five—just as does one of Heinrich Heine's quatrains. Thus came to be written Robert Schumann's *Kinderscenen* and *Bunte Blätter;* and his best works are often nothing more than a kaleidoscopic succession of miniatures, the *Davidsbündler,* the *Kreisleriana,* the *Faschingsschwank aus Wien,* the *Carnaval*—each born of a minute musical seed.

The whole Romantic movement in music is full of discoveries in small, even in very small, matters; and Nietzsche was not entirely unwarranted in his malicious thrust denying to the creator of the monumental music dramas any capacity for creating a dramatic style, and praising him as a master of the miniature, as "in the discovery of the very small and in the tightening up of detail, . . . our greatest *miniaturist* in music, who presses into smallest compass an eternity of feeling and sweetness." [5]

VOCAL MUSIC

Song and opera, on the other hand, were in a much more fortunate situation than pure instrumental music in general, and the symphony in particular. An individual section will be devoted to each of these two vocal genres in the ensuing pages; and it will be shown that, for the first time, the Romantic movement fulfilled the ideal of song—of the complete unity of text and music, the perfect equilibrium between vocal line and accompaniment. Here too there were fluctuations; and since the first great master of the genre, Franz Schubert, was at the same time its greatest, there ensued upon his achievement an unavoidable decline, though it was a descent through highly colorful, fascinating, and abundant fields.

In the realm of opera too one cannot really speak of an overthrow of form, but only of a development or alteration. "Classical" opera—especially *opera seria*—had become a fossil. The 18th century—Gluck, with his

[5] *Der Fall Wagner,* Complete edition, I, Vol. VIII, Leipzig, 1899, § 7, C. G. Naumann.

predecessors and followers—had already perceived that fact and had replaced the Metastasian opera plot of intrigue with simpler, more passionate action, and had resolved the stereotyped alternation of recitative
and aria into a richer whole. The contrast between recitative and aria
became less marked, thanks to the more elaborate orchestral accompaniment. The *da capo* aria gave place to shorter, more varied, more dramatically determined forms. The chorus, following the French model, again
took a lively part in the action—a feature which has led some commentators to consider Gluck a pioneer in the Romantic movement, and as a
matter of fact a direct line of development does lead from him through
Le Sueur and Spontini right on to Meyerbeer. The center of gravity in opera
shifted: it was no longer a concert with pseudo-dramatic associations.
Mozart's failure with *Idomeneo* is, historically, a memorable fact: the
richest, most luxuriant music could no longer help out a dramatic production belonging to an outlived genre.

From *opera buffa* and *opéra-comique* came a very strong impetus
towards the transformation of opera, and—finally—even of the classical
opera seria. It is not here a question of subject matter, which is to be
considered later. In both *opera buffa* and comic opera the solo pieces retired
into the background in favor of the ensemble movements, the *Introduzioni*
and the *Finali.* And these movements required the unification that the
orchestra supplied for them. As early as the second half of the 18th century
there were many finales of "symphonic" character in which the individual
parts were held together by a persistent motif in the orchestral part, and
many *morceaux d'ensemble* that had been structurally developed in both
dramatic and symphonic terms. This connection between the parts that
are separated by spoken dialogue became more and more perceptible—
so much so that, for example in Mozart's *Magic Flute* and Beethoven's
Fidelio, one might reduce the dialogue in general to exceedingly brief
formulae. Then, finally, it disappeared entirely, as, even in the Italian
opera buffa, the burden of carrying the action was more and more transferred from the recitative to the ensemble.

Romantic opera created musical and dramatic *scenes.* In so doing, it
shifted the center of gravity more and more in the orchestra's favor.
Finally, at some of the high-points in Wagner's music drama, the symphonic element preponderates and the vocal part merely comments, as
it were, upon what is taking place in the orchestra. Italian opera had
always insisted that the vocal part be pre-eminent, but even it could not
escape the fusion of recitative and *arioso* elements.

PART II

The History

CHAPTER VIII

The Rise of Musical Romanticism

BACH AS SEEN BY THE ROMANTICS

ONE can get a clear idea of the character of the Romantic era in music by considering its "affinities," i.e., its relationship to the periods and composers of the past who attracted or repelled it. As has already been indicated, it is essentially the first musical period to resume the thread of relationship with a rather remote musical past and to receive impetus from the works of periods opened up to it by music history. And as musical Romanticism constitutes a still living and creative period, misunderstandings continue to follow one another; for Romantics can see the past only in their own, Romantic light.

The first of these misunderstandings is that with regard to Bach—at least, with regard to the church musician Bach, the master of the Passions and the cantatas. As Protestantism lost its fixed liturgical forms and as its means of musical expression declined, Bach was uprooted from his soil of the church and the liturgy, and was transplanted into the concert hall: the church experience became a vaguely religious one, and finally an artistic one pure and simple. In this process, mention need not be made of the truncations, distortions, and alterations that Bach had to put up with in his "revival," beginning with Mendelssohn's presentation of the St. Matthew Passion, or even beginning with the work of Mendelssohn's teacher Zelter, who imagined that Bach would have given him an affectionate pat on the back for all his bowdlerizations, if the great master had lived to see them. At a presentation of one of Bach's Passions at Frankfort in 1829—the same year as Mendelssohn's performance—Bach's recitatives were replaced by those of the director, J. N. Schelble; and in Dresden a colossal performance in the Handelian manner, with no fewer than 342 participants, was organized for Palm Sunday, 1833.[6] How completely a

[6] I have taken this data from the study by Gerhard Herz, *J. S. Bach im Zeitalter des Rationalismus und der Frühromantik* (Würzburg, 1935).

Romantic lieder-composer like Robert Franz changed the instrumental guise of Bach's works is only too well known from his squabbles with musicological purists.

Out of all this welter of activity, however, there emerges a sense of how passionately the Romantics concerned themselves with every aspect of Bach. They were trying to make him at once historically intelligible and their own in a creative way. After Schubert there was hardly a single Romantic composer whose relation to Bach would not be a legitimate subject of inquiry. Even Schubert, at the very end of his life, seems to have felt the need of enriching his own style with the stricter artistic means of Bach's time—a need that was presumably stimulated by the "fugues" in Beethoven's Op. 106 and 110, or the *Grosse Fuge* for string quartet, Op. 133. We recognize this tendency in the touching fact that he, the creator of the B-minor Symphony, wished to become a disciple of Simon Sechter (1788–1867), the Viennese oracle of counterpoint. The only exception to this general Romantic inclination towards Bach is perhaps to be found in Berlioz, the admirer of Gluck (who, like Berlioz, never wrote a seriously intended fugue, and felt very little concern over the subject of counterpoint). Berlioz abominated Bach and made use of the old polyphonic style only by way of parody: for example, in a scene in the *Deuxième Partie* of the *Damnation of Faust,* where the companions in Auerbach's cellar sing their famous Amen fugue—a satire on all the polyphonic pedants whose prototype Berlioz thought was to be found in Bach.

With Mendelssohn, Bach began to appear in the light of Romantic veneration—a mystic, a "Gothic" master of music. Beethoven had incorporated the fugue, "sometimes free, sometimes studied," in his sonatas and in his general instrumental style as a new means of expression; but it did not occur to him to revive the writing of pure fugues. The Romantic era, however, did just that. Mendelssohn brought out his Six Preludes and Fugues, Op. 35, in 1837; and it is highly significant that he closed the first of these fugues, that in E minor, with a chorale in major—a genuinely Romantic mixture and confusion of the secular with the sacred. It was the same spirit and the same mistake that made him introduce chorales and chorale paraphrases in his oratorio *Paulus,* while at the same time Romantic vagueness had given rise to confusion between a Handel oratorio and a Bach Passion. For a Handel oratorio was directed towards a free religious or nationalistic edification, while a Bach Passion was a circumscribed, Protestant liturgical form.

Schumann remained innocent of this error and did not write religious oratorios: what drove him, comparatively late in life, to Bach was rather his need, like Schubert's, for greater profundity of style—a need that caused him to write his Six Studies for the Pedal Piano in Canonic Form, Op. 56 (1845), his Four Fugues, Op. 72 (1845), and his Seven Pieces in Fughetta Form, Op. 126 (1853). This need alone, however, was not entirely responsible for these works. They also originated in the pedagogical tendency of the Romantic movement, in the strange fascination exerted upon it by the past, by historical universality, and in sheer admiration for those infinitely great masters, an admiration that Schumann gave expression to in his cycle of Six Fugues on the name B A C H for Organ or Pedal Piano, Op. 60 (1845), a Romantic imitation of *The Art of the Fugue*—Romantic, because free, expressive, even capricious.

A further, more powerful or more violent expression was then given to this theme by Liszt, with his Variations on the *Basso Ostinato* of the First Movement of the Cantata *Weinen, Klagen* . . . (1863) and his Prelude and Fugue on B A C H (1855, 1870) for organ: both expressions of allegiance, *hommages* to the master whom Liszt called, most significantly, the "St. Thomas Aquinas" of music—and whom he regarded in somewhat the same way as he did the great scholastic of the Middle Ages.

In contrast to Mendelssohn, Schumann, Liszt, and all the many Romantics who—one might say—gave Bach documentary evidence of their esteem, there were some few Romantic musicians who showed their veneration in a much more subtle way, although they never published a fugue as such: Chopin, Wagner, and Brahms (even Brahms, who wrote many fugues but never thought of publishing any of them as free works of art). Bach was assimilated into their work. In that "new world" of music which Chopin wished to inaugurate,[7] provision was made for counterpoint, the strict style of Bach, but at the same time it was so hidden and so completely resolved into the later composer's own personal style that, as in everything perfect, it was unobtrusive. Wagner in *Die Meistersinger* utilized the style of Bach with a violence that was in keeping with his natural propensities for conquest. Completely disregarding the anachronism of his approach, he introduced the polyphony of Bach in place of 16th-century music. In so doing, he secured a point of contrast with his own personal tonal language, without giving up a bit of his own individuality in the very act of imitation. And finally, Brahms, the great stu-

[7] Letter to his teacher Elsner, December 14, 1831.

dent of the past, the great initiate into the company of the old masters, received his best lessons from Bach without divulging the fact.

A special position alongside these three great masters is filled by César Franck. Despite his numerous fugues, both free and strict, he succeeded in fusing the polyphonic spirit, the Bach spirit, with his own colorful, Romantic, and hypertrophic harmony.

THE ROMANTICS AND THE PALESTRINA PERIOD

Bach was anything but a progenitor of the Romantic era. But the Romantic movement saw him in its own light—his organ preludes and fugues with their lofty pinnacles, his cantatas with their mystical symbolism, his Passions with their dramatic power and their Baroque lineaments. Quite similarly, as has already been indicated (p. 46), it also saw the still more distant art of the Palestrina period in Romantic hues. Mendelssohn, and with him many of his contemporaries, looked upon the Masses, Psalms, and motets of the 16th century as the only true church music; and the negative side of this view was the rejection of the whole body of concerted church music, from 1600 to Beethoven, including his *Missa Solemnis.* Even Wagner, who at the end of his years in Dresden (1848) had reworked Palestrina's *Stabat Mater,* made in *Parsifal* a compromise with this style, so much like that of the Nazarene school of painters and so seemingly "other-worldly"; and, just as in *Die Meistersinger,* he achieved his most individual effects by this compromise.

The feature of this style that attracted the Romantics is easy to formulate. They found a link between themselves and the floating "formlessness" of this pure and—as they thought—*a cappella* art. They loved the contrast between these passionless, "objective" sounds and their own passion, their own subjectivity. They saw in the musician Palestrina, just as in the painter Raphael, a seraphic master. In both masters—quite unjustifiably —they neglected to see how closely in the 16th century sacred art was related to secular. The whole tendency was closely connected with the Catholic inclinations of the Romantic era, though it involved Protestants and Catholics alike. The growing misunderstanding, moreover, was not deterred by the realization that the Lutheran or Reformed musicians of the past age cultivated the same style as did Palestrina, Lasso, or Giovanni Gabrieli.

ROMANTIC VIEW OF THE CLASSICS: OF HAYDN

The richest and most notable relationships of the Romantic era in music are, of course, those with the immediately preceding past—with the three great representatives of "classical" music: Haydn, Mozart, and Beethoven. As we have said, in the history of any art, the younger generation, if it is at all revolutionary minded, always is bitterly opposed to its fathers. For the Romantic movement in music, however, this assumption does not prove entirely correct. There is an analogy here with the Romantic movement in literature, at least in Germany. Although its first representatives, namely the brothers August Wilhelm and Friedrich Schlegel, felt themselves to be somewhat—though not essentially—opposed to Schiller and his neo-Classical rhetoric, they yet exalted Goethe as the patron of the Romantic movement, likewise not without a certain willfulness and not entirely to Goethe's complete joy. Although the Romantic era in music did not emphasize its opposition to Haydn and Mozart, and instead held both these names in high honor, it yet set Beethoven on a pedestal as its patron saint and emphasized his "Romantic" traits.

To what extent could Haydn, Mozart, and Beethoven really be claimed by the Romantic era? Least of all, surely, could Haydn, the oldest of the three Classics. He was the "patriarch Haydn," the composer of symphonies full of "sunny clarity"— ". . . heavenly harmony resides in these sounds, so free from traces of boredom, so productive of nothing but gaiety, zest for living, childlike joy in everything, and—what a service he has thereby rendered, especially to the present age, this valetudinarian period in music when men are so seldom *inwardly* satisfied"—thus Schumann-Eusebius wrote on October 21, 1836. Although Schumann—like Mendelssohn—felt the strange melancholy of Haydn's *Farewell* Symphony, even he was in general only too much inclined to underestimate Haydn. In 1841 Schumann wrote that one could not learn anything new from Haydn, that he was "like an old friend of the family, who is always received with pleasure and respect"—but "he is no longer highly interesting for the present day."

Perhaps the only aspect of his vocal works that was felt to be "Romantic" was the new feeling for nature which appeared in his *Creation* and his *Seasons,* and the only such aspect of his instrumental works was the remarkably great freedom in the use of keys within the framework of his piano trios, piano sonatas, and even quartets and symphonies. In a

Quartet in D (Op. 76, No. 5), for example, Haydn wrote a middle section in F-sharp; and in a Piano Sonata in E-flat major (Op. 82), he wrote a middle section in E major. Similarly, in the course of a Piano Sonata in B-flat (Op. 106, completed in 1827), Mendelssohn in his youth wrote the second movement in B-flat minor and the third in E major. There was a relaxation in the tonal framework of the sonata. This tendency, incidentally, had certain precedents even in Beethoven, especially in his earlier works—the Piano Sonata Op. 2, No. 3, the String Trio Op. 9, No. 1, and the first Piano Concerto Op. 15—more so than in his later works.

But, in general, the Romantics felt for Haydn little more than a somewhat patronizing affection. His clarity, his strict mastery, his wit, his spirit—an 18th-century spirit—ran counter to the tendencies of the Romantic movement. For the so-called "neo-Romantics"—Berlioz, Liszt, Wagner—he seemed scarcely to exist at all.

OF MOZART

In Mozart the Romantics respected principally the opera-composer, or —more precisely—the composer of *Don Giovanni*. "The conflict of human nature with the unknown, monstrous powers that surround it, watching its destruction, rose clearly before my mind's eye," writes E. T. A. Hoffmann of his feelings on listening to Mozart's overture, in a fantastic tale entitled *Don Juan: A Marvelous Adventure Which Befell a Traveling Enthusiast*,[8] a tale more profound and penetrating than all that the Mozart biographers of the 19th century had to say about *Don Giovanni,* and yet a tale that sets all its figures in the light of a Romantic opera in the manner of *Der Freischütz* or Marschner's *Hans Heiling.* The Romantics saw in Don Juan a counterpart to Goethe's Faust: da Ponte's "young, extremely dissipated cavalier" (*giovane estremamente licenzioso*) was transformed into a demon; even in the matter of his baritone voice-range, he became the model for the dark, saturnine opera heroes like Marschner's Lord Ruthwen (in *The Vampire*) and Hans Heiling, or like Wagner's Flying Dutchman. Out of Mozart's *dramma giocoso* there developed a Romantic opera; out of *Don Giovanni* there developed *Don Juan*—for so the title of the opera was altered. The other side of this preference for *Don Juan* was the lack of appreciation on the part of the Romantics

[8] Modern English translation in *The Musical Quarterly* XXXI, No. 4: 504–516 (October, 1945).

for a masterpiece like *Così Fan Tutte,* in which the lambent merriment, the iridescent sensitiveness playing between parody and seriousness, was contrary to the Romantic point of view—as much so as was the amorality of the text, which was condemned as immoral.

In the instrumental composer Mozart, the Romantics saw little more than the master, the polisher of formal elements, at best "a master whose passions in their workings are not laid bare to view, but who offers us perfect beauty victorious over turbulence and impurity." This characterization of Mozart from the preface to Otto Jahn's once famous biography (1856) is manifestly directed against the representatives of the neo-Romantic School—Liszt, Wagner, and perhaps Berlioz—who seemed to Jahn to be mere exhibitionists, musicians who expressed their feelings nakedly, without restraining or ennobling them by form. As a matter of fact, Jahn showed a deeper insight into the nature of Mozart than did many of the Romantics—than did Schumann, for example, who saw in the profound, fatalistic G-minor Symphony only the airy grace that we associate with Greek art. Many of the traits in Mozart's works can be considered "Romantic" or proto-romantic: there is, for example, his melancholy, which comes to the fore in the F-sharp minor Andante of his A-major Piano Concerto (K. 488) and which also sometimes forms a background to ostensibly cheerful movements in major; and there is his incomparable sense of sound, which however does not go so far as to lead him to use mere sonority as a means of expression.

OF BEETHOVEN

The real precursor of the Romantic era in music, however, was—of course—Beethoven. As has already been indicated, the Romantics committed an error when they claimed Beethoven entirely as their own; for Beethoven still belonged as much to the 18th as to the 19th century. But it lay in the nature as well as in the fate of Beethoven that he seemed to be the first musician to take up a position *against* the world. The loneliness to which his increasing deafness drove him in a Vienna that delighted in society made a deep impression on all the Romantics. Beethoven became a Romantic figure even as a human being, as one can see from the caricatures by J. P. Lyser, for example, or the short story written by Wagner in his youth, *A Pilgrimage to Beethoven* (1840). With perhaps no other musician did the transformation of a personality into a myth begin so soon as with Beethoven—into a mythical figure which had only a distant resemblance to the actual Beethoven.

The Romantic movement emphasized the tragic features in Beethoven's work, while he, as a child of the century into which he had been born, was an optimist, a representative of the "Nevertheless . . . ," of the "And yet . . ." philosophy, quite in contrast to the anachronistic fatalist Mozart. Not one of Beethoven's works ends with a psychic dissonance; and even the "tragic," the "titanic" works—quite apart from the many works that are plainly full of energy and joy and that the Romantics liked to over-look—express a faith in humanity and in God. Least of all did the Romantics think of Beethoven's humor, either low or sublime: (an example of his low humor would be the Finale of the B-flat major Trio Op. 97, an example of the sublime would be the Finale of the F-major String Quartet Op. 135); for this humor did not fit into the portrait of Beethoven as the musician of the lofty heights. Thirty years after writing his Beethoven story, Wagner in his centennial study of 1870 exalted Beethoven to a veritable saint, who—in contrast to Haydn and Mozart—had "emancipated" music: ". . . as he himself could be no servant of luxury, he had also to free his music from all the marks of subservience to frivolous taste."

In actuality, Beethoven's music did have enough explosive force in it to open up the way for the Romantic era and to make that way easier. The strongest aspect of this force was Beethoven's new passion, which found its clearest expression in his dynamics, in the sharp alternation of contrast in particular, and in the accessions of power in general: the *crescendi* and *decrescendi,* upon which—as in the Scherzo and Finale of the Fifth Symphony—a magnificent, emancipating explosion could ensue. In conjunction with this accession of power, there was also an enlargement and an ostensible freedom in the manipulation of form, which the Romantics eagerly put to their own uses. But this freedom was only ostensible; for even when Beethoven wrote sonatas *quasi una fantasia,* even when he seemed to abandon entirely the usual scheme of the sonata form, as in the "last" piano sonatas or the "last" string quartets from Op. 127 on, there was no break in the unity and completeness of the whole. The Romantics, however, overlooked the inner necessity, the cosmic order, the taming of the chaotic in Beethoven's work; they saw only the freedom, the door thrown wide. The one who went farthest in his interpretation of this freedom was, again, Wagner, who declared that Beethoven had burst form itself asunder in the symphonic field with his Ninth Symphony, through a desire that the last word on the subject of the symphony be said, and that now a new realm was having its beginning: neither cantata nor choral symphony, but—of course—the symphonically conceived opera.

The really "Romantic" part of Beethoven, however, consisted in the content of his sonatas, quartets, and symphonies. In them there seemed to be something new. Beethoven's instrumental music seemed no longer to be "absolute" music, which in itself alone had all its motion and its being; but, behind it, there seemed to be something that explained its originality, its peculiarity, the secret of its formal expansion, its mighty impulse, and the hymnlike quality of the slow movements. And the explanation was found in the "poetic" element. Beethoven was no longer a musician like Haydn or Mozart, but a tone-poet, a poet in tone.

He had himself assisted in the new, Romantic interpretation of his works by ending the Ninth Symphony with Schiller's "Ode to Joy"; for, if this fourth movement, as it were, burst into an explanation, perhaps the three previous movements must also have some "significance." In one of his sonatas he had assigned to the movements the specific meanings of "Farewell"—"Absence"—"Homecoming." By way of "explanation" of the Piano Sonata Op. 90, he had suggested "Strife between Head and Heart—Conversation with the Beloved"; for Op. 101, "Dreamy mood—Summons to act—Return to dreamy mood—The deed." Once when a pupil and initiate of his circle had asked him what his Sonata Op. 31, No. 2, wished to express, he had given the presumably offhand answer, "Read Shakespeare's *Tempest*." Likewise, when the same pupil asked him why the Sonata Op. 111 had no third movement, he replied that he had not had time to write one.

Another pupil of Beethoven's, Carl Czerny, of whom one would hardly expect it, wrote in his *Method for the Piano* (1847): [9] "Each of his compositions expresses some one particular, firmly captured mood or view [!], to which even in the most minute touches it remains true. The melody, the musical *thought* predominates throughout; all passages and agitated figures are always but means to an end." And what did the Romantics esteem as the "end" of Beethoven's instrumental music? The expression of something that lay *behind* the music: if not the programmatic element as in Berlioz and Liszt, then it was the "poetic"—the "poetic idea." No longer did they seek the connection between the individual movements of a Beethoven work within a purely musical framework, but in the composer's poetical intention. They felt that the composer, for most of his

[9] Vol. IV, p. 33.

works, had unfortunately happened to remain silent about this intention, or, for a work like the *Eroica,* had happened to give a mere hint through a vague title.

The one who gave expression to this idea with the greatest air of stating self-evident propositions was again Richard Wagner. In a letter to Uhlig, dated February 15, 1852, he accompanied an "explanation" of the *Coriolanus* overture with these remarks:

> The characteristic feature of Beethoven's great compositions is the fact that they are true poems, that in them an attempt is made to represent a genuine subject. Now, the difficult part of understanding them lies in the difficulty of discovering for certain the subject represented. Beethoven was completely engrossed in it; his most significant compositions are indebted almost entirely to the individual nature of this subject that so engrossed him. In his preoccupation he thought it quite unnecessary to give special indication of this subject, apart from what was given in the composition itself.

Accordingly, the Romantics tried to get at the "content" of a symphony or sonata of Beethoven's by pictures and comparisons, without noticing that in so doing they were getting farther and farther away from its true, purely musical content, and that by "poetically" linking the individual movements they were transforming a Beethoven work with its strict unity and completeness into a novelistic suite.

Finally, tired of the confusion of such poetical interpretations, Berlioz and Liszt themselves, in their works, fixed the imagination of the listener upon certain definite interpretations: the one by means of his programmatic overtures and symphonies, the other by means of his symphonic poems. Meanwhile Wagner went his own special way, and—after he had paid his respects to the program in several youthful works, such as *Christopher Columbus, Polonia, Rule Britannia,* and *A Faust Overture*—he threw the purely symphonic art overboard, in favor of opera, in which stage picture and spoken word explain the symphonic element, or at least provide an interpretation for all the mysterious, unfathomable symphonic features.

The Romantics esteemed Beethoven not only as a revolutionist but also as a rebel, and it lay in their natures to link the veneration of the true Classic with the struggle against the mere imitators of the classical. Cherubini was still greatly respected by the Romantics, while his successor in the "Institute," George Onslow (1784–1853), after deserved temporary success, was straightway plunged into the sea of neglect. "Liberation from the conventional" was a watchword of the Romantics. Schumann started

SCHUBERT

SCHUMANN

ROSSINI

DONIZETTI

his *Zeitschrift für Musik* principally for the purpose of undermining the fossilized *Allgemeine Musicalische Zeitung*. It is a remarkable fact that, in a movement so very inwardly directed, so much inclined to "dream itself away" as the Romantic was, there was never any lack of pugnacious propagandists, much as the Catholic Church has never wanted for valiant defenders. A goodly portion of the literature written by the Romantic musicians consists of manifestoes, controversial pamphlets, polemics, attacks, and counterattacks.

CHAPTER IX

The Romantic Classic: Schubert

THE MAN

IF ONE wished to formulate the external aspects of Franz Schubert's life as simply and concisely as possible, one might make use of the letter he wrote on April 7, 1826—two and a half years before his death—in applying for the position of Vice-Capellmeister at the court of Emperor Francis I:

1. The undersigned is a native of Vienna, son of a schoolmaster, and twenty-nine years of age.

2. As a court chorister, he enjoyed the supreme privilege of being for five years a pupil at the Imperial choir school (*Zögling des k. k. Convictes*).

3. He received a complete course in composition from the late First Court-Capellmeister, Anton Salieri, and is thereby qualified to fill any post as Capellmeister.

4. Through his vocal and instrumental compositions, his name is well known not only in Vienna but also in all Germany.

5. He has in readiness, moreover, five Masses for either large or small orchestra which have been performed in various churches in Vienna.

6. Finally, he now enjoys no appointment whatsoever, and hopes in the security of this permanent position to be able at last to attain completely the artistic goal which he has set for himself.

So far as the outward form is concerned, this application could have been written as well by a musician of the 18th century. In actuality, however, it came from one whose mode of life would have been entirely impossible before Beethoven. The revealing phrase is the statement that he, Schubert, "enjoys no appointment whatsoever." He was also never to "enjoy" one. Like Beethoven, he was independent; yet his independence was of a quite different sort from that of his great predecessor and contemporary, whose livelihood was always secure, despite all his lamentations and hardships. Schubert lived the life of a musical Bohemian, before the term had become current; he lived only for his divine urge to create, without any middle-class support. He considered middle-class support only a means whereby he might be able to satisfy his creative urge. The last passage in his petition betrays this attitude and perhaps was responsible for his not getting the post. The occasional honoraria which Schubert received for his works—particularly his songs—and the receipts from that memorable single concert of March 26, 1828, were meager or quickly spent. Schubert was as unlucky in his applications for positions as he was in his attempts to get away from his Viennese publishers and become connected with the then great publishers of the German Empire. His experiences with Breitkopf & Härtel, Schott, and Peters do not form the subject of the most glorious pages in the history of German publishing. The fact that he nevertheless lived to the age of thirty-one was due to the inexpensive and convenient living conditions in Vienna, and the friendship of certain contemporaries, such as Schober, Mayrhofer, Spaun, and Schwind.

Schubert's failure was fundamentally like Mozart's, though different, too: both came to grief in their attempt to achieve independence. Mozart, in whose times an office at a court was still the accepted position for a creative musician, had established himself as a free artist, relying on Viennese society, on his virtuosity as a pianist, and on the current demand for opera. He was defeated for many reasons—among others, because he was too great and because, in his day, the disintegration of 18th-century society was already in full swing. Schubert was no virtuoso; he shunned "society." He was fundamentally very lonely even among his friends. There is some basis for the saying that he is traditionally supposed to have uttered: "Often it seems to me as if I did not belong in this world at all." After his discharge from the Imperial choir school in the autumn of 1813, he prepared himself to be a schoolmaster, in deference to his father's wishes, and even followed this profession for a few years, until the autumn of 1817. His whole heart and soul, however, were not in this work, as may be surmised from the fact that in 1815 alone he wrote 144 songs, among other compositions, and in 1816 applied for a position as Music Director in Laibach. He would have been as poor a Music Director or Vice-Capellmeister as he was a schoolmaster. After 1817, the only position that he still held was that of a piano teacher for the two daughters of Count John Esterházy, on the Hungarian estate of the Count's family in Zelisz, during the summer and autumn of 1818 and 1824—for free maintenance and two gulden a lesson. Otherwise—except for some professional or pleasure trips to places like Upper Austria or into the Salzburg area—he scarcely ever left Vienna and Lower Austria.

His life would be comparable to that of the hero in the *Taugenichts,* ("Good for Nothing" 1826), a Romantic novel by Joseph von Eichendorff, were this fictional character not the most carefree fellow in the world, who, as Wilhelm Scherer has expressed it, "triumphs over all obstacles, sings the most beautiful songs, and never knows what is going on around him—always dreaming and making love and playing his fiddle and wandering far and wide. . . ." Schubert only "sang the most beautiful songs." Otherwise he suffered deeply, and after his serious illness of 1823, which may well have been of a venereal nature, his life became more and more gloomy. Of himself, he wrote: "Think of a man whose health can never be restored, and who from sheer despair makes matters worse instead of better. Think, I say, of a man whose brightest hopes have come to nothing, to whom love and friendship are but torture, and whose enthusiasm for the beautiful is fast vanishing; and ask yourself if such a man is not truly unhappy. . . ." [10] There are lighter moments, but the fundamental mood remains.

The legend, moreover, of Schubert as a "dreamer" is sheer fiction: he suffered deeply from the political oppression which prevailed in all Germany and especially in Austria after 1815 and which had an unfavorable influence on his operatic ventures. One of his poems, as we have seen, shows how bitterly he regretted the enforced inactivity of the youth of his time. This flight from life to art, here perhaps still involuntary, is genuinely Romantic. Also here is a difference from the attitude of Beethoven, who relieved his political dissatisfaction with vigorous abuse, and who—being looked upon as half a fool—was granted that privilege.

SCHUBERT'S EARLY INSTRUMENTAL WORKS

In contrast to the misfortune of this short and troubled life, full of poverty, humiliation, and disappointment, there stands the luck of that star under which Schubert was born a *musician.* From this good fortune he himself also derived some satisfaction, and posterity must be forever deeply thankful for this happy conjunction of events. As a musician, Schubert came into the world at exactly the right time. He was able to

[10] Letter to Leopold Kupelwieser, March 31, 1824, tr. by G. Grove, *Dictionary,* 3rd ed. (New York, 1935), art. *Schubert,* IV, p. 604.

enter into a rich and still active inheritance, and he was great enough
to use it in the creation of a new world. This fact lies at the basis of his
lonely position as the Romantic Classic. When Schubert began to create,
Mozart's and Haydn's work was complete; and in the same city as Schubert, honored by him timidly from afar, Beethoven lived and worked. It
was, moreover, a piece of good fortune for the younger musician that he
arrived at full maturity before he could be influenced by Beethoven's last
works—the piano sonatas and string quartets, and the Ninth Symphony.
Schubert was deeply disturbed by Beethoven, as was every Romantic. As
a young man (on June 16, 1816), he even made a very critical reference to
Beethoven's "eccentricity, which unites the tragic with the comic, the
pleasant with the repulsive, heroism with rant, the very saint with the
harlequin—unites, exchanges, and even confuses them, driving a man to
distraction instead of resolving him in love." Yet Schubert was not only
the pupil but also the contemporary of Beethoven, independent of him
and one might say coordinate with him—if one can grant any composer
equal rank beside the great creator of symphonies and sonatas, Beethoven.

In contrast to Beethoven with all his energy and power, Schubert has
been characterized as of a "feminine" nature. As a matter of fact, he
was strongly susceptible to external influences. In his early instrumental
works, one can lay one's finger on the motifs, themes, and accompanimental figures in which he followed Haydn, Mozart (whom he spoke of
more than once with glowing enthusiasm), Beethoven, and even lesser
men. He never passed beyond the model of the classical sonata form; it
is touching to see how unhesitatingly and self-assuredly even in a late
work like the Octet (February, 1824) he imitated Beethoven's Septet,
both in the instrumentation for clarinet, horn, bassoon, string quartet
(in Beethoven, string trio), and double bass, and in the succession of
movements. With him, the chief thing was not originality. When Vienna,
around 1815, was stirred by the new Italianism of Rossini, Schubert
yielded also to this influence. He not only wrote overtures in the Italian
style and canzonets on Metastasian texts, more "Italian," more racy than
many a work originating south of the Po, but also introduced into his
German instrumental works many enchanting Italianisms. In a letter to
his friend Hüttenbrenner (May 19, 1819), he also gave verbal expression
to his regard for Rossini: "Otello . . . is far better—that is, more characteristic—than Tancredi. One cannot deny that he has extraordinary

genius. The instrumentation is often highly original, as is also the vocal writing except for the usual Italian gallopades and several reminiscences of *Tancredi*."

Despite all these dependent and derivative features, however, Schubert was from the very beginning a singular personality, with new traits that marked him as a Romantic. Very early, at the age of 17, he began to write symphonies, and by 1818 he had followed his first symphony with five more. In so doing, he did not entirely imitate the model furnished by Beethoven, who by 1812 had written eight great examples of this form, among which were the *Eroica,* the Fifth, and the Seventh Symphonies. Instead, Schubert clung to works like Beethoven's First or Second Symphony, whose Larghetto had made a deep impression upon him. The dangerous model of the *Pastoral* he left quite out of account. He tried the brighter combinations of Haydn and Mozart, as in his very modestly instrumented B-flat major Symphony of October, 1816. Here he was almost writing chamber music, and one can point out the "classical" influence manifested in each of the four movements. Or he enlarged this ensemble along Beethovenian lines when, a year later, he came to write his Sixth Symphony, in C-major, with its passionate introduction and its transformation of the minuet into a scherzo.

Yet he never wrote symphonic music about which one might feel tempted to ask—as one does with Beethoven's—what it "meant." One is scarcely inclined to seek for the "content" even when Schubert wrote a symphony, No. 4 (April, 1816), to which he subsequently appended the title *Tragic*. In the C-minor key of this symphony he showed the influence of Beethoven's String Quartet Op. 18, No. 4, rather than that of the Fifth Symphony; and, in the manner of Haydn, the minor is transformed in both the first and the last movements into the optimism of the major key. Schubert played with the idea of writing discursively, and he wrote graceful development sections; but they were never gathered together in such a way as to achieve the tension or energy found in Haydn or Beethoven. What Schumann, in an essay that has become famous, said about the great C-major Symphony applies even more to these early symphonic works: "Schubert refrains from imitating the grotesque forms, the daring relationships that we encounter in Beethoven's later works, being conscious of his own more limited powers; he gives us a composition of most delightful form and yet of new facture, never departing too far from the center, and ever again returning to it."

Two features, however, mark even these early works: a new sonority, arising particularly from the new, tender, sensitive treatment of the wind instruments, especially the wood winds; and a rather rich harmony —a richness coming from a superabundance of heart. With these, moreover, there is joined a new type of melody, derived not from the development, as so often in Haydn and Beethoven, but self-generated and, one might almost say, cradled in its own felicity. To be sure, there are "beautiful" themes in Beethoven, too—in the Piano Sonata, Op. 110, for example, where after the fermata near the beginning there are eight measures not utilized in the unusual exposition section and present unchanged in the recapitulation. But, with Beethoven, "beautiful" melody is only an element of contrast, like counterpoint or the stricter manner of composition, while with Schubert it is an end in itself. His themes are not small change, but pure, unminted gold.

THE LATER SYMPHONIES

The year 1822 marks the point of division between those symphonies in which Schubert was still somewhat of a pupil, and those in which he took his place as a master standing beside Beethoven and even leading the way on past him. In October of that year he wrote the two movements of the B-minor Symphony, which is referred to as the *Unfinished*. It is not unfinished, even though Schubert may have made some sketches for a Scherzo to follow the Andante and carried them out in score for a few measures. In the two movements everything is said that can be said in music about the abysses and heights of melancholy. In concentration and in the power of explosive forces let loose, the first movement is to be compared only to the first movement of Beethoven's Fifth Symphony, except that in Schubert the contrasts are still sharper.

Within the classical framework, Schubert here ventured to introduce as the second theme a veritable *Ländler,* a true Austrian country dance, not stylized, a gift of the people or of heaven; and only in its syncopated accompanimental figure did he permit it to play a part in the development section. Schubert was thus more Viennese than Beethoven, Haydn, or even Mozart. It was no matter of mere chance that he was born in Vienna, although he was not of Viennese ancestry, for his parents came from the Moravian or Austro-Silesian area. Mozart, Haydn, and Beethoven also composed dances for Vienna; but their pieces are neutral and "classical" in comparison with Schubert's, which are filled with colorful harmony and ingratiating melody and rhythm, yet are free from the slightest traces of vulgarity. The same observation, in the field of military music, applies to Schubert's marches, for which he created a specifically Austrian, or even Austro-Hungarian type, with quick and buoyant step, full of dash, quite unlike the pompous Baroque marches of Lully or their coarser Prussian vulgarizations.

This nationalistic trend had its counterpart in literature, in which the Classical took on an Austrian coloring with Franz Grillparzer. Since Grillparzer, there had been alongside the German a specifically Viennese literature, in the works of such authors as Raimund, Nestroy, and Stifter.

Schubert once uttered this complaint: "Who can do anything more after Beethoven?" An answer is supplied by his own B-minor Symphony, with its reliance upon pure melody, upon that excess of the harmonic element. Its second movement, for example, is not in D, as it would have been according to the classical rule, but in the dominant of the dominant of the parallel key. This symphony, moreover, relies upon pure sound; nothing more enchanting in sound has ever been written than the second movement, with its immortal dialogue between oboe and clarinet above the shimmering background of the strings. The B-minor Symphony has shown that something more *could* be done.

The great C-major Symphony of March, 1828 (the year of Schubert's death) demonstrates this fact, if possible even more clearly. Robert Schumann, who ferreted out its manuscript in the possession of Franz Schubert's brother Ferdinand, in a suburb of Vienna, justly emphasized the "masculine origin" of the work—"the complete independence from Beethoven's work exhibited by this symphony. . . . In addition to masterful technique of musical composition, here is life in all its ramifications, color even to the finest shade, significance throughout, the sharpest expression of individual detail, and—finally—a Romanticism suffusing all that one . . . recognizes in Franz Schubert." The negative evidence of this independence and originality is the fate of this Symphony in Vienna, where in 1828, after a few unsatisfactory rehearsals, it was laid aside again by the Philharmonic Society. Eleven years after the death of its composer, Mendelssohn gave it its *première* in Leipzig. But even in 1844 in London, at its very first rehearsal, it was rejected with laughter by the Royal Philharmonic Orchestra. The first impression that it made is understandable. It has the dimensions of a Beethoven symphony, but not the passion; and passion is more understandable than Schubert's purposeless, entirely unprogrammatic music, full of majesty and depth and at the same time full of jubilation in the first movement, full of enthusiasm and at the same time of sauntering ease in the Finale, full of sonorous and rhythmic magic in the *Andante con moto "all'ongarese,"* in the strong and folk-like Scherzo and Trio. From the very beginning, commentators have noted the original use of the wind instruments in this work, from the flute to the trombone, and the prominent role assigned to that "most Romantic" of all instruments, the horn.

CHAMBER MUSIC AND PIANO COMPOSITIONS

What applies to Schubert's symphonies applies also to his string quartets, with the difference only that the line of division between the experiments and the independent masterpieces is drawn somewhat earlier. Already as a youth of fifteen he had made a beginning with his string quartets; and in the next five years he wrote about eleven works, for each of which one can prove with some certainty that the model was Mozart or the Beethoven of Op. 18. But at the end of 1820, after what had been for Schubert a very long silence, he wrote a quartet movement in C minor which is in itself as finished and as new as the Symphony in B minor—a "fragment" that is complete, compact in form, full of strangeness and magical Schubertian grace. And it was followed by three masterpieces: the Quartets in A minor (1824), D minor (1826), and G major (1826), completely uninfluenced by Beethoven's Op. 59 and the following quartets up to Op. 130, which, though not performed until March 21, 1826, might yet have come to Schubert's attention. In its compactness, the A-minor Quartet is most comparable to the B-minor Symphony, except that it is lyrical in all four movements. The first movement is entirely constructed upon the magical alternation of minor and major, which in Schubert is more elemental, more sensuous than in Beethoven, than—for example—in the slow movement of the Seventh Symphony. There is no model at all, moreover, for the Minuet, with its modulation into the region of A-flat major and with its *Ländler* Trio in A major. In its relationship to a song written in November, 1819, *"Die Götter Griechenlands,"* this work reveals another Romantic peculiarity of Schubert's: his tendency to take a motive with its roots in a song—a motive whose musical expansion was there limited by the presence of the text—and work it out fully in the instrumental realm. Similarly, for example, in the Rondo of his Piano Sonata in A (1828) he took as his point of departure a song written in March, 1826, *"Im Frühling";* or, in his last Piano Sonata in B major, he started out from one of his Mignon songs (*"So lasst mich scheinen, bis ich werde!"*), perhaps having in the back of his mind some programmatic idea whose secret we shall never be able to decipher—and probably never should know. In the gloomy D-minor Quartet there exists a similar relationship with the variations on his song "Death and the Maiden": the gentle answer of Death in the song, concentrated within a few measures, provides the seed which in the Quartet blossoms forth in full lyricism, even to the certainty of blissful release, of most profound peace in the eternal. The G-major Quartet again leads the listener into realms of sound and agitation that were not taken from a model and that have not been imitated.

To the three quartets is to be added the String Quintet in C major, composed in 1828. It is not merely the alteration of the sound, the doubling of the violoncellos instead of the doubling of the violas as in Mozart and Beethoven, that gives the composition its unique character. Rather, it is the new quality of sound in itself that corresponds to, is one with, the new invention of themes. When the C-major triad at the beginning makes a crescendo, bursts into a diminished seventh chord, to come again into the pure heaven of C major, we feel that the door of the Romantic era has been surreptitiously opened. We feel this, even though we realize that this beginning has received certain suggestions from Mozart's C-major Quintet, and that Mozart's C-major Quartet has played a part in the formation of the thematic group. But where are the precedents for the Adagio in E, the Trio of the Scherzo (in D-flat!), and for the lack of restraint in the Allegretto finale?

As with the Classic masters like Haydn, Mozart, and even Beethoven, all the chamber works in which Schubert included a piano part—magnificent as are some of the passages in them—are of less importance than the works for strings alone. The so-called *"Trout"* Quintet (1819), the two Piano Trios in B-flat and E-flat Opp. 99 and 100 (both from 1827), the Duets for Violin or Flute and Piano—all have about them an air of society and the virtuoso. Schubert's period was not only that of the rising Romantic movement, but also that of the *Biedermeier,* of the self-indulgent middle class, of virtuosity.

This aspect, however, does not appear in his purely pianistic works— the sonatas and the individual pieces, the best known of which are the *Moments Musicaux*. Never was Schubert more indifferent to Beethoven —or to any other model—than in these pieces, which stand out amid the panorama of Romantic piano music by the fact that they need no public, and, indeed, scarcely even a listener. What a contrast to Weber's sonatas, polonaises, rondos, and variations, to his *Invitation to the Dance*—works which are inconceivable without some provision for the applauding public! Schubert plays but for himself, and so feels no necessity for concentration. More than ever his themes have their felicity in themselves, and they rather resist dissection, "development." Look at the Rondo of the C-minor Sonata of 1828—what highways and byways until the theme is again found! Beethoven, in all his side-stepping, keeps his eye steadily on the theme; his *divertissements,* his "digressions," are parallel paths from which one can always turn back again onto the main road. Schubert loses himself in the mysterious and highly remote regions of forest and enchantment.

Contrast is supplied by the Impromptus and *Moments Musicaux.* Many of them are as short as they are complete: the one *"all'ongarese"* in F minor is a lyric as finished as a quatrain from Omar Khayyám. Take the Impromptu Op. 90, No. 4, in A-flat with the simple A B A scherzo form, the B being in C-sharp minor, the enharmonic of D-flat minor. There is repetition throughout, for the thought is so beautiful; and at the end there is no coda. What formal primitivism, after Beethoven! But what a magical substitution of sound and of melodic and harmonic inspiration!

SCHUBERT AS CREATOR OF THE LIED

While Schubert's instrumental works became thoroughly his own only in 1820 and thereafter, his songs had already undergone that development at an earlier date. When it is said that the history of song really begins with him, the statement is in a certain sense true, just as in another sense it is not. The history of song is as old as the history of music itself. In order to appreciate its antiquity and scope, one has only to think of the 16th-century Italian canzonetta, of the 17th-century arietta, of John Dowland's lute-ayres, of the 18th-century French chanson.

Especially great were its ramifications and its destiny on German soil. The German lied was hindered by a lack of true, great, heartfelt poetry —a few exceptions like Simon Dach's or Friedrich Spee's in the 17th century, or Johann Christian Günther's at the beginning of the 18th, merely prove the rule. True feeling made itself perceptible almost entirely in the religious sphere alone, where it was too often straightway flattened out into mere moralizing. About the middle of the 18th century, there prevailed three fashionable tendencies: the sentimental, the Anacreontic, and the epigrammatic.

On the musical side, the lied was imperiled by the persistent influence of the Italian cantata, the Italian aria, with its instrumental propensities and its beautifully curved *cantilena* passages. In sharp reaction against this influence, moreover, there came a tendency from rationalistic North Germany that led to an artistic simplicity hardly less undesirable than its opposite. Thus the North Germans such as Johann Abraham Peter Schulz (1747–1800) and Johann Friedrich Reichardt (1752–1814), who favored the genuine strophic song and who, as a matter of fact, did succeed in writing some delicate and wonderful songs, came to be opposed to the Austrians, Haydn and Mozart, whose vocal compositions were felt by their opponents to be too instrumental, scarcely recognized as being songs at all. Where the North put too little music in the song, the South put too much; or, rather, for Haydn and Mozart the poet was still subordinate to the musician, still the one who supplied a text to which music was attached. And since it was all the same to them who wrote the text, they happened occasionally to stumble upon a great poet: Haydn, for example, on Shakespeare; or Mozart, on Goethe. In both instances there arose no real lieder; instead, there were *scenes* with instrumental background. Especially notable is that little masterpiece of Mozart's, *"Das Veilchen"*— half canzonetta, half lyrical melodrama, or recitation with music.

Meanwhile, German song was being influenced by another, new artistic type, the genuine melodrama, in which the spoken word, usually an emotional monologue, was given an orchestral background in the manner of a *recitativo accompagnato*. In this type of composition the orchestra accentuated the feeling, the scenic background—sunrise, thunderstorm and tempest, pastoral strains. From the combination of melodrama and song there arose the ballad, whose first great exponent, Johann Rudolf Zumsteeg (1760–1802) of Stuttgart, made a deep and remarkably lasting impression upon Schubert.

But that is the only strong influence that we can trace as having operated upon Franz Schubert as the creator of the lied. The good fortune of his particular historical position is seen here, perhaps, even more than in the instrumental field. He was born into the greatest period of German literature: he inherited the tradition of Klopstock and Hölty, he was a younger contemporary of Goethe and Schiller, he lived through the revolution of the Romantic movement in literature—that of Tieck, the Schlegel brothers, and Novalis, up to Heinrich Heine. The Romantic movement, moreover, through its translations made accessible to him a considerable body of world literature—Ossian, Petrarch, Shakespeare, Cibber, Walter Scott. Even the texts supplied him by his Viennese friends often bear with them a worthy echo of the excitement of this high-strung period. He wrote over six hundred lieder and other vocal works, among which are a considerable number that represent a definite solution to the problem of the lied—for, like every composite, complex artistic type, the lied really is a problem, scarcely less so than opera, and in every instance the composer has to find the proper balance between melody and accompaniment, between subjective feeling and objective representation.

CURRENTS IN SCHUBERT'S LIEDER

Schubert's type of lied is at once Classic and Romantic. In no other field is one more justified in calling him the Romantic Classic. He is Classical in that he almost always has at his disposal the concentrated energy, the lack of which in his instrumental works has often been made the object of criticism. He wrote songs of some length—and some songs of exceptional length—especially when in his earlier years he took in hand some of the Ossianic lays and the Schiller ballads; but, in so doing, he never gave full license to his purely musical imagination. If we call him Romantic, we do so not because he wrote music for verse of superficially Romantic scenery, of Romantic content, such as grave-diggers' tunes, spectral greetings, and poems in which knights, pilgrims, troubadours, maidens in castle towers, and nuns figure as heroes and heroines. In one of his earliest vocal works, that using Matthison's "Adelaide" as text, he appeared to be competing with Beethoven; similarly, later, in his *"Wachtelschlag,"* he did so once again—and came off the victor by his renunciation of everything Italianate, everything cantata-like, everything predominantly instrumental. Schubert is Classical in that the melody, the vocal writing, and the declamation in his works are in equilibrium, and in that both vocal part and piano part are subservient to the poem. His procedure here is in complete opposition to that in his numerous attempts as a composer of operas, in which he time and again ran aground through his failure to recognize the lack of dramatic content in his texts and his too great reliance on the music—for the hallmark of the opera composer is his critical approach to the text. In his lieder, Schubert is meaningful and succinct, and often more dramatic than Verdi or Wagner.

Schubert is Romantic, compared with his predecessors and contemporaries, in the superabundance, the overflow of music with which he provides both the voice part and the accompaniment. It is characteristic that this overflow was too much for the great poet whom Schubert most deeply honored and whose work he most frequently set to music. This poet, Goethe, envisaged his ideal of the lied as having the music subordinate to the text, as exemplified in the practice of his household composers Reichardt and Zelter. With Schubert, the accompaniment gives everything at once—the feeling, the picture, the atmosphere. It is a kind of painting with the emphasis upon feeling; it is the expression of a kind of feeling most acutely sensitive to all the pulsations of nature. The piano becomes a universal instrument, which in color, capacity for expression, and pure and noble sensuousness has made no greater gains at the hands of any master than at Schubert's. He always appeals to feeling and fantasy at the same time; and one would only stifle the hearer's imagination were one to try (as some, unfortunately, have done) to interpret the role of the piano in orchestral form, to "realize" it—which means to coarsen it naturalistically.

Schubert is Romantic, furthermore, in his relationship to folk song. He does not try to imitate it—in fact, he is completely untouched by the 18th-century theories of simplicity. But he creates it, involuntarily. Some of his songs are folk songs pure and simple, such as his setting of Goethe's *"Heidenröslein."* Others, like that of Müller's *"Am Brunnen vor dem Tore"*—from the second and last of his two great song-cycles, the *Winterreise*—have been taken up by the people, which has done just what it has always done from earliest times: it simplifies the song, "sings it to pieces," until it can sound well from the lips of the most unsophisticated singer. These cycles (the first being *"Die Schöne Müllerin"*), show that Schubert not only had nothing to learn from Beethoven, but also had no desire to learn anything from him; for he must have known Beethoven's greatest contribution to the history of the lied, the cycle *An die ferne Geliebte,* which appeared in 1816 and which, by means of the unifying accompaniment and the return to the beginning, is fused into a musical and psychological whole. The unity of Schubert's two cycles is real, though it cannot be proved, and it is not immediately apparent; as Richard Capell puts it,[11] "a drama is revealed to us in a series of lyrical moments."

Early in his career Schubert succeeded in writing perfect lieder and other vocal compositions: he was not yet eighteen years old when he set the lyric monody *"Gretchen am Spinnrad,"* and Goethe's *"Nachtgesang"* (*"O gib vom weichen Pfühle"*), a marvel of copiousness and concentration. But it would be wrong to conclude that in his remaining fourteen

[11] In his excellent book *Schubert's Songs* (London, 1928).

years of life he did not increase his mastery. Occasionally, he still chose long texts; but where in his youth he had mastered them by alternating recitative and *arioso* passages, in this later period he overcame the difficulties otherwise, by linking the whole together with new bonds, especially those of motivic unity in the accompaniment. This was an artificial means which later all the Romantics were to avail themselves of, not only for the lied but also for the opera, although not always with the same flexibility and artistic necessity as had characterized Schubert's use of it.

Schubert never followed a mere pattern. To the end of his career he kept up the strophic song, which he enlarged into the strophic song with variations only when the text invited his doing so. On the other hand, he dared to try very bold and free forms without their degenerating into mere experiment. The fullness of his production is to be explained only by the almost somnambulistic sureness with which the right tone found its way to each word. The remark of one of his teachers applies more to his mature than to his earlier years: "I can teach him nothing; he has learned everything from the good Lord God himself." The most simple and the most sublime were within the range of his feeling and his mastery.

The only area in which his powers were limited was that of low humor. There Beethoven could have given him a magnificent example in his "Flea Song" (taken from *Faust*). It is characteristic that Schubert time and again set to music the songs of Mignon and of the Harper from Goethe's *Wilhelm Meister;* but he never set any of the songs of the free and easy Philine. He arrived at the borders of the charming and even the sly, but he did not go on beyond. In this respect his Romantic contemporaries and successors, from Carl Loewe and Schumann to Hugo Wolf, were able to furnish a supplement to his universe of song.

But no one succeeded in going beyond him in his work as a whole, and his successors were all the composers of the 19th century who tried their hand at the lied. Schubert made of it a specifically Romantic genre. For a brief period, at first, it aroused only condescending recognition, as manifested in a letter by the editor of the Leipzig *Allgemeine Musicalische Zeitung,* Johann Friedrich Rochlitz, to Ignaz Franz Mosel (April 30, 1826): ". . . several rather new compositions by your Schubert have aroused my great interest and esteem. Perhaps this talented artist needs only a thoroughly educated friend who would gently enlighten him regarding himself: what he is, what he has, what he wishes; whence, it is hoped, he may be able to find out by himself what he should do." Another chattering aesthete, the Swiss Hans Georg Nägeli, in his *Lec-*

tures on Music, also of 1826, knew nothing at all about Schubert. But genuine recognition did come, fairly quickly. How different from these dilettantes were the musicians themselves: Schumann, Liszt (who with his transcriptions did much for the appreciation of Schubert), right on to Brahms and to Hugo Wolf (who so often seemed to challenge comparison of himself with Schubert—not always with complete success).

CHURCH AND CHORAL MUSIC

Yet Schubert still belonged to the vanishing tribe of universal musicians, equally at home and equally great in the vocal and instrumental fields, the secular and the sacred. He wrote seven Masses, of which two, those in A-flat and E-flat, were composed in the period of his full artistic maturity (1822 and 1828)—works of such singular character that they are difficult to classify. Although they were founded on the tradition of Viennese sacred music, on that of Mozart and Haydn, they are much less "Catholic" or churchly than Beethoven's C-major Mass of 1807 and that great work of 1822, the *Missa Solemnis,* the performance of which on March 7, 1824, Schubert had lived to hear. Of Beethoven's vast work, many have said that it far exceeds the dimensions of liturgical practicability and treats the hallowed text far too subjectively; but Beethoven was a faithful member of his church, and the work was intended for that church, even if for an exceptional occasion.

Schubert was much more subjective, more stirred by skepticism, more critical. It is significant that in the Credo of both Masses, as in his earlier ones, he did not compose music for the words *"Et unam sanctam catholicam et apostolicam ecclesiam"*—a feature that, in itself, makes both works unacceptable for church use. This subjectivity is matched by the ecstatic harmony of the work: an example, in the A-flat major Mass, would be the Sanctus, which leaves the major key of F by way of an augmented fifth chord and after a few measures arrives at C-sharp major. Subjective features like these stand in the sharpest contrast to Viennese conventions like the traditional *fugato* passages in the traditional places. This is Romantic church music; and if, in the 19th century generally, there was still a great deal of pious, creative church music still being written, by Berlioz, Liszt, Bruckner, Franck, alongside that epigonous kind which was nothing more than a return to the Palestrina style, this church music was having its difficulties in uniting full belief with the "19th century." It was to have recourse to Romantic ecstasy, which is foreign to genuine church music.

Schubert's versatility also included types of art that had received little or no attention from the Classical composers. All of these had something to do with sound as such—for example, his women's choruses, and especially his men's choruses, which are compositions quite different from the occasional, similar works of the Classical composers, such as Haydn's canons, Beethoven's "Song of the Monks," or the Chorus of Priests in Mozart's *Magic Flute*. They are only very distantly related to those German men's choruses which had their origin in Zelter's *Liedertafel,* or singing society, in Berlin, and which from the very beginning fostered patriotic and nationalistic aspirations. One of the statutes of that first *Liedertafel* (Berlin, 1809) reads: "Themes of the Fatherland and its general welfare, in their entire scope, are recommended to poets and composers. The *Liedertafel* considers itself a foundation that celebrates the longed-for return of the Royal house [that is, from the exile occasioned by Napoleon]; for, in general, one of the primary items of business in the organization is the praise of its King." That is the genre, doubtless not without historical and even artistic worth, to which belong Carl Maria Weber's songs of knights and swords, his drinking songs before battle, etc. A battle song or drinking song is also found occasionally among Schubert's works; but in general his overflowing heart sought texts for his men's, women's, and mixed choruses that he could transmute into pure sound and poetry. After him, the genre divided into two streams: one patriotic, largely a matter of *Liedertafel* activity; the other purely artistic, in which Mendelssohn, Schumann, and Brahms in general followed in his footsteps.

CHAPTER X

Romantic Opera

SPECIALISTS IN OPERA

ALTHOUGH it has already been stated that Schubert was a versatile composer, equally great in the fields of vocal and instrumental music, there is a single reservation to be made: he was no writer of music dramas. True, he wrote operas, incidental music for plays, recitations with music, and an oratorio. Among his works, for instance, there is a comedy dealing with chivalry, *Fierrabras,* in genuinely Romantic style, of the same year as Rossini's *Semiramide* and Weber's *Euryanthe*. But the complete failure of these dramatic works of Schubert's, when they were performed at all during his lifetime, was only too well deserved, hard as that fact was for him to bear. A true opera composer is revealed in his choice of texts, in his eye for the musico-dramatic; and it is not enough for him to do as Schubert did—append the most wonderful music to a text that he liked, as in *Rosamunde,* of which only the instrumental pieces, with their splendid orchestration and sonority, have any vitality. It is unfortunate that precisely in the happiest of Schubert's dramatic experiments—his compositions for Goethe's *Singspiel, Claudine von Villa Bella*—the latter half is not extant. But it is no tragic misfortune, for the real contributions of the Romantics to the history of opera are along a line of development quite different from that of the idyllic *Singspiel*.

It is not necessary, moreover, that a great writer of music dramas be so great a musician as Schubert was: for this role, he must have other qualities. Is it not noteworthy that all the great composers of symphonies and chamber music like Haydn, Schubert, Mendelssohn, Brahms, and even the composer of *Fidelio* were lacking in the dramatic touch, just as the great or genuine dramatists like Gluck, Weber, and Wagner had no real access to the realm of symphonic and chamber music? Mozart is the

single, wonderful exception, while Berlioz and Liszt seem to occupy a
somewhat peculiar position.

At all events, the Romantic era altered the attitude of the composer
towards opera; it made the opera composer a specialist. In the 18th century, Gluck was the only example of this kind of specialization, for, in
general, it was expected of the opera composer, that he would also produce sacred, symphonic, and chamber music. Vice versa, it was expected
of the symphonic composer that he could write an opera if one were ordered. Handel, Jommelli, Hasse, Johann Christian Bach, and Rameau are
more or less typical examples. This situation changed in the 19th century.
When so many Romantic musicians "also composed" or wished to compose an opera, they did not understand that the hour had struck for the
opera, or they were merely deceiving themselves: Mendelssohn began
a *Loreley,* which he did not finish; Brahms concerned himself with opera
plans, which he very wisely did not carry out. Meanwhile, Meyerbeer
also showed his worldly wisdom in the fact that he never even considered dissipating his energies on a symphony; and Verdi and Wagner
either never made an excursion into that region, so strange to them, or frequently had to atone for it if they did, as did Wagner with his *Faust* Overture or his *Emperor* March.

The Romantic movement made the opera composers specialists because it took its opera more seriously than did the 18th century. This
applies even to Italy, the land where opera had been discovered, the land
where opera was endemic, and where the transition to the modern period
took place without the revolutionary disturbances encountered in France
and Germany. One need only recall Verdi's sharp animadversions against
the idea of opera as "entertainment," as "amusement," in order to judge
what a change had taken place in Italy between the time of Cimarosa or
Paisiello and that of the creator of *Rigoletto* and *Otello,* who invested his
operas with his own full, deep passion, his savage frankness, and his hopeless melancholy. In Germany and France, also, the type of the commissioned opera, the "opera of the season," more and more passed out of
fashion.

The composer now took longer to write an opera, and had to count
on a success that would be correspondingly more long-lived. Around 1809,
when Louis Spohr composed his opera *The Duel with the Beloved* (*Der
Zweikampf mit der Geliebten*), he began resolutely "without subjecting
the libretto to examination." [12] That state of things quickly changed.

[12] *Autobiography* (Cassel, 1860–61), I, p. 149.

Around 1829, when a *Faust* (1816) by the same composer was presented in Berlin, Carl Friedrich Zelter wrote to Goethe in amazement at the fact that the score was almost like chamber music: "Now as to the work of the composer, who is clearly recognizable more as a tonal *artist* than as a musician or melodist, everything is carried out most artistically and —astonishingly enough—to the most minute detail, in order to overreach, to outbid the most alert ear. The finest Brabant laces are rough work, in contrast. A copy of the libretto is almost indispensable to the performance, for the expression of the words in respect to high and low, light and dark, tense and lax, and so on, is worked out with hairbreadth precision, like the honeycomb in a beehive." [13] This exactness, moreover, reacted upon the Italian *opera seria,* especially among musicians who no longer wrote exclusively for Italy: Luigi Cherubini, who since 1788 had become a Parisian, and Gasparo Spontini, whose *Vestale* (1807) and *Fernand Cortez* (1809) each required three years to find its way from Paris to Italy, or to return. Above all, the orchestral elaboration of the opera by both Italian masters was something new and of the greatest consequence. Both Cherubini and Spontini were disciples of Gluck in their ideal of the opera, and both helped to establish the "grand opera" idea —Spontini, with his pompous treatment of the brasses and his Napoleonic rhythms, more so than the refined Cherubini—an idea which in the ensuing history of 19th-century Romantic opera played a role that was as unfortunate as it was fruitful.

ANTECEDENTS OF THE ROMANTIC OPERA

For the romanticizing of opera, two centuries had provided abundant subject matter. If one conceives of the Romantic era as a turning away from the Classical, an approach to the medieval, one finds that this approach was very quickly effected, and had already made its appearance in the original circle of the Florentine purists themselves. The imitation of Classical tragedy, which around 1600 was the main point in the program of the Florentine *Camerata,* naturally required Classical subject matter— Orfeo, Dafne, Ariadne, Aretusa. But with Gagliano's *Medoro* or Francesca Caccini's *Liberazione di Ruggiero,* with Michelangelo Rossi's *Erminia sul Giordano,* there came into the opera the chivalric epics of Ariosto and Tasso, which remained an inexhaustible mine of operatic material right down to the time of Rossini's *Tancredi.* Soon there also appeared figures

[13] November 15, 1829.

from Roman history, with Suetonius and Tacitus as sources—an immortal example being Monteverdi's *L'Incoronazione di Poppea.* There also appeared figures from the early Middle Ages and from the period after the decline of the Roman Empire, the personages who emerged from the clash between the Romans and the barbarians. And there was the Spanish drama with its colorful adventures, the Spanish novel—Don Quixote carries the principal role, as hero, in a dozen operas. The purism of the reformers of operatic dramaturgy, Apostolo Zeno and Pietro Metastasio, simply restrained mystical and fantastic opera in favor of ostensibly historical material—no matter whether from sources that were Classical (as in *Didone* or *Temistocle*) or Romanesque (as in *Ricimero Re de' Goti* or *Ruggiero*). And even Gluck, the creator of the half-mythical *Orfeo* and *Echo et Narcisse,* made his offering to the traditional conception of operatic material with his *Iphigénie en Aulide* and *Armide.*

But alongside antiquity and history, there arose after 1750 another source for a new and more colorful world of operatic material; and it is a source that manifested itself throughout the entire operatic field—in the Italian *opera buffa,* the French *opéra-comique,* and finally in the German *Singspiel.* Common to all three national types was the "Turkish opera," with its half comic, half fantastic character. It was no longer merely a matter of Oriental costume, as it had been with Metastasio, who simply presented Viennese court society in a new form of fancy dress, for example, in his *Cinesi* (1735), the music for which was written by Gluck and several others. The "Turkish opera" presented a new exotic world, and as examples of *opera buffa* one need only name Jommelli's *Schiava Liberata* (1768); of *Singspiel,* Neefe's *Adelheit von Veltheim* (1780) or Mozart's *Entführung* (1782); of *opéra-comique,* Gluck's *Rencontre Imprévue* (1764) or Grétry's *Caravane du Caire* (1783). With Grétry we have cited the name of the musician who perhaps contributed most to the transformation of 18th-century opera into Romantic opera. His *comédie-ballet, Zémire et Azor* (1771) is already set in a quite distant part of the Orient, in Persia, where fairies still intervene in the fate of men; and when a German librettist, five years later (in 1776), took in hand Marmontel's libretto for this opera and reworked it for the musician Gotthilf von Baumgarten, it bore the subtitle *"Romantic-Comic Opera."* Thus, for perhaps the first time, the new concept which was to prove so influential in the realm of opera, received explicit verbal expression. And it is anything but accidental that, in the early Romantic period of the opera, the material of *Zémire et Azor* was taken up again—by Louis Spohr in 1819.

The fusion of the fantastic and the comic was also known to *opera buffa* in Goldoni's *Mondo della Luna,* with Galuppi's music, as early as 1750; or in G. B. Casti's *Grotta di Trofonio,* written in 1785 for Salieri. This type of fusion was still vigorous up through *Crispino e la Comare* (1850), by the brothers Luigi and Federico Ricci, even though in their work it was still dependent on the Viennese magic-Singspiel, in the manner of Ferdinand Raimund. In this Italian fusion, however, there was little Romanticism to be detected; but in "The Stone Guest" (*Convitato di Pietra*), the material most used by the dramatists of the 17th and 18th centuries, there were seeds of the Romantic era, and there was at least a general opinion among the Romantics themselves that these seeds had already grown into blossom in Mozart's *Don Giovanni.*

To be sure, the complete fusion of the fantastic with the folklike—and, similarly also, of the sentimental with the comic—was already present in works like Wranitzky's *Oberon, König der Elfen* (Vienna, 1789), which was displaced in the German operatic repertory only by Weber's last work. The fusion was also present in works like Mozart's *Magic Flute* (1791), with which the history of German opera as a whole began, although the work in its serious freemasonic aspects is anything but Romantic and, as a work *sui generis,* has found no successors.[14] But alongside it a German (*teutsche*) *opera seria* had appeared, though it cannot be considered quite seriously until Weber took it in hand. There was even something like a patriotic opera, such as Ignaz Holzbauer's *Günther von Schwarzburg* (Mannheim, 1777), followed in 1780 by the Wieland-Schweitzer *Rosamund*—actually Italianate opera written to a German libretto. There were also operas with Northern material seventy years before Richard Wagner, such as *Baldur's Death* (Copenhagen, 1778) by the Dane J.-E. Hartmann, a "heroic *Singspiel*" with a Valkyrie chorus. To the gloomy, mystical North there belong also the Ossianic operas such as Le Sueur's *Ossian* (1804) or Méhul's *Uthal* (1806)—works whose orchestral color is also full of "Northern gloom." There were fairy-tale operas a hundred years before Humperdinck's *Hänsel und Gretel,* such as *Rübezahl* (1789) by Joseph Schuster of Dresden—the same material that later, in the first flowering of Romantic opera, Louis Spohr dealt with again in his *Berggeist* (1825).

As opera pressed forward with the substance and spirit of such ma-

[14] I hope that no one will consider operas like Süssmayr's *Spiegel von Arcadien* (1794) or Winter's *Labirint* (1798) as belonging to the tradition of *The Magic Flute.* They are mere imitations.

terial, Classical subject matter retired into the background. It did not entirely disappear, and it held on longest in Italy. But Metastasio disappeared. It was, moreover, romanticized; and Spontini's *Vestale* or Rossini's *Semiramide* (1823) had nothing more in common with the operatic ideal of Metastasio. *Opera seria* had been transformed into *grande opéra,* with the strenuous participation of orchestra and chorus, with a new type of scenery that was no longer purely classic and decorative. And it was principally French *opéra-comique* that had contributed to this change. From it, both in terms of the subject matter and the music, evolved Romantic opera. Mere naming of some of the titles of Grétry's operas suffices to show how close we have come to the end and to the new beginning: *Aucassin et Nicolette* (1779), *Richard Cœur-de-Lion* (1784), *Raoul Barbe-Bleue* (1789). The subject matter of *Richard Cœur-de-Lion,* in particular, already fulfills all the requirements for a Romantic opera: medieval chivalry, imprisonment of the hero, discovery and rescue by his faithful minstrel, a castle, forest, nobility, and peasants. Grétry was not yet in a position to mold this material in true Romantic spirit: he still was writing a Singspiel in the 18th-century way; the musical unity of this charming work rests upon the return of the decisive melody of the faithful minstrel, not upon the coloring. But we remember that Robert Schumann fashioned "Blondel's Lied" into one of his finest ballads (Op. 53). "Romantic opera" was at the door.

EARLY ROMANTIC OPERA: WEBER

This door was opened, at least for Germany, by Carl Maria von Weber (1786–1826). He was still a child of the 18th century: sixteen years Beethoven's junior, he died almost a year before Beethoven. Yet he seems a quite different type of musician, a later type than the Classic masters, even than Schubert.

Through Mozart's unhappy marriage to a member of the family, Weber was related to Mozart. The elder Weber—a dubious character, soldier, manager of estates, Capellmeister, theatrical impresario, and high-class swindler when circumstances demanded—tried to make out of his son a child prodigy like Mozart. As a matter of fact, while Mozart published his Opus 1 when he was ten or eleven, Weber brought out his first work, six Fughettas for piano, when he was just twelve. But he turned out quite differently from Mozart. Mozart never learned how to be the master of his own life. Providence simply chose him to be a vessel for musical immortality, which he had to reveal to the world. In the lives of both Mozart and Weber there were crises to be faced by each at about the same age: in Mozart's, the great journey to Mannheim and Paris, in which he went out to conquer the world and from which he returned a completely beaten man; in Weber's, the Stuttgart years from 1807 to 1810, years full of the gravest moral dangers, whose outcome—imprisonment—brought him to maturity.

What followed—his activity as Capellmeister in Prague (1813–1816) and in Dresden (1817–1826)—was a period of sometimes high-spirited and sometimes embittered conflict with middle-class impresarios, aristocratic stage managers, with quarrelsome colleagues and envious rivals, with his public and the world in general—a conflict that Weber fought out with all the 19th-century weapons: manifestoes, open letters, critiques, polemics. In that respect he was something of a successor to Gluck, and certainly a genuine forerunner of Richard Wagner. He was not only a creative artist, a brilliant virtuoso on the piano, and a distinguished conductor, but also a great organizer. In this respect he was again like Gluck, except that he had a much more difficult task than Gluck did, for he had to work within the provincial limitations of Prague and Dresden, and did not have Gluck's violent personality, Gluck's established renown to throw into the balance. Weber conducted the campaign to protect his family, moreover, with more modern means: at this time the rights of legal protection for artistic property began to be established even in music—a development for which the success of Beethoven's works obviously deserves a great deal of credit. Weber's life was so active and eventful that it seems to have been much longer than Mozart's, but it was really only four brief years longer.

In versatility Weber seems to have been a match for Mozart. From an external point of view, the thematic catalogue of his works resembles Mozart's exactly, with Masses and offertories, operas and other dramatic works, songs and arias, choral works, symphonies, and concertos for instruments of various sorts, sonatas and other chamber music for piano solo and ensemble, marches, and dances. But this versatility is only ostensible. Weber was no genuine church composer; in the service of the Dresden court he wrote only two full Masses (together with offertories). To be sure, he felt that he had completed these, especially the first (in E-flat, 1818), "with thorough conviction and a deep feeling for the greatness of the subject." But precisely that phraseology is Romantic: it involves a self-conscious relationship to the noblest celebration in the Catholic

Church. It is not the kind of unquestioned Catholicism, that character-ized Mozart, Haydn, and even Beethoven. Weber wrote his Masses in the same way that he wrote his operas.

Among his early works, he wrote two symphonies—pre-Beethovenian symphonies, as it were—historically of no real importance. Chamber music for strings is entirely lacking among his works. Some 130 songs are extant, but they are in general still in the tradition of the "Berlin School" of Reichardt and Zelter. They are still written in a state of innocence, i.e., without the Schubertian richness, boldness, and sense of artistic respon-sibility. In many of them, Weber toys with the German folk song: he imitates its naïveté and sentimentality, as he also imitates successfully in other works the "national" element, the French and Scottish. In some of the songs he even imitates not merely the national, but also the regional German element—the Low German, the Swabian, and the Bavarian.

There remain for consideration his concert music, his piano composi-tions, and his operas. For the piano he wrote two concertos and one con-cert piece which is still in the repertoire today. He wrote two concertos and a concertino for the clarinet, a concerto and rondo for the bassoon, a concertino for the horn, and also a few recital pieces for various stringed instruments (but none for the violin). In all of these he was quite in his element: the mixing of utmost *espressivo* with utmost brilliance. Even his piano compositions are always *concert* pieces—the variations, rondos, polonaises, waltzes (including the highly eloquent *Invitation to the Dance*), the four sonatas, and the few works of chamber music dominated by the piano. They are of an entirely different order from most of Beethoven's piano sonatas and all of Schubert's. While Beethoven's *Appassionata* and *Waldstein* Sonatas and his Opus 106 are also recital pieces, they are not "brilliant" in the same sense as are Weber's. Weber always thought of the concert hall, and always ended with an exhibition of bravura. His tradition is that stream in the Romantic movement which ran out into broader and broader shoals in the compositions of Thalberg, Dreyschock, Herz, and Hünten—until it was dammed up by Chopin and Schumann, and grew to a torrent in Liszt.

In the domain of opera Weber was that rarest of all phenomena among German musicians—a born opera composer. In this respect he resembled Gluck: he wrote no string quartets and was no composer of genuine sym-phonic music. His calling showed itself very clearly: he was involved with the stage when but a youth of fifteen. An opera written in 1801 and pre-sented at Augsburg in 1803, *Peter Schmoll,* which received the unqualified praise of his teacher Michael Haydn, was already his third dramatic effort.

His peculiar, most personal style which amazed friends and enemies alike, developed very early. In 1812 he brought out in Berlin an opera *Silvana,* which he had written from 1808 to 1810 in Stuttgart. This work already bore the title "Romantic Opera" and contained choruses of hunters, with the sound of hunting horns, the tumult of a thunderstorm, the sharp rhythm of round dances and torch dances, and the mixture of the sentimental and the folklike peculiar to the German Singspiel. On hearing this work, a well-meaning friend, the musician and scholar Von Drieberg, said, "He strives for effects; the instrumental is perhaps the most brilliant aspect of his work, while the voice parts are now and then neglected; and one number rather resembles another, with the result that a certain monotony pervades the whole opera." Although Weber took exception to the latter part of this criticism and at the same time took it very much to heart, he himself acknowledged that there was much truth in the first part.

In his later years he confided the secrets of being a successful dramatic composer to a younger fellow artist: sharpness, clarity—even excessive clarity—of characterization, and lack of restraint. These features differentiate Weber from Louis Spohr, whose orchestra often has the finish of chamber music; and only the fact that Weber never made effect the main consideration clearly differentiates him from Jacob Meyerbeer, his fellow pupil under Abbé Vogler. From the very beginning this quality of melodic and rhythmic sharpness is noticeable in Weber, even in his instrumental works. He was "original," but in quite another sense than Beethoven; he had a manner, though he was anything but a mannerist.

Added to this sharpness, this melodic vivacity, there was also Weber's predilection for the national element, which he likewise inherited from Abbé Vogler. It showed itself in his choice of themes for variations: there are Italian, Norwegian, Russian, gypsy themes. In the six Sonatas for violin and piano which he wrote in 1810 on commission from the publisher André, there is not only a French Romance, but also an Introduction "in Spanish style" (*carattere spagnuolo*), a Russian air, a Siciliano, and a Polacca. When yet eighteen or nineteen, he wrote a "Chinese Overture," the theme for which he had found in Rousseau's *Dictionnaire de Musique.* In a later reworking of this material, he added six marches which (with one exception) modify the theme in the manner of a leitmotif—the whole now serving as incidental music to the Gozzi-Schiller *Turandot.* About 1820 he wrote some pretentious incidental music for a play *Preciosa* by

Pius Alexander Wolff, with overture, marches, choruses, songs, melo-
dramas, and dances, in which the Spanish gypsy character is no less
sharply emphasized than it is later in Bizet's *Carmen,* most of the motives being "modelled after genuine melodies." We are not surprised
that Weber early composed a drama "alla turca," the merry and graceful
Singspiel in one act *Abu Hassan* (1811), with "Turkish music" in the
Overture and Final Chorus, and with the famous Chorus of the creditors
"Money! money! money! I will wait no longer" (*Geld, Geld, Geld! Ich
will nicht länger warten*)—a masterpiece of naturalistic description after
the manner of the *Arabian Nights.* It was a first excursion into the Oriental, which Weber was to take up again fifteen years later, with infinitely
greater refinement, in *Oberon.*

DER FREISCHÜTZ, EURYANTHE, OBERON

In May, 1820, Weber completed a *German* "Romantic opera" in three
acts, *Der Freischütz,* which was to prove epoch-making. He had worked
on it more than three years—a long time, even in view of his official
duties and the many works, great and small, that he had been writing in
the meantime. Rossini, in about the same period, required no more than
a few weeks for any of his operas. This is one of the evidences of the
earnestness with which composers were now applying themselves to the
creation of a German opera. And the first performance, on June 18,
1821, in Berlin, was forthwith recognized and extolled as an event of
national significance. The reason for this lay not alone in the fact that this
date was the anniversary of the Battle of Belle-Alliance, nor entirely in the
fact that the success of a German opera was considered a blow delivered
by a local composer against Spontini, who was then disliked by many in
Berlin, and a blow against Italian opera in general. Instead, the reason lay
in the peculiar nature of Weber's music.

Five years earlier the Germans might have found occasion for a national
exultation in the field of opera, when in this same city of Berlin E. T. A.
Hoffmann's *Undine* was produced. It was a "Romantic opera," quite
similar to the *Freischütz* in character. Later critics have called it a "connecting link between the *Magic Flute* and the *Freischütz.*" A famous
Romantic fairy tale served as the basis for the libretto of *Undine;* the
author himself, Baron Friedrich de la Motte-Fouqué, had adapted the
libretto. The material was genuinely Romantic: the infusion of a soul into
an elemental being, a nymph, and the revenge of the spirits upon human

faithlessness, choruses of spirits of earth and water, medieval chivalric splendor, "folk" in the form of simple fishing people, a pious priest. Hoffmann was much more than a dilettante. Being a contemporary and admirer of Beethoven and of Mozart's *Don Giovanni,* he supplied the work with highly ingenious features: in the music, for instance, one seems constantly to hear water rushing. Weber, incidentally, knew the work very well, and characterized it as "one of the most spirited works that the newer period has given us." In it he found not only a general model for his *Freischütz,* but also a specific one for individual features, such as an aria of Undine's (Act II, No. 10) in polonaise rhythm.

Again, the reason that Weber's *Freischütz* was epoch-making, while Hoffmann's *Undine* and Spohr's *Faust* were not, lies in Weber's stronger, more individual musical talent, in his eye for the theatrical, in the brevity and concentration of all the pieces, and finally perhaps in those mysterious imponderables that are inherent in every individual composition. The *Freischütz* has been called "the most German of all operas." But it is only the material that is German—in the sense of the distinctively German Gothic horror and of the then popular German tragedies of fate (of which the best example is Grillparzer's *Ahnfrau*). A gamekeeper's assistant can win his bride only if he is successful in a shooting match. But his hand is unsteady, and the prospects are not bright. A comrade, who has long since fallen and sold his soul to the Devil, misleads him into casting enchanted bullets, of which six will hit their mark but one will be directed by the Devil as he wishes. At the crucial moment, it strikes the girl. But Heaven has regard for the mortals: a wreath of consecrated white roses protects the victim and deflects the bullet to the villain. A pious hermit, as *deus ex machina,* puts everything more or less to rights. The action is set in the superstitious period after the Thirty Years' War, and in the forests of Bohemia; and the Romantics eagerly seized the opportunity to escape from the rationalism of their fathers for three hours at the theater by abandoning themselves to the titillating horrors of the action. The text is shrill, childish; the characters—with the exception of the sinister gamekeeper's assistant—are pale and inconsistent. But the work is effective; and Goethe was at least not entirely wrong in mentioning the name of the librettist when he said, after the success of the work, "One ought also to give some credit to Herr Kind." As a whole, however, the opera lives only through Weber's music.

If one looks only at the external aspect of the *Freischütz* music, one cannot call it quite "German." The setting-off of the principal woman's role, the "ingénue," by contrast with a "soubrette," was an old rule of dramaturgy both in the *opéra-comique* and in the Italian *opera buffa*. This soubrette was fond of the polonaise rhythm (Arietta No. 7), and sang a romance and aria (No. 13, the last number in the opera) entirely to the French taste. Agatha—the serious, sentimental girl—has a famous Scene and Aria in E, "How could slumber come to me" (*Wie nahte mir der Schlummer*, No. 8), which is unmistakably a *"Scena ed aria"* in the Italian manner. The hero, Max, likewise has an aria that is unmistakably influenced by Méhul, whom Weber rightly esteemed, and with whose *Joseph* he had begun his conductorial activities at Dresden. The main piece in the opera, the melodrama of the "wolves' glen," the finale of the second act, is typically French—a relic of the thunderstorms and tempests of Rameau and his successors.

The "German" pieces in the opera are, after Weber's manner, sharply German: the hunters' choruses, the peasants' march, and the brides-maids' chorus—the popularity of which once drove Heinrich Heine to distraction. It is the customary confusion, or some might call it the customary trick, of nationalistic art history to designate as national what is purely personal style. The *Freischütz* is Weber's own, and because Weber's style is so markedly personal, he set the tone for the entire Romantic German opera.

Weber's characteristic feature consists in the striking power of his melody, which is impelled by his sharp eye for scenic effect. In Agatha's great scene, for example, at the modulation from a seventh-chord on G to the 6/4 chord of F-sharp on the words "What a beautiful night" (*Welch schöne Nacht!*), we *see* with Agatha the whole splendor of a starlit sky in a clear summer night. Another example of Weber's concentration is the villain's inspired drinking song, which Beethoven was highly enthusiastic about, according to contemporary testimony—in this instance reliable. Weber did not have the restraint of the symphonically minded, classical musician. Not only are the melodic aspects of his work more striking, but also the increasing freedom of modulation. Above all, he is one of the greatest innovators in the field of instrumentation. Perhaps the most masterful portion of the opera—exclusive of the overture, which reflects the course of the opera instrumentality—is the "wolves' glen" scene. This would be but a piece of crude Romantic horror—and on the stage it should even be that, according to Weber's expressed intention—were it not softened and ennobled by Weber's refined treatment of the instrumental groups and of the individual instruments: the tight tremolo of the strings, the deep register of the clarinets, the gloomy accents of the trombones, the shrill flutes, the mysterious staccato tones of the horns. The scene also utilizes most cleverly several motives reminiscent of preceding numbers of the opera: thus it is not entirely descriptive or decorative, in the French sense, but it is perceived, felt, and fashioned from within the two "heroes." Weber himself is the one to whom the *Freischütz* is indebted for its homogeneous fundamental tone, and through whom the work has become a German folk opera, in the higher sense of the term.

But Weber had ambitions loftier than merely to have created a folk opera, even a most highly successful one. He wished to build upon this Romantic folklike composition the German Romantic *opera seria:* no longer a Singspiel with spoken dialogue, but a complete opera, or—so the title reads—a "great heroic-romantic opera in three acts." This was *Euryanthe,* commissioned by Barbaja, the Italian impresario of the Kärnthnertor Theater in Vienna, where it was produced in the fall of 1823. It was not well received, and this poor reception has continued to greet the work everywhere and in spite of all attempts at revival. The fault has been ascribed to the librettist, Helmina von Chezy. As a matter of fact, she did everything she could (or, as a result of the prudery of the times, everything she had to do) to obscure the action at its highest point and to transform the four main personages, one "light" and one "dark" pair, into lifeless puppets. The story is that of one of Boccaccio's tales, or of Shakespeare's *Cymbeline.* In the matter of diction, the librettist manifested unusual care. The fault lies perhaps not entirely in the text. Weber was too far ahead of his time in this work, as is shown by the passionately hostile criticism which even his colleagues in art like Schubert and Grillparzer directed against him. The interest in the subject matter of the opera, moreover, quickly waned and thus the favorable time passed in which an opera could gain a footing in the national repertory.

It was this subject matter that had first set Weber's imagination in motion: chivalric Middle Ages ("The scene is alternately Nièvre and the Prémery castle; the time, 1110"), manor houses and citadels, noble lords and ladies, and again peasants and huntsmen. The spirit world, moreover, has a part in this medieval scene, though not quite so obvious a one as in the *Freischütz.* "Medieval" also is the theme of the action: the virtue of a maiden is suspected and eventually vindicated; against the purity and chivalry of the "light" pair, is opposed the raven-hued blackness and the passionate nature of the "dark" pair. Now, Weber would not have composed in the way he did, even after making the librettist revise her text eleven times, if he had not found therein the most moving situations. There are three powerful *finali,* towards which the first act in particular develops with dramatic intensity. There is, moreover, opportunity in the arias and duets for the development of melodiousness, fire, and passion—opportunity in the dances, marches, and choruses for a new colorfulness. But the opera is not merely decorative; it is not merely a combination of chivalric splendor with the mysterious, as everyone knows from the overture. The consistent attention to the recitative—more careful psychologically and thematically than in any of the other examples of *opera seria* in that period—gives the work a new musical unity. The excitement, the high emotional quality of this recitative, moreover, is matched by the ecstasy of the melody at the high points in the drama. In a certain sense, Weber's most violent opponent, Spontini, had prepared the way for him in all this. Spontini, however, had only raised the forms of the Classical *opera seria* to the colossal and monumental, by mass scenes and heightened emotion. Here was a new, more Romantic tone in the opera; and if the public did not appreciate it immediately, at least the musicians of the following generation appreciated him all the more profoundly. No work made a more powerful impression on Wagner as a young man; he found in it all the germinal ideas, both dramatic and musical, for the operas of his Dresden period, from *The Flying Dutchman* to *Lohengrin;* he might be said, during this period, to have been exploiting *Euryanthe.*

After *Euryanthe,* Weber made only one further great contribution to the operatic stage, *Oberon,* which he brought out at Covent Garden in London a few months before his death in 1826. One need but look at the playbill of this presentation to recognize the character of the work: "Oberon, or The Elf-King's Oath; with entirely new Music, Scenery, Machinery, Dresses and Decorations." It was an elaborately mounted piece, the text—by James R. Planché—a conglomeration of Wieland and Shakespeare, somewhat copied after *The Magic Flute,* but without its seriousness and deeper meaning. It was, again, a Singspiel with spoken dialogue; and from the very beginning Weber did not consider the English version of the work as final. What incited him to composition—for he had the choice between this *Oberon* and a *Faust*—was, again, the colorfulness of the work: the "Kingdom of the Fairies," enveloped in enchanting fragrance; the chivalric; the Oriental, with a particular shading of "Arabian" and "Tunisian"; along with all this, a storm at sea and a magical night on the deep; a vision, and a beguiling or grotesque dance. Again everything is brief, striking, and yet presented with greatest care. In the Introduction of the Overture, every instrument—horn, flute and clarinet, trumpets *ppp,* and string quintet—is made to utter sounds with such color as was known to none of his contemporaries, not even to Berlioz. This Introduction alone is evidence that a new realm of Romantic sound had been entered.

MARSCHNER, SPOHR, LORTZING

Out of Weber's work there arose two streams of early German Romantic opera. The one pursued further the ideal of the Romantic folk opera, after the model of the *Freischütz;* the other broadened the channel that had been cut by *Euryanthe.* Mendelssohn in his *Loreley,* which he was prevented by death from finishing, was rather a follower of the E. T. A. Hoffmann of *Undine,* although he knew how to invest the extant finale of Act I with much more dramatic passion and much more enchanting sonority of chorus and orchestra than did the earlier standard-bearer of the Romantic era. Yet his all too highly developed taste may perhaps have hindered the impulsive exercise of his power to achieve the striking effects that were necessary for a successful Romantic opera. The musician who began most naturally in his imitation of Weber was Heinrich Marschner (1795-1861). Weber himself had brought before the public one of Marschner's first operas, *Heinrich IV und Aubigné,* and had expressed himself as of the opinion that "springing from such striving for truth, from such deep feeling, there will develop a dramatic composer who will certainly be highly respected." Three years later (1823) Weber accepted him, not quite willingly, as his own colleague—as Music Director of the Dresden court opera. When Marschner's hope of becoming Weber's successor in office was not fulfilled, he went to Leipzig, where he brought out his first successful operas, *Der Vampyr* (1828) and *Der Templer und die Jüdin* (1829). At last, in 1831, he secured an appropriate position in Hanover, where he soon wrote his best operatic work, *Hans Heiling* (Berlin, 1833).

One need only glance at the subject matter of these operas to see that this "Romanticism" did not hesitate to indulge in the crudest theatricality. The action in *Der Vampyr,* after one of Lord Byron's narratives (*Lord Ruthwen*), centers around a hero who is a demoniac mixture of da Ponte's Don Giovanni and Caspar of the *Freischütz.* Whereas Caspar had to deliver to the Devil only one compensating victim, the Vampire had to

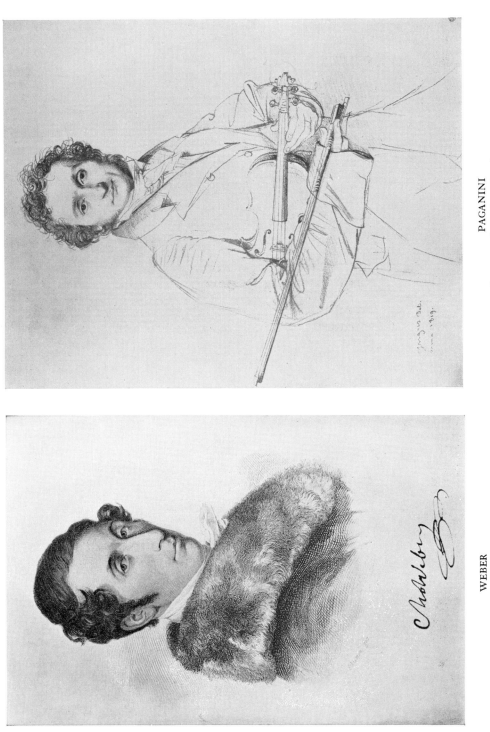

PAGANINI
from a drawing by Ingres

WEBER

BRUCKNER

BRAHMS

deliver no less than three innocent brides within the specified time of twenty-four hours. There was also no lack of wedding and drinking scenes, of quick seduction, and of terrible murder. *Der Templer und die Jüdin* goes back to Sir Walter Scott's novel *Ivanhoe*. But with Marschner it was less a matter of lyric expansion than of robbery, abduction, struggle, ordeal—of romances, arias, prayers, and folklike songs. In the person of the "Black Knight" there is a reminiscence of Grétry's innocent, pre-Romantic opera *Richard Cœur-de-Lion;* but how gaudy, passionate, clumsy, and loud has all this become!

There is a finer quality to *Hans Heiling*. Originally intended by the librettist Eduard Devrient for Felix Mendelssohn, it is based on a legend of the Erzgebirge that had been made into a tale by Theodor Körner. It is the "Lohengrin" theme in a more folklike garb. Heiling, son of the queen of the earth-spirits and of a mortal man, renounces his rule for the hand of a maiden, for whose sake he wishes to become entirely mortal. But like Lohengrin he asks too much of his bride, who breaks faith with her mysterious lover; and after wild outbursts he returns, brokenhearted, to his dark kingdom. Even in this, his best work, Marschner was not Weber's equal; he was a man of cruder stamp than his finely nerved, fiery, inspired, chivalric predecessor. But he had a strange talent for the musical illustration of the mysterious and terrible, and for the heavily passionate. In the dramatic prologue to *Hans Heiling,* which is set entirely in the excited realm of the spirits, he took a step towards the voluntary overthrow of the form of the "Romantic Singspiel": in this prologue there is no longer any spoken dialogue; the scene is "through-composed" (*durchkomponiert*). The unity of this great scene for solo and chorus has a symphonic substructure: we are coming closer and closer to the genuine Romantic opera.

Even a musician so retrospective as Louis Spohr could not help abandoning the number-opera towards the end of his career, with his *Kreuzfahrer* ("The Crusaders," presented in 1845), for which he had himself prepared the libretto, after Kotzebue. His intention has been stated thus: "Entirely deviating from the form heretofore customary, as well as from the style of the composer's own earlier operatic music, he has through-composed the entire work somewhat as a musical drama, without superfluous textual repetitions and ornaments, and with ever advancing action"—to which we might add: with complete avoidance of all melismas. He thus goes not only beyond the Weber of *Euryanthe* but also beyond the Wagner of *The Flying Dutchman* and *Tannhäuser.*

True, the Romantic Singspiel did not die out: in 1845, Albert Lortzing (1801–1851) was composing a "Romantic magic-opera," *Undine,* using the same subject matter as had already attracted E. T. A. Hoffmann. Lortzing was the creator of a whole series of comic operas, effective in the theater, indestructible on the German stage, highly unromantic and in fact rather bourgeois and philistine: *Czaar und Zimmermann* (1837), *Der Wildschütz* (1842), *Der Waffenschmied* (1846). In his *Undine,* Lortzing did not even fill in the outlines drawn by Weber and Marschner: the work is rather a Romantic magic-piece, like those which the Viennese, in particular after *The Magic Flute,* had cultivated and perpetuated in local vulgarizations. In the scenes between some of the comic figures it even comes close to being a magic-farce. This late example of the early Romantic opera, however, is yet Romantic enough, by virtue of its use of themes running through the work for both the supernatural characters —motives which, above all, play out their unifying role in the orchestra. That feature, incidentally, is the mark of Romantic opera in general: the coloring and the symphonic background.

SCHUMANN'S *GENOVEVA*

Lortzing was a man of the theater, and in his operas he had his eye always on the impression that his scenes would make on an average public—that is, on an uncultivated one. What might have come of the German Romantic opera in the hands of a musician of the purest artistic feeling, unencumbered by that *in majorem sui gloriam* theory, is shown by Robert Schumann's *Genoveva,* completed in 1848 and staged in 1850, the same year as Wagner's *Lohengrin*—with complete lack of success. Posterity has accepted, without bothering to verify this judgment of Schumann's contemporaries—one of the saddest misjudgments in the history of music.[15] But it is less our duty to set this right than to understand it in its determining circumstances. The only thing about Schumann's opera that can be criticized is his error in taking up unsympathetic material, which the composer himself freely reworked from the drama of his contemporary and old acquaintance, Friedrich Hebbel—freely, but with high dramatic skill and a sharp eye for the theater, without being afraid of violent effects. The sanctimonious conclusion of the whole is as little—

[15] I myself, in my book, *Greatness in Music,* have been a victim of that traditional prejudice, shared by Wagner and Hanslick in rare harmony.

or as much—to be criticized as that of Richard Wagner's *Tannhäuser*. The true reason for the failure, from the point of view of subject matter, lies in the fact that the work was too *little* Romantic for the period in which it appeared. The only scene in which *Genoveva* still has anything in common with the early Romantic opera is that where the witch Margareta, by means of a few deceptive pictures and mirages, convinces the homecoming knight of his wife's supposed faithlessness. Otherwise, the opera is a highly artistic piece of characterization and psychological delineation, without the tired quality that otherwise customarily mars Schumann's later works, and almost without that gaucherie of orchestration with which his symphonies are afflicted.

It is only the lack of crude operatic theatricality, of that Romantic intoxication to which the audience of the Forties had already accustomed themselves, that explains in part its failure. Also in part it is explained by the critical remarks of one of Schumann's contemporaries, the archaeologist and biographer of Mozart, Otto Jahn, who recognized with surprise the "irrepressibly powerful drive and the really dramatic life of the whole." "But," he continued, "there is something strange and difficult about the opera in the fact that scarcely a single piece of music, isolated in the usual manner, stands apart by itself; instead, in so far as the action is continuous, the music goes on in an uninterrupted stream. What is right and true in this is easy to see; yet, on the listeners' part, a great amount of effort is expected; and, on the singers', the possibility of being accorded immediate applause is eliminated—both very dangerous. No moment in the opera, moreover, is conceived of as merely incidental; every single one is presented and lovingly treated. That too is, in itself, excellent; but it makes comprehension of the work more difficult."

Might one not think that this was a criticism of one of the later Wagnerian operas? It was not Wagner alone who took the road leading from Romantic opera to Romantic music drama, in which the aria is resolved (or, one might say, dissolved) into the scene, the recitative and arioso passages equalized (or diluted to insipidity), the individual scenes tied together by the symphonically conceived orchestra, and the whole opera united by the motif of reminiscence which latter was more and more refined into the leitmotif. *Genoveva* contains a succession of these motifs, and includes but few "numbers" or inserted pieces, which Schumann treats as numbers with a certain embarrassment.

PARISIAN OPERA: MEYERBEER

It belongs to the contradictions—or, better, to what we have called
the polarities—of the Romantic era that, alongside these nationalistic
tendencies in the opera, there developed an international opera which, in
a mixture of unequal proportions, was German as well as Italian and
French. The French element in the compound was the strongest, therefore it is no wonder that the center for this kind of opera was Paris. Or,
one might phrase it this way: since all the opera composers—Spontini,
Rossini, Meyerbeer, Donizetti, right on to Wagner and Verdi—were
drawn by almost magical power to Paris, then the cultural center of
Europe, French operatic taste must be given particular consideration.

The "Romantic" side of this Parisian opera is revealed primarily in the
choice of material. More and more, opera turned away from antiquity,
not only from the mythological but also from Greek or Roman historical
themes; no branch of the lyric stage after 1800 was faced with such rapid
decline as was the 18th-century *opera seria*. The only composer to survive
was Gluck. The veneration of his works, however, was limited to a few
provincial centers, like Berlin, and to a few dissenting and singular spirits,
like Le Sueur and Berlioz; in general, it was little more than lip service.
It is significant that the musician who has been called the "last pupil of
Gluck's," Spontini, went off on another tack after *La Vestale* and *Fernand
Cortez* and *Olympie*. His *Nurmahal* (or *The Rose-Festival of Cashmere*,
1822, after Moore's *Lalla Rookh*) is set in the Orient, his magic-opera
Alcidor (1825) in a courtly wonderland, and his *Agnes von Hohenstaufen*
(1829) even in the German Middle Ages.

The *opéra-comique* and the *opera buffa* maintained their privilege of
snatching up any suggestion whatsoever. In the world of the fairy tale,
for example, Auber wrote an opera *Le Petit Chaperon Rouge* (1818) on
the legend of the German Little Red Riding Hood; and Rossini in *La
Cenerentola* (1817) used the story of Cinderella, which belongs to the
world literature of the fairy tale, and treated it with a great deal of
buffoonery. In particular, the *opéra-comique* grasped at ideas in the realm
of horror, as for example Hérold's *Zampa ou la Fiancée de Marbre* (1831),
the story of the forsaken bride's statue which will not relinquish a ring
placed on its finger in sport; or it grasped at ideas in the realm of the
Romantically comfortable, with a slight element of intrigue, as Boieldieu
did with his very pleasant *Dame Blanche* (1825), after Sir Walter Scott's
Guy Mannering and *The Monastery*. Comic opera too showed a pro-

pensity for Northern themes, especially of the Scottish variety as found
in Scott. Even Auber, the most productive, the driest and most anti-
Romantic exponent of this type, composed in 1823 his *Leicester ou le
Chateau de Kenilworth,* after Scott's novel. The only one who remained
aloof from such tendencies was Hector Berlioz. In his *Benvenuto Cellini*
(1838)—wild fruit of his love for Rome—he wrote an opera about an
artist; and in his *Béatrice et Bénédict* (1862, after *Much Ado about Nothing*) and in his *Troyens* (written in 1856–58) he remained true to his old
enthusiasm for Shakespeare and Vergil.

Although "grand opera," successor to *opera seria* and French opera, became in no real sense historical (for in it the historical element was only
costume and false front), it preserved its historicity. Life stirred in this
historicity only when, beneath the mask, political passions lay hidden. The
first great example of this political purpose was Auber's *La Muette de
Portici* (1828), whose presentation in Brussels on August 25, 1830, gave the
signal for the outbreak of the Belgian Revolution, for the nation's declaration of independence. And the second, coming a year later, was Rossini's
William Tell, which though it did not have the transporting force of
Auber's choruses, yet was of the highest significance in stabilizing the
type—if not in justifying it artistically. Nothing was more characteristic
of the trend towards international opera than the fact that Rossini, who
had given a stronger and sharper national trait to both *opera seria* and
opera buffa than they had possessed before at the hands of Paisiello or
Cimarosa, was drawn to Paris with his *Comte Ory* (1828) and sealed the
result with his *Tell.* As if to atone for the betrayal of his better self, he
then—to be sure—wrote no more operas: the return to *opera buffa* was as
impossible for him as would have been the continuation of *"grande
opéra."*

The real representative of grand opera was Giacomo Meyerbeer (1791–
1864). Under Abbé Vogler's tutelage, he had been a fellow pupil and
companion of Weber's, but had developed inevitably to a position as
Weber's antagonist. His *Alimelek* (1813), a comic opera, had been extolled by Weber himself as a "genuine, truly *German* work"; but, later,
Weber said of the opera *Emma di Resburgo,* which Meyerbeer wrote for
Venice in 1819, that it "bears entirely the stamp of the region in which it
has been created." With the *Crociato in Egitto* (1824), likewise written
for Venice, Meyerbeer took his leave of *opera seria* and followed Auber's
and Rossini's triumphs of 1828 and 1829 with his *Robert le Diable* (1831)
—the text, as a matter of course, by the two experienced grand opera

craftsmen, the librettists Scribe and Delavigne. Someone has called *Robert le Diable* the French counterpart to Weber's *Freischütz;* and so it is, if one thinks of the material and the motley appearance of the musical forms. But what is lacking is precisely the mysterious unity that marks the *Freischütz,* with all its variegated theatricality; what is lacking is precisely the "Romanticism." And what even in Auber's *Muette* and Rossini's *Tell* was still strongly felt passion and fresh inventiveness, here turned into convention—into the convention of *grande opéra.*

Grand opera must have five acts, no longer three; it must include all the sensational features of operatic theatricality—especially the ballet, which in the Italian *opera seria* either was relegated to a position between acts or followed the end of the opera itself. It must, in a fixed order, display a romance or ballade, a few cavatinas and arias for the female and male leads, a passionate duet, and moving scenic effects at the conclusion of at least two acts, to the accompaniment of all available sources of musical power: soloists, chorus, and orchestra. Indeed, the *chorus* began to play a greater and greater role, from that of mere decoration to real intrusion into the action.

Since it has always been the rule in the history of opera that every new discovery, every introduction of fresh stylistic elements, soon stiffens into convention, there was immediately formed a convention of grand opera, for which Meyerbeer in *Les Huguenots* (1836) furnished the prototype. Here was everything, all together: the typical tragic, or serious, pair of lovers, consisting of the "highly dramatic" soprano and the heroic tenor, with whom there stood in contrast another pair, a coloratura soprano and a *basse chantant.* These two pairs were flanked by a rather soubrettish soprano and a *basse profonde;* and the whole was presented on the stage in well-balanced reciprocal action with chorus and ballet, and was given a pervasive background by a more or less massive or refined orchestra. All this is not to say that very great operatic and dramatic effects cannot be achieved, or have not been achieved, within this frame: the fourth act of the *Huguenots* closes with a "grand duet" of an intensity of feeling and a nobility of melody that even Richard Wagner could not help admiring. And it is a thought-provoking fact that precisely the great period of grand opera, the Twenties and Thirties, supplied the whole 19th century with the basis of its operatic repertory, by virtue of the melodic and dramatic innovations thus introduced.

But the Parisian opera was anti-national, or not national enough; it helped itself to all the externals of the Romantic era, but was not Romantic enough; it had hidden political tendencies that were incompatible with the Romantic work of art. The best minds of the time, accordingly, turned against it: Schumann, Wagner, Verdi. Schumann attacked it in a famous discussion of the *Huguenots* in his magazine, a discussion that is at once an artistic and a moral annihilation of the work. Wagner and Verdi, each in his way, surmounted "grande opéra": Wagner through opposition, exploitation, and virtuosity; Verdi through sincerity, simplicity, and the honesty of his feeling and musicianship. In Wagner, notably, the Romantic movement rose to a new phase, which has been called neo-Romantic and which tried to absorb in and *through* opera all the other branches of music. In the late work of Verdi's, too, this phrase was surmounted. We must turn our attention now to those branches that were, seemingly, taken over by Wagner, and then later resume the thread of this chapter.

CHAPTER XI

Symphonic and Chamber Music

MENDELSSOHN, THE ROMANTIC CLASSICIST

AS INDICATED previously (p. 65 ff.), this chapter will present in greater detail the development of Romantic symphonic and chamber music since Beethoven; a development deeply influenced by, and at the same time leading away from, him. For in both fields Beethoven had brought his work to such perfection that his successors had no other alternative than to imitate him or to deviate from him. Naturally, the deviations led farther and farther away from the main line.

One might justifiably ask, with Wagner—but in another sense than the one in which he meant it—why the Romantic musicians after Beethoven still wrote symphonies at all. And one might give this as an answer: just because Beethoven had preceded them in this field. Mendelssohn, Schumann, and Berlioz, as composers of symphonies, settled their accounts with this great inheritance in different ways. Mendelssohn, thanks to his nature and his particular kind of talent, had least trouble in doing so. In the symphony, Beethoven had himself created the means of conveying a great message to all, to humanity; Mendelssohn accepted the given outlines and filled them in with another and more modest content. He was the Romantic Classicist, in contrast to Schubert, who was the Romantic Classic.

His life explains his attitude. He was the grandson of the philosopher Moses Mendelssohn, and the son of a banker; high cultivation and wealth were endemic in this family. Mendelssohn was a child prodigy in music —a fact which did not prevent his receiving a well-rounded education in many other fields as well, through instruction by carefully chosen teachers and through the stimulation of travel. How different from Bach and Haydn, who were musical "artisans," or from Mozart and Beethoven, who were the children of musicians, good and bad! What a difference between a strangely gifted man like E. T. A. Hoffmann, torn by his varied talents, and Mendelssohn, likewise highly gifted as a writer and sketcher, with whom everything subordinated itself without friction to the principal talent, that for music! The harmonious development was so complete that it seems to us almost too easy. Successes presented themselves to Mendelssohn of their own accord; he had almost always a choice between accepting or declining them—almost always, for on one occasion his talent, his youth, and his being a Jew kept him from receiving the appointment to succeed his teacher Zelter as leader of the Berlin Song Academy. His fame spread to and from England, where he enjoyed the patronage of Queen Victoria and the Prince Consort. Even this, however, did not prevent his receiving recognition in his native land; and he ended his days as Director of the Conservatory of Music at Leipzig, having sacrificed himself to his own genius, which drove him on to unremitting creative activity.

The harmonious nature of his creative work appears in the fact that the Classicistic element admitted the Romantic, and the Romantic did not disturb his Classicism. The symmetry of form in his movements and his cycles is unsurpassable. Yet over all his compositions there glistens something subjective, a Romantic shimmer of sentiment (posterity has called it sentimentality), a mingling of grace and humor. When this feature is intended or interpreted as objective, it appears as the elfin music of his *Midsummer Night's Dream* Overture. His music, finally, exhibits a passionate quality that has a Romantic effect through a kind of purposelessness. With no other composer than Mendelssohn does there appear so frequently in the Allegro movements the indication *con fuoco* or *appassionato;* but with no other composer do the fire and passion prove more highly enjoyable in themselves, and remain more their own excuse for being. Another Romantic feature is Mendelssohn's propensity for beginning with an introduction in a light key—his favorites being A major, E major, and G major—and then falling into a main movement in the corresponding minor, in a region of darker passion, of gloomier melancholy.

Mendelssohn, however, never infringes on the laws of inherent musical logic, even where his invention seems to be determined by extra-musical images, as in the *Italian* and *Scottish* symphonies and in the overtures. We can see how completely harmonious the style and expression in his Romantically irradiated Classicism is by comparing him with the composer Louis Spohr, whose operas, such as *Faust* and *Jessonda,* are at least "Romantic" or exotic in subject matter. Louis Spohr (1784-1859) belongs to an older generation than Mendelssohn, to that of Weber; but, unlike Weber, he never entered the mysterious realm of genuine Romanticism. He remained a lifelong Mozartian; nevertheless, he took over some Mozartian chromaticisms—for example, from the slow movement of the E-flat major Quartet (K. 428)—and increased them to a state of hypertrophy which, at least from the standpoint of content, already borders on the chromaticism of *Tristan*. He criticized Weber's *Freischütz* as severely as he did the later works of Beethoven, among which he numbered not only the String Quartets Opp. 59 and 127 to 135 and the Ninth Symphony, but even the Fifth Symphony. Since his nature prevented his becoming a genuine Romantic and since the age with its definite split prevented his remaining in the realm of pure Classicism, he began to experiment.

After a few compositions which belong in the direct line of succession to Mozart's E-flat major Symphony by virtue of their supple and complete form and their general enthusiasm, Spohr wrote a "Characteristic Tone-Painting in the Form of a Symphony" (1834), under the title *Die Weihe der Töne* ("The Consecration of Tones"), which makes use of a poem as the starting-point for revivifying programmatically the traditional form of the symphony. And this symphony was followed by others, such as the *Historical* Symphony, the individual movements of which indulge in a kind of stylistic masquerade, until the Finale illustrates "the latest period of all"; a "Double Symphony," i.e., one for two orchestras, with the title *The Earthly and the Heavenly in the Life of Man;* and a final one, *The Seasons,* which treats the old subject, earlier used by Vivaldi, of the transitions between winter and spring, between summer and autumn. It is clear how very closely Spohr came in contact with Berlioz at this point, in that the pure form of the symphony no longer satisfied him and he needed poetic stimulation to fill the traditional outlines with further content.

Mendelssohn approaches Spohr in his "symphonic cantata" Op. 52, entitled *Lobgesang*. Here the conception is Romantic not only in form but also in the use of the Magnificat theme by the trombones in the Introduction as a kind of leitmotif. He again touches Spohr's orbit in his *Reformation* Symphony. This work is Romantic in its quite un-Mendelssohnian lack of equilibrium among the movements, for the slow movement is quite episodic, and in the use of the "Dresden Amen" in the Introduction and the chorale *"Ein' feste Burg"* in the Finale. This is more like Weber; ideas like this would not have occurred to a Classic composer.

In general, however, Mendelssohn still wrote pure symphonies, pure chamber music, although with less strict unity. As we have already emphasized (p. 68), it is significant that he did not follow so closely the Beethoven of the *Eroica,* the Fifth, the Seventh, and Eighth Symphonies as he did the Beethoven of the *Pastoral* Symphony, with its more pictorial succession of movements. He also followed Beethoven in that he—in contrast to Berlioz—made his *Italian* and *Scottish* Symphonies "more expression of feeling than painting." All Mendelssohn's symphonies, beginning with the one in C minor written when he was fifteen (Op. 11, 1824, for London), shy away from violence; they are conceived and felt lyrically. In their first movements, they display very clever examples of development. But while in Beethoven's *Eroica* one remembers especially the development as the focal point in a mighty conflict, in Mendelssohn's symphonies it is the charming details that linger—in the C-minor Symphony the divided strings with tympani solo in the Trio of the Scherzo, in the *Scottish* Symphony the bagpipe in the Scherzo, in the *Italian* Symphony the Tarantella or the lovely melody in the slow movement. A similar situation exists in his chamber music: in the quartets, one of which, Op. 13 (1827), grew out of a song; others of the quartets often reduce the slow movement to a canzonetta (Op. 12, 1829) or transform it into an intermezzo; in some, the circle of keys is more relaxed than enlarged, as in the Quintet Op. 18 (1831) to A—F—D minor—A. One's memory clings to the originality and amiability of individual movements, usually the middle ones. It also clings to the masterful way in which he formulates his ideas—a high degree of mastery that appears as astonishingly in early works like the Octet (1825) as it does, of course, in late ones like the troubled last String Quartet in F minor (1847).

Mendelssohn administered Beethoven's heritage like a *grand seigneur,* without really taking possession of it. Only when he availed himself of the model of Weber's overture, did he become a genuinely legitimate successor and a true Romantic. This feature of his work is revealed by the perfect rounding-out of the form, which from the musical standpoint is entirely self-contained. Romanticism is also revealed by the externally stimulated invention of themes, especially in the two finest of these overtures, those to *A Midsummer Night's Dream* and *Fingal's Cave.* In both it appears notably in the development sections, enlivened by humor or by love of the vast, northern, elegiac landscape. This is not program music; it is the musical reflection of Shakespeare's figures or of a deeply felt nature experience upon a lovable and sensitive soul. Along with this feature, no essential contradiction arises from the fact that even so early as the *Hebrides* Overture there was also present a greater degree of impressionism than was to be found in Beethoven's *Pastoral* Symphony. Impressionism, too, became more and more an ingredient of musical Romanticism.

CLASSIC AND ROMANTIC IN SCHUMANN

Quite differently divided are the proportions of inheritance and conquest, the relationship of the Classic and Romantic, in Robert Schumann. Schumann had begun his career as a revolutionary Romantic, or Romantic revolutionist of the first water: no other Romantic, not even Chopin, is comparable to him in youthfulness and in originality. In common with Chopin, he used the piano exclusively as the medium for the expression of his "storm and stress" up to his Opus 23. Like Chopin, he was able to say at the piano all that he had in his heart. At the same time, he was able to use his new, virtuoso—and much more than merely virtuoso—piano style as a protest against the empty, shallow, brilliant, drawing room virtuosity which, after Hummel and Weber, was making a great show in his period, along with the activity of really great virtuosi like Liszt or Henselt. This new, bold, original piano music adopted the titles and forms of *études,* toccatas, intermezzi, variations, and dances; but the true title for them all would be the one that was given to only a few: *fantasies* for the piano—Kreisleriana, Jean Pauliana, Eichendorffiana in music. It is only logical that, after twenty-three *opera* for the piano, the twenty-fourth should blossom forth into a song cycle. The discussion, however, of this fusion of poetry and piano music characteristic of Schumann, this "poetic" piano music and its forms, must be reserved for a later chapter.

Among these twenty-three works there had already appeared three sonatas, the *Grande Sonates* in F-sharp minor, Op. 11, and in F minor, Op. 14, and the G-minor Sonata, Op. 22—an apparent compromise of the revolutionary with the classical form. It is apparent only, however, for even these three sonatas filled the outlines of the classical four-movement scheme with very new content. But it is true that Schumann, after the first stormy outbursts of his creative urge which had been so long repressed, felt the need of an agreement, of an act of communication with a less subjective form. The many-sidedness, the strife within him, the fact that "two souls" (and more than two) "dwelt within his breast," he symbolized as a writer by his personification of the fictitious members of his "David's League," the fiery Florestan, the dreamy Eusebius, the wise, meditative, and even-tempered Raro. He was everyone in turn and at the same time—Florestan, Eusebius, Raro. And Raro made it necessary that he express himself in more general, more objective form than he had hitherto used. So, after piano works, songs, and other vocal compositions, Schumann wrote in 1841 his first symphony, Op. 38, and in the following year his three string quartets, Op. 41. These latter remained his only ones.

To begin with the three quartets: they have not become "classics" of quartet literature. They are written after Beethoven, as is shown by the slow movement in each. That in the first is a direct echo of the Adagio of the Ninth Symphony. That in the second—"*Andante, quasi Variazioni*"—is like a variation of the *Adagio ma non troppo* of Beethoven's String Quartet Op. 127; even the key corresponds. Similarly, the *Adagio molto* of the Third Quartet is also a fully developed slow movement—though more passionate, more excited, more agitated than any in Haydn, Mozart, or even Beethoven.

But this lyrical center in each of the three quartets did not cause Schumann to invest the other movements with a similar fullness and depth. In Beethoven's quartets there prevails a complete equilibrium of the movements, from first to last; the structure is always completely stable. In Schumann the first movements (that of Quartet No. 1 in A minor is in F major!) have the qualities of a lyric or ballad; the Scherzo of this first Quartet is a galloping piece, as if taken over from the *Scenes of Childhood* and arranged, with Intermezzi such as might have been taken over and arranged from his songs. The Classical structure falls to pieces, despite the fact that the compositions are reminiscent of Beethoven—particularly, of course, of the late Beethoven, who was considered a destroyer of form. The finest and most original of the three quartets is the last, with marvelous variations ("*assai agitato*") in place of the Scherzo, with the "*hommage à J. S. Bach*"—the imitation of the Gavotte from the French Suite in E—as a "*Quasi Trio*" in the Finale. This is not the place for a critique of the admirable work; we are here concerned not so much with criticizing as with understanding the movement that is referred to as musical Romanticism. The Romantic era *had* to break up the Classical form, if it did not wish to remain academic imitation; for there is no development above and beyond that which is perfect—in this instance, the Beethovenian string quartet.

The same thing applies to the Schumann type of symphony. It becomes more lively, youthful, "Romantic" than Mendelssohn's as it departs further from the Classical pattern. Like Mendelssohn's two great symphonies, Schumann's First Symphony, in B-flat major, is descended from Beethoven's *Pastoral*. Schumann called this composition of his the *Springtime* Symphony and originally gave the movements the following headings: 1. The Beginning of Spring (Andante), 2. Evening (Larghetto), 3. Merry Play (Scherzo), and 4. Spring in Bloom (Allegro animato e grazioso). The impulse to compose this work had come from a poem by Adolf Böttger. But it is significant that Schumann finally suppressed those headings, and that only a rhythmic suggestion of the poem was left, namely of its last line: "Now Spring is blooming in the vale" (*Im Tale blüht der Frühling auf*) in the principal motif of the first movement. This *Springtime* Symphony has much less program, much less "painting," than does Beethoven's Sixth Symphony, if one does not take the use of the triangle in the first movement as a symbol of that "Awakening of Spring," or interpret the horn call and the flute cadenza in the Finale naturalistically. Everything has become an "expression of feeling"; the poetical stimulus has been transfigured and subjected to the laws of symphonic form.

We need not go into the other three symphonies of Schumann's in great detail. The one counted as No. 2, Op. 61, completed in 1846, follows a program similar to that of the First. It was explained by Schumann with only a few words when he called it "a regular Jupiter" (it is in C major) and "somewhat in armor" (*etwas geharnischt*). The Third, in E-flat, Op. 97, written in 1850, bears the cryptic title "Rhenish," and is actually supposed to reflect—according to Schumann's remark—"a bit of life on the Rhine." But it is hard to understand how it is to do that; even the second of the two slow middle sections, which at the *première* still bore the inscription "In the nature of the accompaniment to a solemn ceremony," points only quite generally to something mystical, ancient, Catholic, and not to the specific locality of the Cologne or any of the other Rhenish cathedrals.

The most characteristic symphonic work of Schumann's is his Fourth Symphony, Op. 120, in D minor, which, although reworked and reorchestrated in 1851, actually originated only a few months after the First, in the summer of 1841, and really must be counted as the Second. It joins together five movements—Introduction, Allegro, Romanze, Scherzo, and Finale—into an uninterrupted whole; and, quite logically, in its original form of 1841 it bore the title *Symphonic Fantasy*. This unity is not merely an external feature, for all the movements are developed from melodic seeds that are given in the Introduction; they are blossoms of various colors springing from the same bush. Here again Schumann, after his usual manner, concealed the poetic incentive for this work, and gave only a possible hint in the guitar accompaniment of the Romanze. He did not wish to be more clear than that: the music buries the "program" in mysterious depths. We here stand before a new form of the symphony—one possessed of a thematic homogeneity which Beethoven had felt no need of, although this feature perhaps goes back to the "reminiscences" in the Finale of the Ninth Symphony.

Alongside this achievement of homogeneity, there stands something truly Romantic—disintegration. This trend appears clearly in Schumann's *Overture, Scherzo, and Finale* in E major, Op. 52, which had its origin between the B-flat major and the D-minor symphonies, a work that Schumann in all seriousness wanted to bring out as his Second Symphony, or at least as a "Symphonette." But does not the lack of a slow movement make even a sinfonietta into a suite, a more or less disconnected succession of movements?

Romantic disintegration of Classical structure is found also in one of the most beautiful and most compellingly lovable of all Schumann's works, his Piano Concerto in A minor, Op. 54, the first movement written in May, 1841, the last two in the summer of 1845. We are here not dealing with Schumann's relationship to the problem of virtuosity, which will be taken up later. Instead, we are here concerned with the cooperation of two forces—piano and orchestra—which no longer displays the pure equilibrium that it did with Mozart, nor the dramatic give-and-take that it did with Beethoven. The soloist now is carried, supported, and caressed by the orchestra. In the relative importance of the three movements there prevails a new subjectivity; for the Intermezzo, to which Beethoven's slow movement had shrunk, breathes an intimacy which the heroic Beethoven would never have permitted himself.

Within the Florestan-Eusebius-Raro union in Schumann's creative faculties, Raro achieved more and more the predominance—so much so that one must speak of a dissolution or disruption of this union. In no branch of Schumann's creative activity, except in his songs, does this dissolution admit of such exact observation as in that of his chamber music with piano. The transition from his youthfully free, "unclassical" piano music to these works is afforded by a trio entitled *Phantasiestück* (Op. 88, 1842), consisting of Romance, Duet, and Alla Marcia—a whole, marked by freshness precisely because it seems to be disconnected. Alongside this, Schumann set up a model of Classic-Romantic chamber music in his Piano

Quintet, Op. 44 (1842), the piano setting the pace, brilliant, never virtuoso, a work of high spirits in all the rapid movements, and in the slow or marchlike movement full of mysterious sorrow and indignation. At first slowly, then faster and faster, the descent ensues—in a Quartet Op. 47 (1842), in three Trios Op. 63 (1847), Op. 80 (1847), and Op. 110 (1851), in two Violin Sonatas Op. 105 (1851) and 121 (1851)—to repetitiousness, to mannerism.

Mannerism is a part of the diagnosis of the pathological aspect of the Romantic movement. In earlier centuries copying—even the weaker sort of copying—was a part of the craft; in the new century the heightened conception of the artist demanded ever new creative effort. Fortunate was the man who, like Wagner, Verdi, or Brahms, was equal to this effort, and in his own work increased in stature. Schumann was not such a person. One may say that his real tragedy lay in the fact that he disintegrated in the attempt to do as the "great ones" had done—to become universal. The attacks of insanity are but an outward symbol of this tragedy, a typically Romantic fate. Schumann is a representative of eternal adolescence, of enthusiastic intimacy; the task of becoming a man, in the creative sense, weighed too heavily upon him. Liszt, in a letter to Heinrich Heine on April 15, 1838, understood very well the split in his generation when he said that all the artists of his time were "very badly situated" between the past and the future. "The century is ill." [16] Schumann began as a champion of the future; in establishing a connection with the past he collapsed. But Schumann as a young man did not as yet know anything of the end in store for him. With this youthful Schumann, who is "immortal," we shall be concerned in the chapter on piano music. Had Schumann never passed his thirty-fifth birthday, he would have been the Shelley of music, the star of youth most resplendently gleaming.

BERLIOZ, THE FRENCH ROMANTIC

Quite different, again, was the relationship between Romanticism and Classicism in the work of the symphonic writer Hector Berlioz, although he too, like Mendelssohn and Schumann, was one of the admirers of Beethoven (no musician of the 19th century could ever pass Beethoven by) and although he too, again like Mendelssohn and Schumann, took his special point of departure from the *Pastoral* Symphony. But was Berlioz a Romantic at all? Romanticism, at least in opera and at least so far as

[16] *Gesammelte Schriften* II, p. 200.

subject matter is concerned, was a revolt against antiquity, against Classicism; Romanticism was a Northern, Gothic affair, involving flight into the indefinite, mystical, mysterious. But Berlioz, the man from Southern France, the Latin, cherished a life-long enthusiasm for Vergil and the *Aeneid*. His deepest experience was that of Italy, or more precisely Rome. As we have already emphasized (p. 58), his *Harold* symphony is nothing but a testament of his love for that country, or—as he calls it in his autobiographical sketch—a "Symphony with Viola Solo, in which are recalled the impressions of a trip in the Abruzzi and the remembrance of the beautiful, clear nights of Italy." The clear nights of Italy! He shifts the action in his *Benvenuto Cellini* to Rome; for Rome is, so to speak, more Italian than Florence, and only in Rome would there be a Roman Carnival.

But Berlioz *was* a Romantic. The manifestations of Romanticism in him, however, are different from those in Mendelssohn or Schumann. They involve not only different proportions in the Romantic-Classical combination, but also an entirely different kind of Romanticism. Above all, it is a question of material. Along with his enthusiasm for Vergil, Berlioz had a similar feeling for Shakespeare and for the poet of *Faust*— or, rather, for the subject matter of Goethe's *Faust*—and for English Gothic novels. In France, the land of Corneille, Racine, and Voltaire, admiration for Shakespeare was revolutionary and Romantic; one need only recall that as late as July, 1822, the attempt of English actors to present *Othello* at the Porte Saint-Martin in Paris was thwarted by hooting and whistling. Within only a few years, however, things were different: when from autumn, 1826, to July, 1828, another group of actors headed by Charles Kemble and Harriet Smithson presented *Romeo and Juliet, Hamlet,* and again *Othello,* they captured the hearts of Paris—especially Miss Smithson, who, incidentally, let herself be taken to wife by her most ardent admirer, Berlioz.

The story of this frenzied and desperate love—frenzied and desperate because it was a matter not only of a wife but also of the characters portrayed by her as an actress—was the content of Berlioz's first symphony, the *Symphonie Fantastique,* Op. 14 (1830–31). This is his most astonishing, most alive work; for it is program music based on personal experience. And the astonishing feature of it derives from the coincidence of the programmatic with the pattern of the sonata form: in the first movement, the coincidence of the *"Rêverie"* with the introductory Largo, of the *"Existence passionnée"* in all its changing moods with the customary Allegro. One might say that in this movement the opponent of "program music" proceeds as much at his own risk as does the lover of "program music."

The ensuing four movements—the *"Bal"* in waltz form, the *"Scène aux Champs,"* the dreamlike and sinister *"Marche au Supplice,"* and finally the *"Songe d'une Nuit de Sabbat"* no longer bother with this "coincidence." They are freer and bolder; but, in compensation, they are clamped together, one with the other and each with the first movement, by the *idée fixe,* the reminiscence, variation, or parody of the theme in the first Allegro. There was nothing new in the psychologically (one might say, psychoanalytically) varied return of a theme. One can find examples of it, particularly in the opera, even in pre-Romantic opera. But the *Symphonie Fantastique* brings forth the first example of a very free and bold use of it, and after this work neither Berlioz nor the whole Romantic movement could get along without the reminiscent motif, the leitmotif.

There is no question that Berlioz, by his "program," weakened symphonic form. Schumann, in his famous discussion of the work as transcribed for piano by Liszt,[17] criticized the excessive detail of this program:

All Germany will shy away from it; such guideposts as these always have something unworthy, something of the charlatan, about them. At all events, the five main headings would have been enough; the more precise circumstances, although of interest for the composer's sake who has himself lived and experienced the symphony itself, would have been propagated by oral tradition. In a word, the German, with his delicacy of feeling and his greater aversion to the purely personal, does not wish to be led so roughly in his thoughts; even in the *Pastoral* Symphony, he has taken offense at the fact that Beethoven does not rely on him to guess at its character without the composer's assistance. . . . In this respect, Berlioz wrote first of all for his Frenchmen, who are scarcely to be impressed by ethereal modesty. I can imagine them reading along, program in hand, and applauding their countryman, who has hit everything off so well; they do not much care for the music alone. Whether now, in the mind of one who did not know the composer's intention, this music would awaken pictures similar to those that the composer wished to sketch, I am not in a position to decide, as I have read the program before hearing the music. When once the eye has been led to a certain point, the ear no longer judges independently. If one were to ask whether music really could achieve what Berlioz in his symphony demands of it, then one might try to assign to it some other pictures, perhaps entirely different. At first, the program spoiled even for me all enjoyment, all free view. But when more and more it passed into the background and my own imagination began to work, I found not only everything, but much more, and almost everything in a living, warm tone. As regards the difficult question of how far instru-

[17] *Neue Zeitschrift für Musik* III (1835).

mental music ought to go in the representation of thoughts and events, many view this matter too scrupulously. Yet one should not set too low an estimate on chance external influences and impressions. Unconsciously, alongside the musical imagination, an idea often continues in operation—alongside the ear, the eye—and the latter, the ever-active organ, then holds fast amidst the sounds and tones to certain outlines, which in the advancing music may condense into clear figures and develop. Accordingly, the more that elements related to music carry within themselves the thoughts or pictures begotten of the tones, of so much more poetic or plastic an impression will the composition be; and the more imaginatively or sharply the musician in general perceives things, by so much the more will his work prove uplifting or stirring. . . .

That is more the aesthetic of Schumann than it is of Berlioz, but it is true that to some extent it is also precisely valid for Berlioz.

Never again did Berlioz write for his later instrumental works so detailed a program as he did for the *Symphonie Fantastique*. To the general tendency thereby implied, there is only one notable exception, namely that in his *Rêverie et Caprice* for Violin and Orchestra, Op. 8, written in 1839. The program headed "Note" is so remarkable that it is given herewith:

A soft light envelops Earth in transparence. Mists tremble with the scents of evening, amidst the gusts of breeze. A man beholds this pale light, hears these vague rustlings. But he sees not; he does not hear. . . . He dreams. His heart, wrung by the constraint of suffering, groans secretly. The intensity of his pain reveals to him hitherto unknown delights of vanished happiness. He searches the past. In it there appear some smiles, scattered among the sorrows. . . . O implacable need for thinking and loving! His soul awakens beneath their radiance. All his being fills with sudden eagerness. The future fascinates him. He is about to dart forth into these luminous scents, where life spends itself freely, madly excited. . . . Indecision restrains him, bent beneath its wild embrace. He suffers again; he despairs. . . . The vision, however, pursues him in the darkness. He tingles with mad desires. He struggles against the pain which binds him. . . . Regrets give way to hope. Thirst triumphs over disgust. . . . He revives. He experiences fiery, sensuous joys, feverish transports. . . .

It is self-evident that Berlioz did not compose from this program, but rather read it into his music subsequently. It is so vague that it might be read into every composition of this sort, e.g., Louis Spohr's *Gesangsszene* or Ernest Chausson's *Poème*. In other instances, Berlioz did remarkably little to prevent his listeners from hearing his symphonies as pure music. He was much too French, much too thoroughly a compatriot and contemporary of Eugène Delacroix, who, also, in his "historical" pictures, never prevented the beholder from evaluating them as pure painting. For example, we might take the overtures: that for *Rob Roy* (1831), which Berlioz never published but which he utilized in part for *Harold en Italie;* the *Grande Ouverture de Waverley,* Op. 1 (1827–28); the overture for the *Francs Juges,* Op. 3 (1827–28); that for *King Lear,* Op. 4 (1831); and that for *Le Corsaire* (1831). Roughly, from the point of view of subject matter, they seem Romantic, being based on suggestions coming from Shakespeare, Byron, Walter Scott, and—in the *Francs Juges* overture—a horror play by Berlioz's friend Humbert Ferrand. But actually they are very classicistic—that is, formalistic—and only in a few peculiarities of melodic invention and in some "interruptions of form" does each one betray any direct relationship to its program. The overture to the *Corsaire* has practically nothing to do with Byron; it was originally called *Ouverture de la Tour de Nice,* and the only suggestion that these two titles have in common is simply the poetic or musical depiction of a more or less agitated sea scene. The richest in somber detail is, doubtless, the overture to the *Francs Juges,* which is most delicately modeled both orchestrally and dynamically; and yet in this very piece Berlioz touches upon an overture of his opposite, upon Mendelssohn's *Ruy Blas.*

How new and revolutionary, however, Berlioz appeared to his time may, again, be learned from Schumann, who devoted a long discussion to the *Grande Ouverture de Waverley* in his *Neue Zeitschrift für Musik.*[18] After first speaking of two highly cautious overtures—that of the Netherlander J. J. H. Verhulst (to *Gysbrecht van Amstel*) and that of the Englishman W. Sterndale Bennett (*The Woodnymphs*), he continued:

Other laurels are sought by that raging bacchant, that terror of the Philistines, Berlioz, who appears to them as a shaggy monster with ravenous eyes. But where do we behold him *now?* At the crackling fire of a Scottish manor house, among hunters, hounds, and smiling country maidens. An overture to —*Waverley* lies here before me, to that novel of Sir Walter Scott's which in its charming monotony, its romantic freshness, its genuinely English stamp, is still my favorite among recent foreign fiction. For this, Berlioz has written music. Someone may ask, "For which chapter? which scene? why? for what purpose?" . . . Some explanation, this time, is given by the inscription on the title-page . . . :

> Dreams of love and Lady's charms
> Give place to honour and to arms. . . .

[18] Vol. X, No. 47, 1839.

Schumann then explains that it would be an easy task for him to describe the overture, either by assigning a program to it or by taking it apart mechanically. But he continues thus:

. . . Berlioz's music must be *heard;* even a view of the score is not sufficient, and one might also give himself a great deal of trouble in realizing the work at the piano only to find that his efforts had been in vain. Often there are effects almost exclusively of sonority and resonance, willfully interjected chord-clusters, that play a decisive part. Often there are strange disguises that even the experienced ear cannot clearly imagine after the eye has merely seen the notes on the paper. If one goes to the roots of the individual thoughts, they often seem—considered only in themselves—common, even trivial. But the whole exerts an irresistible charm upon me, despite the many things in it that are offensive and unfamiliar to a German ear. In each of his works Berlioz has proved different, has ventured upon a new field. One scarcely knows whether one should call him a genius or a musical adventurer: he shines like a lightning flash, but he also leaves a smell of brimstone after him; he comes out with great and true passages, and soon thereafter falls to stammering like a schoolboy. . . .

It is then not without irony that Schumann, "remarkably enough," establishes a certain remote similarity between the overture by this "Mephistopheles of music" and that by Mendelssohn to "Calm at Sea and a Pleasant Journey," after a poem of the Olympian Goethe.

Again in his discussion of the *Symphonie Fantastique,* Schumann expressed very sharply what it was that seemed strange to German taste in Berlioz's kind of melody, in the "structure of the individual phrase":

The modern period has perhaps produced no other work in which equal and unequal mensural and rhythmic relationships have been combined and employed so freely as in this one. Consequent almost never corresponds to antecedent; answer almost never corresponds to question. This is so peculiar to Berlioz, so much in keeping with his Southern character and so strange to us Northerners, that the uneasy feeling of the first moment and the complaint about the obscurity are perhaps pardonable and understandable. But with what a bold hand all this is carried out, so that nothing at all may be added or effaced without taking from the thought its sharp penetration and its power —thereof one can judge only for oneself by seeing and hearing it. It seems as if the music wished to tend again towards its very beginnings, where as yet the rule of the downbeat in the measure did not weigh heavily upon it, and to raise itself to unrestrained speech, to a higher poetical kind of punctuation (as in the Greek choruses, in the language of the Bible, in the prose of Jean Paul). . . .

What characterizes Berlioz most of all, as a representative of the French Romantic movement in music, is his daring to send the hearer away with a harsh impression, a dissonance. In the *Symphonie Fantastique,* there is the *"orgie diabolique,"* the blasphemous *"cérémonie funèbre,"* the *"parodie burlesque du Dies Irae."* In *Harold en Italie* there is the *Allegro frenetico* of the *"Orgie des Brigands."* And in the *Huit Scènes de Faust,* which forms the essential part of *La Damnation de Faust,* there is not as yet the apotheosis of Marguérite or the angelic choir which gives the work a conciliatory ending. Only with *Roméo et Juliette* do we begin to find a satisfying conclusion—as peace reigns over Verona, the Montagues and the Capulets have a "serment of reconciliation." And only thereafter did Berlioz feel any necessity for providing the hero of the *Symphonie Fantastique* with a happier evening of life, in *Lelio ou Le Rétour à la Vie.* This "lyric monodrama with orchestra, choruses, and soli offstage . . ." is a continuation of the *Symphonie Fantastique,* quite heterogeneous, and serving more to fill out the biography than to create a unified work of art. It is a patchwork of six movements, and its presentation will never destroy the impression made by the *Symphonie Fantastique* on anyone, despite Berlioz's request: "This work should be heard immediately after the *Symphonie Fantastique,* which it completes and concludes." In this sort of eccentricity, Berlioz had less in common with almost any one of the German Romantics, who were all like-minded idealists, than he did with the poet E. T. A. Hoffmann, whose success in France was not without some basis. With both there is the quasi-intoxicated excitement of the imagination, the coolly fired warmth—a warmth that, however, in so noble and enthusiastic a nature can also become heat and flame, and then —the finest example being the love scene in *Roméo et Juliette*—a purity breathes from this fire, in contrast to which all other love scenes appear impure.

Along with this courageous desire for dissonance, for singularity, for unsavory details, there was a contradictory tendency in Berlioz, his genuinely French respect for "form." With the program in music, the problem was posed of the falling apart of "content" and classical symphonic form, even though this form was capable of extension and, in every case, of variation. But the situation was bound to arise in which the sonata-recapitulation, or the rondo form, was irreconcilable with the "program." The disintegration of the classical scheme then became unavoidable, and the symphonic "self-containedness" had to be sacrificed in favor of a form dictated by something standing *outside* the music. Berlioz did not take this step. In the *Harold* symphony, he relaxed the cyclic fixity of the form he had inherited from Beethoven, in two ways: between the first and last movements he inserted two *episodes* (and it is significant that precisely they are among the finest and most moving passages that he ever wrote), and he assigned to the solo viola a role that is neither *concertante* nor symphonic: it symbolizes or represents the melancholy hero, who (as an admirer of Berlioz's, Peter Cornelius, has expressed it) "stands out as an accessory figure—against what would otherwise be the surroundings."

It was entirely consistent that Berlioz did not wish to destroy the symphony; instead, he set up a new conception of the symphonic that combined the purely instrumental and the vocal. *Roméo et Juliette* (Op. 17, 1839) is a *symphonie dramatique,* "with choruses, vocal soli, and a prologue in choral recitative"; *La Damnation de Faust* (Op. 24, 1845–46) is a *légende dramatique*—a dramatic *tale.* Berlioz never anticipated that his composition would one day be performed as a scenic show-piece upon the stage.

Berlioz himself did all he could to emphasize the symphonic character of *Roméo et Juliette.* "The genre of this work will doubtless not be misunderstood. Although voices are often employed in this work, it is neither a concert opera nor a cantata, but a symphony with choruses." Nothing is more characteristic of him than the reasons for his having recourse to verbal means of expression and yet holding fast to programmatic, pure symphonism. He had recourse to verbal means because, despite his venturesomeness, he saw the limits of instrumental music—because he wished to be exact and objective. He himself has called attention in the score to the difficulty in understanding the grave-scene ("Romeo at the tomb of the Capulets. Invocation. Awakening of Juliet. Surge of delirious joy, interrupted by the first accessions of the poison. Final agonies and death of the two lovers"), and he would surely have liked to compose it as a duet had he not made up his mind to avoid solos altogether. Note how he justified his composing this and the love-scene as symphonic pieces:

If in the famous scenes at the balcony and the tomb the dialogue of the two lovers, the *asides* of Juliet, and the impassioned outbursts of Romeo—if, in short, the duets of love and despair—are entrusted to the orchestra, the reasons therefor are numerous and easy to understand. First of all—and this reason alone suffices for the composer's justification—what we have here is a symphony and not an opera. Second, as duets of that nature have already been treated vocally on a thousand occasions and by the greatest masters, it seemed prudent as well as interesting to try another mode of expression. Finally, the very sublimity of this love makes its depiction so dangerous for the musician that he ought to allow a latitude which the exact sense of the words sung would not have permitted him, and have recourse to the language of instruments, a language that is richer, more varied, more free from limitations, and —in its very vagueness—incomparably more powerful, all other things being equal.

The language of the orchestra, precisely because it is less definite, is more rich, more limitless, and incomparably more powerful than the word! The word is only for *clearness*. In this apotheosis of instrumental music, Berlioz belongs to the Romantic era, even though he stands in opposition to it in certain other aspects of his attitude towards Romanticism.

This apotheosis did not prevent his making use of a solo part in his *Damnation of Faust,* thereby bringing this "dramatic legend" actually close to opera, although originally he had nothing more in mind than to make of *Faust* a "descriptive symphony." Yet, is it not a fact that out of this hybrid work the only pieces that still possess full vitality are the purely instrumental ones: the Hungarian March, merely an inserted number, which has nothing at all to do with Faust; the Ballet of the Sylphs; the Minuet of the Goblins, which is a polonaise; the Pandemonium, in which the human—or rather the diabolical—voices are employed only as instrumental color? Whatever type the work may belong to, it is an evidence of the failure of the "programmatic symphony." Berlioz early saw, after *Harold,* that the union of a "program" and of the Classical symphonic inheritance was no longer possible; and, being a sincere, uncompromising artist, he drew from this state of things his conclusions.

LISZT, A BORN REVOLUTIONARY

Other conclusions were drawn by Franz Liszt. His motto, "Renewal of music through its inner connection with poetry," was somewhat the same as that of Schumann and Berlioz; but he no longer let himself be restrained by the tradition of classical sonata form. He was a born revolutionary; and one might say—if it were compatible with a regard for his magnificent personality—he was a born libertine, a born Bohemian. He has given evidence of his admiration for Bach (though not for Handel), for Beethoven, and for Schubert, by making works of theirs serve the purposes of his virtuosity, or his virtuosity serve the purposes of some of their works. But he did not permit them to have any influence on his own creative activity, the aim of which was "the development of something more free and, so to speak, more adequate to the spirit of these times." [19]

[19] *Briefe* (Leipzig, 1894), III, p. 135.

In his essay on Robert Schumann (1855),[20] he praised the composer who had dedicated his C-major Fantasy, Op. 17, to him and to whom he had dedicated his own B-minor Sonata, for the fact that Schumann "clearly recognized in his mind that music in general—and especially instrumental music—had to be more closely connected with poetry and other forms of literature, even as Beethoven had previously sensed it, though only in the obscure compulsion of his genius, when he wrote his *Egmont* music and gave certain other of his instrumental works definite, objective names or inscriptions."

At the same time, however, Liszt criticized Schumann for not carrying out this closer connection to its logical conclusion:

> Though beauty is not lacking in any of his works, this quality yet withdraws now and then from our perception. At one time it seems hidden beneath the covering of a symmetrical regularity, which is not in keeping with the glowing, inwardly self-consuming enthusiasm of the feeling displayed, and which therefore is not unlike a touch of affectation. At another time it seems to have gone astray along the rough and stony ways of harmony, overhung by the thick and luxurious creeping vines of an iridescently enveloping ornamentation. . . . The result is that both features, since they seem to work against strict form, . . . confuse some listeners and affect others unpleasantly.

One must give Liszt credit for the fact that he himself carried out his ideas to their ultimate conclusion in all the fields of music that he cultivated—in piano, vocal, and even symphonic composition. His strange artistic career and spiritual development caused him to be the most independent and unrestrained of all the Romantic musicians. It is hard to confine him behind national boundaries. He was born in the Hungarian district of Sopron (Oedenburg), but his parents were German, and he never learned to speak Hungarian. At twelve he went to Paris, which remained his real intellectual home, though his virtuosity soon led him also to England and through all Europe. After 1848 he took up residence in Weimar and, at least outwardly, seemed to have given up his nomadic existence. In 1861 he went to Rome; and in 1865, as Abbé Liszt, he fled into the haven of the Catholic Church. This was a typically Romantic step—though one less common among musicians than among poets—the act of a Romantic who, after a hundred approaches to more or less fashionable currents in the stream of "philosophical" development, had become tired and had laid his disappointment and bitterness to rest in the Church's comforting arms. As a matter of fact, no musician of the Ro-

[20] *Gesammelte Schriften* IV, p. 114.

mantic era was more "worldly" than Liszt, none tasted so thoroughly all the triumphs of virtuosity as he did, none came into such direct contact with all the intellectual currents of his time, and none remained in his heart of hearts so lonely and so homeless.

This loneliness, this homelessness, in conjunction with his boundless virtuosity, also exerted an influence on his creative activity. He was a typically "free" artist—but freedom is a negative concept. Although he still used the title "sonata" or "symphony," it no longer indicated a Classical sonata or symphony. Take, for instance, his B-minor Sonata (written in 1852–53), one of his few works that do not proclaim outwardly their connection with poetry. It is a work that Wagner called "beautiful beyond all comprehension, great, lovable, deep, and noble—sublime, as Thou art." The youthful Brahms, however, even as early as 1854 made fun of it.[21] This "sonata" is a great, rhetorical rhapsody on a few motifs, which in the main are set forth as early as the first fifteen measures. No longer is there a separation of the individual movements; instead, there are more or less recitative-like linkages and transitions. No longer is there reliance on the mysterious unity of a movement or a cycle, a unity that in the Classics sprang from deep inspiration; instead, everywhere there is sustained, very spirited motivic work. One might say that this sonata no longer has an exposition and a recapitulation—though it has a first and a second theme, and a contrast between Allegro and Andante—and consists of a gigantic, highly dramatic development section.

The same thing is true of Liszt's "symphonic poems." What a significant title! They all owe their origin to a "poetic idea." But, as has already been suggested (p. 24), they are less dependent on poetry and painting than they may at first seem to be. True, the musician is often indebted to the poets—where Liszt does not follow his own fancy, as in the nuptial *Festklänge,* the *Héroide Funèbre,* or the *Hungaria.* He is often indebted to the painters, as in the *Hunnenschlacht.* Yet, as a musician, he does not follow closely an external program, does not tell a story, but goes to work with considerable independence and self-possession. He seeks to give the essence of his subject. No longer does Liszt write cyclic works of four or more movements, like the *Symphonie Fantastique;* no longer does he write "episodes," finales in bad taste, endings that reflect a spiritual disharmony. In his work there are also no naturalistic touches, as before him there had been in Berlioz (and after him in Richard Strauss); once again, or still, he is quite idealistic. True, this idealism, this

[21] Letter to Clara Schumann, August 27.

absence of passages in bad taste, had been dearly bought, by the absence of spontaneous ideas and impressionistic traits so frequently delightful in Berlioz, by the lack of humor, by an overabundance of emotionalism and rhetoric.

In matters pertaining to "form," Liszt's eager listeners and friendly colleagues—such as Joachim Raff, whom Liszt induced to do some of the preliminary work towards the orchestration of certain of these compositions —tried at first to facilitate the understanding of some of Liszt's works by calling them "concert overtures." As a matter of fact, some of them have served as overtures, such as *Orpheus,* which in 1854 served to introduce a performance of Gluck's *Orfeo ed Euridice* at Weimar, or *Prometheus,* which in 1850 preceded Liszt's composition based on the choruses from Herder's *Prometheus Unbound.* But they no longer have anything in common with the traditional overture—neither with the Classical or Classicistic in sonata form, as found in Beethoven's *Leonore III* or Mendelssohn's *Hebrides,* nor with the potpourri overture in the manner of *Der Freischütz, Euryanthe,* or *Oberon.*

Mazeppa originated from one of the *Grandes Etudes pour le Piano,* the fourth. This symphonic poem consists of an *Allegro agitato,* heightened by *accelerandi,* and a *Marcia trionfale,* the two movements being separated by a short Andante, with those characteristically Lisztian recitative-like interjections which he so frequently assigns to a solo among the wind instruments—separated and linked together by motivic unity and motivic transformation.

Tasso—Lamento e Trionfo (1849) enunciates a solo of this kind as the principal theme, this time the traditional tune to which the Venetian gondoliers sang stanzas from the *Jerusalem Delivered.* The work introduces it in a mood of Byronic gloom, transforms it by variation into a quasi-minuet movement, and heightens it by excited and circuitous routes to its apotheosis. In the minuet movement, which shows the melancholy poet in the midst of the court life of Ferrara and combines the principal motive with a "frivolous" theme and rhythm, there is a characteristic indication in the score: "At this point the manner of orchestral performance takes on a double character: the wind instruments light and fluttery, the singing strings sentimental and graceful." The combination of *doloroso* and *agitato,* of *cantabile* and rhythmic *ostinati,* is typical—as typical as the instrumentation, which partly isolates the *soli* from the orchestra, and partly joins them together into contrasting groups. Structurally, however, Liszt does not follow any one particular type, although he likes to lead a composition from halting beginnings to an apotheosis; and because he feels the danger of this freedom, he also feels doubly strongly the need for grappling the parts of the whole together motivically.

In so doing he did not count upon immediate appreciation. As the form of these works was new and unconventional, he demanded for them also a new manner of presentation, "periodic performance." In this connection he let fall his proud saying about these compositions that "they do not at all claim an everyday popularity." There is here a Romantic inconsistency: to create works for full orchestra, and thus for the great concert hall, which yet address themselves only to a "cultivated" minority! As a matter of fact, the Lisztian symphonic poem is tied up with too many presuppositions of literary and aesthetic culture, and unfortunately it has not always confined itself to impulses from things of eternal value.

Les Préludes go back to suggestions from a sentimental poem in Lamartine's *Méditations Poétiques*. The symphonic poem *Du Berceau jusq'au Tombe* ("From the Cradle to the Grave") even goes back to a pen-and-ink sketch by the Hungarian historical painter de Zichy. This example of late work is a straggler (1881–82), coming well after the twelve compositions of the Fifties.

Although it has already been stated that Liszt no longer wrote cyclic works like the *Symphonie Fantastique,* this does not mean that he wrote no more symphonies. But none of their movements is episodic, as they had been in Berlioz. In both works here being considered, he no longer made the mistake of presupposing a knowledge of Lamartine's or Hugo's or Schiller's poems. Instead, he chose two of the greatest poetical models of world literature, Goethe's *Faust* and Dante's *Divine Comedy.* The choice of *Faust* is something that he had in common with all Romantic musicians. Spohr had begun, at least, to make use of the material, although not in Goethe's version; then came Berlioz with his work of violent adoration, and finally Schumann with his *Scenes from Goethe's Faust* (1844–53), a highly impressive and gripping testimonial to his genuine devotion.

Nor was Richard Wagner silent on the subject; and it is hardly an accident that the title of his contribution is formulated in the same way as Liszt's, "A Faust Overture, for Full Orchestra." It was written in 1840, in Paris, thus precluding any possibility of acquaintance with Liszt's orchestral works; however, it was reworked in 1855, in Zurich, after he had become acquainted with them. The relationship of the two musicians in respect to method is not merely superficial; it is of the essence in their work, for both were Romantic revolutionists. The overture took its origin from the impression made by a performance or a reading of Beethoven's Ninth Symphony, into which Wagner likewise on other occasions was fond of reading a program consisting of *Faust* quotations; and his overture shares with Beethoven's symphony not only the key but also a motif. Externally, the overture looks like a Classical overture or the first movement of a symphony, with a slow introduction and a "very agitated" Allegro; but the motivic unity and the subtlety with which these motives are transformed and interwoven is much more pronounced than in any Classical model. Ostensibly, Wagner represents only one single mood, one single spiritual state of his hero:

> The God that in my breast is owned
> Can deeply stir the inner sources;
> The God, above my powers enthroned,
> He cannot change external forces.
> So, by the burden of my days oppressed,
> Death is desired, and Life a thing unblest!

A troubled inner state is depicted. Gretchen is completely absent. The Mephistophelian element is not lacking (in staccato transformations of a motif which foreshadows that of Beckmesser), but it is more like a reflection in Faust's soul. Yet Wagner would not be Wagner if the transfiguring, "redeeming" shimmer of a hope did not shine forth in the midst and at the end of the composition.

Liszt performed the first version in May, 1852; and here we find one of the instances in which Liszt was spiritually indebted to his younger friend: feeling not only the weaknesses in the orchestration of this version but also the necessity for enlargement and completion, Liszt proposed to Wagner the introduction of a middle movement: ". . . a movement soft, tender, modulated in a Gretchen-like manner, melodious. . . ."[22] Wagner's reply (November 9, 1852) is so characteristic of his principle of thematic economy that it must be given here:

You have wonderfully caught me in a lie, as if I wished to make myself believe that I had written an "Overture to Faust"! Quite correctly you have noticed the place where it is lacking in this respect: it lacks—a woman! Perhaps you would have understood my tone-poem if I were to call it "Faust in Solitude."

Once I wished to write a whole *Faust* symphony. The first part (that which is completed) was the "Solitary Faust," in all his longing, despair, and execration. The "feminine" is present in his mind only as a counterpart of his yearning, but not in its heavenly reality. And this unsatisfying picture of his yearn-

[22] Letter, October 7, 1852.

ing is precisely what he dashes to pieces in his desperation. Only then, the second movement was to present Gretchen, the woman; I already had the theme for her, but it was only a theme—the whole lay unfinished. . . . If now from a last trace of weakness and vanity I do not wish to let the *Faust* composition be entirely lost, I have something to work over in it—but only the instrumental modulation. The theme you wished cannot be introduced; if it could, the composition, of course, would have to become an entirely new one, which I do not have the desire to make. . . .

Liszt then, two years later (in 1854), "made" this composition himself. "A Faust-Symphony (after Goethe)" is the title, with the further indication "in three characteristic scenes, for full orchestra, tenor solo, and chorus of men's voices." It is dedicated to Berlioz—a feature not without an element of irony for us of these later days. To be sure, the composition starts from that principle, that *idée fixe,* through the repetition and permutation of which Berlioz also established the musical coherence, intellectually and thematically, of a cycle of heterogeneous movements. But it leads the application of this principle to a point that Berlioz had never anticipated. The prototypes of these three musical portraits—Faust, Gretchen, and Mephistopheles—go back rather to works like Beethoven's *Coriolanus* or Schumann's overture to *Manfred,* both of which are more important, sincere, and concentrated character studies than Berlioz's depictions of his Lelio and Harold.

One may object that even Liszt in the first and second movements was still "painting" external situations: in the first, that episode in the exposition (*meno mosso, misterioso e molto tranquillo*) which precedes the appearance of the love theme (in C major, *affettuoso*) and points towards an incantation scene; in the second, that play of question and answer which is connected with Gretchen's asking her questions of the flowers. And one may object that even Liszt here, in the first movement, still observed the sonata form faithfully, and thus was guilty of the same compromise as that with which he charged Schumann. But this sonata movement is one which assigns the most important function not to the development section but to the recapitulation, in which the themes seem to operate like chemical substances that enter constantly into new transmutations.

The greatest masterpiece, in this sense, is the last "Mephistophelian" movement, which consists entirely of negative elements, parody, distortion, and mockery of the Faust motifs. Only the Gretchen themes are inaccessible to the Devil. This nihilistic side of Liszt is perhaps the real, the "Romantic" Liszt, who had arrived at the realization that he was a latecomer, member of a generation to which genuine, lively creativeness was denied. This is the Liszt whose manner of playing, in all its demoniac magic, had to be recognized even by a fellow artist who was otherwise not very fond of him, Clara Schumann (in a letter to Brahms, May 5, 1876).

Unfortunately, Liszt added or tacked on to this movement, three years later (in 1857), a vocal ending for men's chorus and tenor solo, which perhaps sends the listener away with a reconciled impression, but is not musically organic with the rest of the work. More organic is the vocal conclusion—for soprano solo and chorus of altos—to the second cyclic orchestral work of Liszt's, "A Symphony on Dante's Divine Comedy" (1855–56), dedicated to Richard Wagner: a Magnificat for a children's chorus, if possible off-stage. But this later work presupposes a rather "literary" background, and is more like a picture book than is the *Faust* Symphony, which remains Liszt's most characteristic work.

There still remain for mention several symphonic works of Liszt's which are among his happiest productions because in them the rhapsodic element is *permitted,* is—so to speak—legitimized, and because they, renouncing a program, emphasize motivic connection: his two Piano Concertos, one in E-flat major and the other in A major (1848–49). It is obvious and not without a certain charm that these two very unprogrammatic works go back to a composition that was "programmatic," Carl Maria Weber's *Concertstück* in F minor (1821), which was one of the virtuoso Liszt's show-pieces, and which reaches its greatest climax in a triumphal march. Liszt imitates Weber, but excels him in boldness of thematic invention and in virtuoso brilliance. The feature especially characteristic of Liszt is the free form, which binds the individual virtuoso passages and the cantabile passages together into unity. In a later concerto, the *Danse Macabre,* a "Paraphrase based on the *Dies Irae,*" Liszt again returned to a program—the famous fresco of (allegedly) Orcagna in the Campo Santo cemetery at Pisa, the *Trionfo della Morte,* which had inspired him to a succession of free variations. It is a composition in which he again established contact with the composer of the finale of the *Symphonie Fantastique.*

The genuinely Romantic features in Franz Liszt's instrumental compositions consist of numerous and strangely mingled ingredients. First, there is the more intimate propinquity of music and poetry. Poetry gives music the stimulus, with which music autocratically does what it likes, no longer having the least regard for the classical or classicistic formulae. Another Romantic feature is the choice of "subject matter"—a product of the "learnedness" of this child of the 19th century, who makes use of all world literature and presupposes the same learnedness among his audience. Above all, a Romantic feature is the fusion of intellectualism and ecstasy. There is intellect, cleverness, in the playful transformation, inflection, and combination of motifs. But the impulse which stands behind this playfulness is fraught with feeling and enthusiasm, sentiment and passion. The listener is to be aroused to the utmost, and thus the equalization of this excitement requires an extreme state—one of prostrating triumph, of mystical exaltation, of ecstasy. What a difference from the serenity of soul with which we are left by the finale of the *Jupiter* Symphony, or even from the sublimity with which we are left by Beethoven's *Eroica* or Fifth symphonies! Music has changed, and with it the entire world.

We know, of course, that the history of the Romantic symphony did not come to an end with Liszt's symphonic poems. Alongside him and after him the stream divided. One group among his contemporaries turned completely away from his "fusion" of music and poetry, and even the adherents of the neo-German school did not burn all their bridges behind them in this matter of form. To begin with the greatest representative of this school, Richard Wagner, we find that he expressly designated his *Siegfried Idyll* (1869–70) in the autograph as a "symphony." In so doing he was justified, for it is anything but a Lisztian symphonic poem or overture. Instead, it is a tightly constructed movement in free Rondo form, of an elegance usually found only in chamber music. The *Emperor* March (April, 1871) went back rather to Mendelssohn's *Reformation* Symphony, in that it contained portions neither more nor less programmatic or poetic than did the Romantic Classicist's composition. There is evidence that Wagner, towards the end of his life, intended to compose some purely instrumental works. Concerning their character, however, the statements of the biographers are widely divergent: one speaks of dialogues in one movement, of subject and counter-subject set apart; another speaks of a symphony with a multitude of themes, without contrasting or interweaving. Neither possibility, of course, sounds very Wagnerian, or entirely plausible. At all events, it is not a question here of a poetically inspired program.

A genuine initiate into Liszt's mysteries was Bedřich Smetana, who seized upon the idea of the symphonic poem with enthusiasm; meanwhile, his younger compatriot Antonin Dvořák in a guileless fashion served both God and the devil at the same time, writing now symphonies, now symphonic poems. But we shall see that, a musician to the core and endowed with genuine inventiveness, Dvořák belongs much more on the side of "absolute" music than on that of programmatic; for the latter presupposes literary taste that he did not have. And—to name a complete contrast—Camille Saint-Saëns (1834–1921), a Parisian of the finest culture, the finest taste, likewise wrote symphonies and symphonic poems side by side; meanwhile, César Franck achieved the goal of his D-minor Symphony along strange paths: his first symphonic poem *Les Éolides* (1876), inspired by Leconte de Lisle's poem, is rather a precursor of Impressionism, while *Le Chasseur Maudit* (1882, after Bürger's ballad) and *Les Djinns* (1884), and also *Psyché* (1887–88), belong in the most unmistakable, most materialistic tradition of Liszt. One could belong on the side of the neo-Germans—at least externally, so far as his party affiliations were concerned—and yet write pure, unprogrammatic, four-movement symphonies, as did Anton Bruckner; one could belong in the narrow group of Liszt's followers and still write a three-movement, genuine (though not very Classicistic) symphony, as did César Franck.

BRAHMS, A POSTHUMOUS MUSICIAN

The composer who is really antipodal to Liszt, not to Wagner, is Johannes Brahms. Liszt was a composer who scorned tradition and in the most real sense of the word stood irreverently before the past, even though he was too good a musician not to recognize the greatness of individual masters; Brahms was becoming more and more conscious of the possibility of finding models in the past, and was reaching back further and further into it. Liszt was a rhapsodist; Brahms adhered to acceptable, strict form, from beginning to end. Liszt proclaimed the fusion of music and poetry; Brahms kept secret all his impulses (the few inscriptions that exist in his works tell us little more about their real content than do the nicknames "Kegelstatt" Trio and the "Sparrow" Mass in Mozart). Liszt was the most European or cosmopolitan or Parisian of all musicians; Brahms was so very national, so much in the main stream of the German tradition as created by Bach, Beethoven, Schubert, Schumann, and the German folk song, that his effectiveness can never go beyond certain limits. Liszt was a child of the culture of his time, a culture which became a burden to him; Brahms was one of those rare 19th-century musicians who were born of simple musician fathers, yet appropriated to themselves all the culture of their time.

Brahms is the greatest representative of the musical Romantic movement, which sought to come to terms creatively with the past, unable to disregard Bach and Handel, Haydn and Mozart, and—above all—Beethoven. Liszt did not write a single chamber music work; Brahms tried to show that it was still possible to write sonatas, trios, and quartets. Wagner looked upon the Ninth Symphony as the closing work in a development; Brahms wrote serenades (though not, of course, serenades in the 18th-century sense of the term) and symphonies.

In so doing, he was well aware of the danger of being a composer born too late, no longer belonging to those happy times when the musician could create at the order of a society to which he belonged, and when the individual still was borne along by the spirit of the community. Wagner and Liszt were revolutionaries. They created against their times; and only the powerful force of will in Wagner was responsible for the fact that he did not succumb, like Liszt, whose creative activity ended in complete resignation. Wagner and Liszt were completely incompetent in professional, "bourgeois" positions. Wagner's six years as Capellmeister at Dresden ended in complete revulsion, flight, and exile. Liszt's "special" Court-Capellmeistership in Weimar ended with a complete surrender of arms before the Philistine world and with the deepest disgust. Brahms, on the other hand, was hurt to the quick and bore a grudge all his life over the fact that his native city, Hamburg, had not offered him the bourgeois position to which he believed he had some claim and for which his short-lived position as director of the Viennese Society of the Friends of Music (1872–75) offered no adequate substitute. Had he been born in the Middle Ages, he would have been a deeply satisfied member of the musicians' guild. In general he did not feel that his status as a free artist was entirely a piece of good fortune, even if his success made it possible for him to spend the last twenty years of his life in the city of Mozart, of Beethoven, and of Schubert.

Brahms's position as a Romantic was due to his feeling that he was a posthumous musician. He did not so consider himself from the very beginning. He began as a genuine Romantic, with a period of storm and stress, with impetuous youthfulness, like Schumann. As a matter of fact, Schumann—having himself become a "master" and feeling that he had failed in his task—greeted the youthful Brahms enthusiastically. The three Piano Sonatas—the first and last that Brahms ever wrote—are genuine examples of "Wunderhorn" Romanticism, and enter the lists with Beethoven, without whose Opus 106 the first movement of Opus 1 would not have come into being. The Scherzo in E-flat minor, to be sure, is Chopinesque, but free from all the shadings that might recall the salon. And with his First Piano Concerto in D minor (Op. 15) he ventured a plunge into the great, the symphonic, which was greeted with as little understanding on the part of his contemporaries as was Wagner's *Tristan.* When Brahms, on January 27, 1859, presented the work to a Leipzig audience, the failure could not have been more complete.

Brahms felt this failure deeply, but it is doubtful if such an experience alone was responsible for his reconsideration of his historical position. He had neither the desire nor the ability to abandon the paths that had been beaten by the very great masters of two or more centuries. He was not able to write operas like Wagner's, nor willing to write rhapsodies like Liszt's; and he was a much more responsible musician than Schumann. The transformation must have taken place in him before he had arrived at the age of twenty-four. In a letter to Joachim, with whom about this time (June, 1856) he was exchanging works in strict style, fugues and canons, there is a significant passage: "I occasionally reflect on the variation form, and find that it must be kept more strict, more pure. . . ." Yet the newer composers—among whom he includes himself and Joachim—"rummage about over the theme more. . . . We keep anxiously to the melody; we do not treat it freely. We really create nothing *new out of it;* instead we only load it down. . . ." However one may interpret these misgivings, at least they indicate the yearning of a Romantic subjectivity towards the strictness and formal sense of the old masters. More and more Brahms came to hate every manifestation of willfulness in creative activity; he yearned more and more for the sureness which he found in the masterpieces of the past, in Beethoven, in Mozart, and—above all—in Bach.

More and more with the passage of time, the past came to seem in his eyes a paradise lost. And if one seeks for the musician whom Brahms most deeply considered to have been fortunate in not being born too late, one would have to name not Mozart or Beethoven, but Schubert. The fact that Schubert had lived in Vienna was certainly the greatest enticement for Brahms to breathe that same air. His Piano Trio in B major, Op. 8, is a composition of Schubertian exuberance, Schubertian naïveté, Schubertian directness of communication. Nothing is more characteristic of Brahms's transformation than the fact that he rescued this very opus by later reworking it—thirty-seven years intervening between the first version (1854) and the second (1891)—and subjected it to his mature demands. The present book cannot devote the space necessary for an analytical comparison of the two; suffice it to quote and subscribe to what Hans Gál says in his notes to the complete edition: "A comparison of the two versions would yield material of unexcelled interest for a study in the technique of composition. The reworking lays bare with relentless critical acumen every weakness of the youthful work and, although the outlines are preserved, has the effect of a new creation. Thus, both as a creative achievement and an expression of an unsurpassable objectivity towards a composer's own work, it is a perhaps unique existing bit of testimony to the character of the artist and the man." What impelled Brahms to this reworking of the youthful composition was the feeling of responsibility before the demands of Classical form; the thoughts that led him in so doing may be brought together into two words: concentration and simplification.

The transformation of Brahms from an adherent of the Storm and Stress school, from an "involuntary" to a "voluntary" creator, to a musician who stands always in a certain relation to other musicians, is revealed in still another essential trait, in his attitude towards folk song. It has already been indicated in the first part of this book that he is hardly to be thought of without his almost mystical veneration of everything created by the "folk": in this respect he was a "Wunderhorn" musician. His veneration remained constant his whole life long: even at the age of twenty he brought together from Schumann's library everything in the nature of folklike melodies that he could find, and his interest in these treasures of seemingly involuntary origin induced him later to concern himself, like Liszt, with a stock of melodies not always free from vulgarity—that of the Hungarian gypsies. In his first, "involuntary" period, he drew folk song into the circle of his discovery and made it an element in his creative activity: the slow movement of his Piano Sonata Op. 1 is a series of variations on a supposedly Lower Rhenish folk tune, whose minor is at the end dissolved into blissful major; in the other two youthful piano sonatas, too, something folksong-like is the seed of the slow movements, and thereby of the whole work. Later, at the age of sixty-one, in his *German Folk Songs,* Brahms once again arranged the song from his Op. 1: but now it had become something sacrosanct to him; to the melody he added only an accompaniment. No longer did he encroach upon it; he had perceived that he, as a composer "born too late," could no longer be so ingenuous as could the old, great masters.

Hugo Wolf considered Brahms a mere copyist, and was willing to admit only one solitary virtue of his talent—"that of artful workmanship. . . . Herr Brahms knows how to vary a given theme as no one else does. His entire creative output, however, is only a great variation on the work of Beethoven, Mendelssohn, and Schumann. . . ." [23] Now, the youthful composer, who himself had already written a D-minor Quartet, might have also added many other masters of the past whom Brahms had "written variations on," particularly Schubert. But it nevertheless seems clear that Brahms was no mere copyist.

Brahms's relationship to the earlier composers may also be differently expressed. Thus Philipp Spitta wrote:

The musical politicians of our day call Brahms a reactionary. . . . Others say that Brahms demonstrates practically that in these [i.e., the Classical] forms something new can *still* be said. Not *still*, but always—so long as our music remains, this will be the situation. For these forms are derived from the very inner nature of this music, and in their outlines could not have been more perfectly conceived. Even those composers who think that they have broken them, and thereby have accomplished an act of liberation, avail themselves of these forms in so far as they still have any desire at all to achieve a satisfying impression. They cannot do otherwise, so long as composition and contrast in music remain. They only do it much worse than does he who enters into the inheritance from the past with full awareness and with the intention of employing it in the service of the beautiful. Power, of course, is required; moreover, many ways lead to the shrine. Weber and Schubert, Schumann and Gade have in many ways loosened Beethoven's firm construction and are, in the matter of musical architectonics, unquestionably lesser masters. They seek to make up for this deficiency through other, magnificent characteristics; and no one to whom music is more than a mere sort of arithmetic will be so pedantic as to look askance at their weaknesses. But the assumption that their willfulnesses are the guideposts to new and higher goals is false. The foundations must remain fixed, and each one builds upon them according to his needs. After Brahms, others will come who will compose in ways other than his. His endeavor was towards concentration and indissolubly firm union, using all the means that are proper to the art of music as such.[24]

The Romanticism in Brahms's work rests upon his relation to the paradise lost of Classical music, and he makes no secret of it for anyone who has ears to hear. This relation gives his work charm and attractiveness,

[23] *Musicalische Kritiken,* December 7, 1884.
[24] Philipp Spitta, *Zur Musik* (Berlin, 1892), p. 416 ff.

with no loss in individuality. The String Sextet in B-flat (Op. 18) would never have come into being without the model of Schubert; in fact, it belongs rather to those compositions in which Brahms is still trying to compete with the classic master of the Romantic era on the same plane. The Waltzes for four hands, Op. 39, Schubertian as they are, already show traces of nostalgia for a vanished happiness. The Violin Concerto would not have found its inner form without Beethoven's example in this genre. The finale of this Concerto, somewhat *"all'ongarese,"* brings us to the observation of how often Brahms, like Haydn, Beethoven, or Schubert, tried to make one or another of his movements more elemental by national rhythmic or melodic coloring and thus to approach that paradise lost of music. In contrast to Schumann, Brahms concerned himself for a long time with writing quartets, and in so doing he entered the ranks more with Haydn and Mozart than with Beethoven. About "originality" he never greatly troubled himse'f, and never avoided the *formula*—in full accord with the old masters, who knew that it was impossible to achieve a style without formulae. The only difference was that he, with his attention directed backwards, did not exert himself to create any further new formulae.

After long consideration he proceeded to the symphonic form—unless one wishes to consider his fateful First Piano Concerto a symphony. After trying out his powers in two Serenades, he set to work on his First Symphony, Op. 68. And what a significant development from this First to the last, the Fourth Symphony! A later admirer of Brahms, deserted from the camp of Liszt and Wagner, Hans von Bülow, coined an unhappy phrase for this C-minor Symphony by saying that it was "the Tenth." It stands only in a certain relationship to Beethoven; and the quality that places it in the genuine "Classical" succession consists only of the concentration and masterfulness of structure, particularly in the first movement. The Second Symphony is pastoral in character. The Third—the most personal of all—is pseudo-heroic. And the last one proceeds from the balladesque to a note of fateful resignation, to a medieval Dance of Death in form of a *Chaconne*. That is the way taken by Brahms the Romantic: the fiery beginning, the perception of the greatness and unaffected happiness of the past, the sorrowful renewal of this happiness, and the resignation of the man born too late. Along this road, the concentration, the simplification, the masterfulness become greater and greater, right up to those farewell works, among which the final piano pieces and the Clarinet Quintet speak out in the clearest accents.

BRUCKNER, RELIGIOUS SYMPHONIST

Anton Bruckner (1824–1896) was almost ten years older than Brahms, but his development was slower and his influence manifested itself much later. Unquestionably, however, he should figure prominently in a history of Romantic music. His Romanticism is not a mere matter of the fact that one of his symphonies, the Fourth, was christened the "Romantic Symphony." Rather, all of his nine or more symphonies—for there are two without numbers—represent in the clearest and most magnificent manner one side of the Romantic movement, that arising from the mystical conception of sound. But there is a question of the connection in which he is to be brought in among the Romantics, for he was different from all the rest and would be a figure to set in contrast to each. He was of rural ancestry, from the schoolteacher tribe like Schubert, but—unlike Schubert, and still more unlike Weber, Berlioz, Schumann, and Wagner —he remained "unliterary" to the very end. The style and content of his letters is obsequious, and one would never expect him to have been able to give an intellectual or aesthetic account of his art.

In this respect, he was the successor and heir of the composer of symphonies and church music, Schubert. The contrapuntal training denied to Schubert was obtained by Bruckner likewise from Simon Sechter, and it was Bruckner's work alone which justified the Austrian type of Mass in the new century. His name was emblazoned on the shields of Wagner and the Wagnerians against Brahms, but he had almost as little in common with Wagner and the neo-Germans as he had with their opponent Brahms. He was in conformity with the spirit of the age only in so far as his art is inconceivable without the precedent of Beethoven and especially of Schubert, and without his adoption of the great symphonic orchestra of the 19th century. Otherwise, his work—in contrast to the posthumous work of Brahms—is almost timeless. Bruckner took over with complete unconcern the great four-movement form of Beethoven's symphonies and of Schubert's C-major Symphony, and again filled in the outline with content that was entirely his own and purely musical.

Bruckner felt no extensively "programmatic" impulse, although in two works, the Fourth and the Eighth Symphonies, he made an awkward attempt to indicate the "content" by a few inscriptions. An idea of their nature may be gained from a manuscript of the Fourth Symphony, which Bruckner himself carefully corrected and which is preserved at Columbia University, New York. In it the first movement actually bears the title

"Dawn Call from the Town Hall" (*Tagesruf vom Rathause*), the Scherzo "The Hunt" (*Jagd*), and the Trio "Dinner Music of the Hunters in the Forest (*Tafelmusik der Jäger im Walde*)! In actuality, however, his symphonic art had nothing to do with such naïve and trivial matters. It sprang from the same source as his church music—from the religious. In the slow movements as well as in the first and last movements, it is always a coming to terms with God. The thematic and symbolic relations between his symphonies and the Masses and his *Te Deum* are easily perceived. In those first and last movements there is no Presto, and not even an Allegro; there is no passion; their movement is always that of the festival, the procession, of motion in rest; but the movement is not that of emotion with personal coloring. The religious element and the feeling for nature converge into the mystical, thus making it possible for one to set Bruckner upon the throne of musical theosophy. We call this Romantic: the purest music within traditional outlines, but connected with a mystery, made palpable to sense in the very radiant emanations from the tone of the strings, and especially from that of the winds, full of mighty crescendos, almost always concluding in a sonorous, almost Baroque halo of the brass choir—in all harmonic and melodic aspects at once monumental and tender.

It is evidence for the opposed, the polar unity of the Romantic era that both Brahms and Bruckner lived and created in the same Vienna and at the same time, and that their symphonies were written during somewhat the same years—the four by Brahms between 1876 and 1885 and the eight completed by Bruckner (the Ninth lacks a finale) between 1868 and 1886. It is one of the wonders of history that in the midst of the full flowering of the Romantic movement, which felt itself cleft, torn asunder, and sick, the timeless, unbroken, monumental symphonic art of Bruckner could still come into being.

CHAPTER XII

Church Music

PROTESTANT CHURCH MUSIC: MENDELSSOHN

WITH his symphonies, his chamber music, and his piano compositions, Beethoven had shown the Romantics the way. He had been essentially a master of instrumental music. The Romantics emphasized and over-emphasized his preference or one-sidedness by entrusting their most intimate and profound thoughts to the instrumental, the wordless medium of music. It is one of the paradoxes of the Romantic era that the recipient of these intimate confessions was to become more and more unable to feel their force except when in a mass of people. With the increasing technical difficulty of symphonies and chamber works, music tended more and more to move into the concert hall. Even in piano music a difference arose between intimate and virtuoso or concert works. Although this had already appeared in Beethoven, it became increasingly marked. The battlefields of Romantic music were the concert hall and the opera house.

No longer was it the house of God. There, from the very beginning, the Protestant church had been at a disadvantage in comparison with the Catholic. The reason was that the Protestants lacked a universally valid form of the divine service, the fixed outlines of the liturgy. Luther had already sounded the keynote, which was taken up by the other leaders of the Reformation, that the order of divine service should belong to those parts of the new faith in which complete freedom is to prevail. The Calvinist utilized this evangelical freedom to suppress entirely or reduce to a minimum the artistic and musical formulation of the liturgy. At the end of the 18th and the beginning of the 19th century, when Romanticism stirred in all branches of thought as a European movement, it no longer found in these barren fields any fruitful soil—quite apart from the fact that church music as such is an area reserved for tradition and is not suited for progress. Where would there have been room, for example, in the manifold species of the Anglican church for creative activity in the Romantic sense of the word—or even in churches where less strictness of fundamental principles prevailed, as for example among the Presbyterians. From early times the freest and most personal musical form within this framework had been the anthem. In the Romantic period—the Victorian age—there were some very attractive exponents of this form of church music: Thomas A. Walmisley (1814–1856) and especially Samuel S. Wesley (1810–1876), the former a friend of Mendelssohn's and both admirers of J. S. Bach. Yet one would do them no injustice to speak of them as free creative musicians who were quite worthy but not exactly great, although they did break away slightly from the merely traditional.

It was for England that Mendelssohn wrote three "church pieces," Op. 69, for *a cappella* chorus with soli. The most beautiful of these three pieces is the third, a Magnificat. It was Mendelssohn, moreover, who in his church music brought out most clearly the cleavage that had evidently taken place within Protestant church music during the Romantic period. In Lutheran centers like Saxony, Prussia, and Württemberg, the 18th century had found itself more and more troubled over the musical adornment of the divine service. On the one side there was Pietism. Being more spiritual and sensitive than the older and more torpid orthodoxy, it frustrated any attempt to give musical brilliance to the celebration of holy worship—and in so doing encountered a fierce opponent in J. S. Bach. On the other side there was that malady of the 18th century, Rationalism. Although it did not rule out the most extreme forms of sentimentality, it worked against the rich cultivation of religious art. Old Bach with his grandiose church cantatas, motets, and Passions, was followed by Philipp Emanuel Bach, Carl Heinrich Graun, and Johann Adam Hiller, with their sentimental compositions—and therewith are named, out of countless musicians, the three best.

The Romantic era felt the state of decay, and recognized also its fundamental cause, the multiplicity and the lack of unity in the traditional orders of divine worship. But it could bring forth no unity out of a new spirit. For that to take place, a genuine, inner renewal of the religious and ecclesiastical life would have been necessary. So the Romantics brought the matter only to a state of historical restoration. It was the "Romantic on the royal throne," Friedrich Wilhelm IV of Prussia, who took the task in hand. Citing Luther as precedent but completely denying Luther's tolerance in these artistic matters, he exercised his prerogatives as head of the church in his territories and proceeded to make the divine service uniform. And as there was a lack of the creative spirit, a return was made to the past, or rather to two mutually exclusive stages of the past and their representatives—to Johann Sebastian Bach and to Palestrina. Since the musical preference of the King had a Catholic tinge, and since he considered the ostensibly pure vocal church music of Palestrina the only genuine and authoritative kind, there was in Berlin at this time actually a school that could proclaim that it had "so penetrated the spirit and technique of that master of pure vocal style that it had brought this music to a state of second flowering." [25]

Even Mendelssohn had to bring his offering to the altar of this antiquarian enthusiasm, notably in the Psalms and motets composed for the Berlin cathedral choir. In these, to be sure, he followed less the model of Palestrina than that of the Venetians around 1600 and even that of the later composer, Benedetto Marcello. He was, however, too deeply impressed by the greatness of J. S. Bach not to make the attempt to give impetus to Protestant church music by the amalgamation of his own style with certain of Bach's traits. From this attempt there arose his great, cantata-like psalm compositions, with large, even unusually large, orchestra—those of Psalms 31, 42, 95, 98, and 115. It was a mistake, although these belong to his most heartfelt and artful works, and are masterpieces in the balance of structure and sound. Mendelssohn could not found a new Protestant church style even upon Bach, one of the most individual of all composers, without completely transforming his own style, and without overcoming everything archaic. For this reason, these works of Mendelssohn's are really homeless compositions, strange both to the concert hall and to their imaginary liturgical setting. This fact has not prevented Mendelssohn's finding successors by the hundreds in this same field. Finally, at the end of the century—again coming from Prussia and, in characteristic fashion, led by an outstanding historian, Rochus von Liliencron—there was set up a strict musical scheme for the evangelical divine service, which made an appeal to creative musicians for its fulfillment.

CATHOLIC CHURCH MUSIC: BERLIOZ

The Catholic Church had it easier. Its liturgy was very old, and from its basic lines every manifestation of willfulness was banished. This fixed

[25] Friedrich Spitta, "Neuere Bewegungen auf dem Gebiete der evangelischen Kirchenmusik," in *Peters-Jahrbuch für 1901*, p. 20.

frame, moreover, was valid not only for Rome or Italy, but also for the whole of Catholic Christendom. Yet within this unity there prevailed no impetus towards uniformity. Instead, there was tolerance—tolerance both for national stylistic peculiarities and for more personal expression. In the course of eighteen centuries the Church had never made an attempt to fetter church music. On only a few occasions—the most famous being that of the Council of Trent—it had tried to eliminate supposed or actual excrescences. In the 17th and 18th centuries it let music go its own way, although there would have been sufficient occasion at hand for intervening. With the so-called "discovery" of monody, particularly, there began an age of concerted church music, in which the musician introduced all the secular forms—the sonata, the cantata—into the church, and filled the holy place with soli, duets, and *concertante* choruses, with subjective expression. The musical *religio,* the musical relation to the divine, became one by no means distant.

One should not for a moment think that there had been any lack of protests against this "secularized" Catholic church music, particularly since the beginning of the 18th century. But this protest acquired a Romantic coloring only at the beginning of the 19th century. The Romantic element in this coloring consisted, likewise, of a return to the past, to the supposedly *a cappella* style of the 16th century, which was considered the only appropriate ideal of church music.

Palestrina became an idol. It was not by mere chance that after 1817 Alexander-Etienne Choron (1772–1834) founded his *Institution Royale de Musique Classique et Réligieuse,* which re-awakened a taste for early church music, and the spirit of which continued operative in the influence of his pupils Niedermeyer and Lafage. It is not by mere chance that in 1828 the great critical—or, rather, somewhat uncritical—enthusiastic monograph by Giuseppe Baini on Palestrina appeared, and that in 1825 a paper was issued by the Heidelberg jurist and musical amateur A. F. Justus Thibaut, *On the Purity of the Tonal Art,* which took the part of the 16th century against the 18th and 19th centuries in a much more exclusive and rigorous spirit than the biography of the Italian had done. Note that all this was *against* the 18th and 19th centuries; for where Palestrina and Victoria prevailed, there was no place for the brilliant, symphonically conceived church music of Mozart, Haydn, and Beethoven.

One might compare the tendencies of these Romantic purists of church music with those of the so-called Nazarenes in the field of painting—men who threw overboard three centuries of development and tried to return to the ideals of Raphael and of the painters before Raphael. The only difference is that the musicians were less radical and fanatical than the theoreticians. In Munich, Kaspar Ett (1788-1847) and Johann Kaspar Aiblinger (1779-1867) wrote church music with orchestra, along with more or less archaistic imitations in the Palestrina style. In the North, however, their Protestant-Prussian colleague, Eduard August Grell (1800-1886), looked upon the rise of instrumental music as a degenerate phenomenon and granted validity only to pure *a cappella* music. During the second half of the century, moreover, the "Nazarenes" of church music were replaced by the "Caecilians," who had their artistic and scholarly center in Regensburg. The discussion of the Classic masters' church music then took on more polemic form, even in South Germany.

This second-hand Nazarene-like church music had the merit of providing to an extensive degree for the practical needs of the liturgy in the greater and smaller churches, while the great creative works of the Romantic masters were unserviceable for the liturgy or were usable only on the rarest occasions. Beethoven, with his *Missa Solemnis,* had given an example of this. Berlioz, in particular, had seen to it that his two works of this type, the *Grande Messe des Morts* (Op. 5) and the *Te Deum* (Op. 22), could be made audible only by the concerted action of the most unusual resources of musical power. This feature is explained by the fact that both are occasional pieces: the Requiem had its origin in a commission from the French Ministry of the Interior, which wished to hold a magnificent memorial service for those who had fallen in the July Revolution of 1830; and the *Te Deum* owes its inception, at least, to the idea of giving a worthy musical setting to the remembrance of Napoleon's return from the Italian campaign and his entry into church—it was not Napoleon III's fault that similar occasions were not repeated in the 1850's. The Romantic element in the composition of the two works is the fact that they are conceived entirely from a subjective and arbitrary point of view. If they are examples of "state music," they are such only in the same sense as are, for example, the great church festival compositions of the late Venetians, Giovanni Gabrieli or Giovanni Croce.

For the old masters, these compositions involved only a special order, requiring unusual artistic ability. Berlioz, however, burst into Romantic flame: "The text of the Requiem was for me a long-coveted prey, which at last was delivered into my hands, and upon which I threw myself with a kind of fury. My head seemed ready to burst with the effort of my ebullient thought. . . ."[26] And to his sister he wrote (on April 17, 1837), "I have taken pains to master my subject: in the first days, the poetry of the *Prose des Morts* intoxicated and exalted me to such an extent that nothing lucid appeared before my mind, my head was in turmoil, and I had spells of dizziness. Now the eruption is under control, the lava has hollowed out its bed, and with God's help all will go well. It is a great affair!" Actually it became a "great affair," for tenor solo, mixed chorus, a gigantic principal orchestra and four subsidiary orchestras, the subsidiary orchestras placed in the four quarters of the heavens, for the beginning of the *Tuba Mirum,* the depiction of the awakening of the dead and their summons before the final judgment seat of God. But it also became in a personal sense Berlioz's principal work: genuinely Romantic—to be sure, *French* Romantic—in its admixture of naturalism, in the utilization of liturgical suggestions, of bits of glowing lyricism, and its contrasts of extreme orchestral and choral magnificence and extreme intimacy.

A more harmonious work is the later *Te Deum* (begun in 1849 and completed in 1855), especially if one leaves out the two instrumental movements (the Prelude and the March), which were written only in consideration of the original military intention. At the first performance, however, Berlioz again gave some thousand participants a share in the work; and along with the double chorus there was a children's chorus of six hundred. He designated the work after the performance as "colossal, Babylonian, Ninevite . . . there is a finale greater than the *Tuba Mirum* of my Requiem." As a matter of fact, this choral hymn is one of the most powerful evidences of Romantic individualism in the 19th century and at the same time one of the mightiest pieces of all Catholic church music. It could have been written only by a French Catholic; yet, in this work as well as in the *Messe des Morts,* this Catholic allows himself to take the greatest liberties in the wording and grouping of the text—in the Requiem he even inserted parts of the Offertory—and thereby made his works unusable for their liturgical setting. Later on we shall see in Anton Bruckner's *Te Deum* and Masses how a genuine Catholic handles liturgical texts without forfeiting his freedom as a creator.

[26] *Mémoires* (Paris, 1870), ch. 46.

LISZT: "DILETTANTE CHRISTIANITY"

The most significant example of what has been called "19th-century dilettante Christianity," i.e., of the Romantic Movement, is Franz Liszt. Quite early in his career, the great virtuoso began to concern himself with the problem of church music, and in the second volume of his collected writings (1887) there is a fragment included from the year 1834 "On the Church Music of the Future"—from the same year as Lamennais's *Paroles d'un Croyant*. It laments the decline of religion; it laments the fact that:

Art has left the heart of the temple and, broadening out, has had to seek in the outside world the stage for its noble manifestations. How often—indeed, how much more than often—music must acknowledge the people and God as its source of life, must hasten from one to the other, to ennoble, comfort, and chasten mankind and to bless and praise God. To reach this goal, it is indispensable that a new music be invoked. This music, which for lack of another designation we may call humanistic (*humanitaire*), should be solemn, strong, and powerful; it should unite in colossal relationships the theater and the church; it should be at the same time dramatic and holy, splendidly unfolding and simple, ceremonious and earnest, fiery and unbridled, stormy and restful, clear and fervent. . . . This will be the *fiat lux* of art!

From these few words one can already perceive the cleavage which the passionate artist and enthusiastic Catholic found in himself all his life—a cleavage which had to be carried over most noticeably in his church music itself. Humanistic music in the church: union of theater and temple, fusion of the dramatic and the holy! One feels that he is reading a characterization of Verdi's *Requiem,* in which—thanks to Verdi's incomparable unaffectedness as a musician and his incomparable sincerity as an artist —the cleavage was successfully obviated. With Liszt, however, the solution was complicated by his acquaintance with Gregorian chant and by his Franciscan inclination to the utmost simplicity. He did not begin with works such as might put into effect his program of 1834, but with —for example—a Mass for four-part chorus of men's voices and organ (1848, considerably reworked in 1869), in a mixture of simple declamation with a cantabile quality, of archaism with Romantic ecstasy, meanwhile using Gregorian idioms in the *Gloria* and the *Agnus Dei*. A similar work is the later *Missa Choralis* (1865), originally for mixed chorus *a cappella,* but later provided with organ accompaniment and given a more strictly contrapuntal character.

Liszt realized his youthful program in his two great instrumental masses, but no longer in the unquestioning manner of his youth. The more modest of these two works is the so-called *Hungarian Coronation Mass,* composed for the festival service on the occasion of the crowning of the Habsburg rulers as king and queen of Hungary in the St. Matthew Church in Buda, 1867. Liszt did not wish the work to be performed in a concert hall, and he even permitted a reduction in the already not too large orchestra for whatever further actual performances the work might be given. But in this respect he was mistaken, for the effectiveness of this Mass rests upon extreme contrasts: a "praying" *Christe* of the solos within the framework of a festal, pompous *Kyrie,* and a quite simply declaimed, sparingly chord-colored, merely organ-accompanied *Credo*—which Liszt took from the *Messe Royale* of Henry Du Mont (1610–1684)—between ecstatic, roaring, wailing subjective movements for chorus and instruments (the Offertory). In the *Agnus Dei,* which—as in Beethoven—is opened by a violin solo, there are ever-present faint suggestions of something like Magyar or gypsy music.

Still more magnificent, particularly in the instrumentation, which even includes a harp, still more unified, and quite in the spirit of that youthful manifesto, is the earlier Mass, written in 1855, the *Missa Solemnis* for the dedication of the basilica at Gran, seat of the Primate of Hungary, in 1856. On May 2, 1855, Liszt wrote to Richard Wagner: "During these last weeks I have been entirely wrapped up in my mass, and yesterday I at last finished it. I do not know how the thing will sound, but I can say this, that for it I have done more *praying* than *writing.*" Beethoven had written concerning the Kyrie of his *Missa Solemnis:* "From the heart! May it again touch the heart!" Here we see the characteristic difference between the Classic, for whom it is well established that a Mass must be prayed for, and the Romantic ecstatic who has to stress the fact. The gigantic work—gigantic, although shorter and more compact than its predecessor from the pen of Beethoven—is the opposite of everything Caecilian: the orchestra, conceived in symphonic and often leitmotivic terms, lays on the ground-color for the liturgical text and unifies it, passionately and dramatically, not resting in God but contending with Him.

And between the dramatic, the ecstatic, and the liturgic, there exist also the numerous other greater and smaller church compositions of Liszt's: five psalm compositions, among which, again, the setting of the 13th Psalm for tenor solo, chorus, and full orchestra (written after the Gran Mass in 1855) is the most fervent and dramatic: ". . . the tenor part is very important; I have let *myself* sing the part and the flesh-and-blood appearance of King David inspire me" (August 29, 1862). A musician of the 17th century could have said that, if such spontaneous confessions had been customary in the 17th century; just as the great Masses of Liszt's in their instrumental power recall works like the 53-voiced festival Mass of Orazio Benevoli for the dedication of the Salzburg cathedral (1628). The only difference is that this Baroque splendor was naïve, while that of the Romantic is ecstatic. And ecstasy, we repeat, is the escape of the Romantic musician to Catholicism, as if into maternal arms of rest and security after years of indifference and even of doubt, of which there had been no lack even for Liszt. Had he been a Protestant artist, he would in the end have turned to Catholicism, as at another time the Romantic German poets Zacharias Werner and Clemens Brentano had done. But since he had been born a Catholic, he became a priest, the "Abbé Liszt," who sought in Rome a sort of defense against his overflowing, life-affirming virtuosity —not always with success, either in his life or, luckily, in his art.

ROMANTICIZED CHURCH MUSIC: GOUNOD AND FRANCK

A counterpart to Liszt, scarcely less torn by conflict, tragically tense, and somewhat smaller in stature, is Charles Gounod (1818–1893), who may be selected as an example of the many lesser figures of this sort who perpetuated the conflict. In his youth, he long vacillated between the priesthood and the musical profession. Even though in the memory of posterity he survives most clearly as the composer of *Marguérite* and *Roméo et Juliette,* he remained a passionate believer to the end of his career, as is attested by his two late, oratorio-like works, *Rédemption* (1882) and *Mors et Vita* (1885). His last work (1893) is a Requiem, and one of his first (1841) is a three-voiced Mass for chorus with orchestra. In all, he wrote no less than fifteen Masses, along with other works for the church—Masses of every kind, *a cappella,* with simple organ accompaniment, with accompaniment of orchestra, among others three *Missae Solemnes,* in fact even a Mass for orchestra alone with voices *ad libitum.*

Here we find the same combination of factors as in Liszt: acquaintance with Gregorian chant, familiarity with the Palestrina style, and courage to be modern. Let us take as an example Gounod's *Messe Solennelle de Sainte-Cécile,* which is his best known mass and which was written in the same year as Liszt's Gran Mass. Is it churchly? Here is a significant trait: it does not follow the text exactly. "Between each of the three settings of the Agnus which are sung by the chorus," he explained, "I have placed a phrase of solo song to the words *Domine, non sum dignus,* which I have thought could be interpolated as being the words of the office at the very moment of communion. The first time, that phrase is sung by a tenor voice, representing the *man,* whose heavy conscience appears in an expression touched with penitence; the second time, it is entrusted, in a slightly modified form, to the soprano voice, emblematic of the *child,* whose fear is less and whose trust greater by reason of the calm given him by his innocence. As to the instrumentation, the piece is based on a sketch for muted violins, begging for mercy; and at the moment of the *Dona nobis pacem* the orchestra subsides, for purposes of recollection, remaining so up to the communion." [27]

It is seen that this Mass is not entirely churchly, for the liturgy does not permit interpolations of this sort. This Mass tends towards Catholicism, but it is not itself Catholic. Despite one or another grandiose and orchestrally unified movement like the Credo, it is poetical, subjective, lyric. It is Romanticized church music.

The same characterization, moreover, applies roughly to the church works of the great organist at Sainte Clotilde, César Franck (1822–1890), who likewise wrote a *Rédemption* (1871–72), a "deliverance" *into* faith, not a resting in faith, reflecting the ardent seeking of the human being for salvation, and of the musician for style. In Franck's church compositions there appear the flaccid and somewhat secular turns of expression that are irreconcilable with genuine church music, with subdued awe before the divine.

GENUINE CATHOLICISM: BRUCKNER, ROSSINI, VERDI

The great church musician of the Romantic era is Anton Bruckner, although—or perhaps because—he never pondered over the aesthetic requirements of church music. As a school teacher and organist, he grew up in the Church; her spirit and her liturgy were the very air he breathed. The instrumentally accompanied Masses of the Classical composers like Haydn, Mozart, and Beethoven—and also Schubert—were still at home in these Upper Austrian churches. Bruckner, moreover, was quite familiar with works from the periods of Palestrina and Gabrieli. Among these, the compositions of the rather agitated and saturnine Jacobus Gallus seem to have made an especial impression on him. But Bruckner did not

[27] Quoted from Camille Bellaigue, *Gounod* 3rd ed. (Paris, 1919), p. 57 ff.

write "Post Classical" or Romantic church music in the style of Schubert; nor did he write archaic music in Palestrina style. As Haydn and Mozart had done, he continued to treat his material in terms of sonata form, in both his orchestral or symphonic Masses, that in D minor (1864, revised in 1876) and that in F minor (1867–68, revised in 1890). Especially did he do so in the *Gloria* and *Credo* movements, which are hard to unify. Characteristically enough, in the *Gloria* he thought of the *Quoniam* as a kind of reprise, and in his E-minor Mass for eight-part choir with wind instruments (1866, revised in 1885) there are archaic effects, even in the modal coloring.

But, unlike Liszt or Brahms, Bruckner felt no self-conscious relation between himself and his predecessors. "In him," Ernst Kurth has written, "are observable the operations of that elemental feeling which prevailed in the early French as well as Netherlandish mass, in Palestrina's reform of church music, in the Roman and Venetian school, and in all the changes that took place in Italian and German instrumentally accompanied church music from the Renaissance and Austrian Baroque right on into the Classic period. This elemental feeling became operative in him and enabled him to settle his accounts with his Classical predecessors in the matter of *form* as well as to reconcile the very ancient churchly spirit with that of the Romantic movement. Bruckner's entire historic position, his penetration upward from medieval-mystic to high-Romantic sensibility, is nowhere more clearly seen than in his church music. . . ." [28] In other words, the mixture of stylistic elements—the chorale, the *a cappella* ideal, Classicism, Romanticism—is so personal, naïve, and unreflecting that it appears, almost more than Bruckner's symphonic art, as a timeless wonder.

A deeply suffering mortal, deeply moved religiously, wrote these Masses; a human being with unshaken consciousness of being a child of God wrote the *Te Deum* (1881) and the 150th Psalm (1892, his last church composition). Yet the personal or seemingly subjective element is so symbolically presented that it appears to us as "Catholic," as necessary as it does in Josquin or Gombert. And this is true despite all the "modernisms," among which the most striking are the "color-drenched, high-Romantic harmonic effects," the monumental unison passages of the choir, and the "primitive" accompanimental figures. The contrapuntal skill of Bruckner is similarly new—and, at the same time, old. It is an art more of thematic *combination* for purposes of achieving fervent or powerful

[28] Ernst Kurth, *Bruckner* (Berlin, 1925), p. 1190.

climaxes. True, this church music is Romantically colored; it could have been written only by a musician whom chance, as it were, had cast into the 19th century. But in it, at the same time, Romanticism was superseded.

A wonder of a similar sort took place in the history of Italian church music. The fact that a biographer and panegyrist of Palestrina had appeared during the first quarter of the century at the very seat of the master's activity was, if not entirely an accident, in any case an archaeological or philological development. But the genuine renewal of the Catholic spirit in the most skeptical of all nations proceeded from one of the great poets of Lombardy, Alessandro Manzoni, in utter contrast to another poet from a nearby region, Vittorio Alfieri, who worked exclusively with material from the Classics and the Old Testament. As a writer of tragedies such as *Il Conte di Carmagnola* and *Adelchi,* Manzoni was an imitator of the historical tragedies of Shakespeare. In the *Inni Sacri* ("Holy Hymns," 1815), he carried out the intention "of dealing with the great, noble, and genuinely human feelings which quite naturally spring from religion, and of carrying them back to this source." At last, in his historical novel *I Promessi Sposi* (1827), Manzoni gave to Italy and to the world the great Catholic work of art, which immediately was imitated in all the languages of Europe.

The Catholic spiritual revival also took hold upon the musicians—except that it could not find expression as with Liszt or the other Northern musicians. For this, Italy was much too isolated before her cultural unification. Musically, moreover, she was much too intensively and exclusively the land of opera, too little inclined to the symphony or to chamber music to be able to cultivate any style other than the operatic even in the music of the Church.

In 1808 Rossini had written a *Graduale* for three concerted men's voices, consisting of an Allegro in D, an *Ave Maria* for tenor in B-flat with bassoon obbligato, and a closing *Alleluia.* In 1847 he wrote a *Tantum Ergo* for the same combination, which even the enthusiast Radiciotti characterized thus: "The music of the first part is not unlike that of a secular romance, and has no lack of sixteenth notes and triplets. The second part, Allegro, is a genuine march with its episodes." [29]

But genuine feeling could very well go along with operatic features such as these, and the time could come when both of Rossini's principal religious or church works, the *Stabat Mater* (1832, reworked in 1841) and the *Petite Messe Solennelle* (1863), might again receive a more just evalua-

[29] *G. Rossini* (Tivoli, 1927–29), III, p. 254.

tion than they had been given during the 19th century. The *Stabat Mater*, for example, received the most villainous sort of criticism in the worst journalistic style of Heine from the pen of the youthful Richard Wagner. This critique was all the more villainous as Wagner could not possibly have known the work. If one rejects the *Stabat Mater*, one must also, along with the Nazarenes, reject all the religious music of the 17th and 18th centuries, including that of Bach, Handel, Haydn, and Mozart. For Rossini simply spoke the language natural to him. Rather, if anything is to be regretted, it is, at most, that he closes this work—which does not serve a liturgical purpose but rather one of religious edification—with an excessively pompous double fugue. To be sure, it includes among the nine preceding parts "arias" and "cavatinas," a "quartet" and an "air and chorus." But this fact does not entirely preclude deep feeling and lofty originality, especially in the two *a cappella* portions (Nos. V and IX). And the same applies to his *Petite Messe Solennelle* for soloists, chorus, two pianos, and harmonium, which Rossini called the last mortal sin of his old age (*le dernier péché mortel de ma vieillesse*). He felt acutely the problem of whether in the 19th century genuine church music was still possible. His awareness of this problem is shown by his well-known dedication to "dear God," behind the farce and buffoonery of which is hidden his serious intention: "Dear God—this poor little mass lies there. Have I written some music that is sacred, or just some sacred music? I was born to write *opera buffa*, well Thou knowest! Scant learning is there contained, but a little of my full heart is there. Then be Thou praised, and grant me entry into Paradise." Even the title, *"Petite* Messe," is one of Rossini's jokes; for the composition is a monumental work, with the "learned," the concerted, the archaic, and the operatic in a childlike mixture that moves and convinces the listener.

When Rossini died on November 13, 1868, Giuseppe Verdi made the proposal to his publisher, Ricordi, that a Requiem might be written by a group of Italian composers, i.e., with different portions assigned to different ones, and on the anniversary of Rossini's death it might be performed at San Petronio in Bologna, "to show how mighty in all of us is the veneration for this man, whose loss is lamented by the whole world." Verdi himself composed the closing *Libera me Domine*. Of all the parts of this Requiem, the *Libera* has alone remained alive, as the conclusion of the Mass for the dead which Verdi wrote a few years later in memory of Alessandro Manzoni (d. May 22, 1873) and which was performed a year later at San Marco in Milan. Verdi, no more than Rossini, had thought of altering the language that was natural to him in order to make it "churchly" or stylized. This Requiem, in which the soloists play a more prominent role than usual and the orchestra speaks as expressively as it does anywhere in Berlioz or Liszt and in Verdi's own operas, is a work of purest sentiment, most heartfelt truth, and highest mastery—a work of the greatest humaneness, and therefore also Catholic.

Here too the Romantic era is superseded, in so far as it is a cleavage, a mask, a yearning for a better past. Nothing demonstrates that fact better than the criticism made by a Wagnerian, Hans von Bülow, who reported the first performance to Germany. In so doing he applied to Verdi such phrases as the "all-powerful demoralizer of Italian artistic taste" who with this Requiem "finds irksome to his ambition the last remnants of Rossini's immortality and presumably hopes to remove them." Von Bülow spoke of the work as Verdi's "latest opera in ecclesiastical garb," and of the closing fugue as a composition "of such industrious work, despite its many schoolboyish, absurd, and ugly features, that many German musicians will experience a great surprise on hearing it." Some twenty years later this same Hans von Bülow wrote to Verdi in deep contrition for this "journalistic bestiality" (*bestialità giornalistica*), of which he had repented a hundred times—as having been committed in a state of madness or mental confusion, of blind fanaticism, of "super-Wagnerian Mohammedanism." What Verdi had praised in the *Promessi Sposi*—that it was a book as true as truth itself—applies also to his own Requiem. His theme is Death: Death as an object of terror, depicted in all its wildness in the *Dies Irae,* Death as a kind emancipator, as a friend and comforter, as in other days it had been represented in Schubert's immortal song and immortal string quartet. There is no Wagnerian "redemption," no Lisztian ecstasy. All heterogeneous stylistic elements—liturgical murmurs, theatrical crescendos, fugal constructions (there is a sort of double fugue in the Sanctus), concertante lyricism—are fused and mastered.

Once again, at the very end of his life, Verdi made some contributions to the church repertoire, in which his rather exact knowledge of the old style and his indifference to it are shown anew, his *Quattro Pezzi Sacri,* written during the years up to 1897. Two of these pieces, an *Ave Maria* and the *Laudi alla Vergine Maria* (to a text by Dante), although both *a cappella,* are as unlike one another as possible. The first is written on a "scala enigmatica," a study in the style of the experiments of Willaert and Rore, with whom Verdi certainly was not familiar. The second is a song withdrawn from this world, for four-voiced women's choir. The *Stabat*

Mater and the *Te Deum* for choir and orchestra belong, in their tenderness, power, brevity, and mastery, to a style in which the personal, the objective, the confessional, and the churchly become one. If church music was ever to be renewed with a new spirit, it was on these compositions of an unorthodox great master that it would have to build.

CHAPTER XIII

Oratorio

MENDELSSOHN AND SCHUMANN

THE Romantic was a movement towards Catholicism; accordingly, liturgical texts exerted a mysterious fascination even upon non-Catholic composers. Robert Schumann did not make a single contribution to Protestant church music, either Psalm or motet; but towards the end of his life, in the Rhenish Catholic city of Düsseldorf, he wrote a Mass in C minor (Op. 147) and a Requiem in D-flat major (Op. 148), both in 1852. The first was performed under his direction, of course not in church but in the concert hall. The second, however, he never heard performed. These are two works of Catholic tendency, rather than purely artistic compositions in the tradition of Beethoven's D-major Mass and Mozart's Requiem. In the Mass, Schumann even paid his respects to the worship of the Virgin Mary which the Romantic era fostered, in that he chose the *"Tota pulchra est"* as the text for the Offertory; moreover, into the Benedictus he wove the words of *"O salutaris hostia."* We are not inquiring here into the value of this work—one finds in the literature on the subject that whatever judgments it has received have been merely patronizing—but into its style. In it we find the Romantic mingling of artistic freedom, inwardness, and archaism—manifested more in Schumann's use of the ancient meters than in the Gregorian turns of phrase.

In general, however, non-Catholic musicians felt deeply how little support their churches gave them in the way of fixed liturgy. They accordingly fled into the realm of oratorio, for which Handel had given them the great model—or, rather, the great models.

Mendelssohn, however, in his first oratorio (1836), *St. Paul,* exhibited the influence of Handel commingled with that of Bach—or, more precisely, with Bach's *St. Matthew* Passion. Significantly enough, Haydn's two late works with their new feeling for nature and their childlike piety had scarcely any part in it. Thus, after a detailed consultation by the composer with theological friends, there came into being this composition, built upon the Biblical text pure and simple. It is a work for the concert hall; yet in it, beginning with the overture, the chorale plays a decisive role—the chorale without congregation. Moreover, it is a work with fanatic *turbae,* the "crowds," as in the Passions—particularly in the first part, which deals with the story of the sufferings of the first martyr, St. Stephen. Finally, it is a work with recitatives, *ariosi,* cavatinas, chorale paraphrases, free and strict choral numbers—full of melodic, choral, and orchestral beauties in a framework that is stylistically impossible—a typically Romantic production.

Ten years later Mendelssohn completed his second great oratorio, *Elijah.* Again he adhered to the Biblical text, but this time with an Old Testament hero and with gentle suggestions of the chorale element. Here he came nearer to the Handel of *Deborah* than to the Bach of the Passions. One principal scene, for example, the competition of the Hebrew prophets with the priests of Baal, is faithfully imitated from a scene of Handel's. This is a work of the greatest stylistic purity, of the highest nobility, of the loftiest spirituality, this time more Classicistic than Romantic. It served as a model for the English oratorio of the 19th century.

Mendelssohn's oratorios reached England, according to Sir George Grove, "not as strangers, but as the younger brothers of the *Messiah* and *Judas Maccabaeus* . . . we are proud of them, as having been produced or very early performed in England; they appealed to our national love for the Bible, and there is no doubt that to them is largely owing the position next to Handel which Mendelssohn occupies in England." [30] The British love of tradition is responsible for the fact that this model maintained its validity too long, and that the revolutionary tide of the Romantic era did not make itself felt in this field in England (and in several other places) until a time that is beyond the limits of our present inquiry. An unimpeachable British witness, Percy A. Scholes,[31] has testified that "the large majority of the British oratorios of the later eighteenth and the nineteenth centuries were mere academic exercises, or popular examples of what may (now that the composers are dead) be called choir-fodder. They served their day and generation and then fell on sleep—like an almost equal proportion of Italian and German operas or German symphonies of the same period (or of any period)." Or, we might close the matter with the

[30] *A Dictionary of Music and Musicians,* 1879.
[31] *The Oxford Companion to Music,* 3rd ed., p. 653.

remark of another competent witness, Ethel Smyth,[32] "Year in year out, composers of the Inner Circle, generally University men attached to our musical institutions, produced one choral work after another—not infrequently deadly dull affairs—which, helped by the impetus of official approval, automatically went the rounds of our Festivals and Choral Societies, having paid the publisher's expenses and brought in something for the composers before they disappeared for ever."

There is another work of Mendelssohn's in the oratorio field that is free of all errors, even in its relation to Handel or Bach—free also of the danger of being poorly imitated. It is a little "secular oratorio," called by him a "ballade," *The First Walpurgis-Night* (Op. 60). Composed in 1831–32, principally in Italy, it was completed in Paris, and reworked very considerably ten years later.

The poem is by Goethe and was presented to Zelter, who of course did not know what to do with it. It is a product of the smouldering hate that Goethe harbored against the "Cross." Goethe expressed himself as officiously as possible on the underlying ideas in a letter to Mendelssohn written on September 9, 1831: "This poem is intended in a spirit of high symbolism. For in world history there must be constant recurrence of the situation in which something old, well-founded, well-proved, and comforting, faced by innovations, will be crowded, pushed back, displaced, and if not destroyed at least penned up in the closest quarters. The middle period, in which hate still can—and quite possibly may—react, is here represented with sufficient exactness; and a joyful, undisturbed enthusiasm blazes up once again, brilliant and clear." No one will possibly conclude from these words that this "old and well-founded" thing is Northern heathenism, and that one of the "innovations that face it" is rising Christianity. Goethe's sympathy rests entirely on the side of the heathen.

How Mendelssohn composed his setting for chorus, solo voices, and full orchestra may be seen from his own description (February 22, 1831): "Since being in Vienna, I have half written the music for Goethe's *First Walpurgis-Night,* but am not in the mood to score it. The composition has now taken form: it has become a large cantata with full orchestra, and can make quite a comical impression; for in the beginning there are spring-songs and that sort of thing in abundance; then, when the watchmen with their pitchforks and prongs and brooms make a racket, the witches' hubbub is added thereto, and you know that I have a special weakness for that; then appear the Druids with their sacrifice, in C major,

[32] *As Time Went On* (London, 1936), p. 172.

with kettle-drums; then the watchmen again, who are afraid, and there I shall bring in a tripping, unearthly chorus; and finally, at the end, the full song of sacrifice—do you not think that this could become a new sort of cantata?"

It did indeed become "a new sort of cantata," so far as Mendelssohn's complete vocal works are concerned—something between the oratorios and Psalms, occupying approximately the same position as the *Hebrides* Overture or the Violin Concerto does among his instrumental works. Robert Schumann, however, as a composer of oratorios, belongs not on the side of *St. Paul* or *Elijah,* but upon that of this secular *Walpurgis-Night,* the first performance of which he heard on February 2, 1843, in Leipzig. The only difference is that Schumann, in accordance with his lyrically and sensuously inclined nature, could not think of such bits of heathen or Classical impudence; his imagination required a Romantic inspiration.

Between 1843 and 1851, at the same time that *Tannhäuser* and *Lohengrin* came into being, Schumann found this inspiration in three oratorios whose fundamental idea, "redemption," shows how deeply all the Romantics had it at heart. The first and last of these oratorios, *Paradise and the Peri* (Op. 50, 1843) and *The Pilgrimage of the Rose* (Op. 112, 1851), both suffer from the softness and sentimentality of the poetry, the first being taken from Thomas Moore's *Lalla Rookh* and the third being based on the verse of an obscure poet, the choice of which by a man of Schumann's poetic sensibilities is hard to understand. Wagner, a dramatic librettist of unerring instinct, at once perceived the underlying weakness in the latter work when he saw the text which had been sent to him. In a letter to Uhlig, May 31, 1852, he wrote: "Why does it not occur to anyone to lay hold of a piece of music like Schumann's by its very basis, that is, to show particularly the appalling wretchedness of the poetry?" But he was not justified in continuing: ". . . and now to ask who it would have to be that would be inspired by such a poor piece of work to write a great composition and what perchance such music would then have to be able to contain." For Schumann had succeeded in appending music in his best manner even to such texts.

Paradise and the Peri centers around the touching figure of an errant Peri, for whom the gates of Paradise reopen only when she is able to bring back home "the dearest gift of heaven." Two attempts fail, but the tears of a repentant sinner bring the wonder to pass. What was the advantage of such a text or subject? It was the limitless change of scenery, the direct appeal to the musical fancy, which Schumann followed out with very great boldness in this first experiment of his in the oratorio field. There is free alternation between recitative, solo numbers, and choral numbers; there are still "numbers," but they are intimately bound together by the leitmotif—yet there is freedom even in the employment of this leitmotif. There are scarcely any remains of that traditional choral style, with its fugues and double fugues; instead, there is a new, sensitive leading of the voices. Above all, there is in the orchestra an oriental shimmer, which in its tenderness and its magic goes even a step beyond Weber.

The Pilgrimage of the Rose, designated by Schumann as a "fairy tale," belongs—according to its basic idea—in the realm of the redemption-operas, like Marschner's *Hans Heiling* or Wagner's *Lohengrin,* in which an elemental being seeks to experience human happiness and sorrow. It its rather folklike, rather Teutonic, and represents a limited type of German musical Romanticism, approximately as does Lortzing's *Undine* in relation to Weber's *Freischütz.*

The "oratorio" which came between these two compositions of Schumann's was the *Scenes from Goethe's Faust* (1844-53). Like the *Peri,* it had no designation of the type to which it belongs. In it, however, Schumann was dealing with the words of one of the noblest poems in world literature. Significantly enough, he began with the third and last part, the "redemption," the "transfiguration" of Faust, to which even Goethe had already found himself unable to give any form other than one tending towards Catholicism. Only later did Schumann add the first two sections, each consisting of three scenes, the first of which could be called "Gretchen," the second, "Faust's supreme moment and death." The overture, which was written last, represents Faust's first monologue. Schumann, moreover, had to entrust to the orchestra the subsequent garden scene or omit it entirely, for it unavoidably falls into the realm of the operatic. Otherwise, he chose only scenes that call for music and that are transfigured by it. Especially in Part III, the unrepresentable has become, as it were, representable, the supersensible, palpable to sense. To be sure, power is lacking in the final chorus ("with the sacrifice of my ultimate powers," Schumann wrote in his journal); and this tendency to render the imperceptible perceptible bears the stamp of Schumann rather than that of Goethe. Yet these scenes represent the most successful union of music with the poem which had already attracted Beethoven and had been an object of concern for every representative of the Romantic era in music.

When Schumann set for himself a problem whose solution was somewhat easy for his lyric nature, he succeeded in writing a complete master-piece: the *Requiem for Mignon* from Goethe's *Wilhelm Meister* (Op. 98b, 1849) for chorus, soli, and orchestra. Something similarly com-pelling, moreover, came into being when it was a matter of a congenial personality and a lesser kind of poetry than *Faust,* as in the music—over-ture, accompanied recitations, and choruses—to Byron's *Manfred* (Op. 115, 1848–51). Liszt helped to secure for the work its first *scenic* performance, in which—during the intermission—Wagner's *Faust* Overture was played. But Schumann's music is so inward and appeals so purely and strongly to the imagination that it may be counted as belonging to the genre of oratorio and as being the highest, the Romantic ultimate of a whole genre, which had begun so classically with Georg Benda's *Ariadne.*

ORATORIO: DEVELOPMENT OF A HYBRID FORM

From the beginning to the end of its history, oratorio exhibits a re-markable, iridescent appearance. Going back farther into the 16th cen-tury, we find that it had an older history even than opera, and therefore a more stubborn tradition. Its development had found a climax in Handel, and in the 19th century this model was again and again revived and emphasized. As in Handel, the material of the Romantic oratorio belongs half to the Biblical or religious sphere, half to the secular or historical. The only difference is that in Handel the secular is limited to the Classical or Ancient—Hercules, Semele, Alceste, "Alexander's Feast"—while in the Romantic oratorio it was enriched by the fantastic and the whole realm of the historical. From the end of the 17th century on, moreover, through the gradual elimination of the *testo* or narrator, oratorio had approached opera to such a degree as to be confused with it. Even with Handel, it is the degree to which the chorus is used that distinguished his works based on Classical subjects. *Arianna* and *Admeto* could also be recast into oratorios, *Theodora* or *Athalia* into operas; and *Acis and Galatea* was pos-sible in either of the two categories.

Oratorio is a hybrid form. One need only name the titles of the oratorios of Carl Loewe (whom we shall meet again in another connection) to see how very much the "profane," the historical, and the religious are mingled: on the one hand, there is the *Walpurgis-Night,* a ballade, *The Marriage of Thetis, The Seven Sleepers, John Huss, Gutenberg, Palestrina;* on the other, material from the Old and New Testament such as *The Brazen Serpent, The Apostles of Philippi, The Atonement of the New Testament,*

The Song of Solomon, The Healing of Those Born Blind, John the Baptist, and *The Resurrection of Lazarus.* Often the historical blends with the religious, as in the *Destruction of Jerusalem.* From the historical material it would have been possible, with somewhat stricter dramaturgic treatment, for operas to have been the result. The Romantic confusion in the form becomes still more strange when the development of instrumental music begins to add its influence. Berlioz's *Romeo and Juliet* is a hybrid work, between symphony and cantata; and *The Damnation of Faust* has been regarded entirely from the point of view of symphony, oratorio, or opera.

Yet even Romantic oratorio retained to a considerable extent its devotional or edifying character. This fact was due to the after-effects of Handel's oratorios, particularly the *Messiah,* and to the effects of two German oratorio-composers, Spohr and Mendelssohn, who were especially influential in Victorian England. One need only recall the success of *St. Paul* (Düsseldorf, Liverpool, 1836) or of *Elijah,* which had been written expressly for England (Birmingham, 1846). But Mendelssohn had predecessors and rivals in such successes in the persons of Spohr—*The Last Judgment* (Cassel, 1825, Norwich, 1830); *The Last Hours of the Saviour* (Norwich, 1842)—of Friedrich Schneider,—*Day of Judgment* (1819); *Deluge* (1823), and of Sigismund Neukomm—*David* (Birmingham, 1834). The series continues in an endless procession, up to Michele Costa's *Eli* (1855) and *Naaman* (1864), and Sullivan's *Prodigal Son* (1869) and *The Light of the World* (1873).

Even Berlioz seems to belong in this series, with his *Childhood of Christ,* in his *Sacred Trilogy,* Op. 25, completed and presented in 1854. But he belongs in it only ostensibly. The scorner of Bach and Handel, the non-historical and anti-historical composer, had here intended to mystify his public, particularly the critics (those "good policemen of French criticism," as he called them). He attributed the composition to an ostensibly forgotten composer, actually a fictitious one from the time of Louis XIV—*Mystère de Pierre Ducré, executé pour la première fois en 1679.* In so doing, Berlioz even set to work to write choruses in fugal form and pieces in supposedly archaic modes. Or, at least, he thought he was so doing when he left out the leading-tone in the F-sharp minor of the overture to the second, previously written portion of the work in order to achieve the "melancholy, somewhat simple mood of the old folk ballads."

As Berlioz not only hated everything historical but was completely ignorant of it, the work became not, as it were, a parody of a style, but

something infinitely original, personal, and modern. The only model that
Berlioz could perhaps have had in mind was the composer whom he
venerated, Le Sueur, with his pastoral oratorios *Ruth et Naëmi* (1810)
and *Ruth et Boas* (1811), and his operas, one of which even toys in a
very childlike way with ancient Greek melody. Despite the choirs of
angels, Berlioz's composition is of an enchantingly tender realism. Significantly enough, he omits the Christmas scene of the Nativity and
dispenses with mere theatrical naturalism, as in the characterization of
Herod. What was important for Berlioz is shown in the orchestral scenes
of the composition: the march by night which forms the background for a
dialogue between Roman soldiers, a "cabalistic suggestion of the sooth-
sayers" of grotesque mysteriousness, a pastorale for the idyll of the "Rest
on the Flight," and a "slow children's dance." Everything seems to be inspired more by the poetry of Italian primitive painting than by the creative fancy, a reflection of the religious aspect in the soul of an artist. The
mingling of operatic and dramatic elements with those from oratorio and
symphony is the same as in the *Damnation of Faust.*

Franz Liszt, too, entered the devotional field with his two oratorios.
Unlike Berlioz, he did not try to mystify the world, to put on a mask;
rather, he wrote partly from inner compulsion and partly under the influence of his passionately Roman Catholic friend, the Princess Carolyne
Sayn-Wittgenstein. As a "Parisian" composer, however, he also derives
from Berlioz. In both works, the *Legend of St. Elizabeth,* written between 1857 and 1862, as well as in *Christus* (completed in 1866), an important and almost independent role is played not only by the orchestra
but also by instrumental music as such.

In the earlier work there is a military and a dead march, and a thunderstorm—in fact, the option is even given of closing the entire work with a
purely symphonic apotheosis. This "Elizabeth Legend" is a typically
Romantic composition in the material, which is closely related to that of
Weber's *Euryanthe* or Schumann's *Genoveva*—the Middle Ages, the
Crusades, innocence persecuted (only this time not by a demoniac lover,
but a demoniacally overbearing mother-in-law), and pious ending. It is
also typically Romantic in the vacillation between the oratorical and the
dramatic; for with suitable abbreviation of the orchestral and choral portions this "St. Elizabeth" can be presented on the stage, and since 1881
it has frequently been given stage performance. In this vacillation between
the concert podium and the stage, incidentally, "St. Elizabeth" found successors in the "Sacred Operas" of Anton Rubinstein: *Paradise Lost,* after

Milton, Op. 54; *The Tower of Babel,* Op. 80, etc. It is evident that the genre had become unsure and hybrid by the elimination of the narrator. In "St. Elizabeth" the elements of piety and operatic theatricality are combined, even in the musical delineation of the principal figure, who is characterized as a saint by a motif that is liturgical and as a Hungarian princess by one that is *all'ongarese.* But in general there is a preponderance of the pious, transfigured, ecstatic.

Quite purely Catholic-Romantic, i.e., Catholicized, is Liszt's *Christus.* It sprang from a liturgically conceived seed, namely from the composition based on the Beatitudes, written as a kind of Gradual, in archaically antiphonal form (solo and chorus). This seed developed into a tripartite oratorio in imaginary scenes: Christmas, Post-Epiphany, and Passion and Resurrection. Here the orchestral element plays so mighty a role that often, as in the scene on the Mount of Olives (*"Tristis est anima mea"*), the word seems to have only the function of releasing a symphonically conceived piece of psychological depiction. On the other hand, Liszt has made greater use than ever of somewhat archaic *a cappella* effects. Nothing is better fitted to give an idea of Romantic or neo-Romantic devotional music than a comparison of this work, greatly conceived and carried out with the most careful consideration and the finest taste, with George Frideric Handel's *Messiah,* which, of course, centers around the same figure and is also cast in the form of a triptych. With Handel there is the very deep inwardness of a free, pious man, the tragic and heroic mood; with Liszt, who emphasizes the scene of the founding of the church (*"Tu es Petrus"*) and the Miracle (the Storm at Sea), there is the ecstasy of mannered Catholicism, together with its converse, the extreme, Franciscan simplicity. One might also speak of the contrast between the Classical as masculine and the Romantic as feminine, between health and sickness.

Both in its material and in its musical style, oratorio operates within the area that Liszt, Berlioz, Mendelssohn, and Schumann set off for it. A mere enumeration of the titles is all that is necessary to see on which side César Franck belongs, at least with regard to the material he used. He stood with Berlioz and Liszt, in *Ruth, a Biblical Eclogue* (1843–46), *The Tower of Babel, a Little Oratorio* (1865), *Redemption, a Symphonic Poem* (1871–72), *The Beatitudes* (completed in 1879), and *Rebecca, a Biblical Scene* (1881)—oratorio of pastoral character and Catholic tendencies, with all the harmonic and orchestral mixtures of color characteristic of the Romantic era. Even Gounod, despite several secular cantatas with orchestra, inclines to this side, in *Peter the Hermit* (1853), *The Angel and Tobias* (1854), *The Annunciation* and *The Nativity* (1871–72), *Redemption* (1882), and *Death and Life* (1885). The German musicians were in part secularly minded, in part also "Lisztians": Max Bruch began with a ballad *Fair Ellen* (1866) and continued with *Odysseus* (1871–72); Felix Dräseke began with the composition of the Easter scene from Goethe's *Faust;* Joseph Joachim Raff wrote a *"concertante"* for chorus, piano, and orchestra, *The Times of the Day,* in the style of Handel or Haydn, but ended with a spacious work in that of Berlioz and Liszt, *The End of the World—Judgment—New World* (1879–80), also performed at Leeds in 1883). A work like *Odysseus* shows that the Romantic movement was again returning to antiquity. This return, however, was no longer inspired by the reverential Classicism of the 18th century, but rather by the indiscriminate and instinctless "learnedness" of the 19th, which rummaged through all the bodies of subject matter of world literature for stimulation.

BRAHMS

As a German and non-Catholic musician, Brahms was not able or willing to undertake a Mass or *Te Deum;* so he composed *A German Requiem* (Op. 45, 1866, with a fifth movement added in 1868) and his *Song of Triumph* (Op. 55, 1871). The *Song of Triumph,* the text after the 19th chapter of Revelation, for eight-voiced chorus and orchestra, was, like all patriotic works, only "born for the moment." Richard Wagner was, at least this time, not entirely wrong when he made fun of the composer for having put on Handel's "Hallelujah wig." But the fact that a great and personal work of art could arise even from the *relation* to Bach and Handel is shown by the *German Requiem,* with which Brahms translated into actuality an idea of Schumann's—the scheme for the composition of such a work is found in Schumann's "project-book." To be sure, the "relation" of Brahms to the old, great masters—also to some earlier than Bach and Handel—is a trait of character in this work more striking to us today, and more painful, than it was to his contemporaries. On the other side of the balance, however, this Requiem is one of the greatest and most personal musical discussions with death, all the more personal and great as Brahms did not make use of the reliance on the liturgical or the Gregorian which was permitted Catholic musicians.

Carrying on from Mendelssohn's *First Walpurgis-Night* and from Schumann, Brahms wrote a few smaller choral works: one based on

Goethe's *Rinaldo* (which, in all reverence, one must admit is textually poor), for tenor, men's chorus, and orchestra, Op. 50; the Rhapsody from Goethe's *Harz Journey,* for alto, men's chorus, and orchestra, Op. 53; the *Naenie,* after Schiller, Op. 82, also a kind of Classicistic requiem; the *Song of the Parcae* from Goethe's *Iphigenia,* Op. 89; and the earliest of these pieces (1871), and the purest and most beautiful, the *Song of Fate,* to a brief, wonderful group of verses by Friedrich Hölderlin. The last named is Classicistic, but it becomes Romantic through the fact that in it the symphony orchestra has the last word and that pure, "absolute" music is able to express the idea where the word fails.

CHAPTER XIV

Song

LIMITATIONS IN ITALY AND FRANCE

IN ROMANTIC song the fusion of music and poetry was *legitimate*—a fusion which had remained of such questionable value and so problematical in the Romantic symphony. Song is no hybrid type like oratorio; it does not have to come to terms with so many externals and traditional paraphernalia as opera. One can, accordingly, speak with justification of song as that artistic type in which the Romantic era expressed itself most purely and freely.

The fact that the work of the Romantic Classic, Franz Schubert, found its center in song suggests that the history of Romantic song is essentially that of its manifestation in Germany. In Italy, everything in the nature of song was too closely linked, on the one side, with folk song and, on the other, with opera, which absorbed the entire interest of the cultivated public. There were *canzonette,* which occasionally even found their way into opera, as for instance the famous one of the Duke in Act III of Verdi's *Rigoletto*. From opera, conversely, melodic material found its way back into folk song. The compositions of a lyric nature written by Rossini, for example, are "ariettas," "cavatinas," "melodies," and—in his French period —"nocturnes" or "romances." His most famous contribution to vocal chamber music, the *Soirées Musicales,* a collection of eight ariettas and four duets with piano accompaniment written about 1835, bears after the title the clear indication "expressly composed for the study of Italian song." Thus he was writing either idealized folk song like the famous "Tarantella" or operatic composition like the duet "I marinari," which was orchestrated by Wagner during his Riga period, quite in the appropriate style. Towards the end of his life, Rossini composed a sonnet "Il fanciullo smarrito" (1861) as a "melodia" for tenor and piano, "for the personal use of the poet," Antonio Castellani. But this was an exception.

The situation, moreover, was no different with Rossini's contemporaries and successors—Bellini, Donizetti, Verdi. In poetry, Italy was experiencing a literary revival, from the work of Pindemonte, Foscolo, Manzoni, and—greatest of all—Giacomo Leopardi, on to Carducci, whose *Odi Barbare* (1877) with their Classical meters might perhaps have been able to attract an Italian Schumann or Brahms. But this new lyric poetry found no musical transfiguration. It took a Hugo Wolf to show what a treasure of burning passion, heavenly simplicity, and mordant humor lay hidden in Italian folk song. There were no Italian song-composers.

There were also no great French song-composers in the early part of the Romantic era. There were many French musicians who incidentally composed songs, or rather "chansons" or "romances"; but there was none in the sense of Schumann, Franz, or Hugo Wolf. As the first "Romantic" song-composer in Paris we might take Hippolyte Monpou (1804–1841). Fétis, as it happens, wrote thus of this pupil of his in the curious article that he devoted to him in the *Biographie Universelle:* [33] "Despite the Classical studies in which he had been engaged throughout his youth, he suddenly conceived a passion for Romanticism, which was at that time the rage; and he enrolled himself among the innovators who dreamed of transforming art." But Monpou's Romanticism consisted solely in the fact that he set to music poems by Musset and Victor Hugo and that he was not bothered by blunders, small or great, in the harmony; in general, even his songs are mere chansons of a sentimental or coquettish nature. A genuine song-composer did not appear in France during the first half of the century.

Berlioz, of course, also wrote lieder and various other kinds of songs, but only as somewhat miscellaneous minor works alongside his symphonies, operas, and dramatic church compositions, even though his first published compositions (1826–27) were a few romances—which he later had his publishers recall and destroy. A little later he came upon Gérard de Nerval's translation (1828) of Goethe's *Faust,* and in the course of his *Eight Scenes* he set the lyrics to music. Among these is Mephisto's demoniac serenade, to the accompaniment of a gigantic guitar, and "Gretchen at the Spinning-Wheel," which unconsciously enters into competition with Schubert's early masterpiece. But, in general, the work turned out half dramatic, half like a romance.

The same thing, moreover, applies to his Op. 2. Like Rossini's *Soirées,*

[33] Vol. VI, p. 175.

it is a collection of vocal compositions for one or more voices with piano on poems from Thomas Moore's *Irish Melodies,* entitled *Neuf Mélodies,* five of which are solos. In contrast to Schubert's songs, which are always coarsened and made less stimulating to the listener's imagination by an attempt to orchestrate the accompaniment, these vocal compositions demand orchestral interpretation—which Berlioz himself provided in one instance (No. 4, "La belle voyageuse").

Significantly enough, moreover, he did the same thing for all six vocal compositions in his outstanding collection *Les Nuits d'Eté,* Op. 7 (composed in 1834, orchestrated in 1841). These six songs are all settings of poems from the *Poésies* of Théophile Gautier, who happened to be himself a master of the descriptive, a Berlioz of poetry. And, as a matter of fact, a unity of the poetical and the musical was here achieved, as personal as seems to have been achieved later only in the Wesendonck-Wagner *Five Poems.* These songs of Berlioz's exhibit compelling grace, as for example in the "villanelle" (No. 1, *"Quand viendra la saison nouvelle"*), and compelling fire, as for example in "Absence" (No. 4, *"Reviens, reviens"*), in that key of heightened feeling—not to mention the heightened key-signature—F-sharp major.

In the three groups of songs (Opp. 12, 13, and 19) in which Berlioz brought together most of his other works in this field, there is an especially significant preference for local color. This predilection is indeed significant both for the Romantic movement in general and for his personality in particular. In writing "The Young Breton Shepherd" (Op. 13, No. 4), Berlioz created a counterpart to Schubert's "Shepherd on the Cliff," which has a clarinet obbligato—only this time, in Berlioz, it was a horn obbligato that gave the simple scene the Romantic tinge of genuineness. "The Captive" (Op. 13, No. 4) is an "oriental song," for which Berlioz supplied an optional violoncello part; "Zaïde" (Op. 19, No. 1) takes us to Spain; the "Danish Hunter" (Op. 19, No. 6) takes us to the North. Above all, however, Berlioz is French: the most beautiful example, perhaps, is his *aubade, "Les champs,"* to a poem of Béranger's, Op. 19, No. 2, a serenade full of grace, wit, and fire. With his lyrical "miscellaneous minor works," Berlioz sowed the seeds for the entire musical lyricism of the 19th century in the French language—in its color, noble sentimentality, and refined sensuousness and grace. But the crop came up only after his death.

SCHUMANN, SUCCESSOR TO SCHUBERT

In Germany, alongside and after Schubert, the flood of song grew to boundless proportions; but the real successor to Schubert did not appear until Robert Schumann. He himself has given a humorous idea of this flood when once as critic, around 1840, he was "seized with the desire to praise something," and dug around in about fifty volumes of lieder for a long time before he finally found three on which he could bestow at least the epithet "good." But even these three bear the names of composers now long forgotten: Wenzel Heinrich Veit, Xaver Esser, and Norbert Burg- müller. The many bearers of such forgotten names may now and then have succeeded in writing a good song—but that does not make them song- composers.

Even Mendelssohn would not have escaped this fate if his fame had been obliged to rest upon his composition of songs—about eighty—among which some, in actuality, were by his sister Fanny. Along with spring- songs and gondolier songs, he chose "Romantic" texts—by Heine, Eichen- dorff, Lenau, Immermann. But in general he treated them in the anti- quated manner of Zelter—too lyrically, too arioso, too much dependent on pretty melodies. When, in setting some texts by his great paternal protector Goethe, he came into competition with Schubert, as in "Suleika" (*"Was bedeutet die Bewegung"*), his work shows up quite miserably in compari- son with Schubert's. If he wished to write something in the folk vein, as he was very fond of doing, it no longer had the folklike exaggeration and masquerade of C. M. Weber, though it was imitation; nor did it have the magnificent insouciance of Schubert. But he would not have been Men- delssohn, the creator of the *Hebrides* Overture, of the Octet, of the Violin Concerto, of the *First Walpurgis-Night,* if he had not created—involun- tarily, as it were—a few highly original and striking pieces, such as the mysterious setting of Hölty's "Witches' Song" (Op. 8, No. 8), the setting of Immermann's "Death Song of the Boyards," which would not have been entirely unworthy of Glinka, the setting of Heine's "New Love" (Op. 19, No. 4), or the melancholy setting of Lenau's "Song of the Reeds" (Op. 71, No. 4).

These are, nevertheless, miscellaneous minor works, as with his opposite, Berlioz. With Schumann, however, song suddenly became the central point in the composer's creative activity—suddenly, but not unexpectedly. Previ- ously, Schumann had written only piano music and, being a genuine Ro- mantic, had thought instrumental music the only fitting means by which the inexpressible could be expressed, and the inmost secret of feeling could be penetrated. He had felt that the word, as something too rational, was a fetter, a limitation. But when with Op. 24, the Heine song-sequence, he began to write lieder, he was like a volcano in eruption. In the first—and, incidentally, the richest—year, 1840, he brought forth no less than 138 vocal compositions. From then on when he composed songs they were lieder of the purest Romantic character. He did not wish to pursue a rational inter- pretation of the word; rather, he wished "to liberate the word from the curse of reason and, by means of the unity of feeling between language and music, to fuse them into something like a universal art-work." [34]

In the matter of texts, Schumann began where Schubert had left off, with Heine. The great German poet who stands in the midst of Schubert's work, Goethe, contributed only a few passages from the *West-östlicher Divan* and—in Schumann's later, brooding years—the songs from *Wilhelm Meister*. There was a new generation of poets, filled with a somewhat more penetrating conception of the Romantic era, who kindled Schu- mann's ardor: Joseph von Eichendorff, with his original feeling for every- thing natural, full of the secrets of night; the Swabian Justinus Kerner, a mixture of simplicity and mysticism; the fine and sensitive Adalbert von Chamisso.

It was highly important for Schumann the song-composer that he al- ready had in his background twenty-three piano works—a world of in- strumental poetry and pianistic, virtuoso perfection and originality. From the beginning on, the piano, the "accompaniment," had to play a different role in his songs than it had done in Schubert's. In Schubert, an equilibrium prevails; in every gentle fluctuation of the balance, the word always leads, the piano subordinates itself. In Schumann, from the very beginning, the piano plays a new role: it is more refined in sonority, more cunning in technique, although it seems to be simple; to it falls the task of emphasizing "the finer traits of the poem," of creating transitions in the song-cycles, of rounding out a group of songs, of supplying a commentary in the prelude and, particularly, the postlude, of giving final expression to the surplus feeling—in short, as Schumann himself has expressed it, of contributing to a "more highly artistic and more profound kind of song."

Schumann loved cycles. Often—as in the Heine song-sequence, Op. 24 —the connection is as little manifest as in the *Carnaval* or the *Kreisleriana* piano cycles; nevertheless, it is perceptible in the relation between the keys and in the contrasts. Contrast often permits Schumann to achieve epigram-

[34] H. Schultz, *Johann Vesque von Püttlingen* (Regensburg, 1930), p. 256.

matic brevity, which is at once extreme tension and fulfillment. Schumann set to music one of Heine's ironic quatrains (*"Anfangs wollt' ich fast verzagen,"* Op. 24, No. 8), with prelude and repetition of the emphatic question at the end, in eleven measures; and it requires no indication of the manner of delivery, so perfect is the musical investiture of the word. The next cycle, *Myrthen,* Op. 25, is marked by a "dedication" and an epilogue (*"Zum Schluss"*) as a gift for his "beloved bride" Clara Wieck. This cycle contains no less than twenty-six numbers, by various poets—Goethe, Rückert, Byron, Moore, Heine, Burns, and Mosen. It is kaleidoscopic and yet unified, forming a compendium of Schumann's complete lyrical expression, with the nocturnally tender eroticism of the *"Nussbaum,"* the mysterious exuberance of the *"Lotosblume,"* the high spirits of the second song out of the *Schenkenbuch,* the intimacy of the Suleika song from the *West-östlicher Divan* of Goethe, or the folk quality of the Highland songs of Burns.

In these songs one sees with particular clarity how greatly the Romantic era had intensified the feeling for everything national. Haydn and Beethoven had also arranged Scottish songs, but in the "Classical" sense: the original melodies were somewhat "leveled off." On the other hand, Schumann's freely devised songs are "more Scottish" than the originals. Schubert came out from time to time in Hungarian costume, for instance in *"Mut"* from the *Winterreise.* Schumann changed costume, with still greater delight; after having come out in "German" dress in the five vocal works, Op. 27, even in the sensitive lines of the closing piece, he showed his love for masquerade in his three songs, Op. 30: in the youthful Romanticism of the "Boy with the Magic Horn," the troubadour-like coloring of the "Page," and the high-spirited bolero of the "Hidalgo"—a piece that the composer of *Carmen* might have envied.

Three ballads (Op. 31) follow, to texts by Chamisso, among which is the *"Kartenlegerin,"* marked with a naturalism that anticipates by several decades comparable pieces of Musorgsky. This goes to show that the Romantic movement could on occasion make an about face; for Chamisso's *"Kartenlegerin"* is a translation from Béranger, and Béranger was indeed the anti-Romantic par excellence, full of disrespect for everything that had "come into being historically," such as the nobility and the priesthood, never inclined to flee into a corner far from the world, a lover of clarity, sobriety, and earthiness. It is characteristic that for Schumann, the apparently dreamy composer, even this opposite was not excluded.

Again and again, until creative exhaustion made its appearance, he succeeded in producing solitary pieces of this sort. Most of these pieces, to be sure, are of overpoweringly Romantic fullness and beauty, especially when Schumann came upon a poet possessed of spiritual kinship with him, like Justinus Kerner, in Op. 35, where are found the enchanting *"Mondnacht"* and the mysterious *"Zwielicht."* Shortly thereafter, in his *"Frauenliebe und Leben,"* Op. 42, he recalled the two Schubert "dramas in pictures," the *Müllerlieder* and the *Winterreise.* But we find even greater delight in his songs when he relaxes the novelistic bond of connection, as in the *Dichterliebe,* from Heine's *Buch der Lieder,* Op. 48, in which the composer exceeds the whole gamut of emotion heretofore exhibited in his lyrics, from pathos, from intimacy, to irony and to grim humor.

With the years—beginning as early as 1840—his exclusiveness changed: he wished to descend to the level of the people. He composed an entire album of songs for the young (Op. 79), without at times being able to prevent its simplicity from becoming highest refinement, as for example in Mörike's *"Er ist's"* (No. 23, *"Frühling lässt sein blaues Band"*). In setting this text even Hugo Wolf can hardly be said to have excelled him. A folk quality became the hallmark also of Schumann's later ballads and romances. Nothing is more significant of this tendency than his "Two Grenadiers" (Op. 49), the text of which, in a French translation, was also set to music about the same time by Wagner. Out of Heine's ballad Wagner made a great, operatic scene, with recitatives and orchestral tremolos, without any regard for the strophic form of the poem; and he placed the melody of the *Marseillaise,* which is a kind of apotheosis and climax of the song, in the *accompaniment.* With Schumann, it is presented by the voice; everything is simple, compelling, completely aware of the limits of the ballad.

Later, in the years of his failing powers, his simplicity became more recherché, with a corresponding loss of the sureness of his literary instinct; and, on the other hand, he fell into a manner, that telltale sign of weakness —into the brooding and the psychologistic, as in the songs and other vocal works from Goethe's *Wilhelm Meister* (Op. 98a), or in some of his ballads where he made so much of the description and yet neither achieved complete pictorial vividness nor gave the whole picture by suggestion— as he had so often succeeded in doing before.

LOEWE, FRANZ, BRAHMS

Besides Schubert and Schumann, there was a musician who cultivated ballads and legends as a specialty, Carl Loewe (1796–1869). From his dates it will be seen that he was about a year older than Schubert, and outlived the younger Schumann by fourteen years. He came from the Thuringian area, the neighborhood where Bach had been cantor and teacher. As a young man he enjoyed the patronage of the merry king of Westphalia and, at twenty-five, became a cantor in Stettin, remaining there until 1866. Along with this activity, he traveled as an interpreter of his own songs and as something of a wandering minstrel in German lands— experiences of which he himself has given an account in an attractive autobiography.

In his songs and other vocal works as well, there prevails a division between genius and Philistinism. Among his most magnificent compositions are "Edward" and the "Erlking," which he set to music at approximately the same time as Schubert (written in 1818, published in 1824 as Op. 1) but in such a completely different way that there is hardly any comparison between them. Loewe never forgot that a ballad is strophic; and strophic it must remain in its musical garb. He never forgot that it had its roots in folk soil and its ultimate source in the mysterious, the fantastic, the uncontrollable, in the dark regions unillumined by the clear light of intellect. This is indeed a realm for Romantic music. And, in genuine Romantic style, he had at once a simple and refined means of linking a folk quality with modern musicianship by varying the melodic incidence of the strophe in the voice part and accompaniment while preserving unity between the most extreme opposites. A typical example is his setting of Goethe's *"Hochzeitslied"* (Op. 20, No. 1, 1832), in which every detail of the situation, the entire merry and delicate nocturnal apparition, is presented with complete and highly refined effectiveness, and yet in the simplest, most well-rounded frame. Another example is "Prinz Eugen," written later, in which, after a few strophic concealments, the old, original melody at last breaks out victoriously—just as, to cite a contrasting orchestral composition, in Vincent d'Indy's symphonic variations *Istar*.

In hundreds of pieces written between 1818 and 1868, Loewe cultivated the whole field of the romance, the ballad, and the legend, Hebraic, French, Spanish, oriental, but above all the Northern in all its varieties, from Scottish to Polish and Lettish—often with very great effectiveness and not seldom with the most easy-going vulgarity. But Loewe possessed one distinctive feature which is entirely lacking in Schubert's lyric production and which is rare in the Romantic movement as a whole—humor. Some of his pieces based on poems by Rückert ("Hinkende Jamben") or Kopisch do not find their counterparts again until the work of Hugo Wolf, who within the field of song commanded the entire gamut of lyricism.

Between Schubert and Mendelssohn, Loewe and Schumann, moved the procession of musicians who contributed to Romantic song-composition. There are very many of these figures the individuals among whom can scarcely be sketched here but would form the subject of a special history of song. How powerfully the constellation of these four stars, particularly the two most brilliant ones, influenced all their contemporaries and successors may be seen from the work of a gifted amateur, Johann Vesque von Püttlingen (1803–1883). He was a diplomat in the Austrian civil service, and published under the pseudonym J. Hoven some three hundred songs. Although older than Schumann, he was primarily influenced by him. His preference among poets likewise was Heine, whose *Heimkehr* he, along with others, set completely to music (1851) in a cycle of no less than eighty-eight pieces, in all shadings of the sentimental, the pathetic, the ironical, and in the iridescent mingling of all these nuances, in the sudden change of the tragic into parody, in cold and daring wit.

Another follower of Schumann was Robert Franz (1815–1892), a pure specialist in song—a "Schumannite," although along with the patronage of Schumann he also enjoyed that of Liszt. He was a "specialist" since, after 1843, except for a few choral compositions, he worked entirely in the narrow field of song lyricism. For him it was a narrow field indeed, for among his 350 vocal compositions there is scarcely one that departs from the idea of the strophic song, the folk song, even to a slight extent. There is nothing balladesque about them, no bold exposition of feeling. There is only pure intimacy and a minimum of concentration, which his enthusiasm for the most concentrated of all musicians, the polyphonist Bach, gave him some means of achieving. These are Romantic miniatures. Many, unfortunately, possess that bourgeois "thoughtfulness" which is the reverse side of the Romantic reveling in feeling, and for which precedent is to be found even in Schumann. Characteristic, too, is Franz's predilection for national and regional coloring—Bohemian, Hungarian, Scottish, and above all "German."

Robert Franz rejected the lyrical compositions of his younger and greater contemporary, Johannes Brahms, as being "too erotic." Actually, however, they are a rich fulfillment of all that Franz himself had been striving to attain. From Opus 3 right on to the last of his numbered works, Brahms expressed himself in song in a more or less interrupted stream, often quite sporadically; and there is no division or subdivision of lyricism that he was unwilling to cultivate. In the central position—as has been emphasized in the first part of this book—stands folk song, on which Brahms bestowed a truly mystical veneration, and to which he often brought tribute even in the archaic formulae of the 16th century. In Brahms there are even more varieties or dialects of the folklike than in Franz—Hungarian, Bohemian, Low German, Wendish.

Where he can cling to the strophic form, he does so; his song is always as strictly formed as his basses. But behind the mastery, the reserve, there stands the Romantic exuberance, which is most clearly attested in the only cycle that he composed, the Magelone Romance, Op. 33, of 1861–62. These are songs which Ludwig Tieck interspersed in a retelling of a medieval tale in that false and arty "Old German style" in which the early Romantics loved to behold the chivalric age. Brahms suffused these verses with a flood of passionate music, just as, later, he almost always utilized poetry in an autocratic manner and never placed himself in its service. A mediocre, though also formally skillful poetaster of his day, Friedrich Daumer, was his favorite as a text writer. In this relation to the text, Brahms rather reverts to a state of things that prevailed before Schubert, back with Mozart, Haydn, or still earlier masters. Also in achieving extreme concentration, as in his balladesque vocal works or in a strophe as brief as that in Uhland's "Schmied," he always preserved the preponderance of the music, the rounding-off of the melody, the fullness of the harmony—in other words, he placed little stress on pictorial or descriptive details. In the course of years, naturally, the instances increased in which he renounced more and more what one might call the decorative-Romantic and became more and more inward. A few examples might be such pieces as his setting of Heine's "Der Tod das ist die kühle Nacht" (Op. 96, No. 1), of Allmers's "Feldeinsamkeit" (Op. 86), of Lingg's "Immer leiser wird mein Schlummer" (Op. 105), or of Liliencron's "Auf dem Kirchhof" (Op. 105). In the end, the last trace of the Romantic mask fell away from him, and he wrote the "Vier ernste Gesänge" upon Biblical texts, an echo of 17th-century monody, and yet most highly personal, one of the great evidences of his resignation and his confidence—and therein, perhaps, once again Romantic.

We need scarcely speak of Schumann's many German successors, for example the pleasant, sensitive, somewhat effeminate Adolf Jensen (1837–1879), nor of the many other musicians who gave a more individual note or variant to the tune called by Schumann. As a song-composer, Peter Cornelius (1824–1874)—strangely enough—belongs in the Schumann group. This artistic affiliation is rather strange because in the "political" grouping of the Romantic musicians he belonged entirely on the side of the neo-Germans, on the side of Liszt and Wagner, as one of their most faithful followers, although a very sharp-eared and critical one. He also had a formal talent of the first rank as a lyric poet; accordingly, he always bore in mind the limitations of singableness, and filled his music with the most sensitive harmonic detail and with highly delicate ideas. Even where he exceeded the strophic form, as for example in *"Zum Ossa sprach der Pelion"* (1862), perhaps his most precious bit of pure expression, he knew how to preserve strict form. Like Schumann, he loved cycles; and approximately in the manner of Schumann's *"Frauenliebe und Leben"* are his *"Brautlieder,"* his *"Rheinlieder,"* his *"Weihnachtslieder,"* his *"Vaterunser."* But his best effort was not bestowed upon the lied, but upon choral song, a genre for which an acquaintance with the old motet art of the 16th century had opened his eyes, as it had done for Brahms. Even this ostensibly "neo-German" musician had his relation to the past.

WAGNER AND LISZT

The genuine neo-Germans, Wagner and Liszt, took up a quite different position towards song than did the Schubertians and the Schumannites. Wagner, however, certainly cannot be called a lieder-composer. His whole interest was concentrated on the opera, and upon the symphony in so far as it could be placed in the service of opera. Nevertheless, his operas, up to *Die Meistersinger*, are full of lyricism; and one need only recall Kurvenal's song of defiance or the song of the young seaman—conceived quite in the spirit and style of the 13th century—to see that even the Wagnerian art-work that is most faithful to the composer's principles, *Tristan and Isolde*, does not disdain the lyric.

At various times in his life Wagner wrote songs: the earliest (1832) are seven compositions for Goethe's *Faust*, among which one is a melodrama. Musically they are apparently as insignificant as they can be; but as soon as they are thought of in their dramatic context, they achieve full life by virtue of their brevity and striking power, especially the serenade of Mephisto and the Rat Song from the scene in Auerbach's Cellar. Even then, as a nineteen-year-old boy, Wagner had an eye for the scenic; the seven pieces were intended for a performance in which Rosalie, Wagner's favorite sister, played the role of Gretchen. Later, in his Riga and Paris period, Wagner contributed a few songs to the magazine "Europe," which from time to time ran music supplements (including, among others, some songs by Meyerbeer). *"Der Tannenbaum"* (1839) is a fatalistic dialogue, composed by Wagner with half flowing, half halting accompaniment and with hesitating declamation in the "Livonian mode," E-flat minor; and there are three songs to French text—to *"Dors mon enfant,"* to Victor Hugo's *"Attente,"* and to Ronsard's *"Mignonne"*—with which Wagner, in his usual way, was himself very well satisfied. They belong entirely to the Berlioz type of vocal work and, like them, far exceeded the French taste of their day; accordingly, they remained of little influence. For us they are of interest because of their relations with later works—with the *Flying Dutchman,* with *Lohengrin,* and indeed even with *Tristan.*

The real contribution of Wagner to Romantic song is his *Five Poems for Female Voice,* published in 1862, the so-called Wesendonck songs. They had their origin in the winter and early part of 1857–58, upon the "green hill" by the Lake of Zürich, the scene of Wagner's deepest and most fruitful love experience with Mathilde Wesendonck, the poetess of the lyrics—an experience which brought to maturity *Tristan* as well as *Die Meistersinger.* In fact, two of the songs, *"Träume"* and *"Im Treibhaus,"* are indicated as being studies for *Tristan and Isolde.* But all five of them are intelligible only in their relation to this exceptional work, whose refined language of dissonance they speak (all perhaps except the first, which shows a relationship with *Das Rheingold*). The music says something other than the poetry, and says much more, showing deeper backgrounds and abysses. With all their freedom, these Five Poems have a definite and songlike form; with all their relation to a music drama they are genuine lyrics. Several years later when Wagner happened to see again the sketch for *"Träume,"* from which had come the climax of the second act of *Tristan,* he was partly right when he wrote to the poetess (September 28, 1861): "Heaven knows, the song pleases me more than the proud scene!"

Through the ballad "The Two Grenadiers," which we have already considered, the song-composer Wagner is related to the song-composer Franz Liszt. Liszt makes the composition scenelike or "dramatic," breaks up the strophic form, and gives the accompaniment more than its due. Therefore, Liszt, the admirer of Schubert's songs had nothing to hand over to Liszt the song-composer. If anywhere, he is in this field the opposite of Brahms. He is literary-minded, even if out of kindness he frequently set to music verse that was very poor and definitely of a drawing room variety. Folk song meant nothing to him: he was internationally minded, and wrote settings of French, Italian, and Hungarian material, although the basis for the greatest part of his output is to be credited to German poets, from Goethe, Heine, and Herwegh all the way down to Bodenstedt and Scheffel.

With Liszt, song lost its form. One need only compare his setting of Goethe's Night-Song (*"Über allen Gipfeln ist Ruh"*) with Schubert's to see how, with him, form runs off into sentimental arioso. One need only compare his setting of Heine's *"Loreley"* with any ballad by Schubert, Schumann, or Loewe, to see how everything resolves itself into details—often very clear details—and is held together only by a single melodic idea. This is a product of the Romantic, Parisian salon. The counterparts to such songs, among which perhaps the happiest are those based on some of the sonnets of Petrarch (first version, 1847), are short lieder or recitations of the utmost simplicity of the melodic line and accompaniment. In these, to be sure, harmonic refinement is almost never lacking; but the character of these pieces is not that second simplicity that is the result of final mastery: it arises rather from resignation.

TREND TOWARDS REACTION: HUGO WOLF AND OTHERS

The history of Romantic song would close with the Brahms-Liszt cleavage (Brahms as a composer born too late, Liszt as an experimenter) were it not that at the end of this history there appears the completely versatile master of song, Hugo Wolf (1860–1903). His life and work fall beyond the limits of this book. His earliest songs, nevertheless, were written five or six years before Wagner's death; and he had made a genuine Romantic beginning with a soaring and impassioned string quartet and a symphonic poem *Penthesilea,* in the Liszt tradition. In the disgusting Viennese party-squabble—Brahms on one side, Bruckner, Liszt, and Wagner on the other—Wolf was forced as a journalist over to the "neo-German" side. But it never occurred to him as a song-composer to sacrifice the unity of a song for the sake of a "program." He was the heir of an entire century, Schubert's and Schumann's as well as Wagner's.

He was the only one whose literary taste made no concessions. Usually in a moment of creation, he turned to an individual poet—to Mörike, to Eichendorff, to Goethe, to the Spanish and the Italian song books in

Heyse's and Geibel's masterful translation, to Gottfried Keller, to Michelangelo. Within such a frame, so remotely placed and yet so uniform, he created individual pieces of the deepest, most intense feeling, the finest grace, the most high-spirited humor. Each of his poems is a sort of "universal art-work" in miniature, in which the voice part and the accompaniment, in reciprocal relationship, vie with each other to extract from the text the most intimate, the final essence—the detail, and the painting, without disturbing the whole. His art includes all of Wagner's, and therefore is more complicated in harmony and coloring than that of all his predecessors—often too, particularly in the longer Goethe songs, more convulsive and tense in the vain attempt to surpass the divine sureness and simplicity of Schubert. He was at the end where Schubert was at the beginning; but Schubert had no need to be ashamed of this, his last successor.

In two of his later books or cycles, the Spanish and Italian song books, Hugo Wolf turned southward. Similarly, after beginning with the adolescent and immature string quartet, he finally arrived at the merry, profound grace of the Italian Serenade for string quartet or small string orchestra. Likewise, after beginning as one of Wagner's enthusiastic adherents, he did not pursue the pathway of so many other of the followers and write music dramas of "philosophical" or tragic pretensions; instead, he wrote a merry opera with a Spanish setting. The Romantic movement was getting tired of itself—tired, at all events, of the heavy passion, the "philosophical" depths, the sentimentality which it had been taking so seriously.

If a change of this sort took place in the mother-country of the Romantic movement, it is not strange that something like it should have happened among musically younger peoples who wished to free themselves from the German model. This did not occur in the North—not in Denmark (Gade, P. A. Heise, P. E. Lange-Müller), nor in Sweden (Emil Sjögren), nor in Norway (Halfdan Kjerulf), where the most productive representative of song, Edvard Grieg (1843–1907), a born lyricist, gave to the Romantic manner only a strong national coloring. Nor did it occur in Bohemia, where song played scarcely any part in the work of Bedřich Smetana (1824–1884). It is significant that his first, Schumannesque songs were composed to German texts, and that only in his last creative years, with the cycle of his *Evening Songs* (1879, texts by Hálek) did he make a great passionate and patriotic contribution to song literature.

The reaction away from Romanticism did occur, however, in Russia, where song was to some extent de-Romanticized. This process occurred not so much in the work of Rubinstein or Tchaikovsky, in which—especially the former—the lyrical vein was too abundant. Rather, it came to pass in the work of Michael I. Glinka (1804–1857), Alexander D. Dargomijsky (1813–1869), and Modest P. Musorgsky (1839–1881). It was not that even with them there was any lack of heartfelt Romanticism, which took on in their work an especially dark tinge: in Glinka's, in the cycle *Parting from Petersburg* (1839, text by Kukolnik), or in the balladesque *Review of Troops by Night;* in Musorgsky's, specifically in his later cycle *Sunless* (1874) or the *Songs and Dances of Death* (1875–77, to texts by his friend Count A. Golenischev-Kutusov). But already Glinka, the lover of the South, of the Italian and Spanish vocal style, was somewhat independent of the German ideal of song. And with Dargomijsky the complete change appeared, not only in the Romantic relationship between voice-part and accompaniment—as, with a more sparing indication of the accompaniment, the expression was concentrated in the carefully declaimed vocal line—but also in the content of the song, as alongside lyric and balladesque matters there also appeared humorous, realistic subjects. Together with Schumann and Liszt, Dargomijsky discovered the anti-Romantic poems of Béranger. Musorgsky, too, felt a quite distinct inclination towards realism, both serious and humorous. The masks fell away; the realities showed themselves: the "ideal personalities" of these songs were no longer the Romantic young man or the Romantic maiden, but the folk: the young wife who, while gathering mushrooms, suddenly has the thought of poisoning her old husband; the orphan; the beggar-child: the mother who, beside the cradle of her child, casts a glance at his joyless future; the village idiot who is in love with the "fair Savishna"; the bride who shrinks back from the ugliness of a goat, but without shrinking marries a goat of a man; the Cossack's wife who gets drunk with a young man. Humor alternates with grim satire. These are Russian figures whom Musorgsky depicted, and he represented them with Russian music—short-phrased melody, sharp rhythm, careless harmony. He loved the people, and especially children. His earliest cycle, *Children's Corner* (1868–72), in which a few "scenes from childhood" are depicted in complete truth to nature, without "transfiguration," is perhaps also his most original and most beautiful work. There is a new humaneness that has herewith grown out of the Romantic movement.

CHAPTER XV

Universalism within the National

I. Literature of the Piano

PIANO: THE REAL INSTRUMENT OF THE ROMANTIC ERA

IF WE consider what instruments the Romantic used in conveying their thoughts, we observe that there was an increasingly limited selection. The orchestra became richer and more many-tongued, but in concert and chamber music the number of instruments employed became smaller and smaller. In addition to concertos and sonatas for the piano and for the violin, Mozart wrote concertos for the flute, the oboe, the bassoon, the clarinet, the horn, the flute and harp, and the violin and viola. Among other instrumental works Haydn wrote a concerto for the trumpet. Weber wrote concertos and concert pieces for the clarinet, the bassoon, and the harmonichord. Even in Beethoven, with the Triple Concerto (Op. 56), the Quintet for Piano and Wind Instruments (Op. 16), the Horn Sonata (Op. 17), the Serenade (Op. 25), and the Septet (Op. 20), the connection with the 18th century was still constantly maintained: it is significant that these are all quite "happy," free-and-easy works. But with Schubert the limitation was already perceptible. The means that sufficed for him were the orchestra, the string ensemble, and the piano. Almost the sole exception is the serenade-like Octet, in imitation of Beethoven's Septet.

It would, of course, be wrong to conclude that the Romantics did not, on occasion, use almost any combination of instruments. Even Schumann wrote a Horn Sonata, and Brahms gave evidence of his increasingly intimate "relation" to the 18th century in his Piano Trio with Horn (Op. 40), in the late Clarinet Sonatas, and in the Clarinet Quintet. But it would not be wrong to conclude that for concert and chamber music purposes the Romantics made more and more exclusive use, on the one hand, of the pure strings and, on the other, of the piano. The virtuosi on the clarinet, bassoon, flute, horn, and the trumpet, did not die out as did those on the Jew's harp or the glass harmonica, but no further literature for them came into being except in their parts in the orchestra, and in the works of very lesser divinities among the pantheon of composers.

The violin and violoncello, however, at least in the concert field, played a more and more prominent role. Mozart wrote almost two dozen concertos for the piano, but only five authenticated ones for the violin. Beethoven, likewise, wrote only one violin concerto as against five for piano. With Mendelssohn, too, the piano predominated; but it might be said that he would have been unable to place a second work beside his Violin Concerto. With Schumann, however, the piano, the violoncello, and the violin are equally represented with one example each, although his Piano Concerto excels the others by far. With Brahms, two piano concertos, a Violin Concerto, and a Double Concerto for Violin and Violoncello stand side by side, as if of equal rank. The violoncello is the instrument used here, and no longer the viola as in Mozart's Double Concerto. It can be said that the Romantic era, as it were, first discovered the violoncello, just as the 18th century did the clarinet. In the second half of the earlier century, to be sure, there were Boccherini and Joseph Haydn. But with Schumann, Robert Volkmann in his Op. 33, and Saint-Saëns in his Op. 33 (not to mention Antonin Dvořák, who does not fall within the period here considered), the instrument acquired a character new, more passionate, opening up more obscure depths—in short, Romantic.

The real instrument of the Romantic era, however, is the piano. It is the Romantic instrument in an inclusive sense, both in its intimacy and in its brilliance. As to the violin, there may be some dispute over which was its great century—the 17th, the 18th, or the 19th. The 17th century, for its part, discovered the violin's potentialities and attained a peak of development in the trio- and solo-sonatas and the *concerti grossi* of Arcangelo Corelli. The 18th brought forth Tartini and Viotti. The 19th produced Paganini, who set an unsurpassable standard of virtuosity. But is it not significant that the model of Paganini had more influence on the piano than on the violin? There came into being for the piano a literature which, owing to the more mechanical character of the instrument, made much more exacting technical demands even upon the amateur than did that of the violin or violoncello. On the other hand, the piano became a universal instrument through the fact that it conquered for its own domain all composition—opera, symphony, song—through the arrangement, the "piano version." How poor, inadequate, sketchy such a version had been in the 18th century, and how limited—to the opera, the oratorio, the melodrama. How much more is offered, from as early as 1814, in the piano version of *Fidelio* prepared by Moscheles and revised by Beethoven, right down to that climax of arrangement, Liszt's piano scores, *Partitions de Piano,* of the nine symphonies of Beethoven, begun in 1837 and completed in the sixties. Besides arrangements for two hands, moreover, one must not forget those for four hands or for two pianos, which to some extent conquered the entire province of musical literature for the home.

The piano, accordingly, became the instrument of the Romantic era, the means of presenting the most intimate as well as the most brilliant display at home and in the concert hall. In part, this development derived, of course, from the fact that Beethoven had written so many sonatas and variations, so much chamber music with prominent piano part, and five piano concertos. But it did so only in part, for Beethoven's effect was indeed not a direct and general one. We must always remember that we write our music history from the point of view of posterity. What appears to us important and worthy of notice often aroused in the world of its day little or no interest. Often we concern ourselves with masters who were far ahead of their time; the understanding of them sometimes came into focus only centuries after their death. For his contemporaries, a more important composer than Beethoven was perhaps Muzio Clementi (1752–1832), in his earlier years a rival of Mozart's, in many original traits of brilliance a model for Beethoven, in the work of his mature years not himself ill-disposed to Romantic ideas. Or there was Johann Nepomuk Hummel (1778–1837), at one time Mozart's fellow lodger and pupil, the musical idol of the German "Biedermeier Period," that age in which the middle class, trying to recover from the heroic terrors of the Napoleonic Wars, wished even in art to avoid everything that excited or led one into mysterious depths, and was satisfied with elegant polish, pleasant wit, and friendly conversation.

MENDELSSOHN'S PIANO COMPOSITIONS

Within the family circle, Mendelssohn had his jokes about Hummel and his "bustling finger-work"—yet a great deal of Mendelssohn's own piano music belongs in this frame, since, in accordance with his serene nature, he did not wish to overstep the bounds of tradition in his piano technique. For him the tradition included this very virtuosity of post-Mozartian, of

Hummel's schooling, which had been transmitted to him by his teacher Ludwig Berger, in his turn a pupil of Clementi and Cramer. Once, in a letter to Moscheles, Mendelssohn himself lamented his "poverty in new turns of phrase" for the piano and admitted that he had taken pains "at last to write a regular, peaceful composition." His possibilities and his limitations appear as early as the first three piano works that he brought out—the Capriccio in F-sharp minor Op. 5, the Piano Sonata in E major Op. 6, and the Seven Characteristic Pieces Op. 7, all written in 1825 and 1826. The sixteen-year-old composer's Capriccio is a brilliant—perhaps the most brilliant—example of that Hummel-like *prestissimo* activity, but in the pleasant seriousness of its motivic aspects it rises far above mere virtuosity. The creator of it knew Bach's Inventions. Once again Rossini showed his keen nose when after hearing this piece (it could hardly have been any other) he said to Mendelssohn, "This thing smells of Scarlatti" —a trace of Domenico Scarlatti.[35] And as to the E-major Sonata, it would not have come into being without a knowledge of the last sonatas of Beethoven—the A major Op. 101 and the A-flat major Op. 110, to which Mendelssohn was indebted for the suggestion of a recitative-like *"Adagio e senza tempo."* But along with this late Beethoven and his free disposition and linking of the movements, there is mingled the most unmistakable and unconcerned Weber in the Finale with its gallant rhythms and violoncello-like melodies. Of the Seven Characteristic Pieces the majority are "Bachian"—the prelude-like Andante, No. 1, the "Invention," No. 2, the Sarabande, indicated to be played "with longing," and Nos. 3 and 5, which are regular fugues of the purest post-Bach stamp.

"With longing"! The phrase hints at the trait of character with which, in general, Mendelssohn's style has been charged—"sentimentality." But it is a trait which Mendelssohn had in common with other Romantics— for example, with Schumann, Liszt, or Brahms—and to which he only gave his special stamp. He would not have found such wide imitation of precisely this trait if this "longing" had not been a general characteristic of the Romantic era—if it had not, one may say, belonged to the general set of symptoms in the Romantic disease.

What is it, this sentimentality? It is the reaching-out for something indefinite, a dissatisfaction which revels in self-enjoyment. In Mendelssohn himself, it is an element in his reaching back towards Bach and Handel—towards, so to speak, the surest, most firmly established masters in the history of music. Mendelssohn's sentimentality comes out most

---

[35] Ferdinand Hiller, *Felix Mendelssohn-Bartholdy* (Köln, 1874), p. 50.

clearly in his eight volumes of "Songs without Words." This title expresses exactly the content: melodies in song-form with delicate, retiring accompaniment, idealized duets, mostly striving for the indefinite, but many of them somewhat in the nature of "characteristic pieces"—gondola songs, spinning songs, hunting songs, cradle songs, funeral marches, folk songs. They are filled with unsatisfied longing for a lost paradise of simplicity, for the original womb of music. Mendelssohn got farthest away from it in works like the last of his Characteristic Pieces, Op. 7, No. 7, "Light and Airy," one of those Romantic elfin pieces, which from his pen sound as enchanting with the staccato of the keyboard instrument as they do with the staccato of the strings in the Octet or of the orchestra, for example in the Scherzo from the incidental music to "A Midsummer Night's Dream."

THE PROBLEM OF VIRTUOSITY

Among Mendelssohn's pieces for piano there are also some *études*—not mechanical, but *poetic études* after the model of so many similar pieces by Clementi, Cramer, Kalkbrenner, and Moscheles. But for him there was no need for coming to terms with virtuosity: he was too completely a past master of music, had too little taste for teaching (although he was the director of a conservatory) not to behold as from a mountaintop the tremendous inundation of piano literature in his day. The three masters who felt themselves inwardly impelled to solve this problem, through a feeling of artistic and moral responsibility, were Robert Schumann, Franz Liszt, and Frédéric Chopin. In all these, this impulse was lively and effective, although in Chopin it had less of a controversial tinge than it did in Schumann, and less of an exhibitionistic attitude than it did in the virtuoso Liszt.

Schumann, Chopin, and Liszt are the three musicians who by their work saved piano composition from the shallowness into which it was in danger of falling or had already fallen, through the merely "brilliant" literature of Henri Herz (1803–1888), Franz Hünten (1793–1878), Sigismund Thalberg (1812–1872), and Alexander Dreyschock (1818–1869). Nothing on the subject is more amusing than the treatment Robert Schumann gave in his magazine to Herz's Second Concerto, Op. 74—a critique which at the same time is of considerable historical significance:

Concerning Herz, one can write (1) sadly, (2) humorously, (3) ironically, or all three at once, as here. The reader can scarcely believe how cautiously and timidly I hesitate to make these remarks about Herz, keeping him always at least ten paces away from me so as not to have to praise him too greatly to his face. . . .

"What is he trying to do but be amusing and become rich at the same time? Does he, in so doing, impel anyone to love or praise Beethoven's last quartets the less? Does he invite comparison with these works? Is he not rather the most giddy fop, who never makes anyone lift a finger to play—and least of all does he lift his own—except to secure money and fame? And is it not ridiculous, the absurd anger of Classical Philistines, who with goggle eyes and drawn spears have now for ten years stood armed and defended themselves, that he might not come too near to their children and their children's children with his un-Classical music, while they secretly themselves took delight in it? If the critics, immediately on the ascent of this comet which has aroused so much talk, had correctly appraised his distance from the vicinity of our artistic sun and had not by their hubbub given him a significance that he himself could scarcely have conceived for his own work, we should long since have recovered from this artistic cold-in-the-head. The fact that he even now hastens to his end with giant steps lies in the customary nature of things. The public will at last become weary even of its plaything and throw it idly into the corner. Towards that end a younger generation has arisen, with strength in its arms and the courage to use it. . . .

"Herz's Second Concerto starts in C minor and is commended to those who love the first. If by any chance in any one concert a certain C-minor symphony be given along with this work, the request is made that the symphony be given *after* the concerto. . . .

In a critique of Thalberg's *Great Concerto,* Op. 5, Schumann proceeded with greater moderation. Yet he always criticized Thalberg's works with special strictness—"only because we have suspected in him a talent for composition which was threatened with extinction by the vanity of the practicing virtuoso." Liszt, on the other hand, without fear of the charge that he wished only to discount the work of an irritating or dangerous rival, criticized some of Thalberg's works in 1837, particularly his *Grande Fantaisie,* Op. 22, with a severity that in actual fact would have been of doubtful justification if it had not been made on serious moral grounds, and if Liszt had not had something other and better to substitute for this kind of virtuosity.

The musician who had created a new ideal of virtuosity was not a pianist, but a violinist, Nicolo Paganini. Paganini belongs to an older generation than the Romantics: he was born in Genoa, in 1782. But even if he himself was anything but a Romantic, he impressed the Romantics strongly as being a Romantic personality, a Hoffmannesque figure. His youth is shrouded in mysterious obscurity. For a few years (1805–8) he lived in the courtly household of a sister of Napoleon's in tiny, venerable, sleepy

Lucca. Only after 1813 did his fame begin to spread in Italy. In 1828 he made a trip to Vienna, and in 1831-2 to Paris and London; and with his playing he aroused an enthusiasm that bordered on sorcery.

Not only did the masses fall under his spell, but also the musicians. They were fascinated not merely by his technical wizardry, but also by the expressive power of his cantilena. Heinrich Heine has captured the unearthly impression of this macabre, possessed musician in a few pages of his "Florentine Nights" (*Der Salon* III). Schubert, on the other hand, in a letter of May 1828—no longer extant—written to Anselm Hüttenbrenner, said of an Adagio of Paganini's, "Therein I heard an angel sing." His virtuoso perfection turned into something unearthly. And the effect seems all the greater when one cannot properly assume that Paganini's compositions were responsible for the character imputed to this wizard, as his larger works—particularly the concertos—were first published posthumously, after 1851, and many remain unpublished to this day.

The effect is, furthermore, all the greater in that his triumphal tour through Europe lasted only a few years: in 1834 he retired to his native land, to his villa near Parma, and thereafter played in public only infrequently and then almost always for charity. Only in 1838 did he come once again into the limelight: after hearing the *Symphonie Fantastique* under Berlioz's leadership, the great violinist—despite his notorious greed —made the composer a gift of 20,000 francs. In 1840 Paganini died, in solitude.

It must be reiterated that the pianists were even more interested in Paganini than were the violinists. The violinists could not imitate him, for he was inimitable. They could add nothing to the technical achievements which are to be found, for example, in his variations for violin and orchestra *Le Streghe* ("The Witches"), 1813. But the masters of the piano could attempt to transfer these achievements to their instrument, and to conquer the differences of technique between the two instruments. And that is what they did: Chopin, Liszt, Schumann, even Brahms, who in his "Studies for Pianoforte"—the Variations, Op. 35, composed in 1861-2 and dedicated to the most skillful piano virtuoso of the 19th century, Carl Tausig—not only used a theme of Paganini's as a basis but also carried it out in the spirit of Paganini, without being false, of course, to his own nature. It is the same theme as that on which Liszt wrote variations in the sixth of his Bravura Studies after Paganini's Caprices.

SCHUMANN'S ART: FIERY AND DREAMY

Schumann and Liszt both transcribed for piano several numbers from Paganini's Twenty-Four Caprices, Op. 1. We shall begin with Schumann, for he—at least as arranger of these particular pieces—was the pioneer. He wrote his Op. 3, the six "Studies for the Piano arranged from Paganini's Caprices," in 1832, and his Op. 10, the "Six Concert Etudes composed after Paganini's Caprices," in 1833. Liszt, on the other hand, did not bring out his Bravura Studies after Paganini's Caprices (*Études d'exécution transcendente d'après Paganini*) until 1838. Neither Schumann nor Liszt—nor, for that matter, Chopin—cared particularly about mere virtuosity. Their mission, clearly realized by all three of them, was precisely that of striking at virtuosity with its own weapons. In the remarks with which Schumann introduced his "Studies," Op. 3, there are a few highly characteristic sentences: "In no other type of musical composition do poetic liberties sound so well as in a *caprice*. But if, behind the lightness and the humor which should characterize it, there may also appear soundness and deeper study, then there is genuine mastery. . . . After elimination of all external difficulties, the *imagination* will be able to move surely and playfully, give its work life and light and shadow, and complete with ease what in a freer representation might be lacking."

The poetic liberties of a caprice! Lightness and humor joined with thoroughness and deeper study! It sounds as if Schumann were characterizing his own work, from Op. 1 to Op. 23. From 1830 to 1840 (Op. 1 to Op. 23), he had written piano works exclusively. During this decade, the piano was for him a universal instrument, capable of expressing his most secret intentions, as it was for Chopin, who for his part—unlike Schumann and Liszt—was content all his life with this universal instrument. In the hands of the three masters, it was in actuality an entirely different instrument from what it had been in the hands of Mozart, Beethoven, Schubert, and even the "brilliant" Weber. It achieved its new, incomparable style. One can orchestrate a Beethoven, Schubert, or even Weber piano work (such as *The Invitation to the Dance*); but one can no longer do that satisfactorily with Schumann's *Kreisleriana*, with a Liszt *étude*, or with Chopin's A-flat major *Prélude*, any more than—vice versa—one can transcribe for piano a Berlioz orchestral work.

Again, it is a matter of the mastery of a new realm of magical sound. This mastery includes, of course, not only technique but also the widening

of the compass, the *hinting* at melodies, basses, and middle voices, the
variety in tone color in the two hands, scales in double-notes, leaps, new
finesse in the use of staccato and legato, etc. It includes a new realm of
style, of freer expression, of more rapid alternation between intimacy and
brilliance, between softness and sharpness. And corresponding to this new
content, which with Schumann always had poetic backgrounds, there was
also the new, kaleidoscopic form. One need only glance at some of the titles
of Schumann's piano works to become aware of his predilection for this
kaleidoscopic form—the *Papillons,* Op. 2; the *Intermezzi,* Op. 4; the
Impromptus on a Theme by Clara Wieck, Op. 5; the *Davidsbündler
Dances,* Op. 6; the "Scènes mignonnes" entitled *Carnaval,* Op. 9; the
Phantasie-Stücke, Op. 12; the *Scenes from Childhood,* Op. 15; the *Kreisleriana,* Op. 16, the *Novelletten,* Op. 21 (named after Clara Novello), the
Nachtstücke, Op. 23, etc.

To understand fully the poetical backgrounds for this form of quick
alteration between contrasting sections, one needs to study carefully
Schumann's two favorite authors, E. T. A. Hoffmann and Jean Paul
Friedrich Richter, known as Jean Paul. In the midst of the *Kreisleriana*
there stands a Hoffmannesque figure, passionate, impelled by mysterious,
demoniac powers, Capellmeister Kreisler, from Hoffmann's *Phantasie-
Stücke,* Part II. It will be observed that in Schumann we again encounter
this title, as well as that of the *Nachtstücke* (among Hoffmann's writings,
the work so named consists of eight tales). A still more mysterious and
veiled role, however, than that of the "phantom Hoffmann" is played in
Schumann's piano works by Jean Paul (1763–1825), the sentimental-
humorous poet, half idyllic and imaginative, who has become for us today
practically insufferable, but who in his time was of greater influence upon
bourgeois Germany than was Goethe himself. In one of his happier works,
the *Flegeljahre,* he tells of twin brothers, Walt and Vult, who—as Wilhelm
Scherer has expressed it—"one awkward, ungainly, shy, with a childlike
dreaminess and impracticality, the other nimble, powerful, brave, stormy,
and satirical, come from his own soul and represent the two sides of his
nature as a poet and as a man. . . ."[36]

Quite similarly Schumann personified the divisions of his own ego: in
Florestan, vehement, enthusiastic, fiery, in Eusebius, youthful, dreamy;
in Raro, mature, calm, the *master.* They are the *Davidsbündler,* the members of David's League, a secret order which has rallied about the great,

[36] Wilhelm Scherer, *Geschichte der deutschen Litteratur* (9th edition, Berlin,
1902), p. 675.

the genuine, the progressive, and which is directed against everything
shallow, merely pleasant, mediocre, Philistine. The fraternity which Liszt
in his Six Essays (1835) wished to organize lived in Schumann's soul.
Florestan, Eusebius, Raro—they are all "Beethovenites," ardent admirers
but not imitators of Beethoven. They seek the key to a hidden, Romantic
realm of the future, upon "new paths." Taking up each of Schumann's
piano works—and not only his piano works—one can say whether it came
from Florestan, Eusebius, or Raro. Sometime at the end of each movement
the composer himself indicated the "author" or pair of authors by initials,
for example in the *Davidsbündler* Dances, Op. 6, whose musical motto
comes from C. W.—that is, Clara Wieck, the beloved, idolized female
member of the society, later Schumann's wife.

In this fiery and dreamy art there is an element of the esoteric, which
excludes the uninitiated. Often Schumann unveiled the secret. In his
Variations, Op. 1, "on the name Abegg" he utilized the theme A-B [B-flat]-
E-G-G to form the opening motif. The *Carnaval*, Op. 9, is a set of *"Scènes
mignonnes sur quatre notes,"* namely on the notes A-Es [E-flat]-C-H
[B-natural]: Asch was the home of the girl whom he at that time loved,
Ernestine von Fricken. Again, in the second number among the *Intermezzi*, Op. 4, the first line of Gretchen's spinning-wheel scene from *Faust*
is unexpectedly quoted above the music. But it requires intimacy with
Schumann's work, and the inclination to search out these matters—to
observe that in No. 6 of the *Intermezzi* Fräulein Abegg once again raises
her head, that in the finale of the *Symphonic Etudes*, Op. 13, a romance
from Marschner's *Templer und Jüdin* well known in that day plays its
part, or that in the first movement of the C-major Fantasy, Op. 17, there
is a phrase from Beethoven's song-cycle *An die ferne Geliebte.*

Later, Schumann chose to refrain from such distinct hints. Like all the
other Romantics, he loved the mask, so that behind it he might behave all
the more sentimentally and exuberantly. He was too completely the artist
to present his confessions baldly and openly.

He did not exactly write program music. What he created was, to be
sure, poetically inspired music, but it was *music;* and the play of contrasts
in his kaleidoscopic "miniatures" does not follow an arbitrary "program,"
but rather conforms to purely musical law. We have here, clearly, the
refined development of the individual parts to which the pianistic art of
Schumann owes its ever-renewed charm. Here there is play with little
seeds of melody; there is alternation between enchanting ornament and
passages formed in strict Bach-like style, between harmony powerfully

definite and that indefinitely floating, gliding in and out, between most simple and most clever rhythm. After the *Intermezzi* and the *Carnaval,* the most original and at the same time most well-developed of these piano works are perhaps the *Novelletten,* Op. 21, the *Faschingsschwank aus Wien,* Op. 26, the *Symphonic Etudes,* Op. 13, and above all the *Kreisleri-ana,* Op. 16, in which all opposites, from the most weird to the most resplendent, stand within a unified frame. A different sort of work, yet one that is immortal and full of Romantic spirit and love for simplicity and innocence, is his *Scenes from Childhood,* Op. 15. These short pieces have their counterparts in the sketches and woodcuts of a German artist, Ludwig Richter.

Even when Schumann did not avail himself of the "kaleidoscopic" form and resorted to the Classical pattern of the sonata, he remained a Romantic, not led by the Beethovenian model or any other Classical model, in his three Sonatas (F-sharp minor, Op. 11; G minor, Op. 22; and F minor, Op. 14—named by the publisher most misleadingly *"Concert sans orchestre"*). The Allegro of the F-sharp minor Sonata originally bore the title "Fandango," the wild dance of a desperate couple—Florestan and Chiara. The F-minor Sonata consisted originally only of a fantastic Allegro and similarly fantastic variations, and it is questionable whether it gained much by the addition of a Scherzo. In the G-minor Sonata the place of the slow movement is filled by a romance of the most extreme compactness and intimacy. A fourth work of this sort, the most beautiful, dedicated to Franz Liszt, renounces the title "sonata"; it is the C-major Fantasy, Op. 17. As to the "content" of the three movements, the original titles, later suppressed, may give some clue: "Ruins," "Triumphal Arch," "Constellation." As to their Romantic intention, note the motto, four lines by Friedrich Schlegel, which Schubert had once set to music:

> Through all the tones there sounds
> Throughout the colorful earth
> A gentle tone, sustained,
> For him who secretly hears.

In this work a dream of the Romantics had become a reality, through the most delicate musical resources, the most carefully considered pianistic means. Here virtuosity stands completely at the service of poetic music, of musical poetry. In his later works for piano—and the last one, of 1853, the *Gesänge der Frühe,* dedicated to "the high poetess Bettina [Brentano]," bears the opus number 133 and the ominous date 1853—Schumann wished

as in other fields to come to terms with conscious "mastery," in the Canonic
Studies for the Pedal-Piano Op. 56, of which at least two combine most
charmingly "learnedness" and Romanticism; the Fugues Op. 72; the
Fughettas Op. 126. Yet again and again he succeeded in writing pieces
which, although not so original as some of his former ones, are yet full
of Romantic magic, like the *Bunte Blätter,* Op. 99, or the *Waldszenen,*
Op. 82.

LISZT, THE CREATIVE TECHNICIAN

A quite different position with regard to virtuosity was taken by Franz
Liszt. He ruthlessly attacked the merely virtuoso musicians of the Thalberg type, and accordingly had to outdo them in virtuosity. In point of
fact, moreover, he did so. In his piano works are found technical ideas
which were not only surprising in his own time but are still so today. Like
Paganini with his violin, Liszt drew from the piano possibilities of sound
that no one before had even imagined. His art, however, consisted not
merely of the transcription of the technical peculiarities of the violin—
or of any other instrument—to the piano. It consisted not merely of the
passages in octaves and tenths, the chromatic chord effects, the technique
of leaps, the crossing of hands, the chains of trills, the arpeggios, the
multitudinous differentiations in the dividing up of cantilena and ornament. All these technical features brand Liszt as an innovator—to be sure,
a *Romantic* innovator. But his art also consisted of a new technique of
invention, especially in the harmony and in the recasting of motives.

It is true that Liszt wrote principally for the public, for the concert
podium; and only towards the end of his life did he begin to write a few
touching pieces that are real monologues. But in most of his work, even
where he becomes more intimate, he is always thinking of the salon and
of a certain feminine audience. From his pen there are no "Scenes from
Childhood," though there is a series—unfortunately too extensive—of
morceaux de salon. There are no *Kreisleriana,* though there is a whole
series of operatic transcriptions from Auber, Bellini, Donizetti, Mercadante, Meyerbeer, etc., including, to be sure, some from Mozart and Verdi
—all pieces that are great technical war-horses. Liszt was an indefatigable
conqueror of new territory for his instrument, and he had almost a copy-
right on the term "transcription." He represents the creative, improvisatory,
rhapsodic appropriation of foreign melodic material to virtuoso purposes,
to the exhibition of *bravura.* For other species within this genus of appro-

priation Liszt had other names—piano scores (among which is the memorable transcription of Beethoven's symphonies onto two staves), reworkings (such as his similarly memorable piano transcription of seven Bach preludes and fugues originally for the organ), fantasies, reminiscences, illustrations, paraphrases (in which category belongs his propaganda for the works of Wagner, from the *"Fantasy-Piece on Motives from Rienzi"* to the *"Solemn March to the Holy Grail, from Parsifal"*).

But it would not be quite right to say that in his work the technical aspect stands in the foreground, much less that it was in any sense its own excuse for being. It is inseparable from the creative—from the creative in the service of Romantic ideas and feelings. As a fifteen-year-old boy Liszt had published an "Etude for the Piano in Forty-Eight Exercises in All the Major and Minor Keys"—technical studies in the style of Czerny, his teacher. In 1837 Liszt took them in hand again, but now they—or at least eleven of them—became the *Grandes Études,* a compendium not only of the new piano technique but also of the Lisztian brand of Romantic poetry. Then, in 1853, in a third reworking, this poetic content was indicated for ten of them by inscriptions, among which are *"Mazeppa"* (No. 4, later used for a Symphonic Poem), *"Feux follets"* (No. 5), *"Wilde Jagd"* (No. 8), *"Harmonies du soir"* (No. 11), and *"Chasse-neige"* (No. 12). One recognizes immediately from these headings the type of Liszt's Romanticism. It is not German Romanticism, but fundamentally French; his background is dominated not by the folk song, Novalis, and Mörike, but by Byron, Lamennais, Lamartine, and Victor Hugo, with their *weltschmerz,* their passion, and their rhetoric.

These are *impressions et poésies.* But they are impressions transmitted by literary ideas. Even before Liszt finally renounced his career as virtuoso, he retired from his triumphal tours to plunge himself into nature, always in "Romantic" regions—on the Rhine, in Switzerland, in Italy. But whatever he saw, he always saw it through the glasses of his reading. Thus there came into existence his *Album d'un Voyageur,* his *Fantaisie Romantique sur Deux Mélodies Suisses,* and his *Années de Pèlerinage,* in part a reworking of that "Album of a Traveler." One piece in it is called *"Vallée d'Obermann":* there Liszt does not see the Swiss valley itself, but he sees it in the light of a sentimental novel by Étienne Jean de Senancour, and —to make the piece understood—the original edition contains a long selection from this "Romantic" work. In Italy this musical journal becomes that of a highly cultured tourist, who lets his imagination burst into flame before Raphael's *Sposalizio* in the Brera Gallery, before Michelangelo's tomb of the Medici (in which Liszt strangely applies to the *Pensieroso* the famous verse on the figure of the *Notte*), in three sonnets thinks of the poet who sang of Laura, and lets his feelings storm out "after a reading of Dante, *Fantasia quasi Sonata.*"

The religious impulse, which had already found expression in his early work, gained strength in his *Harmonies Poétiques et Religieuses* written during the late forties, in ten pieces, among which are the *"Bénédiction de Dieu dans la solitude"* (No. 3), the *"Cantique d'amour"* (No. 10)—piety, which in good part is boredom and flight. There is considerable significance in the performance-indication of the *"Pensée des morts"* (No. 4), the very heart of the collection: *"avec un profond sentiment d'ennui,"* with a deep sense of the vanity of all existence. The triumph of the virtuoso is mingled with *weltschmerz,* the resignation of a highly cultured Romantic. As Liszt grew older, this religious or quasi-religious element became stronger: witness, for example, his *Légendes* written about 1863 (published in 1866), which set both St. Francises in a richly ornamented auriole, *"St. François d'Assise—La prédication aux oiseaux"* and *"St. François de Paule marchant sur les flots";* or the third part, the *"Troisième année"* of the *Années de Pèlerinage* (1877), which ends with a genuine pilgrimage to Rome: No. 1 *"Angelus. Prière aux anges gardiens,"* Nos. 2 and 3 *"Aux Cypres de la Villa d'Este, Thrénodies,"* No. 4 *"Les jeux d'eaux à la Villa d'Este,"* No. 5 *"Sunt lacrimae rerum,"* No. 6 *"Marche funèbre,"* No. 7 *"Sursum corda . . ."* Even in No. 4, the Play of the Waters, a virtuoso piece of the highest sort, the pious turn is not lacking. The revolutionary child of the world seeks, in genuinely Romantic fashion, for rest in God.

Yet, as a musician, Liszt was never able to pacify the revolutionary spirit in his heart. No Romantic pointed so far ahead into the future as did he, and he did so usually when he forgot his program for the bringing of music close to poetry. His Bravura Studies after Paganini, which like the Etudes were unfortunately discussed by Schumann in a highly superficial and almost malevolent way, are perhaps his most highly developed work, for the "mechanical" element here is transformed rather unconsciously into poetry. There is one of his pieces—in fact, that piece referred to as the very heart of the *Harmonies Poétiques* (1834)—which, being without signature of either time or key, may serve as an original model of pure expression. Pure expression suffuses also the sole Sonata, which

Liszt wrote at the beginning of 1852 and dedicated to Robert Schumann in gratitude for the dedication of the C-major Fantasy, Op. 17. He always sought to avoid the sonata form, as his form was that of improvisation, fantasy, and rhapsody. Here too there is something sufficiently revolutionary: a unity seemingly improvisatory, but actually constructed and articulated according to careful plan, arising from five germinal motives which are again and again re-shaped, combined, and intensified. It is one of the few creations (few in relation to the immense number of his piano works) in which Liszt had recourse to polyphony—a *rhetorical* polyphony. Yet the result was still happier, or "more innocent," when he received his inspiration from Bach, as in the Fantasy and Fugue on the Theme B-A-C-H (c. 1871) or the Variations on a Chromatic *basso ostinato* from Bach's Cantata *Weinen, Klagen.*

These are the pieces that stand in contrast to the many works of the Romantic cosmopolite, the traveler Liszt, who belonged to various nations and therefore to no nation and, like Odysseus, "saw many cities of men and learned many customs." According to his birthplace, he was Hungarian; and to this fortuitous circumstance he paid the most splendid tribute in the hundreds of rhythmic, melodic, and harmonic tendencies in his works, particularly in his *Rhapsodies Hongroises,* which are among his most popular compositions, both in the original piano form and in the numerous arrangements. The Hungarian Rhapsodies use mostly gypsy melodies, which Liszt was deeply interested in collecting. What he says in his book *On the Gypsies and their Music* [37] about a Hungarian predecessor in the performance of these melodies, Csermák, applies also to himself: "If a European artist identifies himself by sympathetic divination with the spirit prevailing in this art, he can perhaps succeed in declaiming these songs, in coordinating them, in bringing them together, and in performing them with the way of feeling that has dictated them . . ."—to which, moreover, one must also add Liszt's virtuosity and personal charm. The Hungarian Rhapsodies are perhaps Liszt's best "transcriptions," and in them he appears in his most successful and most characteristic mask. But they are scarcely less a mask than, perhaps, the Italian one in the *"Tarantelles napolitaines"* from the *"Venezia e Napoli,"* a supplement to the *Années de Pèlerinage,* or the Spanish one in the brilliant *"Rondeau fantastique sur un thème espagnol"* ("El Contrabandista," a song by Manuel Garcia, 1836), and no less a mask than the many paraphrases which Liszt wrote on all sorts of national melodies.

[37] *Gesammelte Schriften* VI, 357.

CHOPIN, AN ORIGINAL MUSICIAN

The master of the piano in whose work the national element is united with the highest genius is Frédéric Chopin (1810–1849). It is a strange and certainly not insignificant fact that the greatest Polish national composer was half-French; for his father, Nicolas Chopin, was an immigrant who had come to Poland from Nancy. The national touch, in music as in all the other arts, signifies little or nothing if it does not coincide with personal greatness, or have personal greatness to support it. What is called German music is the indefinite image which Bach, Haydn, Mozart, and Beethoven have created; and Bach, Haydn, Mozart, and Beethoven were not, as it were, representatives of "German" music because there had been something like that before them. Chopin, likewise, also really created Polish music. By asserting this fact, one does not maintain that before Chopin there had not been any regional Polish music or Polish musicians whatsoever. As early as the second half of the 16th century, collections of instrumental dances had included Polish numbers with their characteristic rhythms. The fact that the Polonaise was an internationally fashionable dance in the 18th century, moreover, is attested by works of J. S. Bach and of his sons Wilhelm Friedemann and Philipp Emanuel, of Telemann, Schobert, and Mozart. But not until Joseph Kozlowski (1757–1831) did there appear the first Polish—or, in this instance, Polish-Russian—composer. He was followed by men like Joseph Elsner (1769–1854), born in Schleswig, and Charles Kurpinski (1785–1857). They were all not only Poles but also good "Europeans," i.e., deeply influenced by the styles of Italian opera and German instrumental music. In relation to Chopin, they were perhaps Polish in somewhat the same way that Johann Wenzel Tomaschek was Bohemian or Czech in relation to Smetana. In beginning his career, Chopin relied on melodies by his teacher, Elsner, or—as in the *Grande Fantaisie* for piano and orchestra, Op. 13 (1829)—on a theme by Kurpinski and on Polish songs. Chopin himself called the work a "Potpourri on Polish Tunes."

His life might be called Romantic in its brevity and its suffering ("he was dying all his life," said Berlioz, after Chopin's death), if there had not also been "Classical" careers that were similarly brief, like Pergolesi's, Mozart's, or even Schubert's. Chopin was a *wunderkind,* both as virtuoso and composer. After his first successes in his native land, he went to Vienna and gave two great concerts with the orchestra there in 1829—not without having previously heard Hummel and Paganini in Warsaw.

In 1830 he left Warsaw forever and went by way of Vienna and Munich to Paris, which was for him as well as for Liszt a spiritual and social homeland. He lived there as a free artist, for whom some—not many— concerts, teaching positions, and sales of compositions (the worth of which he was well aware of) assured a degree of independence. It did not, however, assure him independence of women: in 1836 he began his relations with Aurore Dudevant *née* Dupin, known to literature as George Sand, the famous novelist. His relations with her and with her family were not terminated until 1847, after many crises, among which the best known was that in Valdemosa on the island of Majorca in 1838. In 1848, though marked by death, he made one more concert trip to England and Scotland; on October 17 of the following year he died.

His life became, or seemed to be, Romantic, much like Heine's, not by virtue of what he was, but by virtue of what he suffered—his illness, his exile from his native land, whose tragic fate in the unsuccessful resistance to Russia in 1830 he felt deeply though he was far away, surrounded by the admiration of intelligent men and women, the latter more or less beautiful but always passionately intellectual and for the most part aristocratic. In actuality, however, his letters betray a quite different personality—sensitive but never sentimental, witty and ironical even to the point of self-irony, gifted with the sharpest powers of observation both of relationships and of men, devoted to his family, loyal to his friends, sober and matter-of-fact in business matters.

Schumann and Liszt began as purely pianistic composers (although in 1824–25 Liszt wrote an early opera, *Don Sanche ou le Chateau d'Amour*), and only in their later years did they seek or win universality of expression—universality in the sense that they conquered the fields of chamber music, the symphony, and the large and small forms of vocal music. Chopin, however, began and ended as a purely pianistic composer. In the few works in which he combined the piano with the strings, such as the early Piano Trio Op. 8 in G minor (before 1828), the *Introduction et Polonaise Brillante* in C Op. 3, the *Grand Duo Concertant* (composed in collaboration with Franchomme), and the Sonata Op. 65 in G minor, his last work—all for piano and violoncello—the piano insists on all its rights of brilliantly leading, even though Chopin, especially in the Sonata, is much too mature and strong a musician not to grant to the violoncello a word here and there by way of cantabile dialogue. But one can hardly conceive of Chopin as a composer of string quartets or symphonies. In his piano concertos in E minor, Op. 11, and

F minor, Op. 21, the orchestral part is so subordinated that well-intentioned arrangers have believed that they had to enrich it. The same observation applies to the few remaining works of Chopin's for piano with orchestra: the variations on Mozart's "Là ci darem," Op. 2; the *Grande Fantaisie* on Polish songs, Op. 13, previously mentioned; the *Cracovienne,* Op. 14; and the *Grande Polonaise* in E-flat, Op. 22.

It is seen that all these works have early opus numbers: the longer Chopin continued in his career, the more he avoided the concert podium and the expectant masses, which are to be aroused only by very brilliant or very crude means. He turned to a smaller, more choice public. With the highest art and even the highest artistry, he sought to unite the highest type of intimacy. All his contemporaries agree in reporting that his dynamics did not exceed the degree of *forte,* without however losing a single bit of shading.

Chopin's unique position is attributable, first, to the fact that from the beginning to the end of his career he remained an original musician. Schumann, on the other hand, repented of his originality at the end of his career; Wagner, after eclectic beginnings, had to discover and intensify his own highly personal musical idiom; and Liszt, all his life long, remained in a state of eclecticism. But Chopin did not like to emphasize his originality. "Hats off, gentlemen, a genius"—with these words, Robert Schumann in the *Allgemeine Musikalische Zeitung* of 1831 greeted the appearance of Chopin's Mozart-variations. But Schumann, who himself was less inclined to hide his own originality, praised only the Romantic attitude, the "striving," the mastery displayed in the work. No less than Berlioz and Liszt, Chopin was a Romantic revolutionary; but we know that he did not in the least like either Berlioz's bizarre traits or Liszt's rather exhibitionistic and charlatanic brilliance. There are many kinds of musical ore that Chopin smelted together and poured into his mould, and they are so perfectly amalgamated that on hearing his music we are no longer aware that anything but Chopin's own reaches our ears. It is Hummel with his elegance; it is Rossini with the sweet and flowery qualities of his cantilena; it is Mozart with his *second* simplicity and naïveté; it is Bach with contrapuntally or polyphonically conceived details; it is John Field, the pupil of Clementi and composer of ardent nocturnes; it is perhaps the brilliant composer of rondos and sonatas, Carl Maria Weber. Beethoven seems to be lacking: Chopin must have felt that Beethoven, who, to be sure, was still one of his contemporaries, offered him no point of contact. Chopin thought of himself as a *fashion-*

able composer, who wished for and utilized immediate success, although not among the vulgar *en masse*.

Schumann, who accompanied a great part of Chopin's creative career with his criticism, rightly emphasized the mastery that already appeared in Op 2. This mastery developed so fast that after Op. 10—the first collection of *études*—there are scarcely any further unevennesses, and at most only slight fluctuations in the maturity of Chopin's work. The comparison with Liszt's piano works shows us perhaps best wherein this mastery lay. Liszt often tried to astonish the bourgeois, and even to terrify them; Chopin, with all his courage, avoided doing so, in matters of harmony as well as of virtuosity. Liszt's works are rhetorical, often to the point of grandiloquence; Chopin's are eloquent, to the point of extreme intimacy. With Liszt, the form seeks to broaden itself out, mostly to a brilliant climax; in Chopin, the strictest concentration prevails—we have already noted that he was able to say everything in a dozen or score measures, just as Heine was in four brief lines. Liszt's form is rhapsodic; accordingly, he had to concern himself with clever motivic connection in order to produce, so to speak, the tangible evidence for the unity of his compositions—as, for example, in his B-minor Sonata. Chopin creates in all his pieces the illusion of improvisation, but they are firmly formed despite their involuntary or unwillful appearance—as, for example, are his two sonatas, one in B-flat minor, Op. 35, and one in B minor, Op. 58.[38] They are quite un-Beethovenish, both of them, each a whole made up of seemingly heterogeneous parts: two ballades rather than two first movements, virtuoso scherzi, in the first the noted or notorious *Marche Funèbre* and the *étude*-like, ghostly Finale, in the second a nocturne as the slow movement—and yet each is a whole. Schumann hit the mark when he wrote concerning the B-flat minor Sonata: ". . . the fact that he called the work 'Sonata' might rather be thought a bit of caprice, if not of impertinence —he has linked together four of his most mad children . . ." But he added, ". . . who can know whether some day a more Romantic descendant . . . may not dust off and play the Sonata and think to himself: 'Yet that fellow wasn't so entirely wrong after all.' "

It was also Schumann who early sought to differentiate between the national and the universal in Chopin's make-up as a composer. It is true that Chopin was presumably the first and certainly the greatest of all the national composers. More clearly than in any other artist's work, the

[38] A third one in C minor, numbered opus 4, but published posthumously, is a piece of juvenilia, though already very original.

spirit of Poland is embodied in his music; and in all times of Poland's national distress—and when has there not been a time of distress for Poland—this music has achieved patriotic significance. Again it was Schumann who emphasized Chopin's "strong, original nationality" in discussing his two concertos: "And as this national spirit now goes about in the black garb of mourning, it stirs us even more deeply as we find it embodied in the sensitive artist. . . . If the powerful, autocratic monarch in the North [the Czar] knew how in Chopin's compositions, in the simple melodies of the mazurkas, a dangerous enemy threatens him, he would forbid the music. Beneath the flowers in Chopin's work there are hidden cannons."

On the other hand, it is true that the "national" compositions make up only a part among Chopin's complete works. He himself saw forty-two of his mazurkas (Opp. 6, 7, 17, 24, 30, 33, 41, 50, 56, 59, 63, and one without opus number) in print, and thirteen or fourteen more were published posthumously. He saw seven polonaises (Opp. 26, 40, 44, 53, and 61, the *Polonaise-Fantaisie*), with which should be reckoned six posthumous ones. The *Rondo à la Mazur,* Op. 5, too, should be included among the mazurkas. But among his works there are also eight waltzes (Opp. 18, 34, 42, and 64), plus seven posthumous ones, a *Tarantelle,* Op. 43, a Bolero, Op. 19, a Barcarolle, Op. 60, and three posthumous *Ecossaises,* Op. 72. Are they Viennese, Neapolitan, Spanish, Venetian, Scottish? No, Chopin loved to link his imagination to a given rhythm, and on the basis of this rhythm, which might be quite simple, as in the waltzes, to construct the lightest, most blossoming, most imaginative airy fabric.

It is always Chopin who speaks, never the people. Again we must quote Schumann in his discussion of the four Mazurkas, Op. 30. After mentioning the Scherzo, he proceeds, "The mazurka has been likewise raised by Chopin to a little art-form. Though he has written many pieces in this form, few of them are alike. Almost everyone has some poetic trait or other, something new in the form or the expression." Similarly, Schumann feels that Chopin's waltzes are no longer Viennese waltzes, which were the folklike and somewhat countryfied or bourgeois dances of Schubert's local followers such as Lanner or Johann Strauss the elder. Discussing the A-flat Waltz, Op. 42, Schumann says, "Like his earlier ones, this waltz is a salon piece of the noblest sort. If he were to play it for dancing, Florestan thought, half the ladies among the dancers would have to be at least countesses. He is right, the waltz is aristocratic through and through." So also are Chopin's polonaises his own, through and through. He no longer makes use of the national form to create a graceful contrast between two movements. It was for this purpose that Beethoven had used it in his C-major Polonaise, Op. 89 (1814)—"the first original piano polonaise of the master's," it was called in the announcement prefixed to it by way of dedication—and in the Minuet of the Quartet Op. 59, No. 3, which in reality is a polonaise. Nor did Chopin use the polonaise form for purposes of achieving a brilliant effect or of disguising himself piquantly and characteristically as Weber and Liszt had used it. In Chopin, virtuosity, rhythmic splendor, and melodic brilliance are quite subservient to the composer's personal expression.

We must give a certain amount of consideration to the surprising fact that the influence exerted by Chopin was so international. He was imitated not only in Warsaw, but also from North to South, from Oslo to Palermo; from East to West, from Petersburg to Paris. As no symphonic composer of the 19th century could disregard Beethoven, so no piano composer after 1830 could avoid taking account of Chopin.

The same thing applies to the thirty-odd *études* of Chopin, which he brought together principally in two collections, Op. 10 and Op. 25. Treatises may be written on the technical problems of each one, but—more important—each is a piece of dramatic and passionate or lyrical poetry of the utmost concentration. Chopin never allowed himself to give indications of the "content" of these poems. He gave no titles or inscriptions. Again it was Schumann, in a reference to Op. 25, who said of the first and familiar one in A-flat that it is "more a poem than a study" and who proceeded thus to speak of Chopin's own performance (for on the occasion of a visit to Dresden and Leipzig in the summer of 1835 Chopin had played this piece, along with others, for him and Mendelssohn): "One makes a mistake, however, if he thinks that Chopin would have had every one of the little notes there heard clearly; it was more a surging of the A-flat major chord, here and there raised on high anew by the pedal. But one perceived wonderful, great-toned melody running through the harmonies, and only in the middle did there appear at one point alongside that principal part a tenor voice, gradually taking shape as it rose out of the chords."

But Chopin had no need of a pedagogical pretext for writing pure poetry. There are three books of *Préludes,* Op. 28, to which a single composition is to be added, Op. 45—a body of compositions as varied as Heine's *Heimkehr.* There are the four Ballades (Opp. 23, 38, 47, and 52), with which a fifth is to be classed, Op. 49, in F minor, this time called a

"fantasy." There are the Nocturnes and Scherzi, among them the un-
canny and ethereal one in B minor, the Rondeaux and Variations, the
Impromptus. I do not know whether Chopin was familiar with the Impromptus of Schubert, but in common with Schubert he displays in these
and similar pieces melodic and harmonic invention of overpowering
beauty, which is sufficient unto itself, has need of no development, and
does not lose anything by repetition. In no composer's work is there so
much repetition as in Chopin—above all, of course, in the dances. And
there is need for only little ornaments or variations to make the repeated
material appear ever new.

It is a world in little. It is a world seen from a corner, in all conceivable
lights, from the most dazzling (I do not say the most clear or transparent)
to the most shadowy. Compared with Schubert or Schumann or even Liszt,
Chopin is no longer a Romantic, but is already a neo-Romantic, so great
is the sensitivity of his feelings, so bold and new are his means of expression, particularly in his harmony, so rich in modulations and dissonances.
His contemporaries felt this aspect of his compositions to be bizarre, to
be "morbid eccentricity" (Schumann); Field, the composer of nocturnes,
when in 1832–33 he became acquainted with Chopin, spoke of "a sickroom
talent." But the whole Romantic Movement must have appeared in this
light to the representatives of the "Classical" period; and when Goethe
once wrote to Zelter, on February 12, 1829, about the trend of the time
which "runs through and through" the age as one of "dragging everything down into the weak and pitiful," that remark certainly does not
apply to Chopin. It is true that Chopin's sensitivity, developed to excess,
was able to release pathological effects; but also these incidental pathological effects are characteristic of neo-Romanticism.

No one has characterized Chopin's "pathological" manner of working
more accurately than Liszt, who was able to observe it at very close
range. Strangely enough, he does so not in his essay on Chopin himself,
but in one on Robert Franz.

Chopin was . . . of an intensely passionate, an overflowingly nervous nature. He restrained himself, without being able to tame himself. Every morn-
ing he began anew the difficult task of imposing silence upon his raging anger,
his whitehot hate, his boundless love, his throbbing pain, and his feverish
excitement, and to keep it in suspense by a sort of spiritual ecstasy—an ecstasy
in which he plunged in order to conjure up through his dreams an enchanting world of faery, to live therein and, detaining it in his art, to find a painful
happiness. Working in a thoroughly subjective manner, . . . he could not

succeed in diverting for a moment his attention from himself, in order to objectify anything and by the choice and treatment of his material to communicate his feelings more indirectly. Precisely for the reason that he sacrificed himself to the struggle with passions and suffering at once intense and intensely repressed, it became almost impossible for him to win respite for works of longer breadth. The best among his works were embraced within small dimensions, and this could not have been otherwise because each one of these works was the fruit of but a short moment of reflection, which sufficed to reproduce the tears and the dreams of a day.

This characterization is, of course, no less significant of Liszt than of Chopin. We are very grateful for the fact that Chopin in his music did not "objectify anything."

ROMANTIC VIRTUOSI: HELLER, HENSELT, ALKAN

The Romantic era was the time of the great piano virtuosi, of the *discovery* of the piano in its intimate and exhibitionistic potentialities. It is not the task of this book to give a history of piano music in the 19th century, but a few characteristic personalities must be named—representatives of the Schumann type of intimacy and of the Liszt type of brilliance—without thereby pretending to say that any one of them belongs entirely on the one or the other side, although no one of them achieved Chopin's universality within this limited field. Almost completely inclined to the side of Schumannesque intimacy was Stephen Heller of Budapest (1813–1888), a child prodigy like all these virtuosi. His early career was interrupted by illness, but in the provincial quietness of Augsburg between 1830 and 1838 he developed his character both as man and as musician. He then moved to Paris, where despite his friendship with Chopin and Liszt he preserved his individuality—that of a Romantic miniaturist and idyllist. A few titles will give an idea of the nature of his works: *Promenades d'un Solitaire,* Opp. 78 and 79 (after Jean-Jacques Rousseau); *Blumen-, Frucht- und Dornenstücke* (after Jean Paul); *Reise um mein Zimmer,* Op. 140 (after R. Toepffer). Alongside these there are, of course, many sonatas, sonatinas, dances, nocturnes, ballades, songs without words, and especially *études,* as well as all the other forms of piano music of the time. Schumann has again found the right words to characterize young Heller in connection with a discussion of Heller's Impromptus, Op. 7. Schumann says that he is thoroughly tired of the word "Romantic," but what else is one to call Heller?

Thank heavens, our composer knows nothing of that vague, nihilistic monster behind which many seek for the Romantic, as well as of that crude, scribbling materialism with which the French neo-Romantics amuse themselves. Instead, he has feelings that are on the whole natural, and he expresses himself sensibly and clearly. In listening to his compositions, however, one feels that something more stands in the background—an individual, attractive twilight, or rather something like the dawn, which makes one see the otherwise definite figures in a strange aspect. One can never express this sort of thing sharply by words. Perhaps one can communicate it more effectively by a picture; so I should like to compare that spiritual light to the haloes which one will observe in the dawn on certain days about the shadowy outlines of many heads. After all, he has nothing at all supernatural about him other than a feeling soul in a living body. . . .

The majority of his pianistic contemporaries, however, inclined more to the virtuoso, Lisztian side. There may be some significance in the fact that the best representatives of this tendency—of whom the last was Ferruccio Busoni—tired of virtuosity and, in the manner of Liszt, withdrew from the "world."

A rather early example is Adolf Henselt (1814–1889), who was born in Schwabach in Bavaria, studied piano under Hummel in Weimar and composition under Sechter in Vienna, and went to St. Petersburg in 1838. There he abandoned entirely his career as virtuoso and was henceforth active only as a teacher and organizer of musical instruction in Russia. Looking at the list of Henselt's works, one almost has the impression that he is seeing a counterpart to Chopin's. There are only a few pieces of chamber music, always with piano: a Duet with Horn, Op. 14; a Trio in A minor, Op. 24; a Concerto in F minor, Op. 16; Concert Variations on a Theme by Meyerbeer, Op. 11. All the rest are purely pianistic works. It is enough to quote the titles of the first three: Op. 1, *Variations de concert sur l'opéra L'Elisir d'amore de Donizetti;* Op. 2, *Douze études caractéristiques de concert,* all with poetical mottos; Op. 3, *Poème d'amour—Andante et étude concertante.* In addition to these, there are impromptus, nocturnes, romances, ballades, waltzes, and songs without words. There are, moreover, Lisztian items, such as a series of arrangements and "transcriptions." Principal among these are some pieces after Weber, whose piano works—significantly enough—inspired not only Henselt but also Liszt, Bülow, and Tausig to this type of composition. The special ingredient in Henselt's pianistic style, however, came from his enthusiasm for Bach, resulting in a mingling of polyphonic, strict style

with the virtuoso element. Those who are acquainted with his piano concerto know of difficult two-voiced "Bachian" passages in its third movement. It is a strange, genuinely Romantic mixture: Hummel, Weber, Liszt,
Chopin, and Bach!

That remark of Schumann's about the vague, nihilistic monster and
the crude materialism of the French neo-Romantics applies to another
piano specialist who belongs on the Lisztian side: Charles H. V. Alkan,
or, more properly, C. H. V. Morhange (1813–1888). None of Schumann's
writing is more sharp and angry than his critique of Alkan's *Trois
Grandes Etudes,* Op. 15:

The taste of this *Newfrank* reveals itself in a hasty glance at the volume,
and savors very much of Eugène Sue and George Sand. One is horrified by
such disregard of art and nature. Liszt, at least, caricatures with spirit. Berlioz, despite all his waywardness, shows here and there a human heart, and is
a wastrel full of strength and boldness. But here we find almost nothing but
feebleness and unimaginative vulgarity. The études have headings like "Aime-
moi," "Le Vent," and "Morte." Their only distinction, in the course of some
fifty pages, is the fact that they contain only notes without any indication of
how they are to be played. The Caprice might escape censure, chiefly because
one knows without any indication how such music is supposed to be played.
But the inner emptiness now decks itself out with exterior emptiness, and
what is then left? In "Aime-moi" there is a watery French melody with a
middle movement which is not at all in keeping with the title. In "Le Vent"
there is a chromatic howl over an idea taken from Beethoven's A-major Symphony. In the last piece there is a horrible desert of nothing but wood and
sticks and hangman's rope—this last borrowed from Berlioz, at that. We
would protect the wayward talent if there were any there, and if there were
only some music present. But where the former is still dubious and the latter
reveals nothing but black on black, we must turn aside in a bad humor. . . .

Was Schumann right? Did he have the ear for the night side, the
macabre, of the French Romantic movement? Alkan, born in Paris, son
of the proprietor of a private school, likewise a pianistic prodigy—making
public appearances at fourteen—returned from a short concert tour to
London in 1833 and withdrew almost entirely into Parisian solitude, a
solitude possible for a misanthrope and eccentric only in a large city.
Although he was master of a virtuoso technique perhaps equal to Liszt's,
he no longer played in public and no longer wrote for the world. This
tendency is also typically Romantic—more and more to lose touch with
actuality and to withdraw into a pure kingdom of the imagination. Thus
he lost his sense of proportion, with regard to both the performability
and the dimensions of his piano works, seventy-six in number—and he

wrote no others, despite titles like *"Concerti da camera,"* Op. 10, "Concerto," *"Symphonie," "Chants,"* Op. 38, Nos. 1 and 2, 65, 67, 70. A Piano Sonata Op. 33 with a "psychological" program (the only one he wrote) and the "Concerto," in which he differentiated between solo and *tutti* as J. S. Bach once did in the *Italian Concerto,* overstep both the performer's and the audience's limitations: the first movement alone of the G-sharp minor Concerto contains 1,343 measures—more than Beethoven's entire Op. 106. The mechanical aspect—endless transpositions of figurations—is linked with the mysterious.

Alkan wrote pieces "in the religious style" or an Impromptu "on a chorale of Luther's," Op. 69 (for the Pedal-Piano, of which he was very fond). But he also wrote "characteristic pieces," somewhat more bizarre than characteristic, such as his three compositions, each in four parts, entitled "The Months," Op. 74. Here Autumn proceeds through the following images: "Storm at Sea—The Dying Man—The Opera." Or he wrote, several decades before Arthur Honegger's *Pacific 231,* an étude "The Railroad," Op. 27, a study in sixteenth-notes in D minor with staccato basses in eighths, *vivacissimamente,* with several naturalistic features. To be sure, he is happiest in his études and transcriptions (from Bach and Handel to Weber); and, to be sure, he will again and again attract quite great virtuosi, the most recent one being Busoni, who placed him among the greatest luminaries of the pianistic firmament. He is perhaps to be compared with his contemporary, the Belgian painter Antoine-Joseph Wiertz, who likewise combined certain artistic qualities with eccentricity and poor taste. But that he is not to be judged from the German point of view in the Romantic era is shown, perhaps, by his influence on the piano works of César Franck, in which selectivity and strictness likewise do not prevent the occasional intrusions of banality.

BRAHMS AS PIANIST

Does Johannes Brahms belong in this series of Romantic virtuosi, or virtuoso Romantics? Is his body of piano works inclusive enough, in comparison with that of Schumann, Chopin, or Liszt, or in comparison even with the rest of his own works? One might answer the latter question first. Indeed, his list of piano works is not so all-inclusive as Chopin's, and it does not stand so definitely in the center of his own production as does Schumann's or Liszt's. But one ought not to judge it by the two or three comparatively small volumes in his collected edition representing his actual piano works, from Opus 1 to Opus 119. Brahms wrote two great piano concertos, Op. 15 and Op. 83, both of symphonic proportions, the first not only in the key but also in the heroic attitude of the Ninth Symphony, and the second more gentle, more feminine, more "Romantic," being symphonic only in the fact of its having four movements. In his chamber music, Brahms always gave the piano supremacy when he wished to allow free play to his "Romantic" fancy. His chamber music for strings alone, on the other hand, has a tendency to become more a matter of Classicistic retrospect—towards Mozart or Haydn in the quartets and quintets until, in the Clarinet Quintet, the great lesson has been learned.

Brahms was much too good a pupil of Beethoven, who in his works of chamber music with piano had been the first to make serious use of the dialogue or dramatic relationship between the piano and its partner or partners, not to make this relationship even more intense, to fashion it still more dramatically, and accordingly to fill out more and more richly the role that the piano plays. First he wrote a few works in the Schubertian tradition, in the B-major Trio, Op. 8, and the Quartets in G minor and A major, Opp. 25 and 26. Schubertian also is the Quintet in F minor, Op. 34; but the dramatic dialogue between the two bodies of sound is so marked that the work can be refashioned without essential change into the Sonata for Two Pianos, Op. 34 *bis*. What tasks there are for the piano in the Trios (Opp. 40, 60, 87, 101, and 114), in the three Sonatas with Violin (Opp. 78, 100, and 108), the two with Violoncello (Opp. 38 and 99), and the two with Clarinet (Op. 120, Nos. 1 and 2)! Brahms did not need to write pure piano music to be a great master of the piano; in this respect he is like Mozart, whose harvest of piano solo works, in relation to his concertos and his chamber music with piano, is small—though not insignificant.

Like Schumann, Brahms began with piano compositions: the three Sonatas (Opp. 1, 2, and 5) the Scherzo (Op. 4), the Sixteen Variations on a Theme by Schumann (Op. 9), and the Ballade (Op. 10). The difference is that he soon brought to an end his journey along the Schumannesque way, and with Opp. 3, 6, and 7 mingled volumes of songs in with the rest. The author of the Sonata, Op. 5, still called himself "Kreisler junior" —a personality even more impetuous, passionate, fond of making confessions than Schumann's "Florestan." But he soon came to feel that the time of the great sonata was past for a composer "born too late," born after Beethoven.

True, there were variations—Op. 21, No. 1, on a theme of his own,

Op. 21, No. 2, on a metrically unusual Hungarian song, the virtuoso Paganini Variations, Op. 35, the Thirty-Five Variations on an "Aria di Händel" with a closing fugue, Op. 24—variations that became more and more conscious, more and more strict, in which often, as in those on the Handel aria, even a secret historical compendium seems to be intended. In the Scherzo—at least in its main movement, not in the Trios— there is contained something like a "hommage à Chopin"; and in the Waltzes, Op. 39 (1869), something like an act of reverence to Vienna and to Schubert. As for the rest, Brahms wrote only still shorter pieces for the piano—Ballades, Intermezzi, Fantasies, Capricci, Romances, Rhapsodies. Except for the Ballades, Op. 10, these are all—Opp. 76, 79, 116, 117, 118, 119—works from the second half of his creative career, for between 1867 and 1879 there intervened a long pause in his writing of these purely pianistic works. These compositions were no "Bagatelles" in the style of Beethoven, no simple ideas demanding elaboration. Nor were they studies, although many of the pieces present a technical problem— over and above the technical problem that so many Brahmsian piano movements offer because of his manner of setting thirds and sixths in the low register, defying the pianist's efforts to play them clearly. Many are simple songs, like the Cradle Song among the Intermezzi, Op. 117, or like the Intermezzo, Op. 118, No. 2. Several are ballads, among which on one occasion (Op. 10, No. 1) he indicated the source of the inspiration ("after the Scottish Ballad 'Edward' in Herder's *Stimmen der Völker*"). On another occasion, however, he canceled in the course of publication the indication "Nocturne," which he had given as a subtitle in the manuscript of the "Fantasie," Op. 116, No. 4.

These compositions are intimate confessions, often difficult but never virtuoso, retrospective, folksong-like, excited, resigned. It is not simply a matter of personal confession but also of historical intuition. Piano sonatas were still being written, but the time for the sonata was past. Virtuoso composers were still being born, but the Romantic epoch of great brilliance was over. That was what these short pieces, which are not at all miniatures, say with finality.

CHAPTER XVI

Universalism within the National

II. Neo-Romantic Opera

WAGNER: POWER-POLITICIAN IN ART

THE polarity of the Romantic era in music appears most clearly in the fact that it fostered at once the utmost intimacy and the utmost theatricality; and opera, as it had come to be written in the first half of the 19th century, was the very height of theatricality. Even today, when a work of art in another field approaches this extreme, it is sometimes referred to or characterized quite justifiably as "operatic." A great number of Romantics avoided opera entirely, feeling either disgust or indifference towards it. Even if Chopin had not been primarily a piano composer, he can hardly be imagined as having anything to do with opera; and the fact that Schumann wrote an opera is to be explained only on the basis of his later striving for universality and of his feeling that he was morally and artistically obligated to cultivate even this field of music. From time to time Brahms toyed with plans for operas, but in the end laid them all aside. To his Swiss friend and would-be librettist Josef Victor Widmann, Brahms wrote in January, 1888 that he had given up all thoughts of "opera and marriage." It is not by mere chance that Beethoven and Schumann each wrote only one opera, and that Brahms wrote none at all.

The most important opera-sketch intended for Brahms was a libretto based on one of those fantastic *fiabe,* the *Re Cervo,* in which the dramatist Carlo Gozzi (1720–1806), an opponent of Goldoni, strangely combined motives, scenes, and figures from Italian or Oriental fairy tales with those from the *commedia dell'arte*. The cult of this cold, satirical dramatist Gozzi is one of the most curious and significant mistakes of the Romantic movement, which felt that the mingling of heterogeneous elements was

226

per se "poetical." One of Gozzi's German imitators was the Romantic poet Ludwig Tieck, whose *Gestiefelter Kater* is a mixture of fairy tale and caricature much like Gozzi's. But even more enthusiasts for Gozzi's *fiabe* were to be found among the opera-composers, in whose works the new "Romantic" mixture of sentiment and humor replaced the old Classical and childlike distinction between *serio* and *buffo*. It is indeed significant that Brahms, as late as 1877, was thinking of a source of material that had been finally disposed of by a somewhat older contemporary in his initial composition—*Die Feen,* the libretto of which was based on Gozzi's *La Donna Serpente.*

This older contemporary was Richard Wagner. In Wagner's work one finds the embodiment of neo-Romantic opera, the way for which had been prepared by Weber, Marschner, Spontini, Meyerbeer, and many others. But one must bear clearly in mind that despite this preparation, and despite the fact that Wagner had himself pursued this course of operatic development, his opera soon became an art-work of another sort. One must, moreover, bear clearly in mind that Wagner, although he considered himself to be a follower of composers like Weber and Beethoven, was a musician of another order than were his predecessors and contemporaries. He considered himself, justifiably, not as a pure musician, but as a music-dramatist. He saw in himself rather a combination, a fulfillment of the combination of Shakespeare and Beethoven. Since the result of this combination seemed to him, again justifiably, so overpoweringly great and unique, he envisioned the nation and, if possible, the whole world as the recipients of this artistic and philosophical message.

He was one of the revolutionists who consciously took up a position against the world, a power-politician in the arts, who wished to conquer the world and who really did conquer the 19th century. He looked about him for the artistic means to effect this conquest, and found that the strongest means lay in drama—not in the spoken word, but rather in drama with music. Therefore he became a composer. He was the first to use music as a means of influencing, of entrancing, of intoxicating, of conquering. To be sure, all musicians direct their attention to the "world" —to connoisseurs, to a community great or small, to the nation. Even before Wagner a few composers had felt impelled to create a community for themselves because there was none at hand. Handel did so in his oratorios; Beethoven, in his symphonies. So far as Wagner was concerned, however, Handel scarcely existed, being much too clear, humane, anti-barbarian, anti-chaotic, Italian. But in Beethoven Wagner saw his true predecessor—

or, more precisely, in the Beethoven of the Ninth Symphony, with which the reign of pure instrumental music seemed to have come to an end and that of opera, of *his* opera, to have begun.

It took quite a while for Wagner to become a musician, or rather for him to take serious steps in mastering the technical side of music sufficiently well to utilize it for effects. Being the son of an actor—for there is scarcely any doubt that he was the offspring of an adulterous union—he received his first great artistic impression when he attended a performance of *Der Freischütz* given under the direction of the composer himself. Yet it was not so much the music that enraptured him as it was the exercise of power over so great an aggregation of performers by a single individual. "Not being an emperor or a king," he exclaimed, "yet thus standing there and directing!" The second impression, scarcely less intense, was that of the singer Wilhelmine Schröder-Devrient's performance of the title role in Beethoven's *Fidelio*. "Anyone who remembers this wonderful woman at this period of her life," wrote Wagner, "must somehow be able to bear witness to the almost divine warmth which the humane and ecstatic achievement of this incomparable artist cast over her audience." Wagner wished to write a composition that would be worthy of this singer; but since all the prerequisites for his doing so were lacking, he renounced "all striving for art in intense despair."

Without securing a diploma, he turned his back on school and, as *studiosus musicae,* plunged into the most nonsensical and unrestrained student life. Yet from the good cantor of the Thomas-Schule, Christian Theodor Weinlig, he secured incidentally a knowledge of the technique of composition, which he immediately put into practice with remarkable self-assurance and, one might say, almost as if it were a matter of routine. In contrast to Weber, Chopin, or Schumann, he began in a quite unoriginal manner; and one can scarcely consider his Piano Sonata in B-flat major, Op. 1, without embarrassment. With him, however, it was not a matter of *music,* but of the *effect* to be achieved through music. And this is so even in these early compositions, among which are a symphony and a few overtures.

At this time he turned aside completely from the Romantic ideals of childhood and youth, and sought only for the achievement of quick success. Success of this sort was to be achieved by combining, as it were, *opera buffa,* the cantilena of Bellini, and the fire of Auber's *Muette de Portici.* Taking Shakespeare's *Measure for Measure* as a basis, he wrote the libretto for his *Liebesverbot* and set it to music. This work was to represent "a bold glorification of free sensuousness" in the manner of "Young Germany"—not merely an artistic gesture, but also an open declaration in favor of unrestrained, real life. Unfortunately, it had no opportunity of achieving its effect; for the hastily rehearsed initial and only performance at the Magdeburg municipal theater, where Wagner in the meantime (1834) had become engaged—both as music director and as fiancé—"remained . . . a musical shadow-play on the stage, to which the orchestra, with frequently exaggerated noise, did its best to contribute its inexplicable gushes." In Königsberg the fiancé became a married man; and there followed, in Riga, a few years of very unhappy matrimonial disappointments and quarrels as well as very miserable activity as conductor of a provincial theater—from all of which Wagner escaped by an adventurous flight to sea.

His courage, his self-reliance, which never left him even when he was plunged into the most abysmal depths of ill-fortune, is indicated by the fact that he now wished to conquer the world by way of Paris, by way of grand opera. He composed the libretto and music for *Rienzi, the Last of the Tribunes,* an overgrown five-act historical opera, in which greater scenic and musical resources are called for than in Spontini and Meyerbeer combined. In the attempt to stage this work, Wagner experienced, of course, most bitter disappointments, despite Meyerbeer's protection—or perhaps also, as Wagner himself intimates, in consequence of the insincerity of this protection. Somewhat later, this same *Rienzi* opened the way for his going to Dresden and assisted him in securing an assured, "bourgeois" means of subsistence, at a time when he had long since overcome within himself the ideal or inadequacy of grand opera. There is an ironical feature in this situation, for Wagner must have felt that the applause accorded to *Rienzi* was not due to him but to Meyerbeer, though to a "Meyerbeer" of heightened dramatic effectiveness and improved taste.

The Parisian period—two and a half years of the most furious Bohemianism—represents a turning-point in Wagner's artistic attitudes. The change was ushered in by a hearing of Beethoven's Ninth Symphony, performed at one of the concerts of the Conservatoire orchestra under Habeneck ". . . in so perfect and gripping a manner that, all at once, the vision that in my youthful enthusiasm I had divined of this wonderful work . . . now stood before me clear as sunlight, as if I could take hold of it with my hands. . . . The whole period during which I had allowed my taste to run wild—a period which, precisely considered, had begun with my going astray by pursuing the type of expression found in Beethoven's later compositions, and had increased so alarmingly through my depressing experience with the horrible theater—now sank away before me as if in a deep abyss of shame and remorse." [39] It was highly characteristic of him that at this crisis he did not, for example, turn away from the "horrible theater" to which he had made his offering with his frivolous *Liebesverbot* and his pompous *Rienzi* and become—let us say—a composer of symphonies and chamber music. He could not renounce opera. But since he was a German, and since in Germany there were only individual landmarks in the history of opera such as *The Magic Flute, Fidelio,* and *Der Freischütz* and no operatic tradition, he could not—as could someone like Verdi—take the given, national form of opera and refine it into something more and more pure. He accordingly denied the traditional operatic form, particularly that of grand opera.

While still in Paris, he shaped up the material for his *Flying Dutchman,* "whose intimate acquaintance I had made on the sea. . . . In addition, I made the acquaintance of Heinrich Heine's characteristic use of this legend in one part of his *Salon.* Particularly, the treatment of the redemption of this Wandering Jew of the ocean, taken from a Dutch play of the same title [fictitious, incidentally] gave me everything at hand for utilizing this legend as an opera subject." [40] It was still Romantic opera in the sense of *Euryanthe* or *Hans Heiling.* But the customary musical forms of opera, arias, and ensembles began to relax their outlines even more here than in the above mentioned models; and the dramatico-musical *scene* began to take shape as the formative unity. The enhanced role of the orchestra, the increased use of the motif of reminiscence, and the economical limitation of thematic material were but external indications of this change. Wagner entitled the work "a Romantic opera." Yet he might just as well have called it a musico-dramatic ballad, whose three acts could be joined together without interruption.

In Dresden Wagner suffered a relapse. He worked at a sketch for a historical opera-poem set in the time of the great Hohenstaufen emperor Friedrich II and his son Manfred, or in other words the romantic Middle Ages. The heroine was a Saracen maid, a sort of Joan of Arc, half-Arabic by birth, who inspired Manfred, engulfed in inaction and "lyric enjoyment," to heroic deeds and finally died for him, her half-brother, in a death of sacrifice. This sort of thing characterized Wagner's last relapse

[39] *Mein Leben,* p. 210 f.
[40] Autobiographical sketch, covering period up through 1842.

into the historical. He wrote the book and music for *Tannhäuser,* a "drama in three acts," in which the hero is led from sensual enjoyment to "redeeming" contrition and in which the valiant heroine is replaced by a "saint." This opera was the first Wagnerian fusion of lust and piety, the utilization of religious ecstasy for theatrical effect, which returned later in *Parsifal* in more sublimated form. After *Tannhäuser* came *Lohengrin,* again entitled a "Romantic opera," a sublimation of the material which had been crudely presented in Marschner's *Heiling:* the condescension of a higher being to become a mortal and his failing the test of unconditional faith, of "highest trust."

With *Lohengrin,* Wagner again reached a turning-point in his development. The musician in him had, so to speak, overtaken the dramatist. It was here a question of the dramatist, not the poet; for, as a poet, Wagner remained all his life a questionable figure, having only as much command of poetry as was needed for drama. He was unable to give dramatic material a purely poetical form. For confirmation of this statement, one need only glance at the parallel series of dramas and operas in the forties: on the one hand, *The Saracen Maid, Frederick Barbarossa, Jesus of Nazareth;* on the other, *The Flying Dutchman, Tannhäuser, Lohengrin.* The poetical projects remained sketches; the operas got themselves finished. Wagner was unable to express himself either in the purely poetical or in the purely symphonic forms; he could do so only in a combination, the opera.

But the opera-composer, the *opera-dramatist,* was ready from the very beginning. To realize the sharpness of his eye for everything scenic and striking, his dramaturgic skill, one need only compare the libretto of *Das Liebesverbot* with the model supplied by Shakespeare—the clever reduction of the five acts to two, the elimination of everything episodic, the cleanly carried-out crescendos in the operatic manner of the 1830's. In the course of the forties, however, Wagner became more and more independent and individualistic, even as a musician. He was one of the few representatives of the type that begins unoriginally and eclectically, gradually increases and refines his tonal language in his own works without falling into mannerism, and *becomes* original. A musician of this type stands in contrast, let us say, to Schumann, who began with the highest originality and in the end ran afoul of eclecticism or mannerism. In *Tannhäuser* and *Lohengrin* there were still conventional features, but they came more and more to take on Wagner's own personal stamp, the form becoming more and more relaxed, easy, free. Music won a new function alongside its dramatic one—that of absorbing the listener, intoxicating him, and bowling him over. Especially in *Lohengrin,* one can distinguish clearly between the theatrical and the "ensnaring" features of the music. There are scenes of medieval splendor, of musical ceremony, embodied particularly in the figure of the Herald and the scenes which he opens; and there are the moments of "transport," in the role of the hero and his decorative effect, all concentrated in the A major of the Prelude.

How far Wagner had already deviated from the Romantic opera of his contemporaries with the succession of operas that closed with *Lohengrin,* and how conscious he was of his position is shown by a passage in one of his letters to Theodor Uhlig written towards the end of March, 1852. After attending a performance of Marschner's *Vampyr,* he wrote:

> . . . I was very much amused to observe that the public was not at all affected by the crudity of the subject. Their tolerance was due, of course, to their insensitivity, which in the opposite situation would remain likewise unaffected by gentleness. In opera, one can let the people see children being slaughtered and eaten alive in the theater without the audience's being aware of what is happening. This time the music as a *whole* also disgusted me. This singing of duets, trios, and quartets, this whimpering, is quite insanely stupid and tasteless; for it remains entirely without charm for the senses, and thus amounts only to a playing and singing of mere notes. Whatever is an exception to this statement, I shall be glad to admit. But now, at least, I see how very far removed *my* operas are from this so-called "German" type, which is, heaven knows, nothing but Italian music that has been made learnedly impotent, and has been re-soled and re-lined with German leather.

Thus he admitted that the "singing of duets, trios, and quartets" was perhaps still valid for Italian opera, which was no concern of his; but he no longer felt that it had any place in German opera, for which he believed that he had provided the first model.

The more important feature of this opinion, however, is not the criticism of Marschner, but that of the public. *The Flying Dutchman* had been performed not only in Dresden but also, thanks to Meyerbeer's good offices, in Berlin; and *Tannhäuser* had also received a seemingly not unfavorable reception. Yet these operas still remained not really understood. The revolutionist of the arts, accordingly, having obtained a kind of recognition that was not in accordance with his heart's desire, now denied not only the artistic activity and particularly the operatic activity, but also the entire society of his time. He attacked bourgeois "contentment" for its assent to the civilization of the Industrial Revolution. He looked back to Greek tragedy, through which the poet had spoken to an aroused, religiously disposed, *active* congregation. As a new Aeschylus, he demanded the same participation of a congregation in his work, even if for only a few hours. No longer did he appeal to the body of connoisseurs, without which, for example, the true joy in a Mozart opera (not to mention symphonic or chamber works) is unthinkable. On the contrary, he appealed to a congregation of laymen, of submissive, uncritical listeners.

His demand was that one must *believe* in the composer's work, in his mission. All his life he hated to have anyone see him in his workshop or try to discover how he had produced his effects. On one occasion he took it amiss that a member of his circle, Hans von Bülow, questioned the popularity of *Tristan und Isolde:*

> Of what concern is it to you, me, and our few genuine friends—this futile question about popularity? Why give it any attention at all? There are many things which we are willing to allow just among ourselves—for example, that since my acquaintance with Liszt's compositions I have become a quite different person from what I was before, so far as my harmonic style is concerned. But when friend Pohl [Richard Pohl, one of the collaborators in the *Neue Zeitschrift für Musik*] goes blabbing to all the world this secret at the very beginning of a short discussion of the Prelude to *Tristan,* this is—to say the least—plainly indiscreet; and I cannot well imagine that he was authorized to commit such an indiscretion.[41]

He did not wish to pass for a mere musician. Music was a magic potion, and to inquire after its ingredients was an "indiscretion."

In making his demands of his listeners, he especially counted upon the effect that he would create among his feminine audience. Being guided more by instinct, they seemed to him better than the masculine audience as a public. On March 16, 1852, he presented the *Tannhäuser* Overture in Zürich, "with augmented orchestra." Four days later he wrote to Uhlig: ". . . the effect was really *terrible* . . . that is, the women gradually lost their heads. Emotion ran so high among them that sobbing and crying had to come to their aid. . . . The noteworthy thing was the first effect, which manifested itself mostly as abject melancholy. Only after this had been expressed in tears did there come the comfort of supreme, of exuberant joy." In *Lohengrin,* accordingly, there appeared an opera which was specifically designed for its effect upon the feminine audience. A demi-god, the idol bowed down to its worshipers. This feature of Wagner's work, however, did not prevent his pathological effect from manifesting

[41] Letter of October 7, 1859.

itself strongly in a fifteen-year-old boy, who was later to become King Ludwig II of Bavaria. The artistic effect was simply transferred physiologically.

For the artist who has taken up a position in opposition to society, there are only two ways open: either to resign, draw back into himself, become isolated, wait and see whether success will yet present itself, or to take up the fight, if he is not ready to make any compromise. Wagner was not ready for compromise; and since he, as an opera-composer and man of the theater, could not renounce immediate effect, he became a revolutionary. "I bring . . . no reconciliation with worthlessness," he declared in a letter to Theodor Uhlig written in November, 1849, "but, instead, thoroughly unrelenting war. Total worthlessness now prevails in the public state of affairs and particularly in the trade of artists and litterateurs. I can therefore find friends only in those regions which are entirely apart from the dominant reaches of public life. There is nothing here to be persuaded and to be won over—only something to be rooted out. We have the strength to do so—given time—if we will realize ourselves as apostles of a new religion, and will strengthen ourselves in faith through mutual love. Let us hold fast to youth, and let age perish, for there is nothing to hold to in it!"

When Wagner wrote this, he had already made his profession of faith an actuality. A half year previously, the Royal Capellmeister Richard Wilhelm Wagner had taken an unquestionably active, though not mortally dangerous, part in the Dresden Revolution, had been obliged to flee from Germany, and was already living as an exile in Switzerland.

The composition of *Lohengrin* had been completed early in 1848, and for five long years Wagner let his pen lie idle. This fact was due not only to the external events in his life, but also, primarily, to a revolutionary change in his inner life—to his break with the modern theater and with the civilizing relationships in which this theater seemed to take its place. *Lohengrin* was a conclusion; however far it was in advance of its time, it was yet a "Romantic opera"—the final member of a historical series that had begun with *Der Freischütz*. The next work, the *Rhinegold*, belongs to another type of opera.

WAGNER EXPLAINS WAGNER: THE *RING*

Even while working on *Lohengrin,* Wagner busied himself with the Nibelung myth, which he sketched towards the end of 1848 as "an outline for a drama," and of which he presented the last part as *Siegfried's Death* in actually dramatic form. Since he could not derive the purely human element from historical material, and since folk tales and legends were no longer sufficient, as they had been in the three Romantic operas of the forties, he turned his attention to myths and introduced the Norse divinities into the scene. This development had nothing to do with nationalism, and was not, as it were, the artistic manifestation of a purpose which Wagner professed in a pamphlet of about the same time (late summer, 1850), "Jewry in Music"—one of the most infamous pieces to come from the pen of Wagner the pamphleteer, published by him under the shabby cloak of a pseudonym, destined to serve as a veritable arsenal of anti-Semitism for the following nine decades—although Wagner constantly held open for the Jew a way of "redemption" in self-destruction. No, it was the model of Greek tragedy that hovered about the creation of *Der Ring des Nibelungen,* tragedy intended for a religiously minded congregation, unfortunately now prevented from being Athenian or Hellenic; and although Wagner was at this time concerned with the figure of Achilles, he soon saw that it was useless for his purposes.

First of all, he tried to clarify his intentions in a theoretical way, or rather he sought a theoretical justification for everything that he was able and willing to do. All his writings, incidentally, are propaganda; and it would be the height of misapprehension to try to conceive of them as the guiding stars of his career, either from the historical or aesthetic point of view. What he was able and willing to create was the "universal work of art" (*Gesamtkunstwerk*), with which he had the power to move and even intoxicate the public. With rare candor he once wrote to Liszt (on August 16, 1853): ". . . to be sure, my talents, taken separately and individually, are not great at all; I am something and achieve something only when I bring all of them together in an effect and when they and I are recklessly consumed therein. Whatsoever my passions demand of me, I become for the time being—musician, poet, director, author, lecturer, or anything else. Thus I was also for a time a speculative aesthete. . . ." In a precise and felicitous manner, Wagner gave first place to the musician in this schematic analysis of his personality. For it is *music* that in his *Gesamtkunstwerk* wins the real and final victories, though it is music in connection with spectacle; for music—or, rather, good music—*without* scenic presentation was something that Wagner could not write.

The preponderant contribution of music to the effect of his dramatic compositions did not prevent his assigning, in opera, the masculine role to drama and the feminine to music. In his pamphlet "Art and Revolution" (1849), he began with a reference to Attic drama, which he supposed to be the artistic symbol of an ideal commonwealth. Since that time there had occurred not only the decay of this social ideal but also the crumbling of the ancient *Gesamtkunstwerk* into the individual arts—that of the dance, of music, of poetry, and of the plastic arts. In an ensuing pamphlet, "The Art-Work of the Future," Wagner demanded of these individual arts, which had been freed from their original connection, that they give up their independent, egoistic development and return to a state of union, although he was also well aware of the fact that these egoistic developments had achieved noteworthy results. In his main work of a theoretical nature, "Opera and Drama" (1851), he then presented his idea of this *Gesamtkunstwerk* in detail. In this new music drama, music would serve drama—a situation the reverse of that with Mozart, who once said that in a good opera "poetry" had to be "the obedient daughter of music." The most important part in bringing about the new state of affairs, according to Wagner, was to be played by the symphony orchestra, that wonderful instrument which Beethoven had brought to perfection and which Wagner could not forbear putting to the most intensive use.

He availed himself of Shakespeare, and Wagner's reasoning is an excellent example of his way of doing violence to the history of the arts for his own ends. "The tragedies of Shakespeare stand unquestionably above those of the Greeks, for in their artistic technique they have completely overcome the necessity of having a chorus. In Shakespeare, the chorus has been resolved simply into individuals who personally take part in the action and who act out their intention and attitude for themselves quite according to the individual necessity for their doing so, just as does the protagonist. . . ." [42] Opera, however, could not make use of such a multitude of minor characters; moreover, it was not expected to forego an equivalent of the ancient chorus. By this time, accordingly, the modern orchestra had taken over the role of the ancient chorus: it gave a commentary, it indicated the dramatic proceedings that took place on the stage. It did so, moreover, no longer merely at the traditional places at the ends of acts, but in eloquent give-and-take, and in an uninterrupted flow. The separation of the drama into absolute poetry and absolute music was abolished. A new equilibrium of the arts had thus been found in a unified work.

To test his theories by an example, Wagner completed *Der Ring des*

[42] *Gesammelte Schriften* III³, p. 268.

Nibelungen, first the text and then the music. The text he completed in the summer of 1852, taking up the separate parts in reverse order: first *Siegfried's Death* (1848), then *Young Siegfried,* then *The Valkyrie,* and finally the prelude to this trilogy, the *Rhinegold.* This procedure was somewhat the same as he had followed with *Lohengrin,* composing the third act first and only thereafter the first and second. The musical setting of the *Ring* he began, however, with the *Rhinegold.* Of course, a much greater period of time was necessary for the completion of the monster work. The *Rhinegold* was completed at the end of 1854, the *Valkyrie* in the spring of 1856. But in the third act of *Siegfried* Wagner came to a standstill in the late summer of 1857 and did not resume work on it till July, 1865. Finally with *Dusk of the Gods (Götterdämmerung)*—that was the new title for the last part—he brought the whole work to a close in 1874.

Twenty-six years was a long period of time in the development of a genius like Wagner; accordingly, the work had come to be full of contradictions and weaknesses. This observation is not made as a criticism of the work, but rather as a recognition of the fact that was significant for Wagner's Romanticism and for the Romantic era in general. First Wagner changed the hero in the course of his work. In *Siegfried's Death* it had been, of course, Siegfried—or rather Brünnhilde, for Siegfried here plays a passive and equivocal role. The plot had been advanced by a quite materialistic "drink of forgetfulness," a simple drug which occasioned Siegfried's faithlessness to Brünnhilde. But later, in accordance with Wagner's despair over the civilizing influence of the society of his times, the hero became Wotan. This god, since he had lost his power, must leave the struggle against the nether world to a "free" being; and after his tragic end he accepted with resignation the decline of the world and its redemption through woman's love. Wagner's coming to know the philosophy of Arthur Schopenhauer in 1854 called forth still further alterations in *Götterdämmerung.* Wagner immediately took over Schopenhauer's general view of life with the greatest enthusiasm, and made Schopenhauer—who in actuality belonged much more to the "Latin," humanistic, Goethean period—into the fashionable philosopher of the Romantic era.

The mythical, primeval drama of *Götterdämmerung,* peopled only by gods, dwarfs, giants, nixies, valkyries, and heroes, is at the same time mixed up with modern psychology. The saturnine pair of lovers, brother and sister, Siegmund and Sieglinde, for example, may be referred to a model in Wagner's own life; his love affair with Jessie Laussot. The motive which prompts Wotan to forbid the infatuated Siegfried's visiting the sleeping Brünnhilde, moreover, is paternal jealousy. The same cleavage between old and new is to be found in the music. Grand opera, which Wagner had so passionately combatted in its caricatured Meyerbeerian form, again penetrated the *Ring,* with all its pomp. It did not come in by the back door, either: the complicated dramatic machinery of the *Ring,* which so frequently idles along, so frequently creaks, and the "manufactured" dramatic scenes correspond to the purely decorative musical scenes of grand opera, and—particularly in *Götterdämmerung*—to the often merely clever combination of themes and motives. Even Wagner had to pay the price for being born too late, for being a man of the 19th century.

TRISTAN UND ISOLDE

In the period that separated the torso of *Siegfried* from its completion and the beginning of work on *Götterdämmerung,* Wagner wrote his two masterpieces in the neo-Romantic style, *Tristan und Isolde* (completed in 1859) and *Die Meistersinger von Nürnberg* (1861–67). They are both the product of the greatest love affair in Wagner's life (the significance of which he deliberately concealed in his autobiography), his relations with Mathilde Wesendonck, which necessarily had to end in renunciation. Or is this only the result of Wagner's need for creating works of this nature? *Die Meistersinger,* at least, had haunted his imagination ever since the time of *Tannhäuser.* One will never know the answers to all the questions connected with this love of his; but the artistic aspect is with Wagner, as a genuine Romantic, always the primary one, and he was very fond of projecting the figments of his imagination into actuality, as—vice versa— he made use of his experiences for purposes of his art. During the time when he was a partisan of "Young Germany," he rashly married the little actress Minna Planer, who brought with her into the marriage an illegitimate child; and during the time when he came to know Schopenhauer's philosophy with its "denial of the will to life," he entered into hopeless relations with the wife of another man, to whom he was deeply indebted. From the latter experience he created a love-drama which ends with the *Liebestod,* with self-destruction as the highest rapture, the greatest climax, and the transmutation of sensuousness into spirituality.

We have already (p. 194) spoken of a precious byproduct of this experience, the five songs written to texts by the woman who had inspired the work. What was only hinted at there found full expression in the opera, which Wagner called in the printed copy simply "action" (*Handlung*), while in his autograph manuscript he omitted the title completely. This opera became a culmination of the neo-Romantic art-work, and a turning-point in the history of music. It was a culmination of the neo-Romantic art-work in general, not merely of the neo-Romantic opera; for in no field of 19th-century art is there anything comparable to set beside it.

The only criticism that might be made of it—as has already been indicated—is that in it the most intimate experience of the soul is made into an *opera* and presented to the opera-going public, to the mass. Yet how would Wagner have been able, precisely in this situation, to forego his own favorite instrument, the orchestra? In the midst of his work on the *Ring des Nibelungen,* which was to be a philosophical *drama* principally for drama's sake, he wrote a work that was primarily music for music's sake. Wagner indicated the fact—as usual, semi-involuntarily— when he himself spoke the truth thus: "Of this work I have taken the liberty of harboring the loftiest expectations, which follow from my theoretical ideas. I do so not because I may have given the work its form according to my system, for in writing it I completely forgot all theory, but because I here, at last, with the fullest freedom and the most complete disregard of every theoretical consideration, have conducted myself in such a manner that during the execution of my plans I perceived how widely I soared out beyond my system. . . ."

One of the indications of Wagner's independence of his own theories is the nonchalance with which he returned again and again in the verse of *Tristan* to end-rhyme, after he had completely thrown it overboard in the *Ring* in favor of the so-called *Stab*-rhyme, based on alliteration or initial assonance. The "fullest freedom" and "most complete disregard of every theoretical consideration," however, arose from the fact that here Wagner the dramatist was completely overpowered by Wagner the *musician.* One might say that he wrote the work only for the sake of the second act, in which greater part practically nothing happens dramatically, but a great deal happens musically. The first act he wrote only as a dramatic introduction for the duet of the lovers, the third to continue this duet after the interruption of long, masterfully tortured episodes and to bring it to a crowning close.

As symbols for the love-dialogue, Wagner chose the Romantic contrast between "day," which is hostile to love, and "night" as the fulfillment of all yearning. We have already indicated that Novalis was a predecessor in the use of these symbols. We might cite one further remarkable passage from Friedrich Schlegel's novel *Lucinde* (1799). There, under the heading "Yearning and Rest," occurs the following passage in a dialogue between a pair of lovers: "O eternal yearning! At last the vain longing of day, the empty brilliance, will sink and be extinguished, and a great night of love will be felt eternally at rest." Another Romantic, Friedrich Schleiermacher, in an "appendix" to the novel, *Vertraute Briefe,* speaks prophetically of this passage as "the duet." In *Tristan und Isolde,* a wish of the entire Romantic era was fulfilled, thanks to music, much as in the *Ring* there was fulfilled the wish of certain Romantic writers, notably Fouqué with his *Sigurd the Dragon-Slayer* (1808).

This fulfillment was due to the music. For *Tristan und Isolde* is not only a work in which the overt dramatic action now and then stands entirely still and gives place to the music, but it is also an orchestral opera throughout. It is significant that, later, Wagner on one occasion gave his friend Friedrich Nietzsche this bit of advice for enjoying *Tristan:* "Take your glasses off! You must hear nothing but the orchestra." It is significant that Wagner himself sanctioned the procedure, often followed in concert, of adding the *Liebestod* directly on to the Prelude—without the voice part. Actually it is unnecessary, being simply one strand in the fabric of the orchestra. At the end of the first act, when the love potion permits the lovers to express their feelings freely in a duet, the vocal parts are not indispensable, for they contribute scarcely a turn of melody that does not appear in the orchestra. This orchestra says a great deal that the figures on the stage conceal. With the most sensitive flexibility, every agitation of their souls is followed.

This achievement is the triumph of Wagner's art of *transition.* "It is so indispensably important to be understood . . . ," he declared; "and this intelligibility is to be achieved only by the most definite and most compelling motivation of the transitions. My entire work of art rests precisely upon the bringing out of the necessary and willing mode of feeling by means of this motivation." [43] In *Tristan* one does not find the long stretches of musical decoration that one finds in the *Ring:* there is no "Magic Fire Scene," no "Ride of the Valkyries," no "Rhine Journey of Siegfried." Everything is inner activity. For this reason, the way in which the motifs are transmuted and joined musically is more sensitive and more compelling than it is anywhere else in Wagner, except in the later

[43] Letter to Mathilde Wesendonck, Oct. 29, 1859.

Parsifal. The harmony, moreover, in the preponderantly chromatic inventiveness of motifs is more novel and refined. All the elements in this harmony—its suspensions, its alterations, and tensions—had been already present, individually, in Spohr, in Liszt, and even in Mozart. But in Wagner these elements, in a *system* that has turned into something very personal, have a new effect; with *Tristan* one realm of harmony closes and a new one begins. Never before had music had such an intoxicating, or narcotic effect, or been so much to Wagner's taste. He was right when on June 5, 1859, he wrote thus to the woman who had involuntarily helped originate the work: ". . . I have never written anything like it before—you will indeed marvel when you hear it." At the beginning of August, 1860, he wrote her, "To me *Tristan* is and remains a wonder! I shall never be able to understand how I could have written anything like it." And, in the end, he paid tribute to her part in the work: "I shall be eternally grateful to you for the fact that I have written *Tristan.*" [44]

DIE MEISTERSINGER: NATIONAL SOCIAL DRAMA

Many intermingled influences play a part in *Die Meistersinger von Nürnberg,* which in the first version of 1845 was simply called a "Comic Opera in Three Acts," in the second and third "Grand Comic Opera in Three Scenes," and finally was left without subtitle. Like *Tristan,* it is a work *sui generis,* Wagner's only musical comedy—if we leave out of account his youthful "wild oats" in *Liebesverbot.* The tragic creations of Wagner, including the *Ring,* all project into the international sphere; but *Die Meistersinger* is a work of art that is emphatically national—though, to be sure, not "popular" or nationalistic. Even in conceiving of the work, Wagner, being a man of the theater, had thought especially of a performance in Paris, where there was so much affection for the old German costumes on the stage. The German character of the work was not intended; it inhered in the material. In much the same way, Wagner's concern with Wotan and Siegfried in the *Ring* was no longer a matter of Germanism, as it would have been in the beginning period of the Romantic movement, when the literary sources of the primeval and medieval periods were being brought to light again.

Wagner here introduces us to one of the few happy, if not great, periods in German history, the time about the middle of the 16th century when the storms of the Reformation had to some extent subsided and the terrible

[44] Letter to Mathilde Wesendonck, Dec. 21, 1861.

war of the following century had only begun to make its threats felt. He leads his audience into the heart of Germany, to the free city of Nuremberg, industrious in art and trade, with its narrow and secret streets, its churches and towers, its high gables, its old Gothic and fashionable Renaissance features, its inhabitants so eager for a good fight and so eager to engage in a festival, and its guilds, at the head of which stood the noble and somewhat comic guild of the mastersingers.

Tragic tones are also sounded in this comic opera, but for the first and only time in Wagner's work there is no Romantic "redemption"—only a happy, harmonious *resolution*. From an entirely external point of view, it is a perfect *opera buffa*. Here again are "arias"; here again are ensembles like the quintet at the end of the first half of the last act, even though it is no dramatic Mozartian ensemble; here again are grand finales in which the madness of the action is carried to the extreme—finales in which Wagner again takes up the kind of writing he did in the closing ensemble scenes of his *Tannhäuser* and *Lohengrin*. The unique feature of the work, however, is the uniting or linking together of several symbolic plot-motifs, the blending of objective and subjective, of most general and most personal elements.

Die Meistersinger is social drama. The knight is pitted against the burghers, with their guild organization, in an uncomprehending and even hostile relationship. The Philistinism of the guild rejects the member of another class who desires to be admitted to it. After having won the victor's prize, the noble youth defends himself against the community by means of these "burghers." Acting as intermediary between these opposites, there stands a man who through human and artistic experience has come to occupy a position above these parties and who is recognized by the people as their representative, the cobbler and poet, Hans Sachs. In the introduction of the "people" who, so to speak, pronounce God's judgments, we see the Romantic aspect of *Die Meistersinger:* it is not German *opera buffa*, but Romantic comedy.

In addition, however, the work is an autobiographical drama about artists. Sachs and Stolzing are pitted against each other. In the two figures there is symbolized the eternal conflict into which the innovator and revolutionary in art is involved with the old man who is entrenched behind "laws," behind rules. Stolzing is Florestan; but Sachs is Raro, who achieves the reconciliation, not without violent convulsions of the soul. He recognizes the rightness of the new, yet he convinces the revolutionary of the rightness of the old and of the rules. The antagonist of

Sachs and Stolzing is Beckmesser, the "marker," in whose caricatured figure Wagner has personified his great hatred for uncreative criticism, and yet has again so objectified this feeling that we can share his laughter. *Die Meistersinger* was originally planned in 1845 as a sort of comic after-piece to *Tannhäuser,* to the singing contest at the Wartburg: even at that time, all the rancor that the struggle for recognition had created within Wagner's soul was to explode in irony and satire. Wagner was indebted to his experience with Mathilde Wesendonck for the fact that in the creation of Hans Sachs he found the way to resignation, to "conquering the world" without consigning it to perdition.

As a musician, however, Wagner made the most out of the opposition between the old and the new. He symbolized the old, the "guild," by Bach's contrapuntal style, which he did not imitate but handled with his own special art of combination. This was one of the few instances in the 19th century when the archaic style again came to life, became active, without entering into a sort of chemical combination with the Romantic. Other instances are, perhaps, to be found among the works of Chopin, Brahms, Bizet, and César Franck. And this reaching backwards permitted Wagner to lift himself above himself, as it were, and to become slightly satirical about his own personal style. The violent dialogue of the pair of lovers in the second act ("*Ja, Ihr seid es . . .*") becomes, by virtue of its contrast to the general style of the opera, almost a parody of the *Ring* or *Tristan* style. Therein lies the real humor of *Die Meistersinger*—the greatest triumph of self-criticism on the part of its creator.

PARSIFAL: WAGNER'S SERMON TO HIS FLOCK

It is a triumph in the refining of his own style, a sublimation of his art, that distinguishes Wagner's last work, *Parsifal*. We do not here have to pass judgment upon this work, upon this mixture of the deepest mystery of the Catholic Church and the most sophisticated theater. To be sure, the mixture is far more repulsive because it is less naïve theatrically than was that in *Tannhäuser,* and it is not redeemed by its being called "A Festival Play for the Consecration of a Stage." But we do have to understand the work in connection with the history of Romantic opera. The conception of it goes far back, to the dramatic sketch *Jesus of Nazareth* (1848), from which the figure of the repentant sinner Mary Magdalen has apparently passed over into that of Kundry. Later, in 1856, during the *Tristan* period, there was a sketch for a Buddhistic drama, *The Vic-*

tors. In it, a Chandala maiden who in an earlier state of existence had been guilty of a heartless act is, after repentance and "denial of the will to live," at last accepted into the community of the blessed. Soon after sketching this drama, however, Wagner decided, in 1857, to work with the idea of the utmost redemption ("redemption of the redeemer"!), with medieval Christian coloring—to be sure, also for musical reasons, concerning which something will be said later. In 1865 Wagner wrote out a sketch of the work for his royal patron, Ludwig II of Bavaria; in 1877 he published the text; and in the spring of 1879 completed the composition.

Parsifal is the artistic and dramatic counterpart to the numerous essays which Wagner published during his last period at Bayreuth, and among which that on "Religion and Art" is the most significant and inclusive. It is characteristic of his Bayreuth period, for after the struggles which ensued upon his rescue by the Bavarian monarch in 1864, Wagner withdrew again to Switzerland and eventually to Bayreuth, where he built his own theater for the *Ring* and from there through his magazine, led his congregation. The "redeeming work of art" could no longer be presented in places of frivolous enjoyment—and every opera except Wagner's was frivolous. Instead, it had to be isolated. It could no longer address itself to the haphazard masses of the corrupted age, but must be reserved for a worshipfully disposed community that can scarcely be given any designation other than that of a religious art-fellowship—a fellowship that is ready to become "regenerated." "We recognize," Wagner says at the end of the essay referred to above, "the reason for the downfall of mankind in history, as well as the necessity for its regeneration. We believe in the possibility of this regeneration, and dedicate ourselves to carrying it out in every way." The former revolutionary, who still, in 1851, as participant in the Parisian "Assemblée nationale" had hoped for the triumph of the socialistic state, now saw the benefit in a religion of compassion that extends to all humanity—a religion that, among other things, includes vegetarianism, yet does not preclude the most virulent anti-Semitism.

Parsifal symbolizes this profession of faith. It symbolizes it in a horrible dramatic phantasmagoria, in which no single figure is lifelike—not Amfortas, the keeper of the Grail, who is a sort of intensification of the afflicted Tristan; nor Kundry, the temptress; nor Parsifal, who becomes "able to see through the world" by withstanding her arts and thereby "redeems" the sinful Amfortas. What has now become of woman, who previously in Wagner's work—from Senta to Brünnhilde and Isolde—had

WAGNER

MENDELSSOHN

CHOPIN

GLINKA
from a painting by Repin

been glorified as the redeemer through love! What has become of Wagner's type of hero! Now a "simple fool" must by the chastity of his love redeem the world. Out of the decisive scene in the second act, which has its predecessor in the scene between Joseph and Potiphar's wife, there has now developed a philosophical and symbolical sequence of events. In it, both figures almost seem to have their speeches on little bands hanging out of their mouths, as in primitive pictures. To make clear all the dual or multiple meanings of the conflict, Wagner has to precede the beginning of the real action—Parsifal's killing of the swan, the symbolic murder of the living being—with an exposition which is the longest that a dramatist has ever imposed upon his public. As a dramatist, Wagner became himself the victim of his own individual style.

In the music there was a compromise. Wagner knew why he did not compose *The Victors,* why he clothed a work with a Buddhistic basic idea in a garb that was medieval and that tended towards Catholicism. For the Indian drama he would have found no musical point of contact. For *Parsifal* he did find it in his own *Tristan* and in the idioms of Catholic church music, in suggestions of Gregorian chant, of *a cappella* tones, of bell-motifs, etc.—mere suggestions, for he was too strongly individualistic to attempt direct archaism. In comparison with *Tristan,* which is so "full-blooded" musically, and with *Die Meistersinger,* where the echoes of Bach and the Protestant chorale were used so freely, without self-consciousness, *Parsifal* displays a musical language that has become much thinner, more bloodless—it is a work of old age. But all the greater is the mastery in the interweaving of motifs, their transformation, and their overloading with symbolical or psychological force. For the opening of the third act Wagner wrote a Prelude in which he symbolized the wanderings of Parsifal, in the "linearity" of which he seemed to overstep the stylistic limits of his own time.

Parsifal is one of the concluding documents of the Romantic era. The Romantic movement began with a preference for the medieval; in the end, it dressed up a symbolical action in medieval costume. It began with a preference for Catholic mysticism; it ended with the bell-tones and harp-chords of the "redemption of the redeemer." It separated art from life, and found at last a flight from life in an exhilarating art-experience, in intoxication through music. Life and religion were replaced by art. From the very beginning of the Romantic era the tension was maintained between bourgeois finitude and the infinite; in Wagner's operas this tension is most clearly noticeable. In the *Ring* this bourgeois age saw itself reflected in an enlarged, heroic mirror; in *Parsifal* it saw its materialism conquered, its conflict resolved by pseudo-religious ecstasy.

Wagner was not a Romantic musician in the same sense as were his contemporaries, Chopin, Schumann, and Brahms. It is even fundamentally incorrect to place him as one of the three "neo-Romantics" alongside Berlioz and Liszt, although he himself in a letter to Liszt on May 22, 1860, was of the opinion that "in this present period our group consists of but us three fellows, since only we are alike. . . ." His music was of a different sort. It addressed itself not so much to the listener in order to raise him by art, by opening up hitherto unknown, loftier regions of the soul. Instead, it tried to shock him, intoxicate him, overcome him while in a fit of ecstasy, and take him captive.

Liszt never purposed anything like that, either as virtuoso or as composer of his symphonic poems or church works; and, like a genuine Frenchman, Berlioz remained to a considerable extent a traditionalist, despite all his turbulent passion and all his originality. One need only glance at his last operatic work and dramatic problem-child, *The Trojans,* a cycle like Wagner's *Ring,* consisting of two parts (*The Capture of Troy* and *The Trojans at Carthage*), the first of which he was never to see presented on the stage. *The Trojans at Carthage*—presented in 1863, four years after the completion of *Tristan*—is no longer grand opera in Meyerbeer's sense of the term, for which Berlioz was too idealistic, enthusiastic, and artistically tidy. Rather, it goes back to the Classicistic operatic ideal of Lully, of Rameau and Gluck, of Le Sueur and Spontini. It is pathetic-decorative French opera with ballet and descriptive entr'actes. Berlioz compels us by his artistry. His opera is no longer filled with the inventive power of the *Symphonie Fantastique* or *Harold;* it is music in which boldness and Classicistic restraint are strangely mingled. Often Berlioz falls below his own standard, as for example in the appearance of Hector's ghost, where we expect hitherto unheard tone colors. But otherwise his seal is set upon every melodic and coloristic trait in every aria, every ensemble, every choral scene—and *The Trojans* is a great choral opera—as, for example, in the drum and other percussion parts at the procession of the Trojan people, the ominous fanfare before Aeneas's dream-vision, the trumpets in his tale of Laocöon, the rhythmically animated dance-act, and the "royal hunt." Everything is of boundless *noblesse* and tradition, more like Poussin than Delacroix; and often the somewhat pale Classicism is fanned into its old flame, as in the love-duet between Cassandra and Choroebus, in a famous septet, in the love scene between Dido and Aeneas, and in the elegiac greatness of Dido's dying song. But Berlioz never wishes to overcome us as does Wagner.

WAGNER'S PATH TOWARDS INDIVIDUALITY

To reiterate: for Wagner, music was only one means of conquering— the strongest, most bewitching, the finest—but a *means* to an end. One can never consider him as a musician alone. But if one looks only at the musical side of his make-up, one observes the rare phenomenon of an ever increasing originality, of a more and more strongly developed personality. In the beginning of Wagner's career, Beethoven served as his model. Wagner began with a piano arrangement of the Ninth Symphony and wrote some simple piano works—Sonata, Op. 1; Polonaise for Four Hands, Op. 2; Sonata in D minor, in which elements from Mozart, Beethoven, and Weber stand side by side. Among these early compositions only one Fantasia in F-sharp minor shows some individual traits. He wrote overtures and a Symphony (1832) with Beethovenian gestures, which were utilized very skillfully. In a group of overtures that are later, at least so far as the date of performance is concerned, *Polonia, Christopher Columbus* (1835), and *Rule, Britannia* (1837), a new and more modern idea was revealed. It was essentially that of the neo-French opera-introduction in the style of Auber or Hérold, with the use of captivating cantilena passages for the strings and radiant apotheoses for the brasses. Only in the *Columbus* Overture are the brasses really used with poetical intention, as a symbol of ecstatic hope. In 1840, with the *Faust* Overture (see p. 144), this instrumental period of Wagner's came to a conclusion, except for the later additions like the *Siegfried-Idyll,* the *Kaisermarsch,* and the *Huldigungsmarsch.* Wagner used the orchestra for other purposes.

His early operatic compositions were not at all "orchestral operas." There is, for example, a fragment from a wildly passionate bit of early work, *Die Hochzeit* (Autumn, 1832), which consists of a great choral ensemble and a recitative-like dialogue. In this, incidentally, a sort of leitmotif made its appearance in the bass instruments. There is also a "Romantic opera," *Die Feen,* written when he was twenty, in which the dramaturgic motif of "redemption" emerges for the first time. The work is a musical echo of impressions from Weber's and particularly Marschner's operas, fashioned with an almost fatal air of routine. This particular opera even lacks the sure eye for the dramatic that in other situations is characteristic of Wagner.

Vice versa, the *Liebesverbot* or *Die Novize von Palermo* (1836), as has already been indicated, is an early masterpiece on the part of the librettist, who treated freely the model provided by Shakespeare, simplifying it to *opera buffa* and compressing it into two acts. On the other hand, Wagner the musician had almost come to the conclusion that he must deny his personality: "I did not take the slightest pains to avoid reminiscences of French and Italian music. . . . We must seize the age and seek to develop its new forms genuinely[!], and he will be the master who writes neither in Italian or French nor in German style. . . ." Now, as to the "genuineness" of this work, there can scarcely be any question of "reminiscences"; rather, it is a piece of impertinence and shameless imitation. With much more right to do so, Wagner speaks in another place (in *Mein Leben*) of the "light-hearted character of the music." It is light-hearted, too, in its boundless repetitions. Only later did Wagner learn concentration, although a slow development and a breadth of outline are essential even in his later system. The bleating rhythms of Meyerbeer, the roulades of Rossini, the crudeness of the brasses from Hérold's *Zampa,* the amorous and languishing element in Bellini, the rhythmic piquancy and the mass-effects of Auber—all these hold a rendezvous in the music of the *Liebesverbot* and, in a few particularly saucy rhythms, even succeed in reaching the proximity of Jacques Offenbach's operas. A few German traits, too, are not lacking. There is, for example, Marschner's type of lustful melody, sung in the paroxysms of love by the sinister hero, Shakespeare's Angelo. There is an A-flat major reminiscence of Beethoven in the first finale, and an imitation *("Töt' erst sein Weib!")* from *Fidelio* at the climax of the judgment scene. With all this lack of originality, however, one senses already the true Wagner. It is less a matter of a few anticipations, as, for example, of *Tannhäuser,* or the surprisingly clever use of the reminiscent motif. Rather, it is the general character traits: from this unconcerned immorality will some day develop the grandiose amorality of the *Ring* and *Tristan;* and the purpose of the revolutionary of "Young Germany" will be transformed to the inward revolution against his times, under the influence of that will-to-conquer which filled Wagner's heart from beginning to end of his career.

Wagner's following opera, *Rienzi, the Last of the Tribunes,* was no less a bit of "youthful wild oats" than was *Das Liebesverbot*. He himself had a divided attitude towards the work which opened up the way for his success. On one occasion he thought, in looking back, that he had written it only for the sake of success: "Before me stood grand opera, with its scenic and musical glitter, its passionateness so rich in effects and so massive musically." (Is it not suspicious that Meyerbeer declared that the libretto of *Rienzi* was the best book for an opera that he knew of, and that he only regretted it had not fallen into *his* own hands first?) But on another occasion *Rienzi* meant more for Wagner than a mere grand opera. He said that he had not been "imitating" it, but had been wishing "to surpass all its previous manifestations." In so doing, he called on all his own artistic passionateness. *Rienzi* was not to become merely a monstrous historical piece of "ham" opera, with arias, ensembles, finales, processions, marches, ballets, and pantomimes; but the hero was to be a tragic character, whose overweening pride made him become the first Wagnerian *figure,* a sacrifice to politics and the fickleness of the masses. Wagner criticized this figure, but at the same time he loved it. "Rienzi appears as a tribune, dressed in fantastic and ceremonious clothes." But at the moment the work was presented, Wagner had "a strange feeling of the real insignificance of the operatic genre which, in general, I had represented with such great success." He thus blamed the operatic genre for what was the insignificance of the work itself.

Despite Wagner's advance in musical technique, *Rienzi* is yet not much more than a routine product, much more so than Meyerbeer's *Huguenots.* The incongruity between the dramatist and the musician in Wagner is obvious. The theatrical instinct was present in full strength; the dramatist made only a few mistakes, the worst being the unbearable prolixity of the work. But the musician was as yet only a mere routine composer—though one doubly surprising in view of his youth, with a few great ideas, for example the crescendo of the trumpet in the overture, the revolutionary and portentous motto of the whole opera. The routine character of the work was alleviated by the ingenuousness and cocksureness with which Wagner handled it. But even this ingenuousness could not overcome all the unpleasantness and vulgarity of the invention and execution; from *Rienzi,* in fact, a shadow falls upon Wagner's later work, for example upon the second finales of *Tannhäuser* and *Lohengrin.*

In *The Flying Dutchman,* Wagner was no longer a routine composer. In Dresden, accordingly, the opera public which had received *Rienzi* with frantic applause when he brought it out in 1843 no longer understood him. For the time being, the work lived to see only three repetitions. The new feature in the *Dutchman* was its musical unity. The piece that Wagner first worked out textually and musically was the ballad sung by the principal female character, Senta, who sacrificed herself for the redemption of the Wandering Jew of the sea. Wagner confided:

> In this piece, I unconsciously planted the thematic seed for all the music of the opera. The piece was the idea in little for the whole drama, as it stood before my soul. When I wished to give a title to the complete work, I had the not unwarranted desire to call it a "dramatic ballad." . . . In the final working-out of the composition, the thematic picture that I had conceived broadened itself out quite naturally over the entire drama, like a complete fabric. Without further exercise of the will, I had only to take the various thematic seeds which had been contained in the ballad and let them develop further in their own directions and reach completeness. Thus I had before me all the principal moods of this poetry, and they had taken definite thematic form quite of their own accord. As an opera-composer, I would have had to proceed arbitrarily with capricious intention if in the various scenes I had wished to discover new and different motives for the same mood as it recurred. But since I had in mind only the most intelligible presentation of the matter and no longer a conglomeration of operatic pieces, I did not find, of course, the least encouragement to proceed arbitrarily.

This array of statements, formulated from the vantage-point of Wagner's later years, is obviously not entirely true in two points. Wagner was too little an "unconscious" artist not to have achieved the unified thematic structure of the work by an act of will. This unity, moreover, is not quite so extensive as he would have us believe. *The Flying Dutchman* is still a number-opera; the second act consists, for example, of "Song, Scene, Ballad, and Chorus," a Duet between Senta and Eric; and Wagner even divided up the ensuing "Finale" thus: Aria (Daland), Duet (Senta and the Dutchman), Trio (Senta, the Dutchman, and Daland). Traces of "opera" still remain. A few numbers are thematically quite independent; but it is striking that precisely these pieces, such as Eric's cavatina and Daland's somewhat buffoonish aria in which even coloratura is not lacking, are among the weakest pieces Wagner ever wrote. As yet, he had not entirely found himself—a fact of which he was shortly to become aware. In later works, beginning with *Lohengrin,* he never changed a note after he had once completed a work—in contrast to almost all his contemporaries, particularly in contrast to the experimenter Liszt, who recognized no final version for any of his works. When in 1852 he rehearsed *The Flying Dutchman* with the Zürich opera, he mitigated the somewhat coarse instrumentation and reworked the end of the overture and the end of the third-act finale.

Despite the rather limited mastery of compositional technique, *The Flying Dutchman* is a purer work of art than *Tannhäuser,* completed by Wagner in the early part of 1845 and presented later that year in Dresden. Here grand opera again makes its entry in all its splendor, and in a form that is all the more repulsive as it enters surreptitiously, behind a psychological mask, with a bad conscience. The sinful hero and the angelically pure heroine would be possible as medieval figures; but with Wagner they are mere effigies, and remain opera puppets, precisely as are the honest Landgrave or the sentimentally resigned Wolfram von Eschenbach. In this instance, Wagner had not come to a clear understanding with himself about either the musical or the dramatic construction of the work. While still in Dresden he gave the conclusion of the opera various versions. In the first, Wagner only hinted at the reappearance of the Enchanted Mountain and the pious death of the heroine. But he later coarsened these portions by bringing the goddess Venus and the corpse of Elizabeth bodily upon the stage.

It is no mere accident, moreover, that when he wished to gain a foothold in Paris fourteen years later he chose not *Lohengrin* but *Tannhäuser.* In this Parisian version the work became at the same time more Wagnerian and more like grand opera. It was more Wagnerian in that he made the figure of Venus "more profound psychologically," by means of all the musical discoveries that the completion of *Tristan* had meanwhile revealed to him, thus transforming the goddess into a passionately struggling woman, shortening the scene of the singing contest considerably, and above all heightening the pantomime at the beginning of the Venusberg scene, lifting the "Bacchanale" to a state of luxuriance that is unparalleled even in his own work. What in the middle portion of the overture had been only hinted at was here pushed to the very limits; the music, quite as it was permissible for it to do, made use here of sultry tonal excitement, motivic combination, and harmonic refinement in order to express what would otherwise have been inexpressible. To what dimensions, within a short period, the "temptation" scene had grown, in comparison—let us say—with the few innocent A-major measures in Weber's *Oberon!* How very much the role of the orchestra had changed! The overture as well as the entire work finds its life in the contrast between such sensuous music and the pastoral or pious tones. The quick change of the

Venusberg into the "happy valley" of the Wartburg landscape is one of the greatest scenic and musical effects in opera. Yet throughout—quite apart from the lack of stylistic unity in the Parisian version—*Tannhäuser* is not free from irregularities and foreign additions. Mature pieces, like the hero's narrative of Rome or the heroine's prayer, stand beside conventional ones, like the disagreeable prize-song of Tannhäuser or Wolfram's insufferable cavatina to the evening star, or beside semiconventional ones like the finale of the second act.

Lohengrin, completed in 1848, marked the close of the period of German Romantic opera, which had begun in Weber's *Euryanthe.* It was also a conclusion textually. The dramatic motive was about the same as in E. T. A. Hoffmann's *Undine,* Marschner's *Hans Heiling,* and also Wagner's own *Dutchman,* except that here the heroine, unlike Senta, is not equal to the demand of the semi-divine man for unconditional love, for unquestioning faith; the outcome is tragic, although softened by the thwarting of the Evil Principle—embodied in a demonic woman, Ortrud, somewhat like Eglantine—and transfigured by operatic theatricality. But this operatic theatricality, which is linked with Wagner's genuinely Romantic yearning to represent musically the Middle Ages, the 10th century—the patriotic address of the king, the ceremonial of an ordeal, with fanfares and a decorative herald, festive church music, dazzling splendor and chaste accompaniment to a wedding feast, assembly of a bellicose militia—this operatic theatricality is tempered by the fact that Wagner as a musician has at last become a match for Wagner as a man of the theater. The musical mastery is displayed most clearly in the role of the chorus, which vies with the orchestra in giving the work its own proper dramatic and ecstatic color. One could still detach from their scenes certain "arias" or "duets," such as Elsa's narrative of her dream, Lohengrin's warning, and Ortrud's and Telramund's oath of revenge; but the arioso passages more and more dissolve into a sort of speech-song supported by the orchestra. Correspondingly, in Wagner's own words, the orchestral "accompaniment" becomes "more and more significant," more telling, more delicate—one need think only of the new divisions of the strings. If Verdi's *Aïda* may be considered the ideal and ultimate of what is understood by the term "Italian opera," then *Lohengrin* is certainly the ultimate and ideal of German Romantic opera. It is no mere accident that *Lohengrin* was the first opera of Wagner's to make its way on the Italian stage.

The beginning of work on the *Rhinegold* was separated from the completion of *Lohengrin* by more than five years. These were the "theoretical" years in Wagner's career, during which he, according to his abilities, followed or fashioned the history of opera and his relation to it. During these years he also became quite individual in his approach as a musician, quite himself, quite original. The law of his development was a sort of inbreeding, for from now on he developed further only on the basis of his own style. The influence of his contemporaries upon him became less and less. During the Zürich years, he once took in hand the scores of Schumann's symphonies and decided, with the utmost disdain, that there was no longer anything in this sort of work for him, either so far as content or technique was concerned. The first two acts of the *Valkyrie* were already composed and—be it noted—also completely orchestrated when he asked Liszt in a letter of October 3, 1855, to send Berlioz's scores, for Berlioz himself was not able to send them to him. "I confess," wrote Wagner, "that I am now very much interested in giving his symphonies a precise examination in score. . . . I should like to have them soon." But from Berlioz he could then learn at most only a few points of technical finesse in instrumentation, and he had been quite right when he wrote to Uhlig on May 31, 1852: "Whoever in judging my music separates the harmony from the instrumentation does me as great an injustice as he who separates my music from my poetry, my songs from my words!" In this respect the influence, which Wagner according to his own admission (see p. 233) had received from Liszt in the matter of harmony, should not be overrated either. It was a stimulus aroused by the experimenter, and became in Wagner's powerful mind immediately a productive *system*. Wagner was the very opposite of an experimenter. In this respect Liszt was to Wagner as a card player who stakes everything on one play is to a great—though bold—financier.

Wagner's "system" between the *Rhinegold* and *Parsifal* underwent no further change, but only refinement; and the system is carried out most purely and, from the musical point of view, "most full-bloodedly" (his own phrase) in *Tristan und Isolde,* which is least related to grand opera. It is a symphonic opera. Wagner required the orchestra; and even when he wrote a work of the utmost intimacy, like the so-called *Triebschen Idyll* or *Siegfried-Idyll* (1870), with a few strings, flute, oboe, two clarinets, bassoon, and two horns, the work was not one of chamber music but rather a reduced symphony. And he worked out the role of the orchestra in his opera symphonically, by refining the old motif of reminiscence into the leitmotif, with his psychological intention.

Henceforth in each of his operas he secured unity by interweaving and transforming relatively few motifs—rhythmic, linear, and harmonic—singly or in combination. From such interweaving there developed the scene, the act, and the symphonic ebb and flow of the act thus constituted. Wagner, of course, was much too clever to make his work entirely dependent on the symphonic element, on movement in the orchestra plus speech-song. Every experienced singer knows how many cantilena passages, even in the Italian sense of the term, are hiding in a Wagnerian role. The relation between singer and orchestra, between action and music, is constantly shifting. We have already alluded, for example, to the fact that in the second act of *Tristan* the action almost entirely retires in favor of the music. But it is true that the highest climaxes in Wagner's work are *symphonic* climaxes; and precisely in that second act of *Tristan,* in Brangäne's aubade, even the human voice is merely applied as a sounding instrument—as the most beautiful of all instruments.

Wagner's tremendous will power is responsible for the fact that he forced this most highly personal, thoroughly subjective tonal language on his period as the general expression of its feeling. He did not, however, force it on his entire period. Some of the very best spirits of the age—quite apart from the reactionaries—did not join in his retinue. How his music affected the sensibilities of those entirely unprepared for it may be understood from a letter of Leo N. Tolstoy's to his brother S. N. Tolstoy: "Yesterday I was in the theater and heard the famous new opera *Siegfried* by Wagner. I could not sit through the first act to the end but sprang up in the middle of it like a madman, and even yet I cannot speak quietly about it. That is a stupid Punch-and-Judy show, which is much too poor for children over seven years of age; moreover, it is not music. And yet thousands of people sit there and pretend to like it." [45] Similar judgments are to be found in Jacob Burckhardt, the great historian, who had grown up in the tradition of Gluck and Mozart.

Otherwise the effect was international, although a little posthumous; for it reached its high point perhaps only in the last two decades of the century. Wagner soon found adherents in England, which he despised, and in Paris, which in 1861 had given his *Tannhäuser* a very unworthy reception. Characteristically, it was not the musicians who were the spearhead of his conquest, but the literati and the poets, such as in England, or for England, the completely a-musical renegade Houston Stewart Chamberlain, in France, Edouard Schuré, Gobineau, Baudelaire, the circle

[45] *Tagebuch* (Jena, 1932), I, p. 175, note 24.

about Catulle Mendès, the Parnassians (Verlaine, Mallarmé, Villiers de l'Isle-Adam), and the Symbolists. The reason is given by Friedrich Nietzsche, who, after having been one of Wagner's most intimate friends, became the most intimate enemy of his art, and who in his writings about Wagner gave the definitive pronouncements both for and against the composer. "Wagner *summed up* modernity," i.e., the Romantic movement, or the last phase of the Romantic movement. Nietzsche, the cultural philosopher and critic, saw in Wagner as a man of the theater all the mendacity and morbidity of the Romantic movement. He saw the "late" and tired man behind the heroic mask, he saw the contrast between grand opera and miniature. "Wagner's art is sick. . . . Wagner is a great injury to music. . . . But, apart from the hypnotist and fresco-painter, there is another Wagner who incidentally has saved up tiny treasures: our greatest melancholiac of music, full of glances, tendernesses, and words of comfort, in which no one has anticipated him. . . ." Actually, the influence of Wagner upon posterity will always rest on his musical invention: it is Wagner the *musician* who has assured himself of immortality.

THOSE IN WAGNER'S SHADOW

On one occasion (August 23, 1852), Liszt wrote thus to Wagner: "The theater season [in Weimar] will begin with Verdi's *Hernani,* which will be followed shortly by *Faust* with Spohr's newly composed recitatives. . . . In the middle of November I expect Berlioz, whose *Cellini* (with a rather considerable cut) must not be laid aside—for despite all the stupid *bêtises* that are current about it, *Cellini* is and remains a work that is quite significant and is to be rated highly. . . . Raff has undertaken extensive revision of the instrumentation and scene-layout of his *Alfred*. Apparently this opera will be more effective in its new form than in its old, although it was very heartily applauded in the third and fourth performances. In general, I consider it the most talented score that has been written by any of the German composers in the past ten years. You, of course, do not belong with that group—and you stand alone; for that reason you can be compared only with yourself."

King Alfred, by Joseph Joachim Raff (1822–1882), was a failure even in the revised version, a failure which caused Raff to devote himself henceforth almost entirely to chamber and symphonic music: mostly Romantically routine works, none of which have shown lasting vitality. *King Alfred* in particular, and the prolific composer Raff's work in general, may be compared with *King Charles II* (1849) by George Alexander Macfarren (1813–1887), of whose music likewise, as Percy Scholes has said, "practically none is now ever performed—in so brief a period do tastes and standards change." But Liszt was right in saying that he regarded Wagner as an opera composer *sui generis,* not to be compared with any of his rivals then active in the development of opera. To us of a later generation particularly, the history of opera between 1840 and 1883 seems to be concentrated in Wagner's work.

That did not prevent this history from taking its own course alongside and—with some exceptions—independent of Wagner. Liszt might rather have named in place of *King Alfred* some of the works of Gustav Albert Lortzing (1801–1851), who in more modest proportions was comparable to Wagner as a poet-composer: *Hans Sachs* (in subject matter a predecessor of *Die Meistersinger*), 1840; *Der Wildschütz,* 1842; *Der Waffenschmied,* 1846; and the previously mentioned (p. 118) *Undine,* 1845. These later works of Lortzing's, to be sure, do not quite measure up in scenic liveliness and musical freshness to a somewhat earlier one of his, *Czaar und Zimmermann* (1837). In them all—except the somewhat frivolous and satirical *Wildschütz*—folklike humor, German Philistinism, and tenderhearted emotion meet in an ever-varying mixture. In the matter of pleasant and popular melodic invention at least and in that of being composer, singer, and actor combined in one person, Lortzing was most comparable to the Irishman Michael William Balfe (1808–1870), except that the latter's *Bohemian Girl* (1843) was exportable, while Lortzing's type of opera could thrive only on German soil.

Another work that Liszt might have named would be *The Merry Wives of Windsor* (1849) by Otto Nicolai (1810–1849), a North German who was sent to Rome by the Romantic King of Prussia to study the Palestrina style, became in Italy a complete Italian (*Il Templario,* 1840), and made out of the Shakespearian comedy German *opera buffa,* with charming duets, ensembles, finales of Romantic hue, and—above all—a Romantically colored overture. It was an opera that could hold its own in Germany alongside and after the masterpiece of Verdi's old age based on the same material. Of course, Liszt was right when he thought, for example, of the honest Capellmeister Franz Lachner (1803–1890) with his *Catharina Cornaro* (1841), a "grand opera" thunderously Philistine, or when he thought of the clever insipidities of Friedrich von Flotow (1812–1883) with his *Alessandro Stradella* (1844) and *Martha* (1847)—both, to be sure, rather more examples of *opéra-comique* in the Auber manner than of German sentimental-comedy opera. Certainly they were "Romantic" operas only in that they, particularly *Martha,* appealed to the public's special weakness for languishing vicariously in sentimental rags and tatters.

One of the few *non*-Wagnerian operas of the time originated within the very closest circle, that of Franz Liszt. It was the *Barber of Baghdad* by Peter Cornelius (1824–1874), presented at Weimar in 1858, and the cause of an incident worthy of being recorded in the history of music, a theatrical scandal that drove Liszt from his position in Weimar. Cornelius, too, whom we have become acquainted with as a composer of songs (p. 193), wrote his own texts and, in contrast to Wagner, was a real poet who mastered all the lyric forms with playful and, indeed, with true, virtuosity. The *Barber of Baghdad,* too, is a lyric opera, in both acts of which practically nothing happens. In the first, an old owl of a barber, with his ceremonious formality, drives to distraction a lover who is impatient to hasten to his love. In the second, by his rashness he brings to a happy outcome a situation that threatens to become tragic. But all that—or this little—is carried off with so much humor, such unobtrusive formal mastery, pure lyric fire, and delicacy in the suggestion of Oriental color, that one thoroughly understands the work's constant *lack* of success. Later, with the *Cid* (1865) and the unfinished *Gunlöd* (brought out posthumously in 1891), Cornelius came unfortunately under the influence of Wagner's *Lohengrin.* As in his music, so in his life he made the mistake of alternately yielding to and resisting Wagner's inconsiderate egoism. But in the lineage of the *Barber of Baghdad* are the only post-Wagnerian German operas that may lay claim to any worth, precisely because they do not presume to the heroic and generally philosophical pose: *The Taming of the Shrew* (1874) by Hermann Goetz (1840–1874) and Hugo Wolf's *Corregidor* (1896), which, of course, no longer falls within the limits of our consideration.

FRENCH OPERA FROM *LA JUIVE* TO *CARMEN*

In France—or, more precisely, in Paris—grand opera followed the paths that had been marked out for it by Auber's *Muette* (1828), Rossini's *William Tell* (1829), and Meyerbeer's *Robert le Diable* (1831). *Opéra-comique* followed, with some variants, the model that Auber had set up in 1830 with his *Fra Diavolo*—a charming, mechanically military overture in the Rossini manner and a spicy plot, with a few piquant melodies and ensembles. After the success of the *Huguenots,* Meyerbeer wrote some more or less sensational works for both grand opera and *opéra-comique:* for the former, *Le Prophète* (1849) and *L'Africaine* (posthumous, 1865); for the latter, *L'Etoile du Nord* (1854), in the preparation of which he re-used some music from a Berlin patriotic festival play (*Ein Feldlager in Schlesien,* 1844), transferring the material from the "Prussian" to the "Russian," and *Le Pardon de Ploërmel* (1859, also called *Dinorah*), a pastoral subject, the "sensation" of which consisted of the rich coloratura in the madness of the heroine, a shepherdess. (Madness, incidentally, which did not hinder musical exhibition, was a prime requisite to Italian and French opera in the Romantic period.) In all instances and in both genres only the choice of material—historical, exotic, fantastic—had any connection with Romanticism. Otherwise, the convention of grand opera prevailed, demanding a conglomeration of arias, duets, finales, marches, choruses, and ballets in contrasting combination. Within this conglomeration, at least as it was put together by Meyerbeer, alongside passages of the utmost tastelessness, artificiality, and emptiness, time and again there is found a melodic, rhythmic, or orchestral flash of thought. A whole succession of imitators yielded completely to this convention, for example Jacques Fromental Elie Halévy (1799–1862) with his pathetic "history" *La Juive* (1835); and not even Berlioz, with all the purity of his artistic conviction, could escape it.

As to *opéra-comique* and the more "lyric and dramatic" operas of the French stage, the same thing is true on a somewhat more simple and artistic scale. We need characterize only a few of the most significant works. Perhaps the foremost is the opera that—for France—dealt with the most Romantic of all material, Gounod's *Faust* (1859), at first really a "comic opera" with portions of spoken dialogue and only a year later transformed into a full opera, "a repulsive, nauseously vulgar, meretriciously affected piece of bungling work," according to Wagner, "with the music of an inferior talent which tried to make something out of it and in despair seized every means at hand. . . ." At several places in his writings Wagner has passed a similar judgment on *Faust,* which, incidentally, he constantly refused to listen to even once. In a way he was right, and in a way not. For the French and Italian composers—Berlioz, Gounod, and later Boito—in fashioning the *Faust* material were in a somewhat different situation from that of the German musicians, who might not lay hands on Goethe's hallowed text. Gounod's librettists, in making very superficial use of the material, resolved it into its original elements and reduced it to the love-story of Faust and Gretchen. What

does this Faust have to do with Goethe's superman! What does this
theatrical devil with his hocus-pocus have to do with Mephistopheles!
What does Mademoiselle Marguérite have to do with Goethe's Gretchen!
It is but decorative Romanticism, or Romantic decoration. Similarly,
Gounod's music, replete with excessively soft lyrical passages, aspires to
nothing more lofty than the achievements of many lucky song-writers.
There is, however, a passage of peculiarly Romantic intuition in the prel-
ude to the Walpurgis-Night scene.

In somewhat the same spirit Félicien David (1810–1876), in his *Lalla
Rookh* (1862), turned to good account the melodic results of his youthful
trip to the Orient, though it only led him as far as Syria. Within the same
general limitations of purpose, moreover, Ambroise Thomas (1811–1896)
in *Mignon* (1866) and *Hamlet* (1868) has taken the immortal figures
from Goethe's *Wilhelm Meister,* which from Schubert to Hugo Wolf had
enriched German lyricism, and the immortal figures from Shakespeare.
These he has prettified and "rendered operatic." Also among the French
operas of rather limited purpose is to be numbered Gounod's *Roméo et
Juliette* (1867).

In the same general category, moreover, falls *Samson et Dalila* by Camille
Saint-Saëns (1835–1921). Though it is one of the best of the French operas,
it received its christening in Germany, in 1877 at Weimar, where Liszt
was its godfather. Later, Hans von Bülow spoke of it as "the best German
opera in the past twenty-five years, the most significant post-Wagnerian
music drama." At least from the perspective of the present, that opinion
appears as wrong as it could possibly be. A post-Wagnerian opera would
have had to treat the material in the manner outlined by Goethe, who
once wrote to Zelter as he was considering an opera on the Samson theme:
". . . the old myth is one of the most dreadful. An entirely bestial passion
of an overly powerful, divinely gifted hero for the most accursed hussy
on earth, the raging passions which again and again lead him to her,
although every time he straightway knows by repeated deception that he is
in danger; this lustfulness, which escapes from danger; the mighty conception that must be made of the extraordinary presence of this gigantic
woman who was able *so* to enchain such a bull! If you consider the matter,
my friend, you will immediately see that all this must be reduced to nought
in order to produce the mere names according to the conventions of our
time and our theater."

It was both the strength and the weakness of Saint-Saëns that he did not
disregard the conventions of Parisian opera. *Samson et Dalila* is the work

of a French musician who was only too much at home in all periods, regions, and styles. It is a work of perhaps the most "cultivated" musician who has appeared since Mendelssohn. Beneath the smooth, though somewhat iridescent surface of the work, there flow hundreds of currents beside each other and in confused mixture. The duet between Delilah and the High Priest at the beginning of the second act is a draught of "Meyerbeer," strained through Gounod's filter, yet at the same time smacking faintly of the Ortrud-Telramund scene from *Lohengrin,* and in general still Camille Saint-Saëns, the musician of taste, of melodic culture. The choruses in the first act and the great priestly scenes of the last act are inspired by the old classics. They are Handelian, perhaps still more Gluckian, and yet French. Delilah's mocking aria is almost pure Massenet. Since 1867, Jules Massenet (1842–1912) had produced the far too pleasant type of new French lyric opera. But the great duet scene, the melodic climax of the opera, is free from Massenet's somewhat oppressive perfume. The scene of Samson in the mill, finally, is in its seriousness and nobility the work of a great master, who unfortunately utilized the conventions of French opera in a body of material that could no longer be treated conventionally. Saint-Saëns was an elegant exploiter of all possible old traditions and of the newer influences; his is a very French form of the Romantic movement.

The last of the French operas with which we shall here be concerned is also Romantic—*Carmen,* by Georges Bizet (1838–1875). It was produced a little earlier (1875) than Saint-Saëns's *Samson.* Bizet had to go through the same career as Berlioz and so many other young French musicians: the Conservatoire, the trip to Rome, and, in his native land, initial opposition to his first operatic attempts. These were *Les Pêcheurs de Perles* (1863), which became popular only long after his death, and *La Jolie Fille de Perth* (1867), with its "Romantic" scenery after Sir Walter Scott's novel and its unfortunate evidences of Meyerbeer's influence. The main difference was that Bizet, with his rare natural gifts, could take such failures more lightly than the tortured and passionate Berlioz. Now, Friedrich Nietzsche, after his defection from Bayreuth, made the facetious suggestion that the music of *Carmen* should be proposed as a contrast, a cure and medicine against poisoning from Wagner's operas. He set the clean orchestral sound of Bizet over against the "brutal, arty, and seemingly innocent" sound of Wagner, saying that, as music, Bizet's "had the refinement of a race, not that of an individual." Nietzsche praised it thus:

"It is rich. It is precise. It builds, organizes, gets finished: therein it establishes a contrast to that excrescence in music, the 'infinite melody.'" He declared that Bizet's was "Southern music, with which one may take his leave of the damp North."

But *Carmen* is very Romantic in just this Spanish coloring, this look—here not towards the Orient, but at the colorful land beyond the Pyrenees which had attracted so many Frenchmen. Bizet spoke musical Spanish like a Frenchman, and his dialect was felt by the Spaniards themselves to be anything but genuine. One need only compare *Carmen* with an opera about a year older, Musorgsky's *Boris Godunov* (with which we shall concern ourselves in another connection), to recognize what is French *opéra-comique* and what is genuine folk opera.

Nietzsche was right, however, in maintaining that Bizet was the antithesis of Wagner in the use of the closed form and in the resulting brevity. For his system, Wagner needed the broad, careful introduction of motifs or themes at places rich in the power of suggestion, their slow loading and filling up with symbolical force, and their intensification to the point of intoxication. Bizet did not let himself go astray on the leitmotif idea. He used, for example, the "maternal motif" from Micaela's aria only poetically as an interlude when José reads his mother's letter. Escamillo's toreador melody he used as an effective conclusion for the third act. There was only one motif from the overture that he carried through all the acts, Carmen's motif of "fate." What he was seeking for was the rounding-off, the completion of a scene. He obtained the highest effectiveness, of course, when he broke this rule, as in José's "Rose-Aria," which owes its passionateness precisely to its freedom, to the fact that there is not too much "melody" along with it—in contrast, for example, to Micaela's arias, which have proved to have something of a French sweetness and sentimentality about them.

But the uniqueness of the opera, which someone has dared to call a "tragic operetta," rests above all on the fineness of its harmonization and counterpoint, which—as with J. S. Bach—are one and inseparable. It is no wonder that this opera charmed someone besides Nietzsche. That person was a musician who understood such matters thoroughly, Johannes Brahms. In June, 1882, he eagerly besought his publisher to send him the score; and in so doing, not without some seriousness in the jest, he explained that he loved it more than all the other items in Simrock's catalogue —that is, including his own works.

ITALIAN OPERA: THE ROMANTIC-DEMONIC IN ROSSINI

The country that seems to have been least affected by the Romantic era was the motherland of opera—Italy, with its old traditions in this field. As a matter of fact, practically the only object for our consideration in Italy is opera, which became more and more the center of interest for the nation. After relinquishing first place in instrumental music to Germany at the end of the 18th century, Italy had, in the 19th, scarcely a production in the field of symphony or chamber music worthy of mention, and only a small number of noteworthy works for concert and church. There was here a musical self-sufficiency and seclusion, based not only upon the old tradition of the opera but also upon political conditions. The Habsburgs in Lombardy and Venice, even those in Florence, and even the Bourbons in Naples or the Popes in Rome, did not look with favor on an exceptionally lively intellectual exchange between their domains and the rest of Europe.

In addition, the Romantic movement was an essentially "Northern" movement. The Northerners, the closefisted, the disinherited, the "Cimmerians," were seeking for a fulfillment of their true nature in the Southern, the sensuous. The Romantic movement was in great part a yearning for the warmth, naturalness, colorfulness, and freedom of the South. Meanwhile, people in the South—in Provence, in Spain, in Italy—felt no necessity for a Romanticism in this sense. The other side of this yearning for the South was often, among the Northerners, a boasting of the "Teutonic." Peter Cornelius, on one occasion, expressed it very clearly as he lampooned Spontini: ". . . for yet in our *Freischütz,* in our *Heiling,* a breeze of the German forests and mountains, a breeze of the very ancient sacred groves, a bit freer and more heavenly breeze is wafted than that among the palms and coconut trees of his *Cortez,* so that in the Gothic palace of *Euryanthe* and in the Romanic cathedral of *Lohengrin* one may more easily dream of the God of the past and future, and may approach him, than between the temple walls of this composer's *Vestalin.*" [46] The spirit here is still the same as that which, at the beginning of the Romantic movement, made Madame de Staël in her *De la Littérature, considérée dans ses rapports avec les institutions sociales* (1800) emphasize the superiority of Christian civilization over the culture of antiquity and led her to become the champion of the Middle Ages.

[46] "Der Lohengrin in München," *Neue Zeitschrift für Musik* (1867), reprinted in *Literarische Werke* III, p. 95 f.

But Romantic traits were manifested even in Italy. They particularly made their appearance in the perhaps unconscious nationalistic emphasis. We have already seen in the first part of this book (p. 163) that Rossini seems to us more Italian than Cimarosa or Paisiello, not to mention the older masters. This is not owing to his use of musical dialects—from Romagna, Bologna, Rome, Naples—with which, in succession, he became familiar early in his career. Rather, it is a matter of his personal style, with its new piquancies of melody and coloratura, of harmony, and of rhythm, which Louis Spohr took such violent exception to when he heard the *Italiana in Algeri* at the Pergola in Florence in the winter of 1816.[47] It is also a matter of the secretly demonic character of Rossini's music, a character which comes out more clearly in his *opera buffa* than in his *opera seria*.

To find only harmless fun in the *Barber of Seville* (1816), for example, is to be very much in error. Rossini's particular approach consists of his exaggerating the comic element in the situations. An instance occurs in the immortal quintet of the second act, in which Basilio by a special sort of medicine is moved to go and, with irresistibly amiable melodic sinuosity, takes his leave. The motive here is nothing, the situation everything. One would also be in error if he were to think that in the *Barber* the figures of the old guardian Bartolo and of the intriguer Basilio were mere burlesque figures from the *commedia dell'arte*. They are that; yet at the same time they are more realistic, more dangerous figures. The so-called "slander aria" of Basilio is not a mere buffo-aria. Where in a single crescendo the buzzing origin and growth of the rumor is depicted, for example, the number is at once a piece of humor and demonism. The most unearthly passage is that in the very soft *pianissimo* of the triumph before the final cadence, with the ascending and descending scale.

In his *opera seria* Rossini introduced the usual "Classical" or "heroic" material, as in *Ciro in Babilonia* (1812), *Tancredi* (1813), *Armida* (1817), *Semiramide* (1823), etc. At the same time he had also begun to bring "Romantic" material to the stage, in *La Donna del Lago* (1819, after Sir Walter Scott's *Lady of the Lake,* from which Schubert had already taken several lyrics), *Bianca e Faliero* (1819, after Manzoni's nationalistic tragedy *Il Conte di Carmagnola*), and the pasticcio *Ivanhoe* (1826). The presence of this "Romantic" material, however, is of relatively slight importance since, before *William Tell*, Rossini had scarcely anything to do with local color. Even in a legend like *Cenerentola* (1817) he completely divested the

---

[47] *Autobiography* I, 306.

Cinderella story of its legendary quality and made it *opera buffa*. But the Romantic-demonic trait is also discoverable here: in the lack of feeling with which even the moving heroine of the opera is treated, in the wit which suddenly shatters the frame of the presentation and takes the public into the fun. In the second act an example of this sort of thing is to be found in a burlesque sextet (*"Questo è un modo avviluppato"*), which shows the public that the whole performance is nothing but pretence and madness— have fun with it, don't take it too seriously! Something similar is to be found among the Romantics, for example in Ludwig Tieck's *Gestiefelter Kater,* where the public suddenly begins to participate in the play. The model for such pieces of buffoonery is, of course, to be found in the *commedia dell'arte,* as transmitted by Carlo Gozzi in his *fiabe.* But in the 19th century they take on a new, sinister meaning.

Rossini was as unique in his personality as is every great master, but during his short productive period (to 1829) he determined the character of Italian opera, and tended to push the older masters out of the saddle— such men as the fully Italianized Bavarian Johann Simon Mayr (1763- 1845), who wrote his last opera around 1823. Rossini also reduced to minor status contemporaries like the very prolific G. Saverio Mercadante (1795- 1870), who exported his operas not to Paris so much as to Madrid. In Mercadante, Fétis censured the carelessness of the work, the lack of genuine originality, the rough and noisy instrumentation: ". . . however, it is certain that this artist is the last Italian master who preserves in his works the traditions of the good old school. His scores are well written, and one finds in them a feeling for serious art that has disappeared after him."

BELLINI

It was a somewhat younger generation that followed Rossini. They followed him also in the fatal turn towards Paris and in the combination of *opera seria* with grand opera—a connection, incidentally, for which Spontini had prepared the way. Gaetano Donizetti (1797–1848) and Vin- cenzo Bellini (1801–1835) can be called "Rossinists," among hundreds of other opera composers who year by year filled the Italian opera houses with new works of more or less decent or indecent routine.

We shall begin with Bellini, the younger man, since his career and in- fluence were more limited by his early death. Among his contemporaries he passed for a rival of Rossini's. Around 1835, manifestoes and controversial pamphlets flew back and forth on the subject of which was the more significant of the two. But when in 1854 Franz Liszt had been compelled to present Bellini's *Montecchi e Capuletti* in Weimar, he ill-humoredly wrote an essay against this "venerable product of an antiquated school," which he said belonged to the mongrel works "that owe their existence to a mixture of ideas handed down by Rossini and the current principles of the Romantic School." What does he mean here by the Romantic School? The Romanticism in Bellini lies, above all, in the material. Shakespeare, who with his *Othello* had already made himself felt in the work of Rossini (1816), was no more novel as a text-source for Italian opera than was Sir Walter Scott (Donizetti's *Lucia di Lammermoor*) or Victor Hugo (Mercadante's *Il Giuramento,* 1837). "Complete indolence of imagination, the complete carelessness of a pleasant young gentleman, this completely pale, delicate, feeble, meek Bellini, with a trace of the consumptive about him, with his elegant insouciance, with his melancholic *disinvoltura* of intellectual and physical customs—all this has led him to preserve an old tradition of Italian opera from destruction without asking whether it might be squared with the intellectual conceptions of our century and with our demands for dramatic truth or, at least, dramatic verisimilitude." Liszt was right when he thought of Shakespeare and of someone like Berlioz, who with the same material in his symphony-cantata *Roméo et Juliette* had tried to do justice to the demands of the great poet. But Liszt was wrong when he overlooked the naïveté of Italian opera, which dressed up the material from all world literature for its own purposes. The circle about Wagner and Liszt was not very well fitted to deal justly with Italian opera.

Doubtless Liszt was right, however, when he saw in Bellini no great thinker or philosopher so far as the purpose and aims of opera were concerned. Bellini was even a poor pupil in composition, and it is hard to see what he learned during his eight years at the Conservatory in Naples under old Zingarelli. Verdi later gave it as his opinion that "Bellini had unusual qualities which no conservatory could give him, and he lacked those which conservatories ought to have given him." Bellini was a master of the routine of operatic composition, without particular refinement in technical matters. In the ten operas which were crowded together within the ten years of his work, however, he displayed notable progress in knowledge and inner growth.

If one wishes to get an idea of conditions in Italian opera at the time when Rossini laid aside his pen, one need only glance at three of these ten operas, all belonging to a different type of *opera seria*: *La Sonnambula* (1831), *I Puritani* (1835), and *Norma* (1831).

La Sonnambula is a sentimental opera-idyll, the Italian counterpart, we might say, to a German *Singspiel* like Weigl's *Schweizerfamilie* or to certain pastoral species of *opéra-comique,* only of course without spoken dialogue, which was not present in stylistically pure Italian opera. The heroine, a country maiden who sings coloratura, incurs while sleepwalking the suspicion that she is unfaithful to her beloved, until the explanation of her innocent aberration convinces even the most stupid villager of her chastity and of the non-existence of ghosts. It is material for an *opera buffa*. The novelty—and, if one will, the Romanticism—in Bellini's treatment is that this material is taken seriously, and is not presented among a half-dozen soloists but, so to speak, is given in public. After almost two hundred years, Italian opera was rediscovering the chorus. Here the chorus scarcely goes offstage, and when it is not visible it stands in the wings. No longer are there pure arias and duets: everything develops into the ensemble, from which the characters stand out only so much as is permitted by considerations of euphony. Everything is worked out with the greatest simplicity and at the same time with the greatest accuracy of scenic effect.

I Puritani di Scozia or *I Puritani e i Cavalieri* was written for Paris and came to terms with grand opera, although the work was presented only at the Théâtre Italien. *I Puritani* wears historical finery, but that is of little importance since it serves merely to give occasion for introducing sensational situations. The most sensational among these is the outburst of madness on the part of the heroine, who likewise sings coloratura. The action is nothing more than a frame for the exhibition of vocal types. But Bellini's forms became more highly developed, his harmonic palette more colorful, his sense of everything sonorous more refined. Many of his ensembles are of a transparency that could have come only from the most disconcerning practical experience. In Bellini, a new feature was the local color of the military scenery: horns, trumpets, the roll of timpani and drums, and—for Cromwell's pious troops—also bells. It is a work of uncertainty and transition, much of it flat, conventional, antiquated, but much also very noble and replete with music. Bellini in the *Puritani* set out on new paths; and it is all the more tragic that such beginnings are to be found in his last work. Another composer, however, was to carry them on further—Giuseppe Verdi.

Bellini was more fortunate with *Norma*—more fortunate also in that this work won the approval of the German Romantics. Yet even so it is a special case. We know that Wagner called Italian opera a "prostitute," presumably having in mind as the main procurer Rossini, "that sensual son of Italy, smiling his way into the most exuberant lap of luxury." But even for Wagner and the Wagnerians, *Norma* did not entirely have this prostitute character. It was as if, with this work, Bellini had redeemed the virtue, the morality of Italian opera. As a young man Wagner not only wrote an enthusiastic article about *Norma* in the *Rigaer Zuschauer* when he presented the work towards the end of 1837, but also composed for it a great bass aria with chorus as an insertion when in 1840 at Paris he wished to secure an influential singer for his own purposes. Later, of course, he made fun of this "fetching composition," and expressed himself on the subject of Bellini with the same perfidy that marks his judgments of most of his contemporaries in *Mein Leben*.

But, in general, "moral" considerations of this sort have little to do with opera itself. *Norma* ranks higher than *I Puritani* because it is an opera of purer style. It is a genuine *opera seria* just as Piccinni's or Spontini's were, even though the material is transferred to an early Gallic period, the time of the conflict between the original inhabitants of France and the Romans. One might call the material a mixture of *Medea* and *La Vestale,* yet treated with a degree of passion that had been unknown to the *opera seria* of the 18th century. The work still contains heroic arias as did the older opera, for example the hero's narrative of his dream *("Meco all'altar di Venere")*, with the change in the first eight measures from C major to E minor, which Verdi kept so well in mind. But in the main *Norma* is also a choral opera, with solos. The great lyric aria or "cavatina" (e.g., Norma's *"Casta diva"*) is imbedded in very soft and rich choral and orchestral sonority—solos written for a little host of male and female singers, whose names and whose art still live today as almost legendary: Giuditta Pasta, Giulia Grisi, Maria Felicita Malibran, Giovanni Battista Rubini (for whom Bellini in *I Puritani* could write a fourth above high C), and Luigi Lablache. The Romantic element in this opera is the crescendo of lyricism, the satiation with music, somewhat as the prelude to *Lohengrin* or some of its choral scenes are filled with music. Whoever thinks that the Romantic movement passed over Italian opera without leaving its mark is probably not well acquainted with Vincenzo Bellini's *Norma* or *La Sonnambula*. Verdi, in a letter to Camille Bellaigue, May 2, 1898, tried to express it thus: "True, Bellini is poor in instrumentation and harmony . . . but rich in feeling and in a melancholy quite his own, quite individual. Even in his less well-known operas, in *La Straniera,* in *Il Pirata,* there are long, long melodies such as no one before him has written. . . ."

These "long, long melodies" were then much imitated. Bellini brought to perfection the type of aria-opening and aria-development—that riding upon the see-saw of the orchestra, after which the vocal solo begins, with a soft leap of a fourth in dotted, striding rhythms, in soft beginning and smooth dying-away of the *fioritura,* intensified in waves, carried on by the sound of other voices or of the chorus; at the end, the lingering over the high-point, and the cadence. Italian opera was, and remains, based upon the human voice. It knows no "orchestral operas," no symphonic accompaniment.

DONIZETTI

Donizetti was hewn of coarser timber than Bellini, as is shown by his general style and by his greater productivity. Between 1818 and 1844 (when attacks of insanity put an end to his creative work), he had written more than sixty operas. He was a careless worker, without particular ambition, often driven to write by need. Only during a brief period of competition with Bellini did his artistic ambition feel any very strong incitement. To this ambition we are indebted for his best *opera seria, Lucia di Lammermoor* (Naples, 1835), an international success, containing a moving sextet (*"Chi mi frena"*), famous not only in itself but also as the model for another famous ensemble number, the quartet in *Rigoletto.* Donizetti worked so quickly that it was almost pure chance whether a work of his became a success or a fiasco. But whatever he wrote is the product of a great folk-composer. There is scarcely a single melody in his operas that is not Southern, contagious, folklike; yet there is scarcely one that does not bear the stigma of coquetry, of triviality.

In his work there is no distance between creator and public. This advantage makes bearable, in places, a "history" so terrible, though as yet not emasculated by grand opera, as *Lucrezia Borgia* (1833). A second visit to Paris even occasioned a work of specially French charm, the comic opera *La Fille du Régiment* (1840). His masterpiece, to be sure, remains a pure *opera buffa,* completed in eight days, *Don Pasquale* (Paris, 1843), a work which stands in the middle between Rossini's *Barber* and Verdi's *Falstaff,* strangely individual and quite of equal rank with them. Basically, it is a posthumous *buffo* opera; but the tradition of *opera buffa* was so strong that in Italy between 1750 and 1900 this kind of more or less time-less work could come into being at a favorable moment almost any time. Again it is almost pure accident that a similar work, about eleven years older, *L'Elisir d'amore* (1832) did not achieve this height, although Donizetti spent twice as much time—fourteen days—in composing it. This sort of thing was possible because in the *buffo* style everything is fixed, normalized: the arias, duets, ensembles, and choruses are all at their appointed places. In *L'Elisir d'amore* a charming women's chorus gave the same accent that in *Don Pasquale* the famous humorous chorus of the servants was to give. One might mention as a bit of "Romantic gruesome-ness" the fact that *L'Elisir d'amore* in Act II foreshadows the flower-maiden's scene of *Parsifal,* to be sure in *buffo* style, but quite exactly: the rustic beauties crowd about the tenor hero, Nemorino; a girl who leads the chorus sings, "I am the first," until the prima donna by calling out the hero's name dispels the competing throng.

VERDI: A MAN OF HIS COUNTRY

Almost unintentionally, the name of the musician who completed this development of Italian opera has already been mentioned several times—Giuseppe Verdi (1813–1901). It is easy to maintain that one can bring him into a chapter headed "Neo-Romantic Opera" only by stretching the meaning of the term, for Verdi was the antagonist of Wagner. This fact is also shown in the position taken by Wagner's satellites against Verdi—by the satellites, for so far as Wagner himself was concerned Verdi scarcely existed, and one will seek in vain for Verdi's name among the essays and the letters of Wagner. It was as if Meyerbeer "had in his will appointed that puffed-up nullity Ambroise Thomas and his transalpine rival Verdi the heirs of his fame and influence," declared Hans von Bülow in May, 1874.[48] To von Bülow's credit, however, it should be added that three years later (October 25, 1877) he was of the opinion that, in comparison with Thomas, "Verdi, as he was in his earlier rawness, and as he also is in his present confusion, is yet quite a different 'fellow.' "[49]

Even the gentle Peter Cornelius became pugnacious when Verdi was under discussion. With a sidewise look at Verdi, he demanded "a tariff on foreign imports."[50] He likewise fought against the French Romantic

[48] *Schriften* (Leipzig, 1896), p. 350.
[49] *Ibid.,* p. 361.
[50] *Op. cit.*

drama of Victor Hugo which "has not wished to settle down in our legitimate theater, but has found the opera a good enough place in which to ruminate over its caricatures in *Lucrezia Borgia* and *Rigoletto*." At Verdi's plundering of German dramatic literature, Cornelius expressed his indignation thus: ". . . who will marvel if tomorrow we hear Schiller's *Räuber* and *Don Carlos* also on our stage warbling their trills, since obviously for this Don Juan of a Verdi no German tragedy is sacred. . . . Lessing declared war on Racine and opened the way for German poetry. Yet what a noble phenomenon is Racine in comparison with Verdi!" We may wonder that Cornelius did not proclaim himself also Shakespeare's legal defender against Verdi, for the sake of *Macbeth*, which had already been "operatized" at Verdi's hands.

As a matter of fact, Wagner and Verdi have only this in common: they are contemporaries. Both were fighters; but Wagner fought against his time, Verdi for an ennobled ideal of Italian opera, whose outlines he accepted—not, as it were, with the thoughtlessness or naïveté of Donizetti and Bellini, but in full knowledge of its tradition and its natural development. Basically, Wagner always despised his public; it is part of the contradiction in his nature that he nevertheless wanted to conquer it. Verdi took the popular verdict upon his operas as a sort of divine judgment, and bore failure with equanimity. Often he appealed this divine judgment by new versions of a work, but in general he preferred to create a new one. He was not at all "revolutionary"; he simply carried on the work of Rossini, Bellini, and especially Donizetti. Like Donizetti, he was a folk-composer, dependent on and supported by the applause of his nation. Never would he have been able to say of his fellow countrymen what Wagner said of Germany and the Germans in a letter to Mathilde Wesendonck on August 3, 1863: "It is a miserable country, and a certain man named Ruge is right when he says, *'The German is vile.'*" Verdi was an ardent patriot, and participated zealously in the national unification of Italy, thus winning for himself the gratitude of his nation. It is well known that the letters of his name became a symbol of union under the House of Savoy (*Evivva* VERDI, standing for *Evviva* Vittorio Emmanuele Re D'Italia).

No one has expressed the matter more beautifully than the poet Antonio Fogazzaro:[51] "The very soul of Italy, which shines as brightly in the beauty of nature as in the work of the great poets and great artists who secretly live in every color, in every form of our land as well as in every

[51] I am quoting him from Carlo Gatti's *Verdi* (Milan, 1931), II, 400.

heart among our people, has today its voice in the name of Giuseppe Verdi. When this voice wells forth and resounds, every one of us feels himself moved in his heart by the mysterious power of our native land, and he feels that the song somehow comes from himself, from countless others who join with him, from the dear earth which is the mother of all. In such a moment we forget Verdi, and that is his glory." No one could ever write that way about Wagner, not even of *Die Meistersinger.*

Verdi, moreover, watched passionately over the purity of the Italian character in art. His veneration for Beethoven was deep; ". . . before this name," he wrote in a letter to Josef Joachim on May 7, 1889, "we all bow in reverence." But he considered it a misfortune that the younger Italian musicians were suddenly beginning to write symphonic and chamber music. Strangely enough, he himself had written a string quartet— though, to be sure, it was a very Italian one. For him, the national form of musical expression was *opera,* and the national instrument or medium of expression was the human voice. He never concerned himself over Schubert, Schumann, or Brahms—not to mention Berlioz or Liszt.

He followed the development of the Parisian opera attentively, but with critical eye and ear. At the beginning of September, 1847 he heard Halévy's *La Juive* in Paris, but the work bored him unspeakably. In the early part of 1854 he had the opportunity of attending the first performances of Meyerbeer's *Etoile du Nord,* and he informed his friend Clarina Maffei that he, in contrast to the excellent Parisian public, understood little or nothing about it. ". . . I grasped little or nothing, but this good audience grasped everything, and found everything beautiful, sublime, divine!" Another letter to this friend, written on December 17, 1884, seems to give his opinion of German art in general and of Wagner's in particular. He knew who Wagner was. On the day after Wagner's death he wrote to Ricordi: ". . . I was, as it were, prostrated with grief. Here we do not discuss the matter. A great personality has gone from us, a name which will leave the most powerful imprint upon the history of art!"

But he considered it dangerous dilettantism fostered by too much musical criticism, "the new flagellation of the 19th century," to pursue an ideal that is foreign, only half understood, and never to be assimilated. "I am convinced that this art—so artful, and so frequently strange even in its intention—does not conform to our very nature. We [Italians] are positivists and, to a considerable extent, skeptics. We are not inclined to believe much, and are not able to believe for long stretches in the fantastic conceptions of this foreign art, which is deficient in naturalness and simplicity. For art which is lacking in naturalness and simplicity is not art!"

He wished to base his art, his music, on no other presuppositions than truth to his feeling and the directness or fidelity of the melodic expression. And that is precisely the feature that differentiates him from his predecessors, Rossini, Bellini, Donizetti, Mercadante, and all the rest. He distinguishes himself from all the rest by his earnestness. On July 29, 1868, he wrote, "I do not wish to find in art what the Olympian Jupiter of Passy [Rossini] does—simply pleasure." He became angry when people talked about art, and particularly about opera, as "entertainment." "To have been amused! That is a way of speaking that even when I was a young man always made me blush and still arouses my ire."

This striving for simplicity, naturalness, and truth explains the essential nature of his kind of opera. It is the opposite to an orchestral opera. It culminates in the human voice and never lets the orchestral element grow to "symphonic" proportions. It retains all the closed forms and avoids the "unending melody." It looks only to the human beings and listens only to human promptings. The Romantic opera, beginning with Weber, had placed the human beings in a *milieu;* one could call the forest the hero of the *Freischütz,* the elfin world that of *Oberon,* the Grail that of *Lohengrin,* the night that of Act II of *Tristan.* With Verdi—except for *Aïda,* which had to be composed as a showy opera for Cairo—the *milieu* is quite unimportant. If Verdi must give his scene a nature background, he does so with a few ingenious strokes, in contrast to the pompous Wagnerian orchestral painting: for example, the thunderstorm in the last act of *Rigoletto,* the lonely field at the beginning of Act II of *Un Ballo in Maschera,* though it is seen through the hero's eyes, the glitter of the stars in the Nile scene from *Aïda.* When the censor, in the case of *Un Ballo in Maschera,* objected to the historical background of the action, Verdi transformed a Danish king into a simple "Governatore di Boston" without the least harm to the essence of the opera. For the king was also a man. The stage scenery might be ever so poor (though it could not be entirely absent, for Verdi was a man of the theater), yet everything would be all right if only the singers were good.

Thus Verdi could come to terms with grand opera in *I Vespri Siciliani* and in *Don Carlos,* as most of his famous fellow countrymen had done; but he alone could do so without lasting injury. The comparison with Meyerbeer—in, for example, his last opera, *L'Africaine*—can perhaps make clear the difference. The comparison is permissible, for both musicians availed themselves of the same opera form. Meyerbeer, a musician with occasionally great melodic ideas, was no genuine man of the opera like Verdi, but only an exploiter of opera. He sought continually to fill up the gap between convention and refinement, without succeeding in doing so. Meyerbeer relied on proved effect: in *L'Africaine,* for instance, he wrote a great duet at precisely the same place as he had done in the *Huguenots,* at the end of Act IV, but this time it completely missed fire, remained feeble and cramped, because there was no melodic glow born of the situation. He relied on everything conventional in the opera; he wanted only to give it a certain tang. Verdi, too, did nothing revolutionary if he could help it; but in his work the convention came again to life, thanks to his earnestness, his honesty, and his glowing humanity, or in other words, his participation as artist in all his characters. When in *L'Africaine* Meyerbeer sets the words "Ah, the torture is too great" (*Ah, c'est trop de torment*) to music, he does so with all the emptiness of grand opera, all the weight of generations of *recitativo accompagnato.* When Verdi, however, in *La Forza del Destino,* sets "Good night, my daughter" (*Ti benedica il cielo . . . Addio*), he animates the conventional phrase by the entire force and fineness of his feeling, and by the tragic undertones.

PERIODS IN VERDI'S DEVELOPMENT

The long history of Verdi's operas, extending from 1839 to 1893, or almost as long as the reign of Queen Victoria, is the story of an ever greater refinement of musical means within the traditional frame. Unlike the poet-composer Wagner, Verdi was dependent upon a succession of more or less routine librettists. Seldom, to be sure, could they entirely please him, and often they were ordered about by him not only in the laying-out of scenes but even in the versifying, as for example was Antonio Ghislanzoni during the preparation of *Aïda.* As a rule, Verdi's operas are in four acts, or have three acts and a prologue. The three-act *Traviata* is an exception, as is also the ostensibly three-act *Rigoletto,* though with the division of the first act it assumes the form of an opera with prologue and three acts. Both of his "Parisian" operas, of course, have five acts. The stressed portions of Verdi's works, too, almost always come at the same places: the grand finales at the end of the second and third acts, the great duet in the middle of the third, the heroine's prayer at the beginning of the fourth, usually a prayer with chorus, etc. Everything seems to be a matter of extreme routine and of highly conventional machinery.

But, again, it is due to Verdi's seriousness and to what one might call his dramatic morality that all routine and convention in the course of his development became less and less perceptible.

Despite its unity, this development can be divided into several periods. The first extends from Verdi's beginnings, with *Oberto, Conte di San Bonifacio* (1839) to *Stiffelio* (1850). During this time Verdi seemed still to be competing with his contemporaries. The second includes the three operas *Rigoletto, Il Trovatore,* and *La Traviata,* which makes him the most folklike of all Italian composers—the composer of that kind of opera which was characterized once by Nietzsche's musical friend Peter Gast as "barrel-organ nonsense." The third begins with his making eyes at grand opera, but ends with the most Italian of all his works, *Aïda.* The last period, which falls essentially outside the framework of this presentation, was the "Shakespearean" period, with *Otello* and *Falstaff.*

It is one long and great unified development, in which there were no "youthful wild oats" as with Wagner, no "revolutions" or detours, but an unswerving continuity. This was the result not only of Verdi's own merit, but also of his good fortune. If one wishes to compare the fate of Italian opera with that of German, one can put it in the following formula: in Germany, there was no operatic tradition; consequently, after a later beginning, there was only a series of individual, admirable operatic works. In Italy, with its very old tradition of three centuries, there was *opera.* To make clear the continuity of Verdi's creative work, the depth of his roots in tradition, it is perhaps helpful to consider more closely one of his early operas, *Nabucco* or *Nabucodonosor.*

Nabucco (1842) was Verdi's third opera, coming after the somewhat wild and youthful *Oberto, Conte di San Bonifacio* (1839), which, for a first work, met with quite indifferent success at La Scala. It also came after the failure of *Il Finto Stanislao* (or *Un Giorno di Regno,* 1840), the first and, for many years to come, the only attempts of Verdi's in the realm of the comic. *Nabucco,* a Biblical opera, made Verdi all at once a national composer, thanks to a chorus which closes the third act. It should be noted that this is a chorus, not an aria—a fact which points up the altered situation in Italian opera. The captive Jews sit on the bank of the Euphrates and think of their native land: "Fly, my thought, on wings of gold"; and for the torn-up, enslaved, non-unified Italy of 1842 this chorus became an expression and symbol of yearning, hope, confidence, certainty of future liberation. That national opera, which Wagner wanted to create by such long, aesthetic wanderings, that people's opera, was available to

Verdi from the beginning. It is an Italian opera-chorus; one ought not to think of Handel in connection with it. Yet in its tenderness and its swelling power it is, or was, of mighty effect.

One ought not to think of Handel at all in connection with *Nabucco,* despite the material. *Nabucco* is not an oratorio, but a Biblical *opera.* And on the Biblical element much less stress is laid than, let us say, in Méhul's *Joseph* (1807) or even in Rossini's *Mosè in Egitto* (1818). In Italian opera it is of rather slight importance whether it is a matter of Celtic priests and priestesses as in *Norma* or of the destruction of the Temple at Jerusalem as in *Nabucco.* One hardly knows whether the hero of the action is the Babylonian king himself or the Jewish [i.e., the Italian], people. But that is no matter. What is important is the dramatic scene, the living, striking situation, which Verdi demanded of his librettists and in the more fortunate instances carried off with complete success. Verdi's poetical idol was Shakespeare, and the Shakespearean element actually appears at this point among these miserable apprentice librettists, even in the inferior work of Temistocle Solera, who patched together *Nabucco.* And Verdi's sense of the scene, which he shared with Wagner and every other great dramatic artist, is shown in the fact that he wrote his opera upon this libretto, which had been originally offered to Otto Nicolai but had been rejected by him. One may judge for himself whether the action might not have been acceptable to the Shakespeare of *Titus Andronicus* or *Pericles.*

In the first act Nebuchadnezzar rides as conqueror into the Temple at Jerusalem. One of his daughters is living among the Jews as a prisoner, as their secret helper and protectress. In Babylon he demands that the oppressed honor him as a god. Then Jehovah's lightning flash strikes his head and unseats his reason. In this evil plight, he has a scuffle, after passionate duets, with the designing and pugnacious Abigail, who is supposed to be his first-born daughter but is really only a slave, the birth records having been seized and torn up. In the end, the King recognizes the true God and saves his genuine daughter from a sacrificial death. The idol of Baal falls to pieces in the dust, and the prisoners come out into freedom.

Some of Verdi's later great characters are here foreshadowed, such as Philip II of *Don Carlos* or the title role of *King Lear,* which Verdi long planned but never brought out. After a dark prelude of the low strings, Nabucco, like Philip, sits in his chamber lost in sorrow and broods upon his fate. Ishmael, King of the Jews, stands, as tenor between two sopranos, in a great trio, much as thirty years later Radames was to stand between Aïda and Amneris. The pugnacious daughter has a long recitative-like monologue with ensuing aria, like Rigoletto's after the duet with Sparafucile. Immediately thereafter comes a *stretta* with chorus like Manrico's in *Trovatore*. She sits on the throne and watches a military ballet, as later the Egyptian King's daughter is to do. In these beginnings of Verdi's, a good bit of his later work is already at hand—not so much in the framework, which is as yet conventional, nor in the lyric *cabalette* or shortened arias introduced by Rossini, which Bellini or Donizetti could have supplied just as well as Verdi, but rather in certain striking rhythms, in the wild trumpet-sounds of a choral accompaniment, in the mighty expansion of a "Gran Scena di Duetto," and in the sureness with which everything that is oratorio-like is avoided and the great future man of opera is unmistakably revealed.

In the ensuing operas of even this first period, Verdi distinguished himself from his rivals by the full-bloodedness of his work within the frame of convention, by his seriousness. His figures are no longer puppets in costume who sing arias and duets, but they are living beings, with all their passions centered in the tragic situations. Verdi was a deeply passionate, melancholy man. A very frequent indication of the manner of performance in his scores is the word *cupo,* hollow-sounding, of deepest sorrow. No material could be wild enough for him. In 1844 he took in hand Victor Hugo's *Ernani* (1830); and in the gaudiness and incoherence of the text as prepared by F. M. Piave, the opera exceeds even the later *Trovatore*. It also goes beyond *Trovatore* in that the poor heroine stands between not merely two, but even three lovers. Owing to Verdi's impetuosity, however, it became a still greater success than *Nabucco*.

Three of Schiller's plays, for example, were taken in hand by Verdi and made into *Giovanna d'Arco* (1845), *I Masnadieri* (1847), and *Luisa Miller* (1849), without any reverence for the poetic content of the *Jungfrau von Orleans,* the *Räuber,* and *Cabale und Liebe*. He took up these plays purely because of the explosive force of the German poet's works, particularly that of the two revolutionary youthful plays. *I Masnadieri,* the only work that Verdi wrote for London, is considered his weakest operatic composition. Yet it also contains a few musical passages that are most genuine; and it even makes the Germanically inspired Romantic landscape visible through off-stage choruses, off-stage voices, and the remarkably colorful instrumentation. On the other hand, in *Luisa Miller,* Verdi and his librettist, the Sicilian poet Cammarano (who also wrote the

AN AFTERNOON AT LISZT'S

Lithograph by J. Kriehuber; Liszt seated at the piano; around him, left to right, are
Kriehuber, Berlioz, Carl Czerny, and Wilhelm Ernst, the violin virtuoso.

VERDI

libretto for *Trovatore*), make nothing at all of the setting, choosing a somewhat comic and abstract Tirol of the 17th century in place of the corrupt little German principality of the 18th. Nothing remains of the original but the main characters and the bare skeleton of the action. All that Verdi required was the dynamic situation. Much is still conventional and crude, much points entirely back to Donizetti and much entirely forward to *Il Trovatore* of two years later (even in the matter of mixing the sonorities of the stroke of a clock and the organ). But in the last act, one already finds the whole Verdi. There one finds a little aria which, with most simple and moving melodiousness, makes the deepest and purest statement of a resigned soul, a heartfelt duet between father and daughter, the avowal scene of the lovers, and an ending that is compressed into a few measures and yet is deeply moving. Finally, it is noteworthy that the motif from the overture at the beginning of the third act suddenly takes on its significance as a "motif of fate." Verdi disdains all the ingenuities of the leitmotif, being an operatic rather than a symphonic composer; he uses repetitions only in the striking manner of opera.

Once in this period Verdi, while not breaking with the tradition of Italian opera, allowed his love for Shakespeare to occasion his imputing too much to his public—in *Macbeth*. *Macbeth* met with little success both in the first performance at the Pergola in Florence (1847) and somewhat later in La Scala, where people had not grown up to the demands of the work and did not wish to; nor, finally, in the reworking for Paris (1865). For an Italian and French public, it is a very uncomfortable and unpleasant opera, and for an English and German public a very contradictory one, arousing highly mixed feelings, for this public constantly measures it by Shakespeare. A hundred times violence is done to the Shakespearean material, which reaches out into gray and awful, magical medieval regions; and also a hundred conventions of Italian opera have to be here accepted.

But Verdi a hundred times proves to be right in the end. He did not set Shakespeare's *Macbeth* to music, but *transcribed* it into his own operatic style. Where with Shakespeare mist arises, with Verdi something takes on *form;* for Verdi can think only in traditional opera forms which he has adopted. Where with Shakespeare horror and murder arise from a remote age and from the Northern landscape, Verdi knows only human passion. Verdi does not have the sensibilities of a Northerner. A banquet is a banquet, a battle is a battle; only the costume changes. The three witches become a three-voiced witches' chorus, although they are not less unearthly than their sisters in Scotland. The murder of Banquo becomes an assembly of the members of the Maffia, but this four-voiced chorus in staccato eighth-notes takes away from the ensuing murder scene nothing of its terrible realism. Lady Macbeth sings at the beginning of the quartet, conjures up the ghost of Banquo, a veritable "Brindisi" with choral refrain, (as later Violetta in *La Traviata*), which shocks the listener, yet is excellently conceived as an operatic contrast. The whole third act, in which Macbeth again seeks out the witches, seems to be a purely decorative ballet scene with closing duet, but is a dramatic scene of great —and, for Italian opera, new—symphonic power.

There is also a new and "Romantic" coloring about the recitative in *Macbeth*: the voice hovers alone in space, and in the pauses an echo of a woeful cry seems to become audible. Here the recitative is less than usual a mere "preparation" for the closed numbers. Verdi writes arias, duets, ensembles, and finales; everything seems conventional, seems treason against Shakespeare; yet in but very few passages does one find any compromise with "bad opera" or with "grand opera." Verdi rises to his full height in the duet of Macbeth and Lady Macbeth after the murder, or in the "Gran scena di sonnambulismo," as he naïvely entitled Lady Macbeth's sleepwalking scene. Here his probing into the abyss of the human soul is united with what can be characterized only as musical beauty, as the triumph of opera over drama.

Verdi did not repeat the experiment of *Macbeth* in the years that immediately ensued. The group of fifteen early operas are completed by *Luisa Miller* and *Stiffelio* (1850, later reworked, in 1857, into *Aroldo,* a predecessor of *Un Ballo in Maschera*). Passing on into his second period, he wrote *Rigoletto, Il Trovatore,* and *La Traviata,* three folk operas in which he gave quite pure expression to the ideal outlined by Donizetti.

The weakest among the three is the last. Its weakness is not solely due to the disgusting sentimentality of the subject—after Alexandre Dumas's *La Dame aux Camélias,* which Verdi has purified into touchingly human material. Rather, its weakness is due to the fact that Verdi has taken pains to achieve an excessive simplicity of melody.

The most popular of the three is the second, in which one musical explosion follows upon the other, and in which the Spanish Gypsy material seems to have given more richness to the local color of the whole work. One can study Verdi's brevity, his striking power, and his unconscious antagonism towards Wagner nowhere better than in *Il Trovatore:* for example, in the introduction of the story and characters. Whereas Wagner, in such a work as *Parsifal*, requires more than half an act to make the antecedent action clear, or, in the *Ring*, resorts to long recapitulations of the meaning, Verdi takes care of the entire "exposition of the drama" in a short *"Introduzione,"* an aria with chorus.

The most accomplished of the three works is *Rigoletto*, based on the garish drama *Le Roi s'amuse* by Victor Hugo, and originally entitled "The Curse" (*La Maledizione*). It contains several "numbers," which, in the relation of the voices to the orchestra, at once have their roots in the past and point forward into the future. Verdi liked to introduce upon the stage the *banda*, or wind ensemble, playing dance music, which he punctuated by the interjection of dialogues. One of the models in Italian for this procedure was already present in the Fandango of Mozart's *Le Nozze di Figaro*. This *banda*-music—for example in *Rigoletto*, *Traviata*, and *Un Ballo in Maschera*—is mostly of strangely naturalistic triviality. But Verdi refined the procedure, as in the *Allegro agitato* which in the third act of *Rigoletto* introduces the duet of daughter and father (No. 10). Or, still better, Verdi's refinement appears in the melancholy orchestral piece with the muted 'cello and contrabass, followed by the unearthly dialogue between Rigoletto and Sparafucile. Though Verdi did not know any of Wagner's music dramas, he approached the Wagnerian principle of the formative importance of the orchestra without, however, encroaching upon the supremacy of the human voice and without thinking of the symphonic interweaving of leitmotifs. Along with all the explosive force of *Rigoletto* and *Trovatore*, the final scenes, like those in *Traviata*, are not aimed at "effect," but at human movement—Azucena's dream, Rigoletto's desperation. This is one of Verdi's characteristic features: the conception of death as a serious, mild friend.

FROM *I VESPRI SICILIANI* TO *AÏDA*

In Verdi's later works, even in those of the third period, the intervals between the first performances became greater. The production became more careful, without the productive power being lessened. The three folk operas established his world fame, and accordingly he received in this period commissions to write two operas for Paris: *Les Vêpres Siciliennes* (1855) and *Don Carlos* (1867). In *Les Vêpres Siciliennes*, which he himself translated into Italian as *I Vespri Siciliani*, he had to pay the penalty for the fact that he had dealings with the Opéra—or, more precisely, with Meyerbeer's librettist, Eugène Scribe. Verdi was dissatisfied with the libretto, particularly with the last act. "I was hoping," he wrote on January 3, 1855, to the Director of the Opéra, "that M. Scribe (since the situation, in my opinion, is not unfavorable) would have found for the ending of the drama one of those moving pieces that bring forth tears and have an almost sure effect. Please observe, Sir, that this would have benefited the work in general; for it is completely lacking in pathos, except for the romance in the fourth act." Here we have his aesthetic of opera in a nutshell. He required situations of dramatic truth and passion; and as Scribe was much too genteel and conventional to supply them for him, Verdi wrote this opera with a bad conscience. He did everything he could with these historical puppets—among whom, into the bargain, his fellow countrymen play a sinister role. He tried to bring them to life, without succeeding in doing so. Thus the work is rather an echo, and an anticipation, of the genuine "Verdi": the overture with its brightness against a dark background, the duet at the end of the third act (also used in the overture), the magnificent effectiveness of the ends of all the acts. Some features remain feeble; again, others are forceful and thunderous.

In *Don Carlos* Verdi made good these shortcomings. It is significant that although the work had initial success at the Opéra, it was never revived there in the French version. For it *overcomes* "grand opera." Schiller's great, liberty-loving drama is, of course, transported into the operatic realm; and it cannot even forego an auto-da-fé as finale. Even the two French librettists did not succeed in eliminating from the figures of the King, the Queen, with her conflict between love and duty, the Prince, and the passionate lady of the court those "moving" and "emotional" features which Verdi required. He made more of Philip II than did Schiller—a deeply suffering man, whom we understand. To the last act Verdi was able to give an ending in a great scene of the Queen's, both stirring and at the same time heroically tragic and conciliatory—an ending which is a culmination of his art.

There remain, before *Aïda,* three "Italian" operas, in which the note of grand opera is scarcely sounded again: *Simone Boccanegra* (1857), *Un Ballo in Maschera* (1859), and *La Forza del Destino* (1862). *Simone Boccanegra,* in its performance at the Fenice Theater in Venice, was a failure. Shortly thereafter Verdi wrote to Chiara Maffei: "*Boccanegra* suffered a fiasco at Venice almost as great as that of *La Traviata.* I thought that I had made something that was possible, but it seems that I have been mistaken." Then, after a better reception accorded the work in Reggio and Naples, there came a still more decisive failure at La Scala. This time, however, Verdi was convinced of the failure of the Milanese. "Whatever friend or foe may say," Verdi wrote, *"Boccanegra* is not inferior to so many other of my operas that have had better luck . . ." (February 4, 1859). "When, a little later, feelings have been assuaged, it will perhaps be seen that in *Boccanegra* there is much that is not to be despised . . ." (February 9, 1859).

While he would no longer lift a finger for *I Vespri Siciliani,* he later —ten years after *Aïda*—asked Arrigo Boito to rework Piave's old libretto, not for any superficial reasons, but for reasons *"di professione"*—because the *artist* in him impelled him to give his opera the most finished form possible. *"Boccanegra* can make the rounds of the theaters like the rest of her sisters," he declared, "despite the fact that the subject is rather sad. . . . It is sad because it must be sad, but it is stirring . . ." (April 2, 1881). To the music he directed his entire, well-considered artistic skill; the greybeard improved the youth. He destroyed nothing of the impulsive life in the score, but he made out of it a work of the greatest stylistic unity. The performance at La Scala, March 24, 1881, achieved success this time; but again it was not lasting, either in Italy or elsewhere.

The reasons for the short duration of this popularity lay in the relation of the aging, more and more self-refining Verdi to his text. The material of the libretto had come from the Spanish playwright Gutiérrez, who had written the model for the libretto of *Trovatore.* And, exactly as in *Trovatore,* the action is a mixture of political drama, familiar tragedy, and a bit of intrigue, which is scarcely intelligible even to the auditor who is prepared for it. All the actions are, to be sure, motivated; but the economy of this motivation is scarcely surpassable: the narrative of important previous events, important background features of the action, is contained in the *cabalette* of the prelude and first act, and the motives become interlaced into an almost inextricable tangle. But this alarming difficulty, which in *Trovatore* is arrested by the immediate explosive force of the music, proves insurmountable to the master who has become more conscious of the demands of art. He transforms a theatrical scene into a dramatic situation; alongside typical lyric and intrigue roles, he draws two real characters in Boccanegra and his antagonist Fiesco; he leads—and that is the most significant feature for him—the opera from the nocturnal darkness of the beginning to the mild clarity of its denouement, from disunion to rest, from strife to resignation. But he had outgrown libretti of this sort, without perhaps himself having become conscious of the fact.

In *Un Ballo in Maschera* and *La Forza del Destino* Verdi was more fortunate. These are, again, popular operas, as was, for example, *Trovatore* or *Rigoletto,* and have the same variety of action and color. In both, *"grande opéra"* is overcome, although the *Ballo* goes back to an old historical staple of a libretto by Scribe that Auber had set to music. Still more to the point is the similarity between *Forza del Destino* and *Trovatore,* for the former also uses the basic idea of a passion-fraught Spanish drama, most gaudy in action. Verdi does not fight shy of this variety: in the *Ballo* there is a conspiracy, a fortune-telling scene in the cave of a Negress; in the *Forza* there is a gypsy and monastic setting, in which is even found one of the comic figures and scenes which his decision in favor of tragedy after the failure of *Giorno di Regno* had led him to avoid. All the opposites find their complete expression. But one might say that Verdi's landscape of tragedy had become still darker, had won a farther and deeper perspective, for example in Amelia's scene before the great duet in the *Ballo,* or in the famous aria of Leonore's in the final act of the *Forza,* and that as a result even his heavenly denouements had become still purer and more exalting.

The monastery scene in the *Forza* is a climax of purest opera: at once theater and exaltation. One might make an interesting comparison between the function of the organ in Wagner at the beginning of *Die Meistersinger* and here in Verdi: in Wagner, there is the entire historical and harmonic-polyphonic splendor of the Protestant chorale, a radiant introduction to the festive composition; in Verdi, there is the most simple sound, the most simple harmony, mere color, a little monastery church with a poor instrument, but infinitely arresting and moving. Yet in both *Un Ballo* and *Forza* the colorfulness of the whole has induced Verdi to reach back again at significant places in the course of the opera for a few motifs enunciated in the prelude; the most penetrating one is, in the *Forza,* the ever-recurring simple, muffled motive of the wind instruments in three notes—a genuine motive of fate.

With *Aïda* Verdi closed the third period in his work. And with the composition of this opera he returned to the custom of the 18th century, for this is a "commissioned" opera exactly as one of the festival operas of Caldara or Hasse had been. The contrast with Wagner is again striking. From the beginning to the end of his creative activity, Wagner followed only his own law, and forced the result violently upon the world. Verdi composed *Aïda* for the celebrations connected with the opening of the Suez Canal in 1871 and found not the least violence necessary in wooing his muse. His world renown had meanwhile become so great that he had by no means to accept the libretto as submitted. On the contrary, he influenced this text more strongly than any of his others in structure and all details; and one can glean from his correspondence with the librettist, Antonio Ghislanzoni, the entire dramaturgy of his operas.

For the first time he gave special attention to the "milieu": *Aïda* is an opera of ancient Egypt. In the second scene of the first act, a religious scene, a *"Gran scena della consacrazione,"* the ancient temple walls seem to become resonant with the sound of the harp and the monotonous song of the priestesses; and this sound is combined with similarly religious rhythms of the warriors. Aïda, characterized only as a maiden by a yearning motif, becomes an Ethiopian in her Nile Aria, which hovers iridescently between A minor and A major, with its "exotic" accompaniment in the winds. Amonasro is characterized as a savage by his unrestrained musical temperament. The most ingenious ethnographic passage is perhaps, in the first act, the few recitative measures of the messenger from the desert, with the wild melody of the winds against a tremolo of the kettledrum and the strings.

Verdi never forgot his commission: to write a *festival* opera, with ballet, marches, and processions. Above all, the finale of the second act had to fulfill its purpose: *"Gloria al Egitto . . . !"* And yet he never forgot his tragic figures, either: Amneris, Aïda, Radames, who have been imprisoned in a net of love and of rigid law. There are lyric arias, scenes, duets, trios, and ensembles—all richly filled with music. The idea behind Italian opera seems never to have been more completely realized than in this Egyptian festival opera. Yet this festival opera ends *pianissimo* and *con sordini,* with a *Liebestod,* which is not Romantically philosophical, but purely human, and which can be paralleled only by the gentle comfort of Verdi's own *Requiem.*

THE LAST PERIOD: *OTELLO* AND *FALSTAFF*

We take, with Verdi, a step beyond the limits of this book when we concern ourselves with his last two operas, *Otello* (1887) and *Falstaff* (1893). But without these two works the picture of Verdi would not be complete, and they also reflect a new light upon his earlier creative work. With them he returned to the paths at whose beginnings stands *Macbeth,* and to the poet whom among all the rest he honored most highly, Shakespeare. For many years, since 1848, he had been considering the writing of an opera *King Lear.* On February 28, 1850, he wrote to Cammarano, *"King*

Lear seems at first glance so vast, so intricate, that it appears impossible to make an opera out of it. Yet, on closer examination, it seems to me that the doubtlessly great difficulties are not insuperable. You know that it is not a matter of making from *King Lear* a drama in the more or less customary forms; it must be handled in a manner entirely new, magnificent, without regard for any conventions." He outlined a scenario, and after Cammarano's death he obtained a completed libretto from Somma. Yet again and again he postponed the composition, alleging, among other things, that he could not find the right singers for the figures in this drama. They would have to be, he asserted, not only very good but virtually born for the parts ("Believe me," he wrote on January 15, 1857, "that it is a great error to write *King Lear* for a group of singers who are not, so to speak, born for the parts, however good they may otherwise be"). The true reason was that the libretto did not yet suit him, and that he wished to do justice to Shakespeare, not to the traditions of Italian opera.

Then he found the right collaborator in Arrigo Boito; and there came to pass something which Mozart once called the greatest of all possible good fortune, "when a good composer, who knows the theater and is himself able to contribute something, and a clever poet, like a true phoenix, come together." [52] Boito was himself the composer of an opera, one with which he joined the ranks with Berlioz and Gounod and so many others, *Mefistofele* (1868, reworked in 1875 and 1876). It is an unnatural, factitious work, which Verdi with all his friendship for the poet-musician could not be moved to praise. Boito's lasting service to music will always be that he prepared two of Shakespeare's plays—a tragedy and a comedy—for Verdi's needs, without sacrificing any of Shakespeare's greatness in the tragic and comic art.

One should not think that *Otello* now became, as it were, a drama with music. It remained Italian opera, Verdian opera, which preserves almost completely its connection with the composer's earlier work. The Othello-Iago duet occurs at the same place as the Gilda-Rigoletto duet. The third act ends, as usual, with a grand finale. The second has a genuine "footlight piece," Iago's famous *Credo,* which one might wish to eliminate from the score as a concession to melodrama if it were not at the same time a masterpiece. At the beginning of the third act, for the Paris performance of 1894, Verdi even went so far as to provide a great "ethnographic," Oriental-Venetian ballet, which is rightly quite often ignored. But the first act without overture, starting off with a mighty storm and chorus

[52] Letter of October 13, 1781.

scene, and ending with one of the most sublime love duets of all time, is unusual. In the last act, moreover, Boito had, essentially, very little to change in Shakespeare's original. Verdi had remained the same, but he was now seventy, and had behind him the experiences of an entire life. The vocal part still dominates over the orchestra; but it no longer makes so much use of the explosive melody as it does of plastic, expressive declamation. And the orchestra has become richer, finer, more full of secret life, without having become in the least "Wagnerian."

A transfiguration of Verdi's own style, a sublimation, has taken place. It can be observed in the chromatic, somewhat serpentine type of melody that serves to characterize Iago. One might compare, for instance, Iago's description of jealousy ("*È un'idra fosca*") with similar expressions on the part of Azucena or Ulrica. The decisive factor is, to be sure, the strength and fineness with which the aging master followed every impulse in the souls of his characters. Once again the opera shows its superiority over the drama in this last act, where the music raises the tragedy of the proceedings on the stage almost to the limits of endurance, and yet resolves them into harmony.

In *Otello* Verdi, as it were, said the last word on *"opera seria."* In Wagnerian terms, he "redeemed" *opera seria,* which had brought forth at the beginning of the century Rossini's *Otello;* and he resolved it into *"dramma in musica,"* without disturbing the continuity of Italian operatic development. *Otello* stands at the end of the succession that had begun with Monteverdi's *Orfeo.*

Between his seventieth and eightieth years, in *Falstaff,* he accomplished the same thing for *opera buffa.* Approximately the same relationship as that between Verdi's *Otello* and Rossini's *Otello* exists between Verdi's *Falstaff* and Otto Nicolai's *Merry Wives of Windsor,* which in its way was an effective *opera buffa* with German text. Verdi, however, combined his modernity with the older tradition. Boito delivered to him three acts of the strictest symmetry: each one in two parts, the first part "soloistic," the second always uniting all the figures of the farce, as the tradition of *opera buffa* demanded. Verdi accordingly wrote three great finales, comparable in liveliness and masterfulness to nothing in the older Italian opera except perhaps Mozart's *Nozze* and *Don Giovanni* or the endings of Acts I and II in Wagner's *Meistersinger.* Verdi also is related to Wagner in that he resorted, for the conclusion of *Falstaff,* to the fugue "All the world's a joke. Man is born a fool." (*Tutto nel mondo è burla. L'uom è nato burlone*). But the relation to Mozart goes deeper. Mozart's *Figaro* and *Don Giovanni* are not pure *opere buffe*. Donna Anna, the Count, and the Countess are not *buffo* figures. Similarly, the outburst of Mr. Ford, the husband who thinks that he has been deceived, is no *buffo* scene, but a scene of tragic passion. Similarly, too, the comedy of the other figures is no longer buffoonish, has no longer anything to do with the *commedia dell'arte,* but is comedy of character.

Again, as in *Otello,* Verdi creates his own style within the outlines of tradition. The voices move, as a basic manner of behavior, in frantic *parlando,* and the orchestra supplies a commentary of incomparable flexibility and wit. Every melodic feature has become more non-sensuous, one might say, thinner, more spiritual. Even in the description of the magical summer's night in Windsor Forest, there prevails no Romantic exuberance, but sheer loveliness. A very old man, a wise master wrote this work, more for himself than for the world. He no longer really loved the figures which he had created: he found them only droll. He no longer wanted to "conquer" anyone. In a way opposite to Wagner, who overwhelmed Romanticism, Verdi reduced it *ad absurdum.*

OFFENBACH AND THE OPERETTA

The picture of operatic development in the 19th century would not be complete if mention were not made of a variety of opera quite definitely a product of the Romantic era, unknown to earlier centuries: the "operetta" or *"opéra-bouffe,"* and its principal master, Jacques Offenbach (1819–1880). It belongs to Romantic opera as the satyr play belonged to Attic drama.

To be sure, the name "operetta" is not new. In the 18th century any opera of rather small proportions was so called, especially the North German *Singspiel* with its modest musical insertions within the framework of the spoken dialogue. The more demanding Viennese variety, however, such as Mozart's *Entführung,* would hardly be called an operetta. True, another trait of the operetta—at least of Offenbach's—was already to be found in the 18th century, that of social satire or parody. One need recall only Gay and Pepusch's *Beggar's Opera,* the Italian intermezzi, the Parisian Théâtre Italien and Théâtre de la Foire, the French musical farces played at fairs, with their stock parodistic mockery of the Académie Royale.

But at the very beginning of the 19th century the increasing romanticizing, the incursions of sentimentality, of the historical, and of the fairy tale, drove these parodistic and critical tendencies out of the *opéra-comique* and out of the *Singspiel* and brought these forms nearer to serious opera. Owing to the political conditions of Italy, these parodistic and critical tendencies in *opera buffa* would have been almost completely suppressed before 1859. One way to the specifically 19th-century operetta seems to lead from the popular Viennese *Singspiel,* the Berlin "workman's-comedy" with its simple incidental songs, and above all from Auber's *opéra-comique.* All these types of composition, however, which simply reduce the musical dimensions of "serious" works, in no way preclude the most extreme sentimentality. At their best—for example, in Auber's hands— they emphasize the graceful, the piquant, and often slip into the frivolous, as does for example, Lortzing's *Wildschütz.* Yet they all lack the real element of the operetta, which has later been called the "Offenbachiad" —political, social criticism, great parody.

For an operetta competition in 1856,[53] Offenbach himself sent out in advance a manifesto in which he sought to characterize the historical bases of his work. He observed accurately how far the French *opéra-comique* had gone astray through its dramatic and musical ambition, its longing glances cast at the successes of grand opera. He envisaged its salvation in a return to the "primitive and gay type" (*le genre primitif et gai*), as created and cultivated by the 18th-century masters, Philidor, Monsigny, Gossec, Dalayrac, and above all Grétry in the works of an earlier day, when it had not yet been seized with the ambition of competing with Méhul, Le Sueur, Cherubini, and Berton. He let full justice be meted out to these composers, who belong to this "second period of *opéra-comique,*" and with them he associated Isouard, Catel, Boieldieu. He praised Hérold in *La Clochette, Le Muletier,* and *Marie,* but he viewed with concern the darkening of the type in *Zampa* and *Le Pré aux Clercs.* Finally, he saw in Auber, Halévy, Adam, and Thomas the representatives of a mongrel type, which "is not yet grand opera and also no longer *opéra-comique.*" He made an exception for only a few of their works, such as Halévy's *L'Eclair* or the quasi-Italian "retrospective" little operas of Albert Grisar (1808–1869), *Les Porcherons* (1850), *Bonsoir, M. Pantalon* (1851), and *Le Chien du Jardinier* (1855).

What Offenbach wanted to do was to revive the light and graceful type from the early period of *opéra-comique,* "to spin out further the inexhaustible threads of old French mirth," and to stimulate the ambition

[53] I have taken this from the excellent monograph on Offenbach by Anton Henseler, Berlin, 1930.

"of saying things briefly," which incidentally is no slight ambition. He could use none of the libretti which, "instead of remaining merry, lively, and graceful, might have served for operas, darkened the colors, burst their bounds, and complicated the dramatic action." The new genre demanded of the musician "only three things: skill, knowledge, ideas." The idea, however, must be good—the melody must be of sterling worth.

But he would not have been Offenbach and a man of the 19th century if he had been satisfied with this return to the 18th. His personality is worthy of consideration. He was the son of a Jewish traveling musician from Offenbach am Main, Isaac Juda Eberst, who made his living by playing in synagogues and dance halls. By about 1802 the father had settled in Deutz near Cologne, and later he moved to Cologne itself. There Jacques Offenbach, the "most Parisian" of musicians, came into the world. He was a child prodigy on the violoncello, and was early taken by his father to Paris, where he succeeded in getting into the Conservatoire.

His career as a composer began with the writing of waltzes, romances, and salon pieces for his instrument with piano, several of them written with Flotow. He made his first attempt at a conquest of the theater in 1838 with music for the vaudeville skit *Pascal et Chambord,* but the success was not such that he could give up teaching, concertizing, and composing instrumental pieces and comic songs (among compositions of this last type he had already set to music six of La Fontaine's fables). Since the doors of the Opéra-Comique remained obdurately closed to him, he presented his first one-acters partly within the limits of concerts (in 1847, *L'Alcove,* a sort of burlesque-sentimental rescue-opera from the period of the Revolution) and partly at the Théâtre des Variétés (*Le Trésor à Mathurin,* 1852, and *Pepito,* 1853). These early one-acters have been characterized as "something midway between comic opera and operetta, in which Offenbach's very own style does not as yet find full expression." [54] They are, however, full of grace and wit, and are not without satirical allusions, a tendency which had already manifested itself in Offenbach's work, e.g., his parody (1846) on Félicien David's symphony-ode *Le Désert.*

In 1855 he at last followed the example of Florimond Ronger, alias Hervé (1825–1892), organist at St. Eustache, and founded his own theater, *Les Bouffes Parisiennes.* Hervé stands in a peculiar relationship to Offenbach: though preceding him in the opening of his *Folies Concertantes* by at least a year and a half, Hervé was, in his parodies, an imitator of Offenbach and cannot be compared with Offenbach in the music to his comic scenes

[54] Henseler, p. 157.

and pantomimes. But it is significant that Offenbach was not the only creator of this anti-Romantic operatic type: opposition was in the air.

Hervé allowed himself only two actors on the stage; Offenbach at the beginning went as far as three. He has himself described the development in a letter of 1860: "I had a license which specified that I should present only *saynètes* [short, merry scenes] with two or three characters . . . I bought [?] the theater of M. Comté, to transform it into the *Bouffes-Parisiens*. Then my license was somewhat extended in that I was permitted to write on the program, instead of *saynètes,* operettas in one act. Later I was permitted to let four characters come upon the stage. In the last two years the number of characters was unlimited. In the end I received permission to play *buffo* operas in two acts and as many tableaux as I wished . . ." [55]

We scarcely need concern ourselves with Offenbach's small works, by which he made a conquest of the Parisian stage: the idyllic or rustic little pieces in which he really seems to have started from the 18th century—the "bourgeois and military one-acts" which belong with models like Auber's *Le Maçon* or Donizetti's *Fille du Régiment,* and his genuine pieces of buffoonery—although in all of them the trend towards parody is already present. Offenbach's world success—a world success because it was based upon the inconsistencies in the romantic cultural situation of Europe at the time—began with the great operetta *Orphée aux Enfers* (1858), followed in 1864 by *La Belle Hélène.* So far as material is concerned, both operas are a parody of classical antiquity, upon which Offenbach had sworn revenge in the years when he as conductor of the entr'acte music at the Théâtre-Français had to endure the tirades of French Classical tragedy. Satire of medieval legend is shown in *Génevière de Brabant* (1859), nine years after Schumann had treated the material so seriously, and especially in *Barbe-Bleue* (1866), where Offenbach takes the horrible material which leads into the depths of sexual aberration and merrily reduces it *ad absurdum.* In *Pont des Soupirs* (1861), the operatic horror-drama was satirized. In *Grande-Duchesse de Gérolstein* (1867), the satire extended over into the political sphere—or rather more than the political, and it became a satire of the times.

It should, of course, be realized that Offenbach was no moralist. He indulged in criticism so long as he found it amusing. The victims laughed at the more or less obvious objects of satire—idiotic monarchs, military usurpers, profligate ladies of the highest circle, mercenary and rapacious

[55] Henseler, p. 179.

priests. But without knowing it, they were also laughing at themselves. Offenbach uncovered the complete corruption of the Second Empire of Napoleon III, who attended and applauded the operettas of his critic. Offenbach uncovered this corruption while himself making use of it. His *Vie Parisienne* (1866) contributed to making Paris appear, for many years to come, the Eldorado of amusement. The city itself found pleasure in this lascivious picture, behind which grinned Zola's *Nana*. His work, which is unbelievably fertile, is full of contemporary allusions unintelligible to a later time—allusions not only in the characters, situations, jokes, and puns, but also in the music.

What Offenbach took aim at by way of musical parody was, above all, the unnaturalness and the empty pathos of Meyerbeer's grand operas, and the stereotyped insipidity of the Italian *opera semiseria* since Rossini. He tried to satirize even Wagner in a *Symphonie de l'Avenir, marche de Fiancés* and a *Tyrolienne de l'Avenir,* but knew his work too little to make the parody striking and effective. Offenbach's means were, of course, those of exaggeration and contrast, as, for example, when a pathetic recitative changes suddenly into the most impudent dance-rhythm, or when a finale closes with the triumph of a cancan. All in all, in his really important works—for we shall not count the dozens of hollow ballets and empty revues for hundreds and hundreds of performers, the many pot-boilers that he wrote—he is always a dramatist and a melodist of the first rank.

As is to be expected, Richard Wagner has said the worst thing about his contemporary, Offenbach. Wagner speaks of Auber's "cynically delightful coldness and smoothness," the basis of which is nothing but "gracefully hidden smut," and he speaks of Offenbach as an exploiter of this type of music: "There is, at all events, warmth—the warmth of the dung-pile —in which all the swine of Europe could wallow." The culture-moralist might speak this way, but never the musician. The dramatist in Wagner, moreover, should not have failed to recognize the dramatist in Offenbach. Offenbach's secret was that he wrote no insertions; he got his ideas from the situation. He wrote several dozen drinking songs and twenty "letter-arias," but they cannot be transferred from one work into another. And as for Offenbach as a musician, he fulfilled his own demands, the demands for "skill, knowledge, and ideas." Especially he fulfilled the one for ideas.

Opéra-bouffe is the corrupt product of a corrupt period; but Offenbach's music is clean; his melodies, with complete simplicity, are always like blossoms, are genuine ideas. To make the test, one should listen to the music of his last "serious" opera, *Les Contes d'Hoffmann,* presented in 1881 as a posthumous work in already mutilated form. He has not in the least changed his style there, and one will find in this music not the least trace of lasciviousness. His uniqueness becomes clear when he is compared with one of his successful imitators and successors, the composer of Viennese waltzes, Johann Strauss (1825–1899), who, despite the charming *Fledermaus* (1874), directed the decline of later operetta into something disgustingly muddy or greasy.

Nietzsche had a finer sense of appreciation when on March 21, 1888, he wrote to his friend, the composer Peter Gast: ". . . I have . . . heard something—three pieces of Offenbach's [*La Périchole, La Grande-Duchesse de Gérolstein, La Fille du Tambour-Major*]—and I was delighted. Four or five times in each work he reached a condition of most high-spirited buffoonery, but in a form according to Classical taste, absolutely logical—and at the same time wonderfully Parisian! . . . In so doing, this spoiled child has had the luck of finding the cleverest Frenchmen as his librettists: Halévy . . . Meilhac, and others. Offenbach's texts have something enchanting about them, and are probably the only thing so far accomplished by opera that has done a good turn for poetry." Nietzsche sensed in Offenbach the enmity towards the "Romantic," and hailed it, just as he had hailed Bizet's *Carmen.* Incidentally, Henri Meilhac and Ludovic Halévy were also the librettists of *Carmen,* and it was Bizet as a young man who, together with Lecocq (1832–1918), won the prize in the competition mentioned above as having been announced by Offenbach.

The real successor to Offenbach was not one of the Viennese or Parisian operetta composers, but the Irishman Arthur S. Sullivan (1842–1900), who succeeded both in maintaining his independence of Offenbach and in overcoming the influences of his study at the Leipzig Conservatory, at least in this area which is so much his own—for he was a many-sided "serious" Victorian composer. Like Offenbach, he had had the good fortune of finding his equal in a librettist, W. S. Gilbert. Like Offenbach, towards the end of his life he also made an experiment with a romantic opera, *Ivanhoe* (1891)—unfortunately, in contrast to Offenbach's, a tiresome one. His "light operas," of which one, *Trial by Jury* (1875), is even "through-composed," are, despite all their political and social satire, softer and more well-behaved than Offenbach's. In common with his, however, they use the same means: parody of grand opera, quick change from sentimentality to disarming merriment, and innocence and simplicity of melody. If there *was* an English national composer in the 19th century before the awakening of a new nationalistic spirit around 1880, that composer was not Mendelssohn's pupil and Schumann's friend William Sterndale Bennett (1816–1875), but Arthur Seymour Sullivan.

CHAPTER XVII

Nationalism

NATIONAL ELEMENTS IN PRE-ROMANTIC MUSIC

IT HAS already been suggested in the first part of this book that intensified national coloring is an essential characteristic of Romantic music. The word "intensified" is used because there have always been nationally separated developments in music. Even in periods like that of the 15th century, when the universally recognized style of the "Burgundian Masters" prevailed over all Europe, one can perhaps distinguish northern Burgundians of Bruges and Ghent and Hainault from Frenchmen, or Englishmen from Germans and Italians, to some extent—*perhaps,* for it is very easy to deceive oneself into thinking that something represents the nation when it only represents the school of a rather strongly individualistic composer.

Certainly, however, in the 16th century the musical nations began either to develop or to become aware of their national differences. This "creation" or formulation of a national style was most fascinating in Italy, where there appeared a form distinctively Italian, and even distinctively Upper Italian, known under the collective name *frottola*. But about 1525 it was again submerged beneath an overpowering, "international" wave, only to return to the surface decades later in renewed and transfigured form. Beginning with those times, there were French, Spanish, Italian, English, Flemish, and German schools, each of markedly individual character. The national element, however, showed itself much more clearly in secular than in sacred music: in the chanson, the *villancico,* the lied, and the madrigal, while the Mass, motet, Magnificat, and hymn remained more "international," neutral property. Even the separate regions within the national divisions began to make themselves heard: in Italy around 1535, for example, the *Canzon villanesca alla napoletana,* or the *Moresca* in the south of the peninsula. But there prevailed as yet neither a regional nor a national delimitation or barrier. Thus, as the Neapolitan *canzon* was immediately adopted and absorbed by all Italy, similarly the basic idea of reciprocity was recognized by all Europe. The chanson spread to Italy, the madrigal to France and England. Particularly in the instrumental forms there were scarcely any boundaries: the "schools" of the ricercar, whether called fugue as in Germany, *tiento* as in Spain, or fancy as in England, were different; but the spirit and form were the same. At all events, the national aspect was not emphasized.

With the beginning of the 17th century, national distinction was altered in that two nations assumed the rule over Europe in musical matters, Italy and France. Spain withdrew into the status of a province; Germany, torn by religious dissension and the Thirty Years' War, maintained its autonomy only in church and organ music; and not only musicians from Catholic South Germany but also Protestant musicians like Heinrich Schütz looked to Italy as their guiding star. After the great days of the Elizabethan virginalists and madrigalists England withdrew, and, with the death of Purcell, who in his time had been great enough to come to his own terms with both French and Italian influences, ceased to be a musical nation. It was through the "discovery" of monody and its utilization in all musical forms, above all in the opera, that Italy took the lead in European music. Only France opposed this Italian invasion. The failure of Italian opera in Paris at the time of Mazarin is significant of the French resistance to imported opera. We might contrast with it the failure, in 1861, of *Tannhäuser* in Paris, which was only a bit of theatrical scandal, and which rather helped than hindered the shortly ensuing victory of Wagner in France. In view of the 17th-century failure of Italian opera in Paris, it is perhaps one of the ironies of music history that a Florentine, Giovanni Battista Lulli, at that time established the form of French opera, in contrast to Italian, for more than a century to come. He even exerted a retroactive influence upon Italy through the ballet and its particular forms, which were an essential element in this type of opera.

In the early years of the 18th century, Europe recognized only two musical nations, the Italian and the French. No other nation was considered in the literary controversy which was associated around 1700 with the name of Abbé François Raguenet and his "Comparison of the Italians and the French in Music and Opera" (*Parallèle des Italiens et des François en ce qui regarde la musique et les opéras*) and around 1750 with that of Jean-Jacques Rousseau. The style of German music was "mixed," according to the testimony of its representatives such as Telemann. As his

German heritage, J. S. Bach had the chorale and all the forms he needed, but in addition he used the French overture and suite, the Italian aria, the Italian concerto, and the Italian sonata. To judge by his style and nature, Handel, a musician born—like Hasse or Graun—in Germany, in fact in Prussian Saxony, imported Italian music to England. The relationship of the two rival nations was, on Italy's part, one of naïve and unconcerned consciousness of assured possession and, on France's, one of distrustful jealousy. But, on the one hand, even Rameau, the most French of all French musicians, could not prevent Italian elements or seeds of ferment from finding their way into his last operas; and, on the other, there were even in Italy incidental points of entry for French music, such as the court opera in Parma. In his day Gluck passed for an international musician—for one too great to be kept within national bounds; but in reality he was, during the first half of his life, more an Italian, and in the second more a French composer. Above all, he was Gluck.

That state of affairs changed around 1750, and, alongside the two established musical nations, the German took its place as a third. This was by virtue of a few powerful personalities and a great number of smaller composers who devoted themselves to instrumental music. Not all among these lesser composers, whose music inundated Paris and London after the middle of the century, bore German names (so far as the notion of a Germany then existed at all). Stamitz, Holzbauer, Beck, Schobert, and Cannabich came from Bohemia, Moravia, Silesia, and Lower Austria. But the one who contributed most to form our conception of "German music" was Joseph Haydn, who in that day, by virtue of his quartets and symphonies, had the most famous name in music throughout Europe. And with his were soon associated the names of Mozart and Beethoven. Leadership in European music passed over to Germany at the beginning of the 19th century, by virtue of these three masters. The conception of "German music" was derived from the highly individual works of these three great musicians. Many people, however, have not seen clearly how very much the Haydn quartet and the Haydn symphony rested upon an Italian basis and upon the bold amalgamation of popular melody, including Croatian, Slovene, and Bohemian; how difficult it is to isolate the national element in Mozart, who, so to speak, created music out of music, who pursued creative inbreeding; and how many influences Beethoven assimilated in his art. As for Beethoven, at least his contemporaries had the somewhat exciting and somewhat terrifying feeling that, with him, they had to come to terms with a vast originality, which they felt less as "German" than as "Romantic." Even French Romantics—for example, Victor Hugo —in no wise thought of Beethoven as specifically German, Northern, or "Gothic," but rather as the greatest exponent of an art to which they imputed universality.[56]

The process of nationalization in music during the 19th century is perhaps most comparable to a historical occurrence far back in the past: the process by which the universal Greco-Roman gods were displaced by provincial divinities. Their power was regionally limited, rarely extending beyond these limits. Haydn, Mozart, and Beethoven had been universal gods, musically, and their altars remained honored and garlanded. But new, smaller, regional, often only provincial musical divinities made their appearance beside them.

NATIONALIZATION IN ROMANTIC MUSIC: BOHEMIA

The close connection between nationalism and Romanticism is shown very clearly in Bohemia—or, as we must say for the 19th century, the Czech nation. Before the Romantic period there had been no genuine Czech music. There were, indeed, a great number of excellent Bohemian musicians, who not only were active in their native land but also exported their art to all corners of Europe, in much the same way as in the 19th and 20th centuries there have been a number of excellent Swiss musicians —German, French, Italian, and even Romanic Swiss—but no Swiss music. In comparison with the confederated Swiss, the Bohemians were doubtless in an infinitely more advantageous situation by virtue of their common language and their common musical education, which was not reserved for the aristocracy and middle class, but was also available to the lower strata of society for purposes of service to the particularly music-loving nobility. And from the melodic treasury of the people, from its songs and, above all, its dances, there crept into the chamber and symphonic music of these Europeanized Bohemian musicians many melodic and rhythmic idioms which often betray the composers' origin. But even in music of this sort there was far from being what one might call a Bohemian dialect: Johann Stamitz was an "Italian" composer, and even more so was Mysliveček; and L. Koželuch and J. W. Tomaschek were "Viennese" musicians, albeit of Czech origin.

In the formation of national music, the political influence is not to be separated from the influences of the Romantic movement in general.

[56] Leo Schrade, *Beethoven in France* (Yale University Press, 1942), p. 81.

The inhabitants of free nations among the lesser countries, like the Swiss, the Swedes, and the Danes, were less eager for the coinage of a national style than were the people of subject countries. Is it not remarkable that a national musical style springs up most vigorously in times of national misfortune, as in Poland around 1830, where all the feelings of the nation seemed to find expression in Chopin's music? or among peoples denied free public, or other, expression of their essential spirit, as in Russia —itself enslaved, although the oppressor of Poland? A similar state of things prevailed in Bohemia, where, since the times of the Counter Reformation, since the mighty suppression of every "heretical" impulse in a people that had once known freedom, the internal revolt against the Habsburgs had never entirely died out. And a hopeless political revolt always tries to create for itself an escape in art. Such was the case, we have seen, with Schubert in Austria before the Revolution of March, 1848, when Metternich was in power; such was also the case in the border states of the monarchy.

Czech national feeling received its first artistic impulse in literature, through Herder and the German Romantics: in their spirit the first collection of Czech folk songs came into being during the 20's, and was published by Jaromir Erben under the title *Kytice*. Songs were written to Czech texts; after Weber's departure from Prague, operas were presented in Czech translation. In 1826 the first Czech opera was put on the stage, "The Tinker" (*Dratenic*), by the composer of the Czech national hymn, Franz Škroup (1801–1862), followed in 1828 and 1834 by two further operas. "These Czech songs and operas, however, were unduly influenced by the German and French Romantic movement, especially by the German *Singspiel* and the French *opéra-comique,* and were viewed in a false, Romantic light, in consequence of which the creation of a national music was expected from the simple imitation of folk song." [57] But neutral music to "national" texts still does not produce national songs or operas. And, as we have already seen in Chopin, national aspirations lead to nothing unless a superior talent is found as their upholder.

This person was found, for Czech music, in Bedřich Smetana (1824–1884). He was one of the most magnificent examples of the truth that a national composer does not, as the saying goes, "grow out of the very womb of the folk," but that it is first the individual who creates this "folkdom." The period of his youth was precisely a time of musical decay in

[57] V. Helfert and E. Steinhard, *Geschichte der Musik in der tschechoslovakischen Republik* (Prague, 1936), p. 26.

Prague, despite the founding of a conservatory and despite the activity of musicians like J. W. Tomaschek, W. J. Viet (1806–1864), and despite the creative activity of J. H. Woržischek (1791–1825), who during his short life in Vienna belonged to the "Beethovenites" and perhaps incited Schubert to make his excursions into the field of national color. Smetana had to force his nationalism upon his native land, and he carried his point only after violent struggles against a reactionary body of critics, who rejected him as a "Neo-German," a Wagnerite and a Lisztian, a "musician of the future."

He became a national, a Czech musician for the very reason that he was not a "homegrown artist," that he did not stay in his native country, but became a European musician. His fate was that of the prophet in his own land; the years (1856–61) that he spent as pianist, director, and creative musician in Sweden, at Göteborg, are perhaps as memorable as his meeting with Niels W. Gade in Copenhagen. The peculiar situation of a national musician in Bohemia in the 19th century may be gathered from the fact that although Smetana was a member of the national guard in the revolutionary year of 1848, he wrote a triumphal symphony five years later for the marriage of the Emperor Franz Joseph, and from the further fact that when he was impelled by the nationalistic spirit to found a conservatory or lead a concert series, he yet had to get permission to do so from the Imperial-Royal bureaucracy. There was no outward revolution. But political and musical events ran approximately parallel. The so-called "October Diploma" of 1860 became, for Bohemia, a symbol that the absolutist era had come to an end, that a sort of independence within the framework of the Habsburg monarchy had been achieved; and in 1862 Smetana wrote a memorable program for the establishment of Czech concerts, became in 1864 critic on the *Narodni Listi,* and in 1866 conductor of the Czech opera, until in 1874 his deafness compelled him to relinquish all official duties and chained him to his writing desk, and until attacks of insanity put an end to his creative activity and his life.

Smetana's national and international fame was based upon his operas and symphonic poems. He wrote a great number of piano pieces, which border on the work of Schumann and Liszt. Like both of these Romantics, it was impossible for him also to create "absolute" music, music which was not indebted to a poetic stimulus for its very being. It will be enough to mention a few titles: the six *Album Leaves,* Op. 2; the six *Dreams,* from his later period; the *Bagatelles* and *Impromptus,* from his earlier period. In addition, he wrote dances: *Three Salon Polkas,* Op. 7; *Three Poetic*

Polkas, Op. 8; *Impression of Bohemia in Polka Form,* Opp. 12 and 13; and *Czech Dances.* He had no very marked piano style of his own. Also he was never a genuine chamber music composer, although he wrote a piano trio in G minor and two string quartets, the first of which—that in E minor, with the title *From my Life*—became one of the most popular works of world chamber music literature. All three compositions are auto-biographical, full of original and vigorous invention, but formally un-developed and rhapsodic. Yet all three are not only very personal: they are also very "Czech."

In what does this "Czech" element consist? In the use of "genuine folk melodies"? Smetana saw very clearly that the matter did not end there. It is on record that in 1861 he had a memorable discussion with one of the most influential leaders of the national party, Fr. Ladislaus Rieger, on the question "whether Czech folk song could be the basic element in the creation of opera. The conservatively oriented musical circles answered this question in the affirmative. For them, the essence of a Czech national music consisted entirely in the imitation of Czech folk song. Rieger, too, was of this opinion and explained that it would be easy to write a serious historical opera, but that an opera of lighter style based on the life of the Czech people would not be so easy to create successfully. The basis of such an opera, he felt, would have to be Czech folk song. In answer to him, Smetana pointed out that in this way only a potpourri of various songs, a *quodlibet* would result, and no unified work of art." [58] He pro-duced practical evidence for his thesis in his *Bartered Bride* (1866, second version 1869, final version 1870), which came to be the Czech national opera, although it did not contain a single folk song. It was only one in a series of eight operas by Smetana, three serious and five merry; and it shone out among them, although as it happened Smetana himself thought least of it. But it came into being almost of its own accord, as if it had fallen from heaven, and was wedded to an excellent, simple libretto, whereas all the others were more consciously fashioned and suffered from more or less clumsy texts.

To speak first of the serious operas: *The Brandenburgers in Bohemia* (1862, performed 1866) is a folk opera with historical material, conceived in scenes, yet not without "closed numbers," and folklike particularly in its lively, realistic choruses. *Dalibor* (1867, performed 1868) is a heroic opera with tragic conclusion, not uninfluenced by Wagner's *Lohengrin* in musical style, but unusual in the recitative-like and melodic treatment

[58] E. Rychnovsky, *Smetana* (Stuttgart, 1924), p. 135.

of the dialogue. *Libussa* (1872, performed 1881), finally, is a national festival play, in which everything lyric, dramatic, and choral takes on half-decorative, half-mystical form—the last will and testament of a representative individual to his people.

The five merry operas of Smetana's are also very different one from another; and it speaks for his artistry that in none of the four later ones —*Two Widows* (1874), *The Kiss* (1876), *The Secret* (1878), and *The Devil's Wall* (1882)—did he wish to supply a duplicate of the first and most successful one, the *Bartered Bride*. The closest to it is the rustic drama *The Kiss,* though it has much more serious undertones and, with its forest and smugglers' scenes, is not without its "Romantic" traits. *The Secret* is more a light comedy of individualized characters. Smetana then returned to the sharp and variegated demon-opera, somewhat in the manner of Marschner, in the *Devil's Wall;* and, in the *Two Widows,* to the lighter style of dialogue, aria, and ensemble, somewhat in the manner of Lortzing's *Wildschütz.* The merit of all these works lies primarily in the fact that they have preserved their own colorful individuality; neither have they let themselves be overpowered by Wagner, although their creator was one of Wagner's ardent admirers, nor have they let their flavor be affected by that of Italian opera, let alone "grand opera." Nothing was farther from Smetana's thoughts than what is called an international success, and it is all the more paradoxical that with his *Bartered Bride,* his opera closest to the people, he achieved an international success.

Both things, the closeness to the people and the international success, rest naturally on the happy and simple dramatic action and on the bringing of a few simple characters to the fore—the loyal and beautiful maiden, the alert and clearheaded farmer lad, the magnificent talker (the matchmaker), the village idiot—in the midst of the lively village community. These were human beings, not opera puppets. They were farmers from the Bohemian hill-country. Smetana especially contrasted them by bringing out a German circus director from nearby Saxony with his shabby troupe. And while his farmers speak "dialect" in the choruses and dances, the polkas and furiants, in the rhythmic firmness of the melodic style, in the melodiousness which combined simplicity and fineness, they also spoke the universally intelligible language of inspiration. The "Czech" element was not costume or folk masquerade; the spiritual element was not psychology or naturalism: and thus was realized the ideal of a merry folk opera, almost without precedent and almost inimitable.

In his symphonic writing Smetana was dependent upon a model—Liszt.

His three earlier symphonic poems, written during his Göteborg period after a visit to Weimar, *Richard the Third, Wallenstein's Camp,* and *Prince Haakon,* after Shakespeare, Schiller, and Oehlenschläger, respectively, are literarily conceived quite after the Lisztian pattern, and follow also entirely the Lisztian technique of thematic metamorphosis. But in the cycle of six symphonic poems, which he wrote in his last creative period and entitled "My Native Land" (*Ma Vlast*), the Lisztian element plays only a minor part, perhaps only to be found in the wind instruments' apotheoses, which as in Liszt are frequently introduced in too broad strokes. Never has a country, its character, its nature, its heroic or awe-inspiring historical memories received purer glorification than in this cycle, which is also bound together thematically—in the idyllic, elegiac, "dramatic," religious, folk aspects. To be sure, in this cycle—in contrast to the *Bartered Bride*—a musical "dialect" is spoken, so that the cycle can have its full stirring, uplifting, inspiring effect only within the nation. But Smetana has made in this work the dream of so many Romantics come true, that of becoming the rhapsodist of his people.

If Smetana was the protégé of Franz Liszt (and he may justifiably be called that in both a material and a spiritual sense), Antonin Dvořák (1841–1904) stood in somewhat the same relation to Johannes Brahms. That, too, is understandable. For Dvořák overcame the influence of Wagner rather quickly, as if it had been a children's disease (although in later years the germs of the disease were again to become active), and turned his attention to the "absolute" forms of music. He wrote symphonies (of which one in F, No. 3, and one in D minor were written before the middle of the '70's), string quartets, string quintets and chamber music with piano, and piano works—although no piano works in sonata form. To Brahms, Dvořák must have seemed almost the ideal musician, which Brahms himself was prevented from becoming through his being too heavily burdened with the past. In historical perspective, as a matter of fact, Dvořák appears as the member of a young musical nation; and in his relation to Smetana he seems as fortunate as was Schubert in his relation to Beethoven, except that the development of the Romantic movement and the existence of Wagner had shifted the situation. Dvořák took over the heritage of absolute music quite naïvely, and filled its forms with an elemental kind of music of the freshest invention, the liveliest rhythm, the finest sense of sonority—it is the most full-blooded, direct music conceivable, without its becoming vulgar. He drew always from the sources of Slavic folk dance and folk song, much as Brahms had drawn from those of German; the only difference was that with Dvořák everything was childlike and fresh, whereas with Brahms there was always an overtone of yearning or mystical reverence.

In his writing Dvořák was less regionally limited than Smetana; although he still wrote polkas, dumkas, and furiants, he also wrote waltzes and mazurkas. And while he still wrote Moravian duets and Slovak men's choruses, he also wrote quite general Slavic dances for piano four-hands (Opp. 46 and 72) and Slavic rhapsodies (Op. 45) for orchestra. He was interested in the folk songs of *all* Slavic peoples, even during his later years; and folk song secretly influenced his inventive processes, although during the last decade of his life in his nationally colored "Classic-Romantic" symphony he approached the neo-Romantic, more descriptive symphonic poem. He was at his best, perhaps, in his songs and choruses; and one of his greatest and most deeply felt works is his *Stabat Mater* (1876-7), with which he had very great success in England and in which he held up a mirror to the academic-Victorian oratorios. That a musician who created so easily and richly should also have tried his hand at opera is not to be wondered at; but likewise little to be wondered at is the fact that a musician so naïve, so little "intellectual" could not become a genuine dramatist.

Only a small part of his creative activity falls within the limits which have been set for this book. A history of music during the most recent period would have to concern itself in detail with Dvořák, and would have to show that his historic position, at the end of the Romantic era, at the beginning of the great musical fair which announced this end, was yet not so happy as one would think at first glance. Dvořák, too, was a late-born musician. With Smetana he was the founder of Czech music, but both composers stood alone and could no longer found a genuine school. Subsequent developments proceeded along other ways.

RUSSIA

Even in Russian music of the Romantic era—or, better, in Russian music of the 19th century—there was manifested the paradox of musical nationalism: that the national trend is young, but comes late and finds its place in a long development on the part of the older music-nations. The situation is somewhat like that of a savage people which comes into contact with European civilization and suddenly is placed in the position of using the achievements of a civilization it has not created, such as guns and "fire-

water." And as in such cases there has usually been one party that passionately resisted every influence from without, another that plunged
completely into the foreign wave, and a third that was ready for compromise, so has it also been in the history of music. In Russia the only
difference was that the first party was completely absent.

The musical soil on which a national music developed among this
musically gifted people consisted of an immeasurably rich, regionally
differentiated storehouse of folk melodies and a highly festive liturgy
derived from Byzantine and Oriental sources. An indication has already
been given in the first part of this book of the way in which, since the
days of Peter the Great, this soil had been overrun, at least at its western
gateway, in St. Petersburg, and among the higher or "more cultivated"
circles. In the 18th century, Russia was a province of Italian operatic music, and the Italian spirit entered into even the courtly church music with
the work of Maxim Beresovsky (1745-1777) and Dmitri Bortniansky
(1751-1825). There was an uninterrupted succession of Italian composers
who were active in St. Petersburg, beginning with Francesco Araja (*La
forza dell'amore e dell'odio,* 1736) : Manfredini, Galuppi, Traëtta, Paisiello,
Sarti, Cimarosa, Martin. In the first quarter of the 19th century, Clementi
and John Field brought their virtuoso and expressive art to the aristocracy
of St. Petersburg; and, principally among the aristocracy, composition
was pursued as a dilettante pastime—variations and bagatelles for piano,
"romances," canzonets, and other chance bits of song. In 1798 Paul I
closed the gates on Italian opera for a short time, but they were soon re-
opened. The director of the Imperial Opera, as has already been indicated,
was the Venetian Catterino Cavos (1776-1840), who with his light touch
provided dramatic music for the three opera companies of St. Petersburg
—the Italian, the French, and even the Russian. But whenever he exercised his art on Russian material, as in a version of Kauer's *Donauweib-
chen,* with the title *The Dnieper Nymph* (1803), in *Ilya the Hero* (1807),
and in *Ivan Sussanin* (1815), a work that was considered a model of
national opera up to the time Glinka's masterpiece appeared, the result
was always Italian music, despite occasional use of Russian folk melodies.

After all, the Russian enthusiasm for Italian music cannot be explained
entirely by the "passivity of the Russian character," the ability to receive
everything strange. It must be based on an affinity in the sensuous sphere,
in the yearning of the people of the North for completion by something
Southern—a yearning which is Romantic. The only memorable Russian
predecessor of Glinka was the Music Inspector of the Imperial Theater in

Moscow, Alexis Nikolaievich Verstovsky (1799–1862). Three of six operas are *Pan Tvardovsky* (1828), *Vadim, or Twelve Sleeping Virgins* (1832), and, above all, *Askold's Grave* (1835), a work that had not lost its force even for Rimsky-Korsakov's generation.

Verstovsky, however, in his charming dilettantism, his naïve imitation of Italian and French models, was only a forerunner. The real founder of national Russian music was Michael Ivanovich Glinka (1804–1857), with his two operas *A Life for the Tsar* (1836) and *Russlan and Ludmilla* (1842), with his overtures, and with his songs; and only his premature death prevented his also becoming the founder of a Russian church music that was both modern and national. Glinka was the first Russian composer who was not a dilettante, although he too began as a dilettante. And he was like Smetana, in that he also kept his eye open to Europe in musical matters, although he never felt the inclination to give in completely to European music. It might have been possible for him to write for the Parisian grand opera, but he declined.

Illness drove him for many years to Italy (1830–34) and Spain (1845–47); but, unlike Meyerbeer or Otto Nicolai, these foreign experiences led him in spirit more and more back to Russia. In the same way as he prepared a collection of Little Russian (Ukrainian) melodies, he occupied himself in Spain with the restoration of genuine Spanish folk tunes, free of Italianisms, and was thereby inspired to compose two overtures, *Jota Aragonese* and *Souvenir d'une Nuit d'Été à Madrid,* which exceed in originality anything previously composed by Spanish composers themselves—the first, originally called *Capriccio Brillant,* being a set of variations in scintillating dance-rhythm, the second being a symphonic transcription of two Castilian *seguidillas.*

What he did for Spain, he also achieved for Russia with the incidental music to Kukolkin's tragedy *Prince Cholmsky* and with his orchestral fantasy on two Russian folk songs, a wedding-song and a dance-song, known the world over under the title *Kamarinskaya.* What distinguishes these symphonic works is not only their brevity and melodic raciness, but above all what one might call their orchestral counterpoint. Glinka was one of the greatest masters of orchestral color, the equal of Berlioz, independent of him (although acquainted with him personally), and his superior in the apparently *un*intentional quality of his effects.

Glinka's real national influence, however, came from his two operas. Each sounded a note that has reverberated in Russian opera, and not only in opera, until deep within the 20th century—the national and the legendary. But both operas have the quality of folk song and are at the same time modern. An ironical whim of history decreed that the libretto of the national opera *A Life for the Tsar* should come from the pen of a German, a Baron C. F. Rosen, as well as that the music of this anti-Polish opera should come from a musician who was not entirely "pure Russian," for Glinka himself had Polish blood in his veins. The material was the same as that in Cavos's *Ivan Sussanin:* a Russian farmer sacrifices his life to save his prince, the first Romanoff, from being taken prisoner by spies of the Polish invaders—four brief acts and a moving and festive epilogue with the populace in jubilation and the bells pealing. Particularly in this final scene, with its elaborate apparatus of three choruses, orchestra, two wind ensembles, trumpet fanfares, and bells on the stage, Glinka provided the model for similar scenes in Borodin and Musorgsky; and in the melody of the *tutti,* which serves as a sort of rondo-theme, the deep ceremonial obeisances of a whole mass of people seem to become audible.

The opera, however, is not Byzantine in its aspirations. The people are simply people, represented in the chorus and in a few simple figures: Ivan and an orphan boy whom he has adopted, Vanya. Only in the characterization of a pair of lovers, Ivan's daughter and her betrothed, Glinka was still a victim of his times—they are strongly "Italianized." Musically, also, this opera has Italianate features, with its separation of recitative and "closed" numbers, and with its cantilena and coloratura passages. But they constitute a mere tint which, alongside the "Russian," scarcely obtrudes; and the Russian features, the simple folk-idioms in melody and rhythm, are set off more sharply by contrast with the "Polish" features, for Glinka characterized the Polish soldiery and their leader, quite unconcernedly and without any animosity, by means of polonaise, cracovienne, mazurka, and other national rhythms. When one considers that in the same year, 1836, Meyerbeer's *Huguenots* and the piquant light opera *Le Postillon de Longjumeau* by Adolphe-Charles Adam, one of Auber's imitators, received its first performance, one begins to appreciate the complete naturalness, the fineness without sophistication, the feeling without sentimentality, that prevail in Glinka's opera.

Of no less significance is Glinka's second opera, *Russlan and Ludmilla,* the first opera to take its material from one of the poems of Pushkin, the Romantic source of so many other Russian works for the stage. It is a dramatic legend, and the opera has justifiably been compared with Weber's *Oberon.* There is the same lack of dramatic skill in the transformation of the epic source into a libretto. Both operas have the incoherence of a succession of bright pictures. Yet in both there is the same colorful and fanciful sequence of national or regional scenes. The mixture of the fantastic with the comic (the duet between the foolish knight Farlaff and the sorceress Naina) is also reminiscent of *Oberon;* moreover, the "Russian" element is still mixed with "Westernisms" that are merely brilliant, as is immediately felt in the all too resplendent overture. But alongside these features there are also such things as a definitely national chorus in 5/4 time, a "Persian" dance-chorus, a wild Causasian ballet, and new harmonic idioms like the use of the whole-tone scale to characterize the unearthly. In this opera Glinka really discovered the Russian Orient, and captured it in tones of the most delicate magic.

In proportion as *A Life for the Tsar* had been a great success, *Russlan and Ludmilla* was a great failure—a work in which Glinka was far ahead of his time. Like Smetana, he was not spared the fate of the prophet in his own country; and the consequence was that a subsequent operatic plan, the composition of a music drama *The Volga Robbers* or *Double Marriage* (after a drama by Prince Shakhovskoi) was never carried out. The real hero of this opera would have been, again, the Russian people, as before in *A Life for the Tsar* and later in Musorgsky's *Boris Godunov.* In St. Petersburg and in Moscow the beginnings of national opera were again submerged by the Italian inundation. Glinka's *A Life for the Tsar* was degraded by indifferent performances to the status of a festival opera, with which it became traditional to open every opera season officially, and *Russlan and Ludmilla* did not again come to the surface.

A change did not come until the sixties. The way for it was prepared by the activity of the musician who stands between Glinka and the later generation of those years, Alexander Sergeyevich Dargomijsky (1813–1869), one of those "dilettantes" who play so great a role in the history of Russian music. In the winter of 1833–4 he made Glinka's acquaintance, and later received from him the notebooks which Glinka had kept during his studies with S. W. Dehn in Berlin—Dargomijsky's only experience in the stricter discipline of composition. In contrast to the versatile Glinka, he was almost exclusively a "vocalist," interested only in the intoned word, in song and opera. Only in his later years did he come to write a few instrumental works, which might be best characterized as symphonic trifles: a Polish Cossack-dance (*Kasatshok*), a Russian fairy tale (*Baba Yaga, or From the Volga to Riga*), and a *Finnish Fantasy*—orchestral scherzi, in which one may recognize prototypes for so many later pieces of Musorgsky's, Rimsky-Korsakov's, or Anatol Liadov's, suggested by national landscape or national legend. To be sure, there is a certain relationship here with Berlioz; but the "Western" element plays scarcely any part in Dargomijsky's creative work, even though he visited Paris, Brussels, and London in the manner of a *grand seigneur,*—and even though he began his activities with an opera in the style of Hérold or Halévy, *Esmeralda* (completed in 1839, but not performed until 1847), after a wildly Romantic novel of Victor Hugo's. A cantata or opera ballet *The Triumph of Bacchus,* after Pushkin, did not see the light of day; thus in his dramatic output there intervened a break, filled in with the creation of his colorful, deeply felt, sometimes satirical romances or songs (see p. 196 ff.), with which he became a forerunner and model of Musorgsky.

Finally, in 1855, utilizing a text which Pushkin left at his death as the fragment of a drama, Dargomijsky completed his *Russalka* (performed in 1856), which might be called a Romantic opera somewhat in the manner of Hoffmann's or Lortzing's *Undine:* it is the same tragic legend of the faithless knight drawn to his destruction by an elfin being. But the musical combination is partly new: the choruses of country people speak Russian dialect, the nuptial celebration is more lively, and in place of the Philistine comedy as in Lortzing or the Romantic yearning as in Hoffmann there appears genuine, rough humor and—especially in the figure of the insane old miller—a terrible kind of realism. Where Glinka's operas still showed traces of Italianism, Dargomijsky's developed from the spirit of the Russian language a new type of speech-song, full of character and with the harmonic ground-color freely painted in—new enough for his contemporaries to deny to the work the unqualified success which began to greet it only after 1865.

After Dargomijsky, in 1860, had abandoned a comic opera in its very beginnings, he began in the last years of his life to think of a new work, which had to be finished eventually by César Cui and Rimsky-Korsakov, *The Stone Guest,* the legend of Don Juan and Donna Anna in the Pushkin version. Dargomijsky set Pushkin's drama to music word for word, as a dialogue opera, almost without any points of rest provided by the "closed" forms, entirely dependent upon his new type of recitative, without any attempt at symphonic or motivic unity in the Wagnerian manner. It was an experiment, the sort of thing one calls in artists' parlance a "studio piece"—meaningless and ineffectual so far as the great mass of people is concerned, but memorable as a point of departure towards something new.

From 1859 on, Dargomijsky's house was the meeting-place for a circle of younger musicians who represented national Russian music among a second generation, and whose lives extended beyond the limits that have been set for this book: Mili Alekseyevich Balakirev (1837–1910), César Antonovich Cui (1835–1918), Alexander Porfirevich Borodin (1833–1887), Modest Petrovich Musorgsky (1839–1881), and Nikolai Andreyevich Rimsky-Korsakov (1844–1908). The characteristic situation of a musically young nation finds expression in this very point, that such a group would separate itself from the larger circle of Russian musical life and inscribe a stricter nationalism upon its banner. The direction in which the struggle was to proceed had by no means been determined, so little unity prevailed within the group itself. Rimsky-Korsakov in his autobiography has depicted, not without humor, how Balakirev, as leader or captain of this troop, and Cui, as his argumentative and learned assistant, looked somewhat condescendingly upon Borodin, Musorgsky, and even young Rimsky himself. They were united only in their opposition to the internationally minded and Teutonophile Anton Rubinstein (1829–1894), who had established in 1859 a concert association, the Russian Musical Society, with a German program as a basis, and in 1862 a national conservatory with exclusively German instructors, and who personally as one of the greatest virtuosi of his time and a learned composer—like Glinka, he had been a pupil of S. W. Dehn—harbored only disdain for this host of "amateurs." As a matter of fact, all the members of the group except Balakirev were only incidentally musicians: Cui was an authority on the construction of fortifications, Musorgsky was a public official, Borodin was a physician and chemist, and even Rimsky-Korsakov, the only one who felt the necessity for stricter training, was at first a naval officer. One is reminded of E. T. A. Hoffmann, who was able to maintain his artistic and official careers all his life long.

The spokesman for the group was the journalist Vladimir Vassilievitch Stassov (1824–1906), who later became the biographer for them all. Not on the opposite side, and yet not within their circle, was the critic and composer Alexander Nicolaievitch Serov (1820–1871), one of the earliest and most passionate defenders of the neo-German school in Russia, of Liszt and especially of Richard Wagner, with whom he had some personal dealings. This fact, however, did not prevent his composing three very un-Wagnerian operas. He wrote a Biblical drama *Judith* and a grand opera *Rogneda*—both of which might be characterized as merely gaudy Meyerbeeriads. Later, he composed a rustic drama after Ostrovsky (*The Power of the Evil One*), in which the folk tone is sounded and imitated in a purely intellectual fashion. Even Serov, however, tried to make Western influences Russian.

It cannot be our task and intention to provide a history of Russian music; we can concern ourselves with the five musicians who received the nickname of "The Invincible Band" only in so far as they have any relation to the Romantic movement. Most strange are the relations of the half-French Cui, who drew his material as an opera-composer from Romantic sources—*The Captive in the Caucasus* (1859) from Pushkin, *William Ratcliff* (1869) from Heine, *Angelo* (1876) from Hugo—but who was not essentially a dramatist. The intimacy of his expression and the finish of his workmanship are inconsistent with the theatricality of his material. He was much more at home as a composer of songs or piano pieces. Balakirev, on the other hand, was a close follower of Glinka, whose Spanish and Russian overtures he echoed in works like his overtures on Spanish march-tunes, on Russian tunes (three folk songs), on Czech themes, and like the symphonic poems *Russia* and *Tamara,* projected in the Lisztian manner but of much more elementary strength of invention and instrumentation. Balakirev proceeded—as did Glinka with *Russlan and Ludmilla*—into the more distant, more fantastic Orient with the piano fantasy *Islamey*. A strange relationship to the German Romantic movement is revealed by the circumstance that Balakirev at the beginning of the 70's, after the failure of his "Free Music School," devoted himself to religious mysticism, from which the musician Balakirev henceforth seldom emerged.

The "youthfulness" of the national movement in Romanticism, the peculiar relationship of the new musical nations to the old West, is best represented in the work of Alexander P. Borodin. It is not extensive—Borodin, the illegitimate son of a Georgian prince, merry, independent, kindhearted, hindered by hundreds of obligations from composing, always had to be forced to complete his works. Basically, they consist of only two symphonies, a symphonic poem, two string quartets, and one opera. Except for a third symphony left half-finished at his death, the rest are only minor works. With a great master, however, a great deal depends not only upon the quality of his work, but also upon its quantity. Philip Heseltine has said, "So far as traditional symphonic form is concerned, the master craftsman of the last quarter of the nineteenth century was not Brahms, but Borodin." [59] The comparison is valid in that Borodin, despite all his

[59] I have taken the quotation from the monograph *Borodin, the Composer and his Music,* by Gerald H. Abraham (London, 1927), p. 175.

admiration for Liszt, was a pure, an "absolute" musician. Even for the most zealous exegetes or interpreters it would be difficult to read a poetical program into his symphonies and quartets. But where Brahms had *inherited* the art of the symphony and of chamber music from Beethoven and Schubert and was inclined to write music that stood in a conscious "relationship" to theirs, Borodin wrote his symphonies and quartets without concern for the past and, as it were, with a clear conscience. In this respect he was rather more comparable to Bruckner. Brahms was posthumous; Borodin and a few other national musicians were young.

Borodin was not without his presuppositions, any more than Brahms was. The first quartet, for example, is consciously linked with a motif from one of the last quartets of Beethoven (Op. 130, Finale). The first symphony was not unjustly characterized by Musorgsky as the "Russian Eroica," for it bears the heroic stamp of Beethoven and the rhythmic quality of Schumann; yet these elements are fused with the true and personal expression of the composer. But in the Second Symphony (B minor) and the Second String Quartet (D major), Borodin succeeded in writing two works of a freshness, immediacy, colorfulness, and raciness that a composer of the older musical peoples could no longer succeed in capturing. What is here referred to as raciness is a quality of melodic invention which has its roots in the intervals, the rhythm, and—not to be overlooked—the ornamentation of the Russo-Oriental folk song, in the mixture of the barbaric and the intimate, in the contrast, the wild repetition, and the resounding instrumentation.

Even more clearly than in these works, Borodin's greatness as a musician is shown in his single, posthumous opera, completed by Rimsky-Korsakov and Glazunov, *Prince Igor,* on which he worked from 1871 until his death. Its dramatic worth is very slight. Borodin himself was partly responsible for compiling the prologue and the following four acts, with Stassov's help, from the ancient *Tale of Igor's Campaign,* a literary monument ascribed to the 12th century. In 1185 the Russians clashed with a nomadic people, the Polovetsians, and suffered a terrible defeat: Igor and his son were taken prisoner, and Igor's wife Yaroslavna remained, like Schumann's Genoveva, in the care of a treacherous villain. To show Borodin's lack of dramatic skill, one need only point out that this villain, Galitzky, completely disappears after the first act. A happy ending is assured only by the barbaric chieftain's turning out to be as kindhearted as a tame bear. But a wonder comes to pass like that in the first half of the second act of Mozart's *Don Giovanni,* in which the action likewise stops and is filled out with dramatic trivialities—a gap bridged over by music. The same thing is successfully achieved by Borodin, in deeply felt and purely fashioned scenes which are at once dramatic and arioso, in the choruses expressive of the psychology of strange peoples, and in the orchestral pieces which seem to realize in sound for the first time the Russian Orient, that profoundly medieval land. Merely to mention the pieces that Borodin, according to Rimsky-Korsakov's statement, completed and orchestrated himself is to rehearse a list of pure masterpieces: "the first chorus, the Polovetsian dances, the lament of Yaroslavna, the recitative and song of Vladimir Galitzky, the arias of Kontshak, of Kontshakovna, and of Vladimir Igorevich, as well as the final chorus." Here was a new, more unsophisticated form of Romanticism, in which the costume was genuine and not masquerade.

The most original, though not exactly the most unsophisticated of the group, was Modest P. Musorgsky. It is significant that he was the only member who did not visit the West and who never left Russia; in fact, a journey to the South of Russia itself in one of his last years was the only interruption in his short, rather Bohemian life in St. Petersburg. His way of living resembled, in a strange Russian variant, that of Schubert, sharing the room of one and another of his friends, without whose self-sacrificing help we should not possess even the fragmentary works that he left behind. These works find their culmination in his songs (see p. 197) and in his operas. As with Dargomijsky, his compositions for orchestra and for piano are only secondary works, with two exceptions. The symphonic poem *A Night on Bald Mountain* is a fantastic echo of Liszt's *Danse Macabre.* The *Pictures at an Exhibition* for piano (1874) is a demonic and humorous counterpart to Schumann's *Carnaval,* but is still more definitely in closed form (it might even be called a rondo with varied theme and alternating episodes) and is still richer in its changes of expression by virtue of the drastic realism in the individual "pictures."

Realism is the word with which many commentators have tried to encompass Musorgsky's individuality. As a matter of fact, Musorgsky does in many respects negate Romanticism; but at the same time he still remained a Romantic. This feature is revealed in the very choice of material for his operas. He began, in 1863–66, with *Salammbô,* after Gustave Flaubert's famous novel, in which, however, it was not so much the human aspect of the characters that attracted him as it was the combination of the barbaric and the sophisticated, the African feature of the setting. It remained in fragments, among which are an Oriental women's chorus and some sketches. Then followed, in 1868, *The Marriage*. Meanwhile Dargomijsky's *The Stone Guest* had become known among his circle of friends. As Musorgsky himself indicated, *The Marriage* was an "experiment towards a dramatic music in prose"; that is, he began to set to music in dialogue, word for word, a comedy of Gogol's. He completed four scenes of the first act, in a style which might be called *recitativo accompagnato buffo*: what Dargomijsky had done with Pushkin's impassioned verse was here applied in still more sensitive and flexible manner to Gogol's rapid prose. This was the negation of the entire Romantic "heroic" attitude; but there was also no lack of the fantastic and the unearthly, in which Gogol is outstanding. As Gogol has justly been called the E. T. A. Hoffmann of Russia, so Musorgsky might be called the Gogol of music.

Finally, in 1868–72, came Musorgsky's masterpiece in the field of opera, a work to which he gave the subtitle "A Musical Folk Drama," *Boris Godunov*. What are we to make of it? It is a musical "history," perhaps most comparable to Shakespeare's historical plays. It takes us into the wild period before 1600, a generation before that in which Glinka's first opera was set, into the time when a usurper seized the throne in Moscow and was cast out by another usurper, the "false Demetrius." Once again the material is from Pushkin, from a dramatic work which is like a succession of pictures and which even Musorgsky with the help of his friends could not succeed in reducing to genuine drama. This weakness is not a matter of drama in the conventional operatic sense. In fact, the subsequently inserted "Polish" scenes, which provide brilliant instrumental music and culminate in a passionate duet, seem "grand opera" and something foreign to the whole.

Rather, the important thing in this opera seems to be the psychological aspect of the characterization of the hero, the other figures, and the people, who are not treated here as a mass, a "chorus." There is nothing truer, less operatic, more affecting in the literature of opera—one may go back all the way to Monteverdi—than the "mechanical clock" scene, which synchronizes its tick-tock with the usurper's qualms of conscience. All the other figures are sketched in with like force: the old and venerable monk who in his cell is writing the history of Russia, the drunken mendicant friar, the coarse barmaid, the motherly nurse, the children of the usurper, the sweet and treacherous nobleman, the idiot—all members of *one* people, the Russian. The musical means that Musorgsky avails himself of for purposes of characterization are at the same time primitive and sophisticated. Luckily, we do not have to enter into the controversy over Musorgsky's "dilettantism," and over the justice or injustice of revising his works and of eliminating his "crudities."

He later expressed himself (in a letter to Vladimir Stassov, December 25, 1876) on the principle he had followed: ". . . You know that before *Boris* I placed the whole stress upon folk scenes. My present intention, however, is directed towards the melody that partakes of life, not towards Classical melody. I explore human speech; thus I arrive at the melody created by this kind of speech, arrive at the embodiment of recitative in melody (excepting, of course, the passages of dramatic action, where each interjection may become important). One might call this a melody justified by sense. Labor such as this is a joy to me; suddenly and unexpectedly something will sound out that is opposed to the so-much-beloved classical melody and yet will be understood immediately by everyone. If I should reach that goal, I would consider it a conquest in art. . . ." This "melody justified by sense," i.e., by character and situation, is entirely designed in terms of lifelike and changing harmony, which also does not avoid absolute dissonances, "mixtures," mere masses of color, audacities which in Musorgsky's time appeared unpardonable mistakes. Clearly, in the relation of the voice to the orchestra Musorgsky was like Verdi, but not in the formation of the melody; and he was the very opposite of Wagner. He hated them both.

After the performance of *Boris,* Musorgsky began to decline, not only as an artist but also as a man; in his loneliness he sought consolation in drink and did not complete any of his further works. From 1872–80 he worked on a second "history," the setting of which was a century later, around 1682. It took as its material the struggle of ancient Russia, embodied in Prince Khovanchin, against young Tsar Peter, whence the title *Khovanchina*. Again there was a mixture of operatic and folk elements: the basic colors were savage Russian, "Western," and even "German" in a narrow ethnological sense. His last work, *The Fair at Sorotchinzk* (1875–80) again utilized Gogol, this time a rustic comedy set in Little Russia—the regional coloring new, and marked by a new spot of color in the gypsy music. One is involuntarily led to compare it with *The Bartered Bride,* though here everything is more earthy, more naturalistic, more free from presuppositions—or it would have been so, could it only have been completed.

Musorgsky was a revolutionary. Shortly before his death he wrote an autobiographical sketch in which he said, "neither in the character of his compositions nor in his ideas about music does Musorgsky belong to any of the prevailing musical trends. A formulation of his artistic creed can be derived from his ideas about the duties of art: art is a means towards communication with human beings, not an end in itself. This principle determines his entire creative activity. Since he proceeds from the conviction that human speech is governed by strictly musical laws (Virchov, Gervinus), he sees the duty of music to be the tonal reflection not only of accesses of feeling but also of the pulsations of human speech. To be sure, he recognizes that in the field of music reformers like Palestrina, Bach, Gluck, Beethoven, Berlioz, and Liszt have shown the art its laws. Yet he holds these laws to be not irrevocable, and believes that they are subservient to progress and change. . . ." This sounds very anti-Romantic, and the invocation of Virchov and the dry German pope of letters, Gervinus, is as significant as the list of names of composers whom he recognizes as reformers of music.

There is a story that Musorgsky was playing the first movement of Schumann's E-flat major Symphony for Borodin, but broke off before the development section with the remark, "Well, now the musical mathematics begin." For Musorgsky, art for art's sake did not exist; he did not write any development sections. He hated the "salon composer" Chopin. He was an expressionist; his art addressed itself directly to the listeners, the "folk." And in precisely that respect he was Romantic.

The last and youngest of the group of Five, who devoted years of his life to bringing out Musorgsky's works, was N. A. Rimsky-Korsakov. He, alone of the group, felt a need, in his thirties, of acquiring mastery of all the technical means of musical composition. All of the works that he had written previously were then subjected to revision. Rimsky-Korsakov was a master of his art. He was also the only one who—in his later years, beginning with 1888, when *The Ring of the Nibelung* was performed in St. Petersburg—did not entirely resist the influence of Wagner. Of course, this influence was limited to music: none of the Five laid claim, as did Wagner, to the whole man, none wished to regenerate, none wished to "redeem" him. They were Romantics, but not neo-Romantics.

Even Rimsky-Korsakov did not go back to Russian myth, but only to the Russian fairy tale, which—particularly from 1893 on—he decked out in colors of clearer and clearer brilliancy. He was a Romantic in that he was one of the greatest masters of color, in this respect quite as independent of Berlioz as he was, even in his later years, of Wagner. He himself has spoken of this art of his in connection with a reference to his

Capriccio Espagnol (1887), a piece which he justly characterized as nothing more than "a purely superficial, effective composition of sparkling, lively color." He further said, "The opinion that has become current with critics and with the public that the *Capriccio* is an unusually well-orchestrated piece is wrong: the *Capriccio* is a splendid composition for orchestra. The change of tone color, the felicitous selection of melodic lines and of secondary figures which always correspond to the character of the particular instrument playing them, the little virtuoso cadences of the principal solo instruments, the rhythm of the percussion, etc.—all this creates here the real nature of the composition, not merely its orchestral garb."

Rimsky-Korsakov embodied within himself the connecting link between the Five and the next generation, which for the most part profited by instruction under him, as did his favorite pupils Glazunov and Stravinsky; and his own creative work, to a considerable extent, no longer belongs within the limits of this book. The same thing is true of the work of Peter Ilich Tchaikovsky (1840–1893), although a considerable number of his significant works came into being before 1880: five of his six symphonies (1866, 1873, 1875, 1878, 1880), the symphonic poem *Romeo and Juliet* (1869), three quartets (1871, 1874, 1876), the piano concerto in B-flat minor (1874), and the lyric opera *Eugene Onegin* (1878, performed 1879). Tchaikovsky kept aloof from the group of the Five, although he was on fairly good terms with most of the members and even dedicated two of his symphonic poems to Balakirev. He was a pupil of Anton Rubinstein. From twenty-six on he was no longer a "St. Petersburger," but lived and did most of his composing in Moscow. He is also to be contrasted with four of the Five—Rimsky-Korsakov being excepted—in that his work as a composer, however completely versatile it appears at first glance, did not culminate in the vocal sphere, but in the instrumental, the symphonic. Along with his symphonies and concertos, he also wrote overtures and symphonic poems as unconcernedly as Dvořák—the orchestral fantasies *The Tempest* and *Francesca da Rimini,* the festival overture *1812,* the four-movement symphonic poem *Manfred,* and the fantasy-overture *Hamlet;* but basically he was a composer of absolute music.

Of course, he filled his purely instrumental music to the brim with a program of feeling. For example, we might take the "program" of his Symphony in F minor as contained in a letter to his patroness Mme. von Meck:

The Introduction is the germ of the entire symphony, the idea upon which all else depends—Fate, unconquerable, inescapable. Despair and discontent grow stronger . . . at last a sweet and tender dream appears and little by little possesses the soul; but it was only a dream and Fate awakes us. So life is a persistent alternation of hard reality with evanescent dreams and clutchings at happiness.

The Second Movement expresses another phase of suffering—the melancholy that comes when memories crowd upon us. One regrets the past, though there were happy moments. One is too weary to begin life anew; it is easier to be passive and to look back; it is sad and sweet to sink thus into the past.

The Third Movement is a succession of capricious arabesques, when the mind is empty and the imagination begins to draw intangible designs—a drunken peasant, a brief street song, a military procession. The pictures are disconnected, out of touch with reality, wild and strange.

The Fourth Movement depicts a peasant festival. You forget yourself in this spectacle of the joy of others, but merciless Fate reappears to remind you of yourself. The others remain indifferent to your loneliness and sadness. Enter into such simple, deep joys and life will be bearable.

As Tchaikovsky let himself be led in his creative work by melodramatic and sentimental programs such as this, he seldom succeeded in a complete mastery of form. And as he was a neurotic, yielding unreservedly to his lyric, melancholy, and emotional ebullitions, he marked most distinctly a last phase of Romanticism—exhibitionism of feeling. We shall abstain even here from criticism, from demonstrating that along with his cheap chains of sequences he achieved genuine climaxes, that along with his unbearable vulgarities he created some genuine flowers of melody—and vice versa. He intensified everything to the extreme, which is a general sign of Romanticism. It was not by chance that he was indifferent to Bach ("I do not consider him a great genius," he declared) and that he considered Handel a fourth-class composer; for in both of these the feelings are held in check and mastered. It was also no accident that, among the German Romantics, he gave only grudging credit to Schumann, who likewise often wore his heart on his sleeve. But in favor of the flooding of works with feeling, Tchaikovsky might have invoked the name of almost every Romantic, of Liszt and Wagner, only not that of Brahms, who always hid or veiled his emotion behind the mask of art and who accordingly incurred Tchaikovsky's open disdain. As a classic example of his boundless emotionalism, the Piano Trio Op. 50 in A minor might be cited, written to "the memory of a great artist," namely Nicholas Rubinstein—a work in whose two movements, a *"pezzo elegiaco"* and a set of variations with finale and coda, there is a veritable orgy of sequences and naked feelings. In his last symphony this exhibitionism found a final escape-value.

A revulsion against such exaggeration had to ensue. As the so-called New Music was in part a protest against the ideals of the preceding generation, it was directed principally at the "exhibition of feeling." Here too we stand at the end of the Romantic movement.

SCANDINAVIA

In much weaker, paler colors than among the Slavic peoples, nationalism in music manifested itself among the Scandinavian countries—in Denmark, Sweden, Norway, and even Finland. They all were more or less oriented towards Germany. Like Germany, they all harbored the Romantic yearning for the true South of Italy and Spain; and especially in Denmark—or, rather, in Copenhagen—they showed an affinity for the French. There was no nationalistic group in the Northern lands. There was, moreover, no outstanding personality who with his music re-influenced Europe, as did, in literature, the Danes Kierkegaard and J. P. Jacobsen, the Norwegian Henrik Ibsen, or the Swede August Strindberg. National coloring was often so weak that it merely suggested a region and should be thought of simply as native rather than national art.

It was especially so in Denmark, which during the 17th and 18th centuries had already received its musical impulses mostly from Germany, with Schütz, Scheibe, Naumann, Schulz, and F. L. A. Kunzen. It has already been said (p. 162) that the patriarchs of Danish music were born Germans: Christoph E. F. Weyse of Altona (1774-1842) and Friedrich D. R. Kuhlau of Uelzen (1786-1832), who nevertheless complied with the national needs of their new home by glorifying the Danish folk song in their songs and in their modest *Singspiele,* e.g., Kuhlau in his "Elves' Hill" (*Elverhøj,* 1828, really only a play of Heiberg's with incidental music).

As in other lands, the way was here prepared for Romanticism, particularly on the stage, by collections from the national storehouse of folk song. The most noteworthy of these collections came from a genuine Dane, A. P. Berggreen (1801-1880), a pupil of Weyse's and a teacher of one of the genuine Danish national composers, Niels W. Gade. The way for the appearance of Gade, however, was prepared especially by another pupil of Weyse's, Johann Peter Emilius Hartmann (1805-1900), the real founder of the Romantic movement in Denmark and even in all Scandinavia. He had also been principally trained according to German patterns —Weber, Marschner, and Spohr. But underlying these were occasional manifestations of French influence, Auber and the unavoidable traces of Italianism: e.g., his opera "The Ravens, or the Trial of the Brothers" (*Ravnen eller Broderproven,* 1832), with text by the master of the fairy tale Hans Christian Andersen, after Carlo Gozzi. But in the same year occurred the performance of a play with his music, Oehlenschläger's *The Golden Horns,* which struck a soft, new, "Northern" note; and he intensified this note in a series of operas (e.g., *Little Christine,* after Andersen, 1846), in opera-ballets using Northern material (*The Valkyrie,* 1861, and *Thrymskviden,* 1868), in overtures to the dramas of Danish poets, in choral works, and even in purely instrumental music.

This note, characterized by folk song idioms and strong rhythm, was taken up by Niels W. Gade (1817–1890), though he tended more and more to restrain it in the course of his career. Gade belonged to the German Romantic circle. In 1843 he went on a royal scholarship to Leipzig, where he became a friend of Mendelssohn and Schumann. After a visit to Italy he returned to Leipzig, where he became Mendelssohn's successor as director of the Gewandhaus concerts. From 1848 on, he was active in his native land. His friendship with these two Romantics, however, was not alone responsible for the complete lack of opera in his creative output. As with the Dutch and also the British composers, the dramatic explosiveness, the free and natural passion that belongs essentially to opera, was not vouchsafed these Scandinavian composers. He wrote no less than eight symphonies, of which the first in C minor (performed by Mendelssohn in 1843) and the last in B minor sound most markedly "Northern," while the fourth in B-flat major (1871) is regarded as his most important one. Of his overtures, the first two, *Echoes of Ossian* (Op. 1, 1841) and *In the Highlands,* are the most thoroughly his own. In his choral ballads and dramatic cantatas he tended more towards Schumann, in his chamber and piano music more towards Mendelssohn. He was an idyllist, and fundamentally—like Mendelssohn—a Classicist with Romantic coloring. His national tone was not challenging. He lacked the quality of proud protest which made Czech and Russian national music so strong and full-blooded. Nevertheless, his efforts established a national school, in which Peter A. Heise (1830–1870) was particularly excellent as a sensitive song-composer, a sort of Danish Robert Franz.

No less than Denmark, Sweden also began its musical history under the influence of Germany, or more precisely of Lübeck and Hamburg—in the

17th and the first quarter of the 18th century, principally through the Düben family, a member of which, Gustav the elder (1624-1690), was in touch with Buxtehude and Christoph Bernhard. The only difference was that in the 18th century Sweden brought forth a native composer, Johann Helmich Roman (1694-1767), who, as a pupil of Pepusch and under the influence of Handel, treated the Swedish texts of his church and festival music in Italian style. His instrumental compositions, oboe concertos, flute sonatas, are of considerable interest. A center of musical life was supplied, under Gustav III, by a magnificent court-opera, of half Italian and half French tendencies, for which the Dresden composer Johann Gottlieb Naumann in 1786 wrote a "national opera," *Gustaf Vasa*. The text of this opera originated with J. H. Kellgren, the most important man of letters of the period, and possesses important historical and political traits which, unfortunately, have lost their topical value for us. The opera, which excells in great choral, ensemble, and ballet scenes, is consciously aligned in certain of its aspects with Gluck, whose works were well known in Stockholm. A number of its melodies have survived to our own day. In addition there were also in Stockholm *Singspiele* after the French model, in which national songs were not entirely absent, thanks to Karl Stenborg (1752-1813). There was instrumental music wholeheartedly after the Haydn pattern: Joseph M. Kraus (1756-1792), a highly gifted composer, who hailed from Mannheim and Göttingen, and a folk bard K. M. Bellman (1740-1795), whose repertory *Fredmans Epistlar och Sänger,* edited by Olaf Ohlström, achieved very great popularity.

Here too the Romantic movement began with the collecting and publishing of the old national treasures of folk song—full of feeling and dance-like, the folk songs of sentiment being often modal, the dancelike ones (polskas) being related to the mazurka. First there appeared a group of Swedish song and choral composers, among whom Adolf Fredrik Lindblad (1801-1879) is considered the most significant. Opera, as it had been in Russia before Glinka, was completely internationalized until in Ivar Hallström (1826-1901) there appeared a composer who kept to national themes, at least so far as his subject matter was concerned, and who also in his music tried to sound a national note. A later major work of his was "The King of the Mountain" (*Den Bergtagna,* 1874). But he was an opera composer without being a genuine dramatist. The initiator of Swedish Romantic instrumental music, the most original personality of 19th century Swedish music, was Franz Berwald (1796-1868), with a G-minor symphony (*Symphonie Sérieuse,* 1843), another one in C major (*Sym-*

phonie Singulière), and works of chamber music. As in Copenhagen, this early Romanticism in Stockholm had mostly a Leipzig coloring, in the work of Albert Rubenson (1826–1901), the lyric piano music of Ludwig Norman (1831–1885) or Jacob Adolf Hägg (1850–1928), and the songs and choruses of Johann August Söderman (1832–1876), who stressed especially the national element, notably in the popular choral suite *Bondebröllop* ("Peasant Wedding"). The so-called neo-Romantic school of Swedish musicians, headed by the composer of operas and symphonies Andreas Hallén (1846–1925), already had aligned itself with the successors of Wagner and Liszt.

Last of all, Norway took its place among the musical nations of the Scandinavian peninsula. At the beginning of the 19th century, all the musical needs of the Norwegians were being provided for by their town musicians, in the secular field, and by their organists and choir directors, in the sacred. But one of these organists, coming like Bach from an old family of choir directors, Ludwig Matthias Lindeman (1812–1887) was also the first and most significant collector of Norwegian folk tunes and country dances. Many of these dances show evidence of great age and uninterrupted tradition—the leaping dance (*springar*) in 3/4 meter and the *halling* in duple meter. With all their regional varieties, and in their strong rhythm and their melancholy or carefree melody, they form perhaps the most distinguished of all the bodies of Northern folk music. One should not forget how long even Norway, under Danish rule, belonged to the subject nations.

One of the first musicians to sound the national note was Waldemar Thrane (1790–1828), with his incidental music to Bjerregaard's "Mountain Adventure" (*Fjaeldoeventyret*, 1824). Another, with constantly intensified emphasis, was Ole Bull (1810–1880), known as a bizarre virtuoso violinist, with his fantasies and caprices on Norwegian folk themes. The most significant of this Early Romantic group, however, was Halfdan Kjerulf (1815–1863), a sensitive lyricist, whose songs and piano pieces have been justly compared with those of Adolph Jensen.[60] Neither he nor, even less, the generation after him escaped the danger inherent in the spirit of the Leipzig Conservatory, or Romantically inspired Classicism—not even the most prominent among them, Johan Svendsen (1840–1911), in whose work the national coloring, despite his "Norwegian" rhapsodies for orchestra, almost completely faded away.

The genuinely national musicians of Norway were Rickard Nordraak

[60] Walter Niemann, *Die Musik Scandinaviens* (Leipzig, 1906), p. 68.

(1842–1866), the creator of the Norwegian national hymn, and Edvard Grieg (1843–1907). Nordraak did not live long enough for his music to develop a distinctive character; his service consisted principally in preventing Grieg from falling entirely a victim to Classicistic Germanism. Like the "German" in Weber and the "Russian" in Glinka, the "Norwegian" in Grieg was not one hundred per cent pure: his great-grandfather Greig was a Scotchman. That does not alter the fact that in Grieg's music not only the Norwegian but also the Northern in general is most marked in strong, original, and very sensitive harmony and in the charm of his similarly strong and refined rhythm. He was, however, a miniaturist. His works in Classical form—the Piano Concerto in A Minor (a sister work of Schumann's Concerto), the String Quartet in G minor (Op. 27), the three Violin Sonatas in F, G, and C minor (Opp. 8, 13, 45)—each show individual ideas that are ingratiating (though often vulgar), but the structure as a whole is cramped and brittle. In his piano pieces and songs, however, he was a great master—in miniature. He carried on the Schumann tradition of the characteristic piece; and as with Schumann, the title in this kind of piece always conceals an intimate experience. He was, of course, familiar with all the new and choice features of Liszt's and Wagner's harmony; but he compressed them into the smallest space and made them entirely his own possession. Many of his ideas, in their boldness and tenderness, began to step over into the territory of the "impression," and a history of post-Wagnerian impressionism would have to concern itself with him as one of its ancestors, or at least as one of its godfathers.

Finland also comes between Sweden and Russia in its musical development. Political reasons inclined it to its Western neighbor rather than to its gigantic Eastern one. There were the same bases and developments here as in all the "border" nations: a very old epic, the *Kalevala*, in the vocal rendition of which a five-stress rhythm played a part; the collecting and arranging of sacred and secular folk melodies; and the cultivation of songs and choruses, especially choruses for men's voices. An ironical whim of history also decreed that the founder of the Finnish national school, Frederic Pacius (1809–1891), should be born in Hamburg and should be a pupil of Spohr and Hauptmann, both in the matter of training and in the character of his music. Yet he not only gave the Finnish people a few of their national songs but also organized for the first time their whole musical life. About him congregated a small circle of followers, among whom Martin Wegelius (1846–1906) stands out slightly.

The first composer really to sound the Finnish note was Robert Kajanus (1856–1933), with symphonic poems, an orchestral suite, Finnish rhapsodies, etc.—though the nationalism of his works had to make its way against European influences. Finland's greatest musician, Jan Sibelius (b. 1863), began as a Finnish-national Romanticist; later, however, he often approached the symphonic music of Finland's Eastern neighbor, especially that of Tchaikovsky. The boundaries of this book do not permit further study of him. In a certain sense, he too was at once a "young" and a "posthumous" musician.

HOLLAND

In the course of the 19th century the other European nations also became articulate in the field of music. The impetus and value of the nationalistic trend, though not its distinctness, depended in each instance upon the appearance of an outstanding personality. In Holland the trend was not at any one time especially distinct, despite the existence of a store of excellent ancient melodies, in part assembled at the beginning of the 17th century by Adrian Valerius and entitled *Nederlandtsche Gedenk-Clanck*. At the end of the 16th and beginning of the 17th centuries in Amsterdam there was a great composer, Italian or more precisely Venetian in his training, but of world-wide significance for he was the teacher of a whole international generation of musicians, Jan Pieterszoon Sweelinck. But after him Dutch music declined to a state of mere friendly and bourgeois music-making, which cannot in any way be compared with the painting of the same time, not to mention the immeasurable greatness of Rembrandt. In the 18th century there was a complete absence of all the prerequisites for significant composition in the fields of opera, of great vocal music for the church, of oratorio, and even of the symphony. Amsterdam, through the engravers and publishers Etienne Roger and Michel Charles Le Cène, became simply a center for the dissemination of the new instrumental music—not, however, of Dutch composers, but of Italian and French.

At the beginning of the new century, there appeared a native musician of apparently great significance, Jan Georg Bertelman (1782–1854), who wrote not only chamber music but also a Requiem and a Mass; and one of his pupils, Jan Bernard van Bree (1801–1857) even produced an opera (*Sappho,* 1834). But the next generation came completely under the spell of German or Leipzig Romanticism. Its propagandist was Johannes Verhulst (1816–1891), who, in very close association with Mendelssohn, had himself been at one time director of the Euterpe concerts in Leipzig, and who after returning to his native land—to Rotterdam, to The Hague, to Amsterdam—fought for the ideals of his youth and against the neo-Romantic movement. Along with him there was Richard Hol (1825–1904), composer of choral works, an oratorio, four symphonies, songs, and even, late in life, of some operas. He was also one of the many organizers of Holland's highly developed musical life, which can truly be called national. But in the 19th century there was no national *music* corresponding to this national musical life, and after the Schumann-Mendelssohn period only the neo-German or Wagnerian gained further territory.

BELGIUM

Remarkable development took place within the boundaries of Belgium, the state that won its independence in 1830. No section of territory could look back on a greater musical past than could the land which was once the northern part of the duchy of Burgundy. It is sufficient merely to mention names such as Joannes Ciconia of Liége, Guillaume Dufay and Gilles Binchois of Hainault, Joannes Ockeghem of Flanders, and Josquin, also of the old province of Hainault. To the very end of the 16th century, in which the way was slowly being prepared for the Italianizing of music, the laws of this Italianization were dictated by composers from the Belgian region: Willaert of Bruges, Rore of Antwerp, Monte of Mechlin, Lassus of Mons, and Macque of Valenciennes. With the beginning of the 17th century, the tide began to ebb; and just as Holland had no musicians even half-way worthy of being placed beside Rembrandt van Rijn, so Brussels had no one to place beside Rubens. The only composer of any rank, Henry du Mont of Liége, went as a church musician into the service of Louis XIV, just as at the beginning of the 18th century the only one of any rank, Jean-Baptiste Loeillet, went to England. On the other hand, a whole family of Italian musicians, headed by Joseph-Hector Fiocco, later established itself in Brussels. Belgian composers enthusiastically embraced the new instrumental style that had come out of Italy and had spread over Vienna and Prague and Mannheim to Paris and London: Pierre van Maldere of Brussels, François-Joseph Gossec of Hainault, and Jean-Noël Hamal of Liége, who was the eldest of the three and in this connection the most noteworthy because of his four Walloon operas—works in Italian-French *buffo* style, with text in Walloon dialect. His great successor, André-Modeste Grétry (1741–1813), emigrated to Paris and became the most significant representative of *opéra-comique;* and somewhat the same thing was done by his lesser countryman F. A. Gresnick (1755–1799). Gossec, too (1734–1829), early became a Parisian, and along with Grétry and Méhul, the latter from Givet in the Ardennes, became "one of the titled bards of the Revolution." [61]

What might be called Belgian art began to achieve new life only in 1830, after a period of lethargy and with the revolutionary movement that led to the establishment of a Belgian state under a king. Belgium, which united within its boundaries Flemish and Walloon peoples, was somewhat in the same cultural situation as Switzerland: just as there the three elements of the nation were oriented towards the cultural centers of their language affiliations, so the Flemings with Antwerp as their center tended towards the Dutch or Teutonic, the Walloons towards the French. Unlike the situation in Switzerland, however, where even some of the German-Swiss musicians felt themselves more and more attracted by the Romanic-French ideal, the cleavage in Belgium took on a polemic or separatistic character among the Flemish musical propagandists: Peter Benoît (1834–1901), a composer of very colorful oratorios, and his pupil Jan Blockx (1851–1912), a composer of similarly gaudy operas. A Walloon counterpart to this bit of surrounding territory is the district of Liége, from which came a number of violinists and violin-composers, led by Henri Vieuxtemps (1820–1881)—all of them inspired by the French ideal of elegance and sentimental charm. Credit for founding the Walloon school of composers goes to Adolphe (Abraham) Samuel (1824–1898), whose work seems not to have been influenced too much by his trips to Germany and Italy for purposes of study.

How little, however, a musician's extraction has to do with national style is shown by the figure of the greatest musician born in Liége, César Franck (1822–1890), whose name has already been mentioned at several places in this book. Is he a Walloon, as his birthplace would indicate? Is he a German, as his mother's Rhenish ancestry would indicate? Is he a "Belgian," because he dedicated his Opus 1 to the First King of the Belgians? He went to Paris early, as his fellow-countryman Beethoven fifty years before had gone to Vienna; and Franck founded a school of French musicians—but he never became a fellow-countryman of Saint-Saëns any

[61] Charles van den Borren, "La Musique belge du Moyen Age et sous l'Ancien Regime," in *La Revue Franco-Belge,* November, 1932.

more than Beethoven did of Gänsbacher or Hummel. Yet Franck was the glory of French instrumental music in the 19th century, alongside and in contrast to Berlioz, with whom he would not have the least to do, any more than he would with his "predecessors," like Georges Onslow (1784–1852), in the field of French Classicistic chamber music. In a certain sense Franck was an untimely or timeless musician, like Anton Bruckner, with whom he also had in common a deep and childlike Catholic faith. But he was more many-sided than Bruckner. He wrote operas—one "premature" (1851), and later disowned, with a typical Paris libretto by Alphonse Roger and Gustave Vaes, and two posthumous (*Hulda,* after "Northern" material, and *Ghiselle,* left unfinished). Mention has already been made (p. 166) of his oratorios, from the Biblical pastoral *Ruth* of his early period to the Nazarene *Béatitudes.*

But his significance rests upon several of his instrumental works, which, however, do not fit themselves easily into a history of Romantic music: works of pure chamber music and a symphony, which contrast with some of his own symphonic poems written in the style of the transition from Liszt to Debussy. Franck began, when he was about twenty years old, with four piano trios, Opp. 1 and 2. One of these he himself characterized as a *"trio de salon."* But another—Op. 1, No. 1 in F-sharp minor—is one of the most amazing works in trio literature, even granted that the "last" piano sonatas and quartets of Beethoven had loosened his tongue. Franck constructed the entire three-movement work on two themes—one contrapuntal unit and a song-theme, which gives the composition great unity along with a passionate abundance of invention and feeling. It was a foreshadowing of that Piano-Violin Sonata of 1886, in which the fantastic and rhapsodic were introduced into the frame of this thematic and contrapuntal unity. This Trio, incidentally, doubtless influenced Liszt's sonata; and thus not only was Franck a rather late follower of Liszt's, but Liszt was also one of Franck's. As Peter Cornelius noted in his journal on March 22, 1852, Liszt knew and played the Trio. Franck loved Bach, Beethoven, and Schubert's songs; but throughout his career he was, like Bruckner, also a child of the 19th century, which welcomed his refined system of harmonic tensions as a real musical achievement. In a Piano Quintet in F minor (1878-9), a String Quartet in D major (1889), and in the D-minor Symphony (1886-8), polyphony and this system of harmonic tensions entered into a new and inimitable synthesis. This synthesis was also present in a series of monumental organ and piano compositions, for which Franck chose a form reminiscent of Bach and of apparent improvisation: *Prélude, fugue et variation; Prélude, choral et fugue; Prélude, aria et finale*. Finally, it appears quite simply in his last work, the *Trois Chorals*. It has already been pointed out that along with his highly distinctive masterpieces of most intense inner passion, he also paid tribute to his times with hundreds of tasteless and trivial pieces. Strangely, his church music itself often belongs in that category in which the devout sentiment of the 19th century was blended with saccharine theatricality.

HUNGARY

If it is difficult to classify César Franck and many other "Western" composers nationally, it is superficially all the more easy to do so with members of national groups whose folk music has been given a specially distinctive stamp. That is the situation in Hungary. To be sure, the original source of Hungarian music, uncontaminated by Western influences, was often disturbed in the course of the centuries: what the 19th century accepted as Hungarian music was the practice of fiddling folk musicians (János Bihari, Anton Csermák, and Johann Lavotta), characterized by rubato in performance and by a sharply dotted and syncopated rhythm, a passionate use of coloratura, and a melancholy major-minor tonality. The gypsies, into whose hands Hungarian folk-music fell, carried this melodic material still further and gave it almost an air of caricature. How early and how intensely it attracted Northern and Western musicians is shown by precious examples of it in the works of Joseph Haydn and Franz Schubert. In its peculiar character, the Hungarian-gypsy idiom is so easy to adopt that the international and versatile Parisian, Franz Liszt, could even deck himself out with it like a genuine Hungarian, and that Johannes Brahms, born in Hamburg, could find it quite as becoming to him as did his Hungarian friend, the great Classically-minded violinist Joseph Joachim.

One of the most sensitive adherents of the Romantic movement, somewhat along the lines of Schumann, Robert Volkmann (1815–1883), from Lommatzsch in Saxony, early settled in Hungary. Along with many other chamber and orchestral works of general Romantic character, he wrote a Symphony in D minor, the first movement of which could pass for the ideal of Hungarian national composition. Native musicians, accordingly, did not find it especially difficult to create a national style. In opera, Franz Erkel (1810–1893), the composer of the Hungarian national anthem, wrote two pieces for the national repertoire, *Hunyady László* (1844) and *Bánk*

Bán (1861). In the symphonic field, Michael Brand (1814–1870), who wrote under the name Mosonyi, decided in 1859, in characteristic fashion, to adopt the national dialect. A number of imitators began to speak this dialect in virtuoso fashion. That it had only a patriotic, decorative, and artful character, despite its wide dissemination, became evident only in the 20th century, with the sincere work of Béla Bartók.

POLAND

The situation in Poland was similar. No subsequent Polish musician succeeded, as did Chopin, in raising the "national" to a world language and in expressing the most intimate and personal feelings in the most enchanting national coloring. Again one is reminded of that comparison with Roman times when, alongside the universal gods of the Greeks in the late Roman empire, the provincial and regional divinities took their places.

Stanislaw Moniuszko (1819–1872) became the creator of the Polish art-song, and of the Polish national opera, particularly with *Halka* (performed 1847 in concert, 1854 in the opera at Vilna, 1858 in the final version at Warsaw), and *The Haunted Castle* (1865), two colorful works of far more than merely patriotic character, like *A Life for the Tsar* and *The Bartered Bride*. Moniuszko and his successors developed a flourishing Polish musical life, both with respect to composition and performance. The most significant names among this group are the following: Vladislaw Zelenski (1837–1921), a musician of rich versatility; Sigismund Noskovski (1846–1909), a symphonic writer of note; and finally, the somewhat Gallicized violinist Henri Wieniawski (1835–1880).

SPAIN AND PORTUGAL

If we turn to the Iberian peninsula, we find there scarcely any traces of genuine "Romanticism." The Romantic movement is a "Northern" affair, is to a great extent a yearning for the lost paradise of the South, for a simple, more natural, more happy state of existence. What Jean-Jacques Rousseau in the 18th century called "return to nature" changed, at the beginning of the 19th, to Romanticism. Perhaps the only expression of the Romantic Movement in Spain was a new national self-consciousness, a re-nationalizing of music. The great musical heritage of the 16th and 17th centuries had never been entirely lost in Spain; but it is true that the way was being prepared for the Italianization of Spanish music as early as Calderón's period, which brought forth the old *zarzuela,* a mixture of song and dance with spoken dramatic dialogue. In 1629 an eclogue after the Florentine-Mantuan model was presented before Philip IV; and even the *zarzuela* of this century was somewhat too heavily garnished with the mythological and pastoral spirit of Italian opera, the only difference being that it also permitted a more earthy, rustic tone. The Italianization seemed to be complete with the entry of the Bourbons into Madrid around 1700; but at the same time the national tradition also began secretly to stir.

It is true that Spanish opera-composers like Domingo Terradellas of Barcelona (1711–1751) and Vicente Martin y Soler of Valencia (1754–1806) became completely Italianized; and it is also true that Carlo Broschi, known as Farinelli, sang the same four Italian arias for the melancholy king Philip V every night for years. But it is likewise true that Domenico Scarlatti, during nearly four decades that he spent on the Iberian peninsula in Lisbon and Madrid, received almost as much of its musical spirit as he gave to it. His capricious rhythmic and melodic invention is full of this Hispanic spirit, with which his pupil, Padre Antonio Soler (1729–1783), soon became imbued. Something similar, though to a lesser degree, was true of Luigi Boccherini, whose chamber music did not remain uninfluenced by the thirty-seven years he spent in Madrid. The occasional light Spanish coloring gives it its greatest charm. Boccherini's influence, in remarkable fashion, then facilitated the entry into Spain of Haydn's art.

It was in the dramatic field that Spain sounded its own national note. After the middle of the 18th century, the old Calderón type of *zarzuela* became closer to the people, more natural, by the same development that in France infused life into the *opéra-comique.* As a famous example might be cited the *"zarzuela burlesca"* in two acts *Las Segadoras de Vallecas,* with text by Ramón de la Cruz (1731–1794) and music by Antonio Rodriguez de Hita (d. 1787). Still more strong in their expression are the so-called *"tonadillas escenicas,"* lively dialogue scenes with interspersed music. They are perhaps related to the Italian intermezzo (though the latter had of course recitatives) and are comparable to Offenbach's early *bouffonneries* or *folies.* During the few decades after 1750 they were produced in great numbers, with Louis Misón as the leading master of the form—if one may speak here of mastery.

The fashion, however, was short-lived; for the nadir of Spanish music, which lasted to about 1830, coincided with the Napoleonic era, the years of deepest national misfortune. The most celebrated composer in Spain was Gioacchino Rossini. Again it is one of the ironies of history that an Italian, who had been in Madrid since 1827, was the one to plead for a national Spanish style. He was Basilio Basili (1803–18. .), the son of the Francesco Basili who won eternal notoriety by refusing young Verdi admission to the Milan Conservatory. The works decisive in bringing out this national style were a one-act "The Fiancé and the Concert" (*El Novio y el Concierto*) of 1839 and a three-act "The Smuggler" (*El Contrabandista*) of 1881: *zarzuelas* in the realistic manner of the *tonadilla,* full of folklike character types and folklike music.

The real master of this light-opera form, however, was Francisco Asenjo Barbieri of Madrid (1823–1894), himself a man of the people, although he also later rose to achieve very high honors as conductor and musicologist. He wrote some eighty zarzuelas, making a rather Italianate beginning with such pieces as "Playing with Fire" (*Jugar con Fuego,* 1851). "Bread and Bulls" (*Pan y Toros,* with Francisco de Goya as one of the principal characters, 1864) and "The Little Barber of Lavapiés" (*El Barberillo de Lavapiés,* 1874) are considered his masterpieces. Barbieri, however, was only one of the most successful among many: Hernando, Gaztambide, Oudrid, Arrieta, Chueca, etc.

Some had erroneously believed that these folklike zarzuelas could be "raised" to operas, by substituting more or less pretentious recitative for the dialogue; but thereby their charm was destroyed. An experiment of this sort was made by Emilio Arrieta (1823–1894) in his *Marina* of 1855, which in 1871 was enlarged into a three-act opera. Alongside it there was also no lack of attempts to rival Italian opera: Baltasar Saldoni (1807–1889) and Miguel Hilarión Eslava (1807–1878), in particular, continued in the 19th century the work of Terradellas and Martin, although they remained in Spain. The real protest against this Italianism was made by the contentious Tomás Bretón (1850–1923) and the idealistic champion for a new national style Felipe Pedrell (1841–1922).

Portugal, which from 1580 to 1640 was joined to Spain by personal union within the reigning monarchy, also had a fate similar to that of its larger neighbor. Portugal had a brilliant musical past, around the end of the 16th and beginning of the 17th centuries, with composers like Duarte Lobo in the vocal field and Manuel R. Coelho in the instrumental. To be sure, it had a Royal amateur of incomparable stature in John IV (1604–1656), whose music library perhaps might have been the basis for a national culture had it not been destroyed in the great earthquake of

1755. In the 18th century, Italianism prevailed. As had done Terradellas or Martin, Marcos Antonio Portugal (1762–1830) went to Italy when he was about thirty; and the last twenty years of his life were spent in Brazil. The only difference was that alongside his many *opere serie* and *buffe* for Venice, Florence, and Milan, he also wrote some for Lisbon, or at least had his *opere buffe* translated into Portuguese for his fellow countrymen. And unlike Spain, where the nationalization took place almost entirely in the field of opera, Portugal had an instrumental composer, João Domingo Bomtempo (1775–1842) who, trained not in Italy but in Paris and London, followed the model of Haydn and Mozart in his symphonies and chamber works.

As usual, the national consciousness in music was preceded by the collecting of folk songs in all regions of Portugal: the first of these collections, in fact, goes back to 1793. The activity of a generation of more nationally-minded musicians—for example, Augusto Machado (1845–1924) or Alfredo Keil (1850–1907)—did not come until the post-Romantic period, when these musicians can be classified roughly according to their training in Germany or in Paris.

NORTH AMERICA

In the United States of American there was no unified Romantic movement, and no great national music, simply because the nation was still too young to form a unified spiritual basis and because—at least in the 19th century—there were no outstanding masters whose work was able to *create* a national style.

The Indian aborigines, confined to reservations, were isolated from the cultural life of the nation. But their melodies, more and more zealously collected and studied, supplied a number of composers with the material for compositions written in the Western European manner. Strangely enough, one of the first composers to do so was Anthony Philip Heinrich (1781–1861) from Schönbüchl in Bohemia, who lived for a time among the Indians in Kentucky. In 1820 Heinrich published a book entitled *The Dawning of Music in Kentucky*. He also wrote symphonic and choral works of large dimensions, in which he used Indian melodies "for his singular and somewhat empty works." [62]

Although the Negroes do not belong to the original inhabitants of the land, they form a unified group by virtue of their ancestry and social

[62] Carl Engel, in Adler's *Handbuch der Musikgeschichte,* 2nd ed., p. 1195.

exclusion. Transplanted from a foreign continent, they proved to be a people of the highest gifts in musical assimilation, i.e., the creative imitation of European impulses. Evidence of this ability is supplied by the so-called "Negro songs" and "Negro spirituals," full of passionate, unrestrained warmth and childlike mysticism, with most simple harmony and anglicized rhythm. But it is significant that the most beautiful of these songs, *Old Folks at Home, Old Black Joe, My Old Kentucky Home,* and many others, were written by a white man born in Lawrenceville, Pa., Stephen Collins Foster (1826–1864). Of his songs, *Oh! Susanna* was one of the oldest (1848) and was most widely circulated by the "minstrel shows." And although he himself did not know the deep South very well, his tunes have been accepted by the Negroes as an expression of their inmost feelings—"They are probably the most typically American expression that any composer has yet achieved." [63] They are, at the same time, the earliest evidence of the Romantic movement in America; and, like the Indian melodies, the Negro material has, of course, furnished the basis for Romantically nationalistic compositions of every type.

One of the earliest exploiters of Negro material was the somewhat charlatanic piano virtuoso Louis Moreau Gottschalk (1829–1869), born in the South (New Orleans), a French Creole despite his German-sounding name, and trained in Paris, where he came in contact with Chopin, Berlioz, and other composers. In 1844 he made his debut in Paris, and 1852 went to Spain, where by virtue of his temperament and his romantic appearance he caused a very great sensation—success which, beginning with his first appearance in New York in 1853, continued for him in both North and South America. He was a somewhat eccentric salon-composer, writing not only "Spanish" virtuoso-pieces—*Le Siège de Saragosse, La Jota Aragonese, Souvenir d'Andalousie, Manchega, La Gitanilla,* etc.—but also pieces characteristic of the South, with musical impulses from the slums of New Orleans, from Cuba and Brazil—"The Banjo" (*Bamboula*), *Ojos Criollos,* habaneras, tangos, *guajiros*.

The northeastern part of the United States, whose musical taste was long determined by England, showed Romantic inclinations of different origin and different nature. It would be incorrect to believe that New England was satisfied with crude congregational singing in the church: Francis Hopkinson (1737–1791) was already an American composer of "secular" music, and William Billings (1746–1800), originally a leather

[63] *The International Cyclopedia of Music and Musicians,* ed. Oscar Thompson (New York, 1943), art. Foster., p. 616.

dresser, not only published hymns and congregational songbooks but also wrote some exceedingly original "fugue tunes." Handel's *Messiah* was performed in Boston as early as 1770, Mendelssohn's *St. Paul* in New York as early as 1838. A prominent figure in the East was Lowell Mason (1798–1872) of Medfield, Mass., who in 1822 fitted sacred texts to melodies by Haydn, Mozart, and even Beethoven. He stood out as a great musical educator, both of youth and of adults. It was, however, only an education for greater receptivity of European imports. The fame of the so-called Viennese Classics made Germany appear to be *the* land of music, and made Leipzig or some other German conservatory seem the center of higher musical education. Accordingly, John Knowles Paine (1839–1906), the first occupant of the chair of music at Harvard, was an organ pupil of C. A. Haupt in Berlin; and George Whitefield Chadwick (1854–1931), who wrote symphonies and chamber works, choruses and operas, was a pupil of Jadassohn and Reinecke—which, however, did not prevent his writing works of a specifically Anglo-Saxon character.

In the period of the Romantic movement it became all the more difficult for the American musician to preserve his independence when, even in the field of performance, all the more or less sensational great ones of Europe were being imported, beginning with Manuel Garcia, Jenny Lind, and Henriette Sontag, all the way to Anton Rubinstein and Hans von Bülow, Tchaikovsky and Dvořák. At the end of the period the influence colored by Mendelssohn and Schumann changed more to that of Wagner, who himself occasionally during his lifetime—not quite in earnest—toyed with the idea of emigrating to the New World.

In contrast to the mighty Western nation whose mixture of inhabitants —a conglomerate of the most heterogeneous elements—constantly compelled it to *create* a new artistic unity, Europe was impelled by the Romantic tendency to establish in musical matters the national boundaries more and more sharply. Gradually the rather small, even the very small, musical units became musically articulate: in the Baltic countries, the Esthonians, the Letts, the Lithuanians; in the Balkans, the Rumanians, Bulgarians, and modern Greeks; within the South Slavic area, the Serbs, Croats, and Slovenes. All were striving for national separation. And, each time, the process went on as before: the collecting and sifting of old traditional melodic treasures, which formed the basis for a creative art-music —or was to have formed it. The final consequence of this separation was the attempt to separate even the national music of the old musical peoples into regions—German music, for example, into Bavarian, Swabian, Saxon, Rhenish, Lower German, Wendish, etc., or Spanish music into Catalonian, Basque, Andalusian, Castilian, Asturian, Galician, etc. Many attempts were made to do exactly that. It was a process of regionalization in music, the end of that movement which had begun at the start of the century with Italian music becoming "more Italian," French music "more French," German "more German"—or seeming to become so.

This was the complete antithesis to the Classic trend, whose great glory had been that it stood above the nations, that it spoke the language of humanity, that it corresponded to Goethe's opinion: "There is no patriotic art and no patriotic science. Both belong, like everything nobly good, to the whole world; and they can be furthered only by the general, free give-and-take of all contemporaries, with constant regard for what survives and is known from the past."

PART III

The Philosophy

CHAPTER XVIII

Musical Aesthetics and Musicology

AESTHETICS

IN TWO chapters of the first part of this book, two principal articles of the Romantic creed have already been formulated: first, that in the association of the arts music stands in the center, that all the other arts are related to it as to their original basis; and, second, that among the various manifestations of music itself instrumental music—wordless, "ambiguous," autonomous music—has a claim to primary importance.

The change from the rationalistic 18th century to the Romantic 19th could not have been greater. In the 18th, music was classified by the philosophers—so far as they concerned themselves with it at all as aestheticians —very low in the scale of the arts. It was useful in so far as it served the purposes of devotion in church and, incidentally, of polite social intercourse. Really the only writers who had a deeper conception of it were the theological zealots who fought against its excessive cultivation in church and home. They were afraid of its sensuous power or sensuous seductiveness; there was still a suspicion of the dark, orphic power of music. The idea of music as occupying a subordinate place in the hierarchy of the arts continued to show its effects in Kant's *Critique of Judgment* (1790). He recognized thoroughly that music was able to move the mind in an even greater variety of ways and even more intensely than poetry itself. But since he evaluated the worth of the arts in proportion as they contributed to the expansion of the "cognitive faculties" (*Erkenntnisse*), to the increase of what he called "culture" of the mind, he concluded that music was "rather enjoyment than culture" and, in contrast to the other arts, "does not bear frequent repetition without producing weariness." Therefore, like all enjoyment, it requires rather frequent change, and "in the judgement of Reason it has less worth than any other of the fine arts." [64]

Kant's critique of music was still influenced not only by the idea of music's subordinate position but also by that of its therapeutic effect. It gratified because it promoted the feeling of health; it was a proof "that we can reach the body through the soul and use the latter as the physician of the former."

But Kant was also still intensely possessed by the so-called "theory of the affections" (*Affektenlehre*) of his time, that is, by the idea that the sense of music consisted in its "imitating" the various agitations of the soul. The family tree of this idea is very old: it goes back to antiquity, when there was a current slogan about the sense of art being *imitatio naturae*. The 16th century piously revived this catch phrase, and the 18th played variations on it in all keys and meters. Kant, too, repeated it: "Thus as modulation [of human speech?] is, as it were, a universal language of sensations intelligible to every man, the art of tone employs it by itself alone in its full force, viz., as a language of the affections, and thus communicates universally according to the laws of association the aesthetical ideas naturally combined therewith." Kant always seemed to recognize music as an art, as an organ for the communication of aesthetic ideas. But his slighting estimate of its rank did not diminish: in his *Anthropology* (1798) he characterized it once again as a communication of the feelings into the distance round about, to all who are within its radius—a state of things with which he was not entirely in sympathy, for people cannot avoid receiving this communication. Again he emphasized, not without displeasure, the orderly play of sensations without concepts in music, the social enjoyment. "Music was for him a beautiful (as distinct from a merely pleasant) art only because it served as a vehicle for poetry." [65]

It is evident that in this kind of musical aesthetics there was but little place for instrumental music, and none at all for its peculiar merit. Instrumental music was mere play, with no more value than the arabesque on a piece of tapestry. In this point Kant was in agreement with Jean-Jacques Rousseau, who likewise still had as part of his musical creed a considerable underestimation of pure, "absolute" music—almost fifty years after the composition of the *Well-Tempered Clavier*. For Rousseau, the

---

[64] *Critik der Urteilskraft* I, § 53; trans. J. H. Bernard (London, 1914), p. 217. Cf. the excellent book by Paul Moos, *Die Philosophie der Musik von Kant bis Eduard von Hartmann* (Stuttgart, 1922), p. 15.

[65] Moos, *op. cit.*, p. 18.

linguistic origin of music was axiomatic. One might characterize him not only as the father of the aesthetic forerunners of Wagner but also as the father of musical nationalism. In his supposedly happy original state of mankind, when language came into being, speech, poetry, and music were one—there was no other music than melody and no other melody than the varied tone. Incidentally, this Rousseauesque theory of the linguistic origin of music, basically wrong as it is, still reappears even in professional psychological literature of the 19th century. From passionately intensified speech—so Rousseau thought—melody was differentiated only by the duration of the tones. Hence music was also dependent upon the *differences* in speech: "It is the accent of languages that determines the melody of each nation; it is the accent that makes people speak while singing, and makes them speak with more or less energy, according to whether their language has more or less accent. . . . These are the true principles. . . ." [66]

It is clear that for Rousseau, just as for Kant, pure instrumental music was nothing but music of secondary rank. "If music is able to depict only by melody, and draws from it all its power, it follows that all non-vocal music, however harmonious it may be, is only an imitative kind of music and can neither move nor depict with its beautiful harmonies, and soon leaves the ears, and always the heart, cold." [67] Rousseau immediately used this final inference for a diatribe against counterpoint, against the simultaneous combination of two melodies which, however beautiful they might be in themselves, could only neutralize each other—"it is as if one were to find a way to recite two speeches at once, to give more force to their eloquence."

In vindication of the 18th century's honor, the opinion of Johann Gottfried Herder (1744–1803) might be cited. Herder began as one of Rousseau's adherents in aesthetic matters. But later, in contrast to this arrogant dilettante, he discussed polyphonic music, having in mind perhaps one of Haydn's development sections, as an "affectionate dispute," which finds "after the bitterest struggle its harmonious resolution."

NEW EVALUATION OF "ABSOLUTE" MUSIC

We need not trace the changed conception of music in post-Kantian philosophy in detail—not, for example, in the work of the philosopher of

---

[66] *Dictionnaire de Musique* (Paris, 1768), art. *Mélodie*, p. 277.
[67] *Ibid.*

the Romantic era, Friedrich Wilhelm Joseph von Schelling, who, in his lectures on the philosophy of art (1802–1805), considered music as that art "which to the greatest degree divests itself of corporeality and is borne upon invisible, almost spiritual wings"—an idea which then led to the assertion that true, ideal music is not heard at all, but is non-sensuous and suprasensuous. In contrast to him, the Danish scientist Hans Christian Oersted (1777–1851) in his dialogue *On the Bases of the Enjoyment Elicited by Sounds* (1808, first published in 1851) conceived of music as spiritually inspired sensuousness. A Romantic feature of his philosophy is the assertion that the inner agitation occasioned by hearing a good piece of music does not arise from conscious reflection, but from obscure depths of consciousness.

For Georg Wilhelm Friedrich Hegel in his *Lectures on Aesthetics* (written about 1820 but published only after his death), music was an art of feelings and moods. Its task consisted of "reproducing not only the objective aspect . . . but, on the contrary, the manner and the way in which the inmost being, according to his subjective nature and ideal soul, is moved." It is possible that music, under certain conditions, may also awaken in us definite attitudes or ideas, but these are then ideas that we ourselves have read into it. Hegel was not a very "Romantic" philosopher: he preferred vocal music, which wins definiteness through the word, to instrumental music, in which he saw little more than formal movement, a simple and purely subjective play of form. His attitude towards instrumental music then led him to characterize it as a truly Romantic art.

In this respect he stood in contrast to a philosopher who passionately opposed and despised him, Arthur Schopenhauer. In *The World as Will and Idea* (1st ed. 1818, 2nd ed. 1844), Schopenhauer saw in words only "a foreign addition, of secondary value." He claimed that music had a right to exist for itself, completely independent of text and, in opera, of the proceedings on the stage. He considered it entirely effective even without text; in fact, he noted it as an advantage when it had no need of words and manifested its full effect in purely instrumental performance.[68] In this respect, to be sure, he agreed with Hegel that for him, too, music was an art of indefinite expression; it did not express "this or that particular and definite joy, this or that sorrow, or pain, or horror, or delight, or merriment, or peace of mind, but joy, sorrow, pain, horror, delight, merriment, peace of mind themselves, to a certain extent in the abstract, their essential nature, without accessories, and therefore without their

[68] Moos, *op. cit.,* p. 162.

motives. Yet we completely understand them in this extracted quintessence." Music tells the secret story of our "will."

In the first part of this book we have already seen (p. 237) how deeply Wagner was affected by his acquaintance with Schopenhauer, how, with some violence to Schopenhauer's meaning, he made this aesthetic doctrine grist for the mill of his *Gesamtkunstwerk*. To be sure, Schopenhauer never spoke of the "end" of instrumental music, and he also very neatly pointed out the doubtful validity of reading a program into it: "If we now cast a glance at purely instrumental music, a symphony of Beethoven presents to us the greatest confusion, yet with the most perfect order at its foundation, the most vehement conflict, which is transformed the next moment into the most beautiful concord. It is *rerum concordia discors,* a true and perfect picture of the nature of the world which rolls on in the boundless maze of innumerable forms, and through constant destruction supports itself. But in this symphony all human passions and emotions also find utterance—joy, sorrow, love, hatred, terror, hope, etc.—in innumerable degrees, yet all, as it were, only *in abstracto* and without any particularization; it is their mere form without the substance, like a spirit world without matter. Certainly we have a tendency to realize them while we listen, to clothe them in imagination with flesh and bones, and to see in them scenes of life and nature on every hand. Yet, taken generally, this is not required for their comprehension or enjoyment, but rather imparts to them a foreign and arbitrary addition: therefore it is better to apprehend them in their immediacy and purity."

Lesser spirits, too, like the professor of philosophy at Breslau, August Kahlert, in his *System of Aesthetics* (1846) placed music in the foreground of all the arts and considered pure instrumental music as the most effective of all the artistic means for expressing freely "the as yet inexpressible neutrality of the soul." [69] It is remarkable, and quite in the Romantic spirit, that instrumental music, like landscape painting, seemed to him to have come more from the "Teutonic" than the Romanic spirit—a false conclusion, explicable only because Italy had centered its attention exclusively on opera during the 19th century. In an earlier day Corelli or Vivaldi or Domenico Scarlatti had been quite notable exponents of instrumental music. But it is axiomatic that philosophers do not need to know anything about music history.

Once again, it is not necessary to pursue the attitude of the 19th-century philosophers towards Romantic music in detail. The representatives of

[69] *Ibid.,* p. 179.

philosophy in almost all instances dispensed with the technical preparation that would have enabled them to express themselves authoritatively
on problems of music. Where they happened upon the right thing, it was
mostly an intuitive perception. The only thing characteristic of them was
the elevated position that was more and more generally accorded to music
in the hierarchy of the arts as the century progressed. In contrast to the
18th century, which always was at great pains, in its aesthetics, to get rid
of pure instrumental music, the 19th prized and exalted precisely this
branch of music.

England in the 18th century had considered music mostly from a low,
sensualistic point of view. Burney, for example, wrote in 1776: "Music is
an innocent luxury, unnecessary, indeed, to existence, but a great improve-
ment and gratification of the sense of hearing." ". . . an art that unites
corporal with intellectual pleasure, by a species of enjoyment which gratifies
sense, without weakening reason." Again, William Mason, in the first of
his Essays on English Church Music (York, 1795) wrote: "Music, as an
imitative art, ranks so much below Poetry and Painting, that is, in my own
opinion, which I have found confirmed by many late Writers of the best
judgment, it can hardly be so termed with propriety (See Harris's Three
Treatises, Dr. Beattie on Poetry and Music, and particularly Mr. Twining's
Second Dissertation prefixt to his Translation of Aristotle's Poetics). Not-
withstanding this, it has certain qualities, so analogous to those which constitute Metre or Versification, such as Accent, Rhythm, Pause, and Cadence,
that it thereby becomes, equally with Poetry, an object of criticism . . ."
It was a triumph, then, for music when the psychologist Herbert Spencer
in his essay On the Origin and Function of Music (1857) said, ". . . music
must take rank as the highest of the fine arts—as the one which, more
than any other, ministers to human welfare. And thus, even leaving out
of view the immediate gratifications it is hourly giving, we cannot too much
applaud that progress of musical culture which is becoming one of the
characteristics of our age." And it was a triumph when James Sully (Sensation and Intuition: Studies in Psychology and Aesthetics, 1874) spoke thus
of the refinement and intensification of music in the 19th century: "Since
instrumental music won the upper hand, this process has been going
mightily forward. And although in the evaluation of vocal and instrumental music individual preferences must be permitted their place . . . ,
the highest attainment of music is the simultaneous realization of lofty
beauty of form and of deep emotional expression . . . to be found, not in
the opera or any form of word-bound music, but in that free development

of pure tone which has certainly reached a beauty and a splendor of power unattainable by song, and which nevertheless retains, in the folds of its own intimate structure, abundance of force for stimulating and satisfying the deepest emotional cravings of the human heart." [70]

Herein we note that Spencer also considered the increase of the sensuous life, to which music contributes, as one of its virtues. It was one of the particular traits of the Romantic movement that it placed music so high because it was the most *exciting* of all the arts; and Wagner was for that very reason an arch-Romantic, because there is no more exciting, more orgiastic music than his. Already in another connection [71] I have alluded to the fact that music is not in all periods the direct expression of the spirit in a century. Many periods create for themselves the music that they need. The 16th century, for example, was wild, torn by religious strife, thrown off balance by the destruction of all the finest traditions of the Middle Ages. It looked upon music as a gift of heaven, as a sedative, as a means of regaining composure, as a medicine for the soul. In contrast to it was the century that was born of the Revolution, that had the shocks of the Napoleonic wars behind it and, in general, since 1815, enjoyed bourgeois peace. For it, music was a means of exciting, of whipping up the emotions. It no longer had any right to the heroism of Beethoven, but it still liked to look at itself in this heroic mirror; and even Wagner owed his general victory to the "bourgeoisie," for whom he presented very modern, and very intimate conflicts in a heroic exaggeration, in the key of highest passion.

CONVERGENCE OF THE ARTS

The tendency of the Romantic era proceeded in the direction of effacing the boundaries of the arts. The real observations regarding the position of music, accordingly, are not to be sought so much among the philosophers, whose method leads or should lead to separation, but among the poets. And they are found, first of all, among the poets and other writers of the early Romantic movement in Germany. The beginnings are very sharply outlined. Wilhelm Heinse (1746–1803), who was, after a fashion, an exponent of *Sturm und Drang,* reduced Rousseau and his linguistic theory of the origin of music to absurdity, and showed the superiority

---

[70] Cf. Carl Stumpf, "Musikpsychologie in England," *Vierteljahrsschrift für Musikwissenschaft* I: 266 and 299 (1885).

[71] *Greatness in Music* (New York, 1941), pp. 166 ff.

of opera over drama, in his *Musical Dialogues* (written *c.* 1776 or 1777, but first published 1805). In his "musical novel" *Hildegard von Hohenthal* (1795–6) he exhibited what might be called a foreshadowing of forthcoming developments in the Romantic movement by his recognition of the inclusive power of instrumental music and his regret that Gluck lacked a sense of the national. But Gluck was the "most modern" composer he used as an example; so far as he was concerned, his contemporaries like Haydn and Mozart scarcely existed as yet, and his real household divinities were the older Italians, especially the neo-Neapolitans Pergolesi, Jommelli, and their retinue. Heinse still belonged entirely to the 18th century; he spoke of music simply as a cultivated musician, and avoided effacing its boundaries. Fundamentally, his conception of music was still purely hedonistic—a simple pleasure.

But in the following year, 1797, there appeared *The Outpourings of the Heart of an Art-loving Cloister-brother—Fantasies on Art for Friends of Art* by Wilhelm Heinrich Wackenroder (1773–1798), edited and interspersed with some contributions by his friend Ludwig Tieck. In place of Greece, the Middle Ages (or what was thought to be Middle Ages) now appeared as the ideal; in place of Rationalism, appeared Christian mysticism. The world became a product of the ego. The ego had the right to fashion it in its own way; so it fashioned it in the artistic way: life was nothing, art everything.

Where the Classicist Herder, completely recognizing the justification for instrumental music, had yet considered the union of poetry and music the culminating point and thus had remained within the aesthetic field, these early Romantics permitted religion and art to fuse into one. To one of the heroes in Wackenroder's confessions, the South German *Kapellmeister* Joseph Berglinger, who died "in the prime of life," it seemed logical that sacred or church music be the summit of all art; in him there already appeared evidence of that cult of the past which was so characteristic of the Romantic era, the Palestrina style, "that ancient, chorale-like church music, which sounds like an eternal *Miserere mei Domine!,* and whose slow, deep tones like sin-laden pilgrims creep along in deep valleys."

As the boundaries between religion and art, between thought and poetry were effaced, so were also effaced the boundaries between the individual arts. August Wilhelm Schlegel was already propagandizing for a mutual convergence of the arts: statues should be enlivened into paintings, paintings should become poems, poems should become music. Music always stood at the end of the sequence. Goethe—who harbored the deepest

theoretical interest in music, who in characterizations of it as "completely
form and substance" showed most profound understanding of it, and
who experienced with a sense of shock its "releasing effect"—yet never
considered it the "center of art." The Romantics, on the other hand, headed
by Novalis, despised language as a means of communication: the soul of
language was the vowel, its final aim was its emancipation into music.
Everything tended towards establishing the primary importance of instrumental music, precisely *because* it could not communicate any no-
tional perceptions, because it was indefinite, an art of the unconscious.

Finally, the sense of music blended with pantheism. E. T. A. Hoffmann
said, "The spirit of music pervades all nature." Thus the creator of music,
who as late as the 18th century had been little more than a craftsman, became himself a priest, a Romantic figure. Goethe had given the Romantics
a fictional model with his *Wilhelm Meister;* now it came about that when
the heroes of novels were not specifically musicians, they were usually at
least artists, mostly unfit for life.

One can see how closely the figure of Beethoven must have corresponded
to these Romantic ideas. In Germany they had been in large part formulated even before Beethoven's symphonic and chamber music had become
widely known. They were but specially strengthened by the interpretation
that E. T. A. Hoffmann gave to Beethoven's music in general, to Beethoven's instrumental music in the *Kreisleriana,* and to individual items
among his works—the *Coriolanus* Overture, the Fifth Symphony, the two
Piano Trios Op. 70, the music for *Egmont,* and the C-major Mass. In
France these Romantic ideas actually attached themselves to the direct acquaintance with Beethoven's works. Mme. de Staël, in her book *De l'Alle-
magne* (1810), which conveyed to the French people the first conception
of German Romanticism, had only literary connections; but what she said
incidentally about the difference between beautiful verses and true poetry
sounds like an echo of Schlegel's ideas about music: ". . . To conceive
of the true grandeur of lyric poetry, one must wander in ethereal regions,
forget the sound of earth while hearing celestial harmony, and consider
the whole earth as a symbol of the emotions of the soul. . . ." What revelations she would have had to make for her fellow countrymen if she had
had any connections with music! In the years when she visited Germany
and Austria, the *Eroica* and the *Appassionata* had long since been written.

What she had neglected was abundantly supplied by the ensuing generation of French writers and poets. In the wake of Stendhal, whose en-

thusiasm for music was but part of his enthusiasm for Italy and whose principal interest was in Italian opera—though he seemed but little concerned over the difference between Cimarosa and Mozart—came the generation of Balzac, Victor Hugo, and George Sand, for whom music stood above all other arts, even as it did for their German fellow Romantics. For George Sand, who had special reasons for becoming Chopin's friend, music was an incentive to let the imagination roam in fields of the infinite and the unknown. Balzac, in his two novels about music and musicians, *Massimilla Doni* and *Gambara,* placed music, the language of which he considered a thousand times richer than the language of words, at the head of all the arts, and especially in his *Gambara* depicted the man "bewitched by music," for whom Berlioz might have served as a model—a Hoffmannesque figure, like *Kapellmeister* Kreisler.

The greatest contribution to the change of the French attitude towards music from the Classicistic to the Romantic was naturally made by the writer and critic Berlioz himself, especially through his passionate propaganda for Beethoven.[72] In Berlioz's friend and counterpart ("the angelic pendant to the diabolical Berlioz"), Chrétien Urhan (1790–1845), who played the viola at the Grand Opéra and composed two *Quintettes Romantiques,* the enthusiasm for music in general and for Beethoven in particular already assumed a form of exaltation that we meet with more commonly only in the later years of the neo-Romantic period, in the Wagnerian cult. What Alphonse de Lamartine said about the secret voices of music which pervade the whole universe agrees precisely with that quatrain of Friedrich Schlegel's which we have already cited (on p. 208) as the motto of Schumann's Fantasy, Op. 17.

THE CULT OF MUSIC: LISZT AND MAZZINI

By a thoroughly logical development, it was the land of the Revolution in particular that assigned to music, and above all to the music of Beethoven, the role of *world-improvement*—a moral-political-social role. As the Revolution had torn the musician—the composer, the performer, the virtuoso—out of his old social connections and set him over against the masses as a free individual, it became all the more necessary that a new relation between him and the whole be found. This came to pass through

[72] Cf. Leo Schrade, *op. cit.,* especially the excellent chapter "Enthusiasm of a Poet," pp. 39–69.

the attempt to raise music to a new state of dignity, to set up a temple for it and assign to the musician the role of priest in this temple. The Saint-Simonian movement, especially the manifesto of Emile Barrault *To the Artists of the Past and Future in the Fine Arts* (1830), formulated this new role of the artist in general. For the musician in particular, it was then formulated by Berlioz and Liszt. Berlioz, with his cult of Beethoven, used all forms of ridicule, despair, and irony in his passionate criticism of the conditions of music in Paris. Liszt, with his manifesto of 1835 whch has been already referred to (p. 30), tried to reorganize concert life, instigated the establishment of music schools and libraries, proposed the stimulating of creative activity by conventions of musicians and by prizes for exceptional works, and, in general, took his stand against the inferior quality of public criticism and the ravages of poor instruction.

To gauge how much conditions had changed since 1800, one need only imagine how Bach, Haydn, or Mozart would have been received in this new order of things. And how far the disintegration of the old order seemed to Liszt to have proceeded may be inferred from the fact that he, "in the name of all artists, of art, and of social progress," demanded that music instruction be introduced into the elementary schools, that thereby a new church music would be brought to life. He also demanded that the most significant works of all the old and new masters be made available in cheap editions. The masses must be educated to receive the revelations of music and its priests. "We believe as steadfastly in art as we do in God and Man, both of whom find therein a voice and type of elevated expression. We believe in one unending progress, in one untrammelled social future for the tonal artist; we believe in these with all the strength of hope and of love!" [73] This was an ecstatic, thoroughly Romantic creed.

Strangely enough, it resembled another manifesto on the place of music in the past, present, and future—the pamphlet *Filosofia della Musica,* which Giuseppe Mazzini wrote in 1836 and dedicated to the "unknown divinity" (*ignoto numini*).[74] This was one of the strangest publications in the world —youthful, enthusiastic, written by a person who spoke to the masses of music only as a layman. He named Mozart's *Don Giovanni* and Meyerbeer's *Robert le Diable* in one breath and placed them on the same artistic level. Like a genuine Italian, he was confused or uncertain about everything outside the field of opera; and he saw in Donizetti's operas, particu-

[73] *Gesammelte Schriften* II, p. 30.
[74] *Scritti letterari editi ed inediti* II (Imola, 1910), pp. 117–165.

larly in *Anna Bolena* or *Marino Falieri,* beginnings towards the realization of his ideals. (He would have been able to find this realization later in Verdi; and I do not know whether he *did* find it—at all events, he did not express himself on the subject.) But his ideas were much too comprehensive to be realized in opera. He clearly stated that it was impossible to revive an exhausted epoch, but he did not exactly preach revolution—only a powerful evolution.

The strange thing was that he condemned *Romanticismo* quite as much as persistent Classicism. He envisioned the Messiah of music as a son and pupil of Italy, who, however, would have to develop Italian music into European music, who would fuse the "creative elemental forces" (*elementi generatori*) of Italian and German music, in "individualistic" melody and "social" harmony, into one, towards "social music, the musical drama of the future" (*alla musica sociale, al dramma musicale dell'avvenire*). "I am speaking of a time when the public and the drama will exercise a reciprocal and beneficial influence . . . , when the musical drama will be performed to a public neither materialistic, idle, nor frivolous, and itself regenerated by the consciousness of a truth to be taught, will possess a high educational mission, while the beneficent power of music over the mind will be aided and increased by the combination of every other form of dramatic effect." [75] Amid all the dilettantism and all the rhetorical confusion, it is clear that in Italy, too, there was an audible cry for genius, for a higher evaluation of art, for a new relationship of music to the life of the whole.

In this pamphlet of 1836 there were also strange parallels to later demands of Wagner's: for example, when Mazzini demanded a stronger, more active participation of the chorus in opera. One thinks of *Lohengrin* when one reads in Mazzini: "Wherefore should not the chorus—which in the Greek drama represented the unity of impression produced upon the judgment and conscience of the majority, acting upon the mind of the poet—assume more ample proportions in the modern musical drama, and be raised from the passive and secondary position now assigned to it, to the solemn and complete representation of the popular element?" [76] or when he demands that *recitativo accompagnato* be made a matter of major importance, to achieve more highly dramatic effects than are possible in the closed forms in opera. These ideas are like a presentiment of the Wagnerian "endless melody."

[75] *Ibid.*, p. 155.
[76] *Ibid.*, p. 152.

AGAINST FUSION OF THE ARTS: HANSLICK

In view of the polarity within the Romantic movement, it is not strange that the group of poets, writers, and musicians who demanded the most intimate fusion of the arts were opposed by another group who tried to preserve the independence of music and did not want to hear of its being bound together with poetry, or of its social mission, or of its regenerative power. This group is represented by the name of Eduard Hanslick (1825–1904). Although Hanslick had been one of Tomaschek's pupils in Prague, he was originally a lawyer. Quite early, however, he began his journalistic activity in the field of music—activity which was to end in his becoming, from 1864 on, the influential critic on the Viennese *Neue Freie Presse*. A performance of *Tannhäuser,* which he attended in the fall of 1846 at Dresden, occasioned his writing an enthusiastic article about the work; and in a significant letter (January 1, 1847) Wagner thanked him ("I am entirely convinced that adverse criticism is far more helpful to the artist himself than praise . . ."). Hanslick's attitude towards Wagner, however, and his support of him soon underwent a fundamental change. Though his pamphlet *On the Beautiful in Music: A Contribution to the Revisal of Musical Aesthetics* (1854), Hanslick became the spokesman for all those who saw in neo-Romanticism or the "music of the future" a wrong road and a danger, and who stigmatized Wagner's "endless melody" as "formlessness exalted to a principle." The passionate party struggles which developed from this antagonism—Wagner, Liszt, Berlioz, Bruckner, Hugo Wolf on the one side, Schumann, Brahms, and all the exponents of Romantic Classicism on the other—are not without a certain element of the comic, so far as posterity is concerned. They are a little comic because we who have been born later see only too clearly how much the enemies, grouped into two Romantic poles, had in common. Suffice it to note that Wagner took Hanslick seriously enough to perpetuate the name of his hated enemy in the original version of Beckmesser ("Hans Lick").

As a matter of fact, Hanslick is to be taken very seriously. He was not unaware that an emotional response is indispensable to any aesthetic comprehension—"the ultimate worth of the Beautiful will always rest upon the evidence of the feelings." [77] But he turned against the thesis that music exists to arouse the feelings; he expressly criticized Robert Schumann, who had "caused much harm" by his way of writing: "The aes-

[77] Foreword, 11th ed., p. v.

thetics of one art are those of the other; only the material is different." In contrast to so many Romantics, Hanslick favored a clear separation of the arts. Quite justifiably, he cited by way of example pure instrumental music. He pointed out—like Schopenhauer—that music with its own means alone cannot represent or express definite, individual feelings and emotions: it is completely denied the capacity for depicting unequivocally precise stirrings of the soul, such as friendship, love, hope, anger, hate, jealousy, or despair. The musical construction of a sonata or a sonata-movement does not follow real or idealized feelings, but develops according to purely musical laws. Music is an autonomous art.

The English psychologist Edmund Gurney (*Power of Sound,* 1880) said the same thing of music, only in different words: that its function is "to give impressions of unknown things, namely of tonal forms, which do not appear outside of music and whose beauty cannot be derived from any external principle. Music is not, like the other arts, a representative art, but a presentative one; perhaps it appears to us through a psychological illusion as a sort of expression, but that is not to say *what* is expressed in it." [78] It should be added that, in pure music, simply *music* and naught else is expressed. Gurney's "presentative art" corresponds exactly to the definition given by Hanslick who attributes "self-containedness" (*Immanenz*) to music. "Composing is an activity of the human mind, working in the material capable of becoming the symbol of spirit. We have found this musical material abundant, elastic, and pervious to the imagination of the artist. . . . But the tonal combinations, in whose relationships the beautiful in music consists, are secured not by the composer's stringing them together mechanically, but by the free creativeness of his imagination. Thus the spiritual power and individuality of this particular imagination imprints itself upon the result as *character*. As the creation of a thinking and feeling spirit, accordingly, a musical composition has to a high degree the potentiality of being itself full of spirit and feeling. We shall demand this spiritual content in every work of art, yet it is not to be ascribed to any consideration other than the tonal configurations themselves." [79]

The artistic worth of a composition is thus not determined by the effect upon the feelings, but by the spiritual consideration; and while the layman or uncritical person asks whether a work is happy or sad, the connoisseur asks whether it is good or not. Music becomes unambiguously

[78] Cf. C. Stumpf, *op. cit.,* p. 275.
[79] Hanslick, *op. cit.,* 11th ed., p. 65.

operative upon the affections only in connection with poetry, which assures it a *definite* expressiveness. "The union with poetry," however, "extends the *power* of music, but not its *boundaries*." [80] This power, incidentally, is very great: composing to words is much more than the coloring-in of indicated outlines—a task with which Gluck had been satisfied, as he had set it for himself. In union with poetry, music always has the stronger power; it can transform a mediocre poem into the most inward revelation of the heart.

"Music," Hanslick said, "is tonally animated form." He did not, however, advocate empty, purely formal beauty; for he emphasized again and again the idea that "the forms established by the tones should not be empty, but full, not mere boundary-lines of a vacuum, but spirit taking shape from within." His aesthetics were narrowly conceived, but impeccable within their limitation. One understands, however, the opposition which they must have aroused among those of that day who passionately proclaimed the reconciliation, the closer union of the arts, who considered Beethoven great not because he was a great musician but because he was a "tone-poet," the originator of the idea of the symphonic poem and the *Gesamtkunstwerk*. And one understands the disagreement with his thesis that music does not address itself to the feelings but to the imagination, if one thinks of the tendency of Romantic music to address itself not merely to the listener of aesthetic interests but to the entire human being, as individual and as member of the multitude, of the whole.

Hanslick expressly attacked this pathological, narcotic effect of music; and presumably he had his eye on the Wagnerian public when he wrote:

> Curled up half-asleep in their easy chairs, these enthusiasts let themselves be carried away and rocked to and fro by the pulsations of the sound, instead of considering it with sharpened attention. As it more and more increases, subsides, exults, or dies away, it transports them into an indefinite state of feeling, which they are so innocent as to consider purely spiritual. They form the "most grateful" public and the one that is fit to discredit most surely the value of music. The aesthetic feature of *spiritual* enjoyment escapes their listening entirely. . . . The principle is the same whether one person sits there thoughtlessly comfortable or another is wildly delighted: the joy in the *elementary* aspect of the music.[81]

Hanslick here touched upon the question of the spiritual soundness, the mental health of his Romantic contemporaries—as Friedrich Nietzsche did later. And there is no question that the musically receptive person of

---

[80] *Ibid.*, p. 34.
[81] *Ibid.*, p. 122.

the 19th century was more *pathological* than were his less music-loving contemporaries.

MUSICOLOGY

It has already been observed in the first part of this book that the Romantic period was the first one in the history of music to cultivate a relationship with the more distant past. The Romantics discovered the "Middle Ages," including in that period the 16th century, the time of Palestrina; and they discovered Bach. They could not have done so without the help of musicology; or perhaps it is even better to say that musicology, in many instances, gave the impetus for a creative approach to the past. Without Johann Nikolaus Forkel's book *Ueber Johann Sebastian Bach's Leben, Kunst und Kunstwerke* (1802), the Berlin Singing Academy under Carl Friedrich Zelter would hardly have thought of concerning itself minutely with the art of Bach's cantatas, and the date of the first concert performance of the St. Matthew Passion would presumably have been much later than 1829.

Musicology too is a child of the Romantic era. One realizes this fact clearly when one looks back at the first great 18th-century ventures in music history, Padre Giambattista Martini's *Storia della Musica* (1757, 1770, 1781), Charles Burney's *A General History of Music* (1777–1789), and John Hawkins's *General History of the Science and Practice of Music* (1776). The work of the learned Franciscan is entirely antiquarian, and would not have lost this character if it had extended out beyond the history of Ancient music. And the same observation applies in almost equal degree to Forkel's similarly fragmentary *Allgemeine Geschichte der Musik* (1788–1801). The works of the two Englishmen, however, are the reverse of the antiquarian. Both, especially Burney, consider the whole development of music from the point of view of the present, from the point of view of progress, which in their time had reached its height. To these two scholars it was unthinkable that there could have been periods of development in which music had already achieved a much higher degree of mastery and honor than in their own day—that, for example, a cantata of Carissimi's could have greater worth, to take an extreme example, than an aria of Jommelli's, or a fugue of Bach's than a sonata of Galuppi's. The effect of ideas like that is echoed by William Mason (see p. 339) in his Essay on Cathedral Music (re-published in 1795, p. 112), when he states that the art of the old masters was deficient in both the essential points of the use of music: to please the ear, and to "convey sentiment, and to affect the passions."

This state of affairs changed as early as the first quarter of the 19th century. The change is linked particularly with the name of a great Belgian savant, François-Joseph Fétis, of Mons (1784-1871). One need but glance at his principal works to recognize the altered condition. His *Traité de la Fugue et du Contrepoint* (1825) was no longer a didactic work in the "mechanical" sense of the 18th century, as is still, for example, the *Gründliche Anweisung zur Composition* (1790 and 1818) by the worthy Johann Georg Albrechtsberger, Beethoven's teacher. A further work of Fétis's, published in 1830, makes it known even in the title that music is no longer a privilege of professionals, nor is it a mere hedonistic affair, but a social matter: "Music Reduced to Everybody's Level" (*La Musique Mise à la Portée de Tout le Monde*). This was followed by the *Biographie Universelle des Musiciens* of 1837, the *Resumé Philosophique de l'Histoire de la Musique* of the same year, and finally (in 1869) the *Histoire Générale de la Musique Depuis les Temps le Plus Anciens Jusqu'à nos Jours* (1869, planned as eight volumes, with two more of appendix—of which, however, only three volumes were published by Fétis himself and two more brought out from material which he left behind at his death).

Fétis's universality was essentially something entirely different from Hawkins's or Burney's. He not only knew about past ages of music history, but also compared them and evaluated them apart from their period. In the preface to the second edition of the *Biographie Universelle* (1868) he expressed this point clearly: "One of the greatest obstacles to the fairness of judgments on the value of musical works is found in the doctrine of progress applied to the arts. I have long striven against it, and I had to endure lively altercations when I maintained that music changes, and that it progresses only in material elements." This was a new, anti-Rationalistic, Romantic point of view, that the past could be greater than the present; and it led to the formation of new "affinities" with the past, which constantly changed so long as a period of art still maintained a spark of creative life. In the Romantic era it was the affinity with Bach and with the Middle Ages—though that with Bach was more a sentimental than a living relationship, and that with the Middle Ages was more a learned than a really creative one.

A friend of Padre Martini's, the prince-abbot of St. Blasien, Martin

Gerbert, had edited in 1784 a series of medieval tracts on music, the celebrated *Scriptores Ecclesiastici de Musica Sacra Potissimum;* a reader of Fétis's critical magazine *Revue Musicale,* Edmond Henri de Coussemaker (1805–1876), continued this series (*Scriptores de Musica Medii Aevi,* 1864–76), but in a new, vividly scientific, no longer purely antiquarian spirit.

The same change occurred in the Romantics' attitude towards a later period, the 16th century. Romantic patriotism and pride in nationality had already begun to play a part when Baini in 1828 published his monograph on Palestrina. In 1826 the Royal Netherlands Society of Sciences set this question for a prize competition: What were the merits of the Netherlanders in music, principally in the 14th, 15th, and 16th centuries? The competition turned into a contest between Fétis and the Viennese public official Raphael Georg Kiesewetter (1773-1850), the latter proving the winner.

At the same time as such matters were being considered in Rome and Paris and Vienna, in Berlin Carl von Winterfeld (1784–1852), distinguished jurist, was occupied with the sacred and secular music of the 16th century, and published (in 1834) his "Giovanni Gabrieli and his Period" (*Johannes Gabrieli und sein Zeitalter*), in which—among other things—the significance of Monteverdi was revealed for the first time after Padre Martini. This work was followed (1843–47) by three volumes on "Evangelical Vocal Church Music and Its Relation to the Art of Composition" (*Der Evangelische Kirchengesang und sein Verhältnis zur Kunst des Tonsatzes*). Both of these are monumental works in which language and treatment are at once scientific and Romantic. While Fétis, as a great writer at home in every field, also criticized the development of his own time (so critically that he elicited very angry reactions on the part of Liszt, Verdi, and lesser personages), Winterfeld was already one of those men who live entirely in a distant past. For him, the 18th century scarcely existed.

Another, later type is represented by August Wilhelm Ambros, Kiesewetter's nephew (1816–1876), with a likewise uncompleted history of music, which broke off at his presentation of the 17th century. It is quite obvious that Ambros's favorite field was the period that his contemporaries called "the Renaissance," quite in harmony with the inclinations of the period between 1850 and 1880, which liked to think of itself as reflected in the age of Titian and—in Germany—of Dürer and Hans Sachs. For the first time, there appeared in Ambros's work the continuous parallel between the development of music and the developments in the plastic arts, the attempt to see all the arts as the expression of a unified cultural complex.

There was thus a transition to the philological or purely historical research into facts, as it was realized most fully in the biography of Beethoven by the American A. W. Thayer (vol. 1, 1866). With the appearance of this book, the writing of Romantic music history had virtually come to an end, and it is not without interest to note that this is what the later anti-Romantic Nietzsche, after coming across Thayer's book, observed immediately and with satisfaction.

CHAPTER XIX

Conclusion

ROMANTICISM in music—and not merely in music—has appeared to us as two opposing poles, the opposites being united in a great, broadly flowing movement. But at the *end* of this movement the opposites could no longer be quite brought together. At the time of Richard Wagner's death there was no longer a style in art, as there had been, of course, in earlier centuries. Of this new development, Richard Wagner himself offers the best example. In his *Gesamtkunstwerk* all the individual arts were supposed to give up something of their own nature in order to create a higher unity. In actuality, his work reached its culmination in his music, or—more precisely—in his symphonic orchestra. Not only the voices but also drama, poetry, and the plastic arts had to subordinate themselves to this orchestra and make it their vehicle. In the plastic arts he, the creator of the "art-work of the future," was only too much a "contemporary": his naturalistic stage-setting is the despair of every artist: a sort of diorama with little moving figures of men and animals, and finally even moving stage *décor*. His Venusberg and flower-maiden scenes are the direct counterpart to the fulsome paintings of Hans Makart, one of the "most decorative" exponents of the art of painting in Germany's Gilded Age.

It was unavoidable that poets, painters, sculptors, and especially the musicians themselves should react against the idea of the *Gesamtkunstwerk,* and should reclaim most passionately the rights of their special arts. They again insisted, as Lessing had done in the 18th century, on cleanness and clarity of distinctions. But what a difference in the situation of the two centuries! The separation of the laws and possibilities of poetry on the one side and of the plastic arts on the other had been in the 18th century a purely aesthetic matter, a question of style, resting upon the sure basis of a homogeneous culture. But now, at the end of the 19th century, there was no longer this sort of homogeneous culture, and a basis had first to be re-established. Earlier, art or style was an unquestioned form of life: now art was to reform life which had lost its style. This was the aim that Wagner had in mind with his regeneration through art, in association with Friedrich Nietzsche, in the earlier part of his career, and with several others of like mind. After the deeply disillusioning experience of the first Bayreuth festival of 1876 when Nietzsche turned against him, Wagner felt Nietzsche's defection not merely as the loss of his best follower and propagandist, but also as a final condemnation of the ultimate object towards which the Romantic movement in its culminating work had led the way.

Nevertheless, Wagner wished to go forward. His work was born of despair over his age's artistic deformity, or *Unform*. Especially in his native land, this *Unform* more and more hid itself behind the *Uniform*, behind a dead sameness. Elsewhere, for example in England, there was a compromise with an old tradition, in which art—particularly that of music—assumed a rather decorative place. The only art-form still truly living and national was, perhaps, opera in Italy. But precisely in this national passion for opera, Italy stood somewhat aloof from Europe, and paid for its aloofness by atrophy of all the other branches of music. Brahms looked backwards, and it is a new indication of the significance of his "retrospective" work that he achieved style and permanency by virtue of his personality, which was so warmly human, and his mastery in matters of craftsmanship, at a time when otherwise, in the field of the arts, the century was exhausting itself in the uncreative imitation of all the styles of past centuries.

The Romantic movement, by the end of its development, had transformed itself into a carnival of styles. This sounds harsh, but it is not too harsh when we think of the *average* composer and listener, and not of the exceptional ones, in terms of whom we of a later generation are accustomed to judge the worth of a period. In a way we are justified, for the justice of an estimate demands that we measure its loftiest productions; but in another way we are not, if we consider how intensely most of the creators of these productions had to struggle to bring them to recognition in their own time, against the competition of the fashionable, the mediocre, the poor, and the low.

If one wishes to measure the degree of cleavage at the end of the Romantic period, one must also look at the cleavage among the masses in their attitude towards the business of music. The lavish patronage of the aristocracy in the field of music had practically disappeared; and only the leaders of the German aristocracy, the German princes, regarded it as an inherited duty to indulge in this sort of patronage. But they limited it mostly to continuing their more or less brilliant cultivation of opera. Otherwise, the support of music fell to the lot of the cultivated middle classes, which had come together in associations to promote oratorios and other choral works and—as an inheritance from the old *collegia musica* and "academies"—contributed to the perpetuation of orchestras. They filled the opera houses and the concert halls. But this bourgeoisie was now anything but an ideal congregation.

The contrast with the 18th century is striking, even in the few large cities where there was a mixed public of the aristocracy and the upper middle classes, both in the manner and in the quality of the art-works offered. In the 18th century, audiences heard *opera seria* and *opera buffa* in London as well as in Italy; in France, there was *tragédie lyrique* and *opéra-comique;* in Germany, there was a mixture of everything together, with *opéra-comique* represented only in a somewhat Philistine variant, the *Singspiel.* Audiences heard good and bad opera—that has always been true. But the enjoyment of opera was not of so disparate a character as it was to become at the end of the Romantic era. The bourgeois opera-goer of 1880 had not only the opportunity of hearing an international repertory—Beethoven's *Fidelio* today, *Aïda* tomorrow, *Carmen* day after tomorrow—but they could also hear *Tristan und Isolde* today and *La Fille de Madame Angot* tomorrow. It cannot be argued that there had already been something like this around 1750, for example in Paris, where alongside Lully's and Rameau's operas in the Académie Royale there were also parodies of them in the Théâtre de la Foire. Here there was still a relationship between the high and the low; but at the end of the Romantic movement the art-consumer became an omnivorous creature, who devoured acorns and oysters with the same relish. It is understandable that Richard Wagner set his art-work apart from this kind of audience, that he wished to transform the mass of people who enjoyed art into a *congregation.* But it is essential to the idea of a mass of this kind that it be large, and to the idea of a congregation that it be small.

Also in its relation to the past, the end of the Romantic era showed its omnivorous character. It appropriated more and more to itself—so much that it was no longer able to digest the heaped-up material. Goethe said in *Faust:*

> Really to own what you inherit,
> You first must earn it by your merit.

But the inheritance had grown too big to permit its being earned again. Thus the past took on more and more of a museum character. More and more people lived off the past, and the great past began to be played off against the little present.

A symptom of that process of "living off the past" was the appearance of the "interpreter" in the concert hall, in contrast to the virtuoso. The great virtuoso had been, so to speak, the original phenomenon of the concert hall: it was taken for granted that he would provide for his own repertory—Paganini for his violin, Liszt for his piano. The virtuoso tradition did not die out. It reappeared again and again with unquestionably great effect in Rubinstein and Busoni, in Sarasate and Ysaye. But with Liszt and his Beethoven interpretations, which to the 20th century would presumably appear examples of violence done to the original, the change had already begun. Liszt's pupil, Hans von Bülow, became the first "interpreter" of all the works which he played. Despite all his vivacity, he was of a sterile, uncreative nature; he showed how the compositions ought to be played. And what he did for the piano literature of the past, Joseph Joachim did for violin literature.

Bülow, in connection with Liszt, was also the one who changed the type of the conductor to that of the interpreter, and—strange to say—to the type of the subjective, virtuoso interpreter. Liszt, in the preface to one of his symphonic poems, *Hungaria,* had already demanded the change: he demanded not only careful rehearsal of the separate instrumental groups within the orchestra, which even honest conductors of the old sort sometimes failed to require, but even more: "At the same time I should like to observe that the *measure* in works of this type needs to be managed with more feeling for the musical periods, more flexibility, and more knowledge of the effects of color, of rhythm, and of expression than is still customary in many orchestras. It is not enough for a composition merely to be regularly beaten and mechanically executed, more or less correctly, so that the author may feel satisfaction in the way his work is performed and can there recognize a faithful representation of his thought. The vital nerve of good symphonic execution lies principally in the conductor's comprehension of the work being performed, which, throughout, the conductor should possess and communicate. . . ." To be sure, one scarcely understands what the composer and listener could demand that might be different from or better than "a faithful representation" of the work. However that may be, what Liszt demanded of the interpreters of his symphonies was achieved by Bülow even for the symphonies of the past—a willful rendition, a fluctuation of the tempo, a dismemberment which obviously did not always succeed in attaining a new synthesis.

Wagner, in many passages in his famous essay *On Conducting* (1869), appears to sanction this sort of "vitalizing" of the classics. What came of it may be shown by the criticism of an unimpeachable witness—of so good a Wagnerian as Hugo Wolf. On February 6, 1887, he wrote of his regret at observing that Bülow seemed to have fallen out with Beethoven: "Above all, the living Beethoven terrifies him. To get at him, however, he simply strikes him dead. Then his real activity as a Beethoven-player begins. Carefully the corpse is dissected, the complex of organs is traced out into its most subtle ramifications, the entrails are studied with the seriousness of a haruspex, and the anatomical lecture proceeds. . . ."

The period of musical Romanticism was nearing its end. And, as always, when a period in art approaches its end, these are the symptoms: lassitude or exhaustion, and exaggeration. Against the exaggeration, there is registered a protest; and in the exhaustion there is manifested, at first scarcely noticeably, the seed of the new. The protest was most vigorously directed against the overly strong effect of Wagner's art. The stronger the force of his conquest became, the stronger was the reaction; the more international his success, the more nationally emphasized was the counter-effect. Under the pressure of Wagner's conquest, even the old musical nations began to reawaken: first and most decidedly, France.

On the other hand, there were manifestations of lassitude and exhaustion. Types of art began to die out, apparently with most people unaware of the fact. A bibliography of piano music would certainly show that after Schumann and Chopin, after Liszt's B-minor Sonata, after Brahms's Opp. 1, 2, and 5, countless piano sonatas were still written. Rubinstein, for example, wrote four of them. But the piano sonata *as such* experienced no further development, precisely because it always had to be measured by the greatness and completeness of Beethoven's sonatas, and because there had been a decline in that Romantic enthusiasm which had inspired Schumann and Chopin and Brahms.

The same thing applies to the lied. One may say that in Hugo Wolf the genre displayed a magnificent sunset glow, but it was nevertheless the glow of a sun that was setting. One may say that French vocal lyricism first came into bloom at the end of this period in the work of Gabriel Fauré (1845–1924) or Henry Duparc (1848–1933); but actually the great period of the lied was past, although time and again well into the 19th century many lieder were still written. Similarly in the field of chamber music Brahms had been the last great master, the model for a group of inferior successors.

To only two genres did the Romantic era in its changing or declining stage hold fast with unyielding strength—to the symphony and the opera. These are, it should be noted, the genres with the richest resources for producing musical power, the greatest possibilities of gaining an effect by sheer sound. Along with the effect by sound, there was a related exaggeration of the harmony. One could also represent the essential history of Romantic music as a history of the incipient disintegration of the elements of music: melody, rhythm, and harmony. In Beethoven they were still in complete equilibrium. But with the mention of his name we suddenly realize that he was the last great master of rhythm. The Romantic musician thought, above all, of the refinement of the harmony, an element in which he had his real ideas. And the "most Romantic" of all the works of the Romantic movement, Wagner's *Tristan,* was a culmination and a turning-point in the history of the dissonance, not in that of either melody or rhythm.

Out of the neo-Romanticism of Liszt and Wagner there came hyper-Romanticism. Especially through the intoxicating impression of Wagner's operas or Wagner's orchestra, there began a period of musical intoxication, a deification of art, contrasting sharply with an extreme narrow-mindedness also current. (The most characteristic example of this idolatry of music appears in the work of Scriabin.) The self-deception of the enthusiasts from the neo-Romantic circle often assumed grotesque forms. "We stand at the beginning of a new era; we live in a great movement that mankind since the Reformation has been furthering. We go out to meet an immeasurably higher and finer conception of man. As yet, with respect to this end, we are still in a very primitive state; but towards the year 2000 a remarkably beautiful efflorescence of mankind, like the century plant, will develop"—so wrote Peter Cornelius on January 9, 1861, to one of his Weimar friends. The same exaggerated hope for regeneration through art, for the "redeeming" role of music, expressed itself in the youthful writings of Friedrich Nietzsche. Nietzsche, incidentally, had always been a "misplaced" musician, an artist whose real means of making himself understood would have been music, and who availed himself of language only through necessity. At the same time and in the same place as this youthful Nietzsche, there was active the representative of profound cultural pessimism, the true prophet of the future, Jacob Burckhardt.

This is the sum total of the Romantic era in music. But while one adds it up, a contradiction at the same time manifests itself: one feels an urge to set over against it the most glowing apotheosis of the Romantic movement. What a period of music! At the beginning stood Franz Schubert, the purest incarnation of the musician; and at the end stood the creator of *Tristan*, Richard Wagner! What names between these two, so bitterly opposed, so truly great! What a *heroic* age of music, with a task so difficult!

Peter Cornelius in his prophecy was wrong in considering that the age was still "in a very primitive state." It was sensitive to the finest tremors of the soul, and its sensitivity already included the beginnings of impressionism, which it was still too much alive and too inclusive to develop into a specialty. The Romantic movement in music was at once young and old. Music justified the faith that the early Romantics in literature had placed in it—justified it completely. It fulfilled the task assigned to it—that of standing in the center of art. However great achievements the other arts of poetry and painting may have brought forth in all the nations during the 19th century, music excelled them. And where the other arts refused to act, music stepped into the breach.

If one thinks of the works of the past which are still alive today, the Romantic counterbalances the Classic. We should have been immeasurably poorer if the history of music had stood still with the death of Beethoven. To be sure, the music of the Classical period is like the starry heavens. We cannot reach the stars; we cannot even envy them. But the music of the Romantic period is *our* music, at once fulfillment and boundless yearning.

There is no eternity in the history of art: not only individual works die out, but also individual periods. But the Romantic era, as a symbol of cleavage and of the will to overcome this cleavage, is an eternal principle of art. In Romantic music of the 19th century this principle found its most illuminating, its most "eternal" realization.

INDEX